Forgotten but Not Gone

Forgotten but Not Gone

The Origin, Theology, Transmission, and Recurrent Impact of Landmarkism in the Southern Baptist Convention (1850–2012)

James Hoyle Maples, Jr.

WIPF & STOCK · Eugene, Oregon

FORGOTTEN BUT NOT GONE
The Origin, Theology, Transmission, and Recurrent Impact of Landmarkism in the Southern Baptist Convention (1850–2012)

Copyright © 2018 James Hoyle Maples, Jr. All rights reserved. Except for brief quotations in critical publications or reviews, no part of this book may be reproduced in any manner without prior written permission from the publisher. Write: Permissions, Wipf and Stock Publishers, 199 W. 8th Ave., Suite 3, Eugene, OR 97401.

Wipf & Stock
An Imprint of Wipf and Stock Publishers
199 W. 8th Ave., Suite 3
Eugene, OR 97401

www.wipfandstock.com

PAPERBACK ISBN: 978-1-5326-4414-6
HARDCOVER ISBN: 978-1-5326-4415-3
EBOOK ISBN: 978-1-5326-4416-0

Manufactured in the U.S.A.

Chart reproduced from *The Trail of Blood* herein used by permission of the publisher, Ashland Avenue Baptist Church, 483 West Reynolds Road, Lexington, KY 40503.

To Robyn, Hillary and Michael,
James and Becky, Abigail,
Avery, Jacob, and Asher
with much love

Contents

Preface | ix
Acknowledgments | xi

Chapter One: Introduction | 1

Chapter Two: Early Landmarkism: An Evaluation of Theology | 15

Chapter Three: An Evaluation of Baptist Church Succession | 66

Chapter Four: Controversies Generated by Landmarkers | 90

Chapter Five: Gone in Name but Present in Doctrine | 149

Chapter Six: Conclusion | 207

Appendices | 219
Bibliography | 237
Index of Names | 253
Index of Subjects | 259

Preface

ONE CAN HARDLY WATCH television today without seeing a commercial for various forms of DNA testing which purport to give various kinds of information about one's makeup, from potential health issues lurking within one's body to information regarding one's ancestral heritage. Many of the commercials feature people who for one reason or another believe they hail from a certain country, region, or ethnic background. The point of the commercial and the "hook" to motivate one to purchase the service is the testimony of the people in the commercial that they were completely surprised about their heritage or ethnic makeup when they received their test results. If such tests were available for denominations within the church the results might be equally surprising.

Having been born, raised, and a member of various Southern Baptist churches for almost forty years, I for one never heard the term *Landmarkism*. My father was a bi-vocational Southern Baptist pastor for several years. In retrospect, he was not one who espoused Landmark beliefs, but it was never even a topic of discussion. As a member of seven different Southern Baptist churches in forty years I never heard the term Landmark or Landmarkism. However, having become familiar with the Landmark movement and looking back at various pastors, sermons, teachings, and affirmations to which I was exposed, it is easy to see some traces of Landmark influence, some more visible and dominant than others.

It is this strain of Landmark influence, these "markers" which are imbedded in the DNA of the Southern Baptist Convention, that shape some areas of Baptist thought and practice like DNA, to greater or lesser degrees, depending on the ancestral heritage of a particular church or region. As in my own case, these influences are not known or named but are generally accepted as Baptist doctrine and practice. It is the purpose herein to trace the origin, growth, and transmission of traits (beliefs and doctrines) which owe their development to the Landmark movement, but which today are unseen, largely unknown, but still a defining part of the makeup of many Southern Baptist churches and members. It is just who they are even if they are unaware of the heritage and its influence upon their beliefs.

James H. Maples

Acknowledgments

SEVERAL LIBRARIES WERE OF special assistance to me in my research. A special thanks to Elizabeth Wells, Special Collections, Samford University; Al Lang, Archivist, Carson-Newman College; Jonathan Jeffrey, Curator of Manuscripts, Manuscript and Folklife Archives, Western Kentucky University; and Taffey Hall, Director and Archivist at the Southern Baptist Historical Library and Archives.

Drs. James Patterson, Union University, Merrill Hawkins, Carson-Newman College, and Kenneth Roxburgh, Samford University, were particularly helpful in facilitating student surveys incorporated into this project. Dr. James McGoldrick was also very gracious in sharing his experience and insight as one who has researched aspects of the church succession issue discussed herein.

Soli Deo Gloria

1

Introduction

Background

THE LANDMARK MOVEMENT WAS perhaps the greatest controversy ever within the Southern Baptist Convention, the largest Baptist denomination, and the second largest denomination in America. The Landmark movement was highly sectarian and the attacks of the Landmarkers focused on other denominations, but also included mission boards, seminary presidents and professors, denominational boards and leaders, and even other churches and pastors within the Southern Baptist Convention. Many see Landmarkism as a movement which appeared for a few decades preceding and following the American Civil War but one which was largely forgotten in the twentieth century. It is true that a majority of Southern Baptists today cannot define Landmarkism or articulate anything relative to the controversies that were spawned by the Landmarkers. This is odd because many Landmark principles and doctrines are very visible within the Southern Baptist Convention today. The explanation lies in the fact that to many Southern Baptists these doctrines and principles are not strange or aberrant at all even though church historians or theologians would view them as such. Many Southern Baptists view some tenets of Landmarkism as basic Baptist doctrine and recognize nothing aberrant or Landmark about them.

The Southern Baptist Convention has been gripped by several major controversies during its 173-year history. The denomination was birthed as a direct result of the slavery controversy which ultimately led to war in America. Landmarkism began its ascendency during the first decade of the Southern Baptist Convention's life and firmly planted itself within the fabric of the denomination. Although many would not agree in toto, the position set forth herein is that all the major controversies which have gripped the Southern Baptist Convention have at least some roots in or connection to Landmarkism in doctrine, principles, or practice.

This relationship and influence is striking because many Landmark beliefs are contrary to historic Baptist beliefs and various positions proceeding from the convention. These Landmark beliefs, however, have insinuated themselves into Baptist life, belief, and practice to such an extent that Landmark principles are seen by many as Southern Baptist principles. The difficulty herein has several facets.

The Landmark view of church history (both a history of the church and as a discipline of study) is unsupported by critical, historical research. If there are any Baptist historians who hold to a strict succession of Baptist churches from the first century to the present, they are an incredibly small minority. However, decades of teaching Baptist church succession in the seminaries and in the churches have produced numbers of pastors, leaders, and teachers who have inculcated such beliefs into the mainstream of Baptist life. Acceptance of such by large numbers of Southern Baptists is often seen as a curiosity rather than a cause for alarm.

Landmark ecclesiology presents a different set of challenges which center around the autonomy of the local church and its actions. The "high-church"[1] attitude of Landmarkism has seeped into the Southern Baptist Convention and there is an attitude of congregational authority which rivals in some cases anything Rome has put forth regarding papal authority. This view has manifested itself repeatedly in various controversies, in relations or lack thereof with other denominations, in mission work and support, and in the workings of the Southern Baptist Convention itself. One's ecclesiology, however, cannot be considered in isolation. By definition, it has influence upon other areas of doctrine.

The father of Landmarkism was James Robinson Graves (1820–1893). The author of the tract from which Landmarkism derived its name (*An Old Landmark Re-Set*) was James Madison Pendleton (1813–1891). Much has been written about these two men, but I believe there is more to be found in the sermons, letters, and other unpublished material which may shed more light upon their theology particularly in the area of ecclesiology.

The extent to which Landmark theology, doctrine, and practice have made their way into current-day Southern Baptist thought is somewhat remarkable. This was expected and reported in the decades when Landmarkism was a major force within the Southern Baptist Convention but the extent of that assimilation into current beliefs, attitudes, and practice is

---

1. From Tull, *High-Church Baptists in the South*.

of great interest to and presents a great challenge to this historiographical research. The theology and historical view of the church fostered by Landmarkism was molded by a group of strong personalities within the Southern Baptist Convention. Rather than being condemned by Southern Baptists these views were embraced by the vast majority of Southern Baptists particularly in the Southern regions of the United States. These doctrines of Landmarkism, far from being a forgotten curiosity in Baptist history, have become part of Baptist faith and practice in the minds of many Southern Baptists and have exerted a significant influence in many controversies within that denomination even to the present day.

Rather than being a curious and to some an embarrassing part of Baptist history from which the Southern Baptist Convention has long since moved on, Landmarkism has proven to have amazing staying power, so much so, that it continues to influence Southern Baptist life today. Many do not recognize the distinctive Landmark doctrines and, if questioned, do not attribute these beliefs and practices to Landmark influence, if indeed they even recognize such influence, but categorize these doctrines as Southern Baptist doctrines. Many Baptist historians have demonstrated conclusively the faulty scholarship behind the Landmark view of Baptist church succession but there is still much in print even in recent publications which support, defend, and promote the Landmark position.

One area that is noticeably lacking in the history of Landmarkism and its influence is the time immediately preceding the Civil War. In addition, the loss of the war in the South, the period of Reconstruction, and the Landmark assessment of that time is curiously missing from or is treated very lightly in most studies. This was a time of high emotions. The American Civil War has been described as a religious war. Both sides in the conflict believed they had divine warrant for their position and in many cases the loudest denunciation, condemnation, and excoriation of the other side came from the pulpits and the pages of the religious press. The issues of slavery, states' rights, and republicanism were front and center, and the loss of the war did nothing to change the minds of those in the South on these topics. After the slaves were freed the attitudes of most within the South did not change regarding the Negro. Most have ignored or skipped this part of history as if the Landmarkers had nothing to say on the subject. Research has proven that not to be the case. In fact, the twin doctrines of anthropology and the *imago Dei* and the Landmark interpretation of the same figure prominently in the Landmark-controlled press in what was then called the Southwest where Landmark influence was greatest. These doctrines would prove to have profound influence in the Southern Baptist Convention in later controversies which grew out of the aftermath of the Civil War and the

Lost Cause mentality of many in the South. These connections and their Landmark roots are explored here.

Most of the studies of Landmarkism have terminated in the early twentieth century. After many Southern Baptist churches with strict Landmark beliefs split from the Southern Baptist Convention and formed their own convention it appeared that Landmarkism as an issue within the Southern Baptist Convention was a thing of the past. In addition, the tracing of Landmark positions during the last century has proven difficult and imprecise. Such a study is one of the primary goals of this work.

These are the reasons behind this work. It is intended as a detailed and in-depth history of the areas noted above. Every effort has been made to let the Landmarkers speak for themselves rather than respond to individual apologetic challenges. At times it is necessary to call some of the Landmark apologists to account but every effort to do so has sought foundation in the words and works of the Landmarkers themselves. It is the author's stated purpose to go beyond what has been presented in other works and add to the historiography of the Landmark movement and its influence. This treatment, particularly in the areas noted above, seeks to better understand this movement and particularly its current influence and the foundations on which that influence is grounded. There will be, no doubt, much that can be advanced upon following this work, and it is hoped that this writer's contribution will be useful in future research into this subject.

Naturally not everything written, preached, or said about Landmarkism can be included. This work is limited to pastors, editors, persons in positions of influence within the Southern Baptist Convention, and those of other denominations who were often the target of their attacks. The significant participants in the controversies which took place or persons who exercised considerable influence in propagating and extending the influence of Landmark beliefs among the members of the churches of the Southern Baptist Convention are the focus of this research.

From a historical point of view, a review of the theology of various groups claimed as Baptists in the successionist view of the history of the Baptist church will be examined. It should become clearer to what extent both the Landmarkers and the adherents of Landmarkism were willing to overlook theological inconsistencies and even heresies[2] if the key marks of what they considered the true church and true church doctrine were present.

---

2. It should be noted that the use of the terms heretical, unorthodox, aberrant, error, or other such terms throughout this book mean that the doctrine or view expressed is out of step with the historic confessions of the church at Nicea, Constantinople, and Chalcedon and more particularly out of accord with historic Baptist confessions of faith as articulated in the First and Second London Confessions and the Philadelphia Confession.

Further, it is the aim here to document the presence of the Landmark views of ecclesiology and the church ordinances of baptism and the Lord's Supper within the Southern Baptist Convention and give relevant examples of the extent of that influence.

Achievement of those aims will address certain questions/objectives:

a. Can it be demonstrated that certain theological aberrations are overlooked if one's ecclesiology and view and practice of the church ordinances are correct according to Landmark doctrine and practice?
b. Is this the *sine qua non* of what it means to be a Southern Baptist?
c. What part did Landmarkism play in shaping responses by Southern Baptists to critical events in Baptist life like the Civil War, the civil rights movement, the conservative-moderate controversy, the missions controversy, and the debate over Baptist cooperation with other evangelicals?
d. How pervasive is Landmark doctrine and belief in the Southern Baptist Convention today?

Historiographical Method, Chronology, Authenticity, Meaning, and Context

The historiographical method focuses on the critical analysis of sources and the synthesis of those sources into narrative. The heart of the historiographical method is not merely the collection of data but the interpretation of that data. Certain patterns emerge in the analysis of data that make historical facts meaningful. The goal of the historical researcher is not only to present the facts but also to present a rationale supported by those facts as to the cause or reason behind the events surveyed. This research must try as much as possible to evaluate original sources, i.e., newspaper articles, diaries, letters, eyewitness accounts, and other pieces of the historical record from which insight into the meaning of events may be gleaned. Historical events take place in space and time and thus must be evaluated both with respect to chronology and where those events took place. This data must be examined on two levels. First, is the document authentic? Second, what is the meaning of the contents of that document? Much of chapter 2 makes use of the biographical method wherein events during the lives of key individuals are examined to determine the impact of the cultural, religious, and political climate of the period on those individuals. Additionally, the perpetuation of beliefs and ideas, the political and cultural influences and their effect on beliefs and doctrines necessarily enter the analysis.

The sociohistorical dimension also gives a clear view of the background against which Landmarkism was planted, grew, and matured. Over twenty thousand documents, a significant portion of which were unpublished handwritten journals, letters, sermons, notes, and speeches, were examined to gain better insight into these issues. Many of these, naturally, were not used but were still of value in understanding the sociohistorical background and the many complex personal relations, plans, and unrecorded reactions to various events. The examination of so many original documents adds confidence to the authenticity of the documents as one soon begins to recognize handwriting, figures of speech, and modes of expression of various writers.

The primary sources include miscellaneous unpublished sources and archival collections and papers. The largest of these include: original writings of J. M. Pendleton consisting of correspondence, sermons, journal, and notebooks (Benjamin Franklin Proctor Collection, Western Kentucky University, Bowling Green); collections of the records of First Baptist Church, Nashville, Tennessee (Dugan-Carver Library, Nashville); archives of religious periodicals including but not limited to: the *Baptist*, the *Tennessee Baptist*, *South West Baptist*, *Baptist World*, *Baptist and Reflector*, *Western Recorder*, the *Texas Baptist and Herald*, and the *Christian Index*; historical collection at Oklahoma Baptist University; special collection Samford University; and the annuals of national, state, and associational Baptist organizations and archival papers and collections at the Southern Baptist Historical Library and Archives, Nashville, Tennessee. Secondary sources include books, theological journals, encyclopedias, and sound recordings.

The Landmark Conversation

The distinctive beliefs of the Landmark movement have been regarded by some as accurate historical research and scholarly exegetical interpretations of Scripture. Others see them as unscholarly and clearly uncritical, not to mention unorthodox. The theological views of Graves and Pendleton have been hailed as pillars of orthodoxy and indeed have been the basis for much instructional material in both the seminaries and the churches. Some of what Graves wrote was clearly unorthodox and the Baptist successionist view of history he put forth claimed as Baptists many groups who would be rejected by discerning Baptists today. However, if his contemporaries contradicted these views, there were many who were ready to come to his defense with aggressive and antagonistic diatribes against any such offenders.

One of those offenders who felt the wrath and retribution of the Landmark forces was W. H. Whitsitt, professor of church history, and president of Southern Baptist Seminary, Louisville, Kentucky. Whitsitt was hounded out of the seminary because of his views that Baptists as a denomination arose in seventeenth-century England.[3] There was a time when many Southern Baptists desired to establish a visible succession of Baptist churches back to the apostolic age. Any theory which traced the succession of Baptists back to John the Baptist had a ready audience—witness the popularity and longevity of J. M. Carroll's *Trail of Blood*, which continues to sell at an annual rate of approximately fifteen thousand copies, and over two million copies have been distributed since its first printing in 1931.[4] Carroll's position has been refuted by able scholars but even the literature coming from the Sunday School Board of the Southern Baptist Convention (and its successors) has accorded Landmark positions on the history of the Baptist Church some respect if not standing.

The doctrines of ecclesiology and the ordinances of baptism and the Lord's Supper have been and continue to be the ground on which the Landmark influence is less susceptible to attack. Even though the Landmark position distorted the doctrine of the church and the ordinances by overemphasis, much of what they believed and taught is still the fundamental belief and practice of many Southern Baptist churches. The Landmark position made the doctrine of the church, baptism, and the Lord's Supper the point of division between themselves and other denominations. These points of division were magnified beyond the doctrines themselves and became the focus of attention in all relationships with other denominations and in their own internal struggles.

Landmark Writings

Among the early Landmarkers, Graves was the most prolific writer, publishing over two dozen books. These works break down categorically into works on ecclesiology and the ordinances of baptism and the Lord's Supper, critiques and attacks upon other denominations, and church history. His magnum opus is *The Work of Christ in the Covenant of Redemption, Developed in Seven Dispensations*. In addition, Graves was involved as either editor or a major contributor to various denominational periodicals from 1847

---

3. Whitsitt, *Question in Baptist History*.
4. Published by Ashland Avenue Baptist Church, Lexington, Kentucky.

until his death in 1893. He wrote editorials almost weekly promoting the Landmark doctrine and often responded with letters to the editors of other denominational periodicals which challenged his views or differed in their theology and practice from the Landmark view. This was during a period in which, as James Tull says, the "denominational newspaper was one of the most powerful instruments in forming denominational opinion."[5]

J. M. Pendleton wrote relatively little compared to Graves but his work, *An Old Landmark Re-Set*, written at Graves' request, is the source of the movement's name. Pendleton's works were more scholarly, and his *Christian Doctrines* and *Church Manual* were used in some Southern Baptist seminaries for decades. Several of Pendleton's other works defended some Landmark principles but not as stridently as Graves. Pendleton was a frequent and regular contributor to numerous religious periodicals and served on the staff of the *Tennessee Baptist* as assistant editor with Graves.

The analysis of the theology of Landmarkism and particularly the early Landmarkers is somewhat limited and it focuses primarily on the theology of Graves. This is primarily because certain aspects of Graves' theology are quite troubling, giving his critics ample reason to criticize and requiring explanation and defense by his supporters. Graves' opponents like William G. Brownlow, a Methodist minister and later governor of Tennessee, took on Graves' attack of Methodism in *The Great Iron Wheel Examined*. Brownlow was as truculent as Graves and accused Graves of perpetrating twenty-nine falsehoods in one chapter of only twelve pages. Adversaries from other denominations engaged Graves in debates which usually centered on the validity of their recognition as a church of Christ. These debates were often serialized in the pages of the *Tennessee Baptist* or the *Baptist* newspapers, and some like the Graves-Ditzler debate were later published in book form. Contemporaries such as J. J. D. Renfroe, another Landmarker, wrote attacking Graves' views on close communion.[6] Renfroe objected to the highly sectarian antagonism which he said Graves' view promoted even among Baptist churches.[7] There were far more who were sympathetic to Graves' cause and who were quick to defend certain tenets of Landmarkism and in many cases collaborated with Graves in defense of Landmarkism or certain Landmark principles.

---

5 Tull, *High-Church Baptists in the South*, 121.

6 Renfroe, *Vindication of the Communion of Baptist Churches*. This practice is known as "closed communion" today but it was more common in the nineteenth century and early twentieth century to refer to it as "close communion." See chapter 2, footnote 17 for Pendleton's explanation.

7 Ibid., 47.

Baptist Successionism

As W. Morgan Patterson points out, Graves did not originate the idea of the succession of Baptist churches back to apostolic times.[8] Graves was, however, the leading promoter and defender of that view by popularizing G. H. Orchard's *Concise History of Foreign Baptists* which he reprinted in 1855. The succession of Baptist churches and the authorized administrators of the ordinances became integral to Landmark ecclesiology. John Tyler Christian later produced a Baptist history that sought to justify the successionist theory on historical grounds.[9] Christian's work was under the auspices of the Southern Baptist Convention and was one of the keys in the minds of many in refuting Whitsitt's research. Christian was professor of church history at what would later become New Orleans Baptist Theological Seminary. Willis Anselm Jarrel opted for a change of terms, preferring the word perpetuity rather than succession, but his work was basically a defense of Baptist church succession.[10] Tellingly, it was dedicated to Graves among others. It should be noted that Jarrel's scholarship was no better than Orchard's. Hugh L. Tully produced a short recapitulation of the Landmark theory of church succession near the middle of the twentieth century.[11] It contained nothing new but demonstrated the tenacity of those holding the Landmark position even in the face of conclusive scholarship to the contrary.

Of course, there were some dissenting voices who, like Whitsitt, sought to answer the Landmark view of history with scholarly research. At the time of the Whitsitt controversy other works appeared, most notably those by George Augustus Lofton, who refuted Christian's claims that Whitsitt's scholarship was faulty and rested on fraudulent documents. Albert Henry Newman produced a scholarly rebuttal of Baptist claims which identified with the various groups opposed to the Roman Catholic Church and infant or other unauthorized baptism (the heart of the Landmark identification system). Few if any Baptist historians today hold to any view of church succession. Competent scholarship has ably refuted this view. Other works have addressed the orthodoxy of the medieval groups claimed by the Landmarkers as true Baptists. Scholars have addressed various questionable aspects of the groups the Landmarkers claimed to be the true church and the successors of the first Baptist church they contend was founded by Christ.

---

8. Patterson, *Baptist Successionism*.

9. Christian, *Baptist History Vindicated*. Christian's history included material from his earlier work *Did They Dip?*

10. Jarrel, *Baptist Perpetuity*.

11. Tully, *Brief History of the Baptists*.

Ordinances of Baptism and the Lord's Supper

The largest volume of work produced by the Landmarkers has been in the area of baptism and the Lord's Supper. These works address the question of the authorized administrators of these ordinances, participants, and the mode in the case of baptism. Graves published eight works specifically on these topics. Due to the nature of the question they almost always found their way into his other writings, particularly when addressing the authority of the Baptist church or the lack of authority in other denominations. R. B. C. Howell, Graves' mentor turned antagonist, from whom Graves gleaned much of his doctrine, produced several works.[12] The central question surrounding the Landmark doctrine of the church and the ordinances centered on the questions of alien immersion, an authorized administrator, and the mode, particularly in what many scholars claimed were the beginnings of the Baptist church in seventeenth-century England.

Much of the Landmark doctrine was spread through the Baptist periodicals and it was often marked by polemical editorial exchanges with other religious periodicals of the day. Many of Graves' works were serialized in the pages of the *Tennessee Baptist* and later the *Baptist* which were published in Nashville, Tennessee, and Memphis, Tennessee, respectively. James E. Tull and Albert W. Wardin Jr. made the greatest use of these periodicals but left much unsaid that flowed from the Landmark pens. Wardin's massive history of Tennessee Baptists only devoted two chapters to Landmarkism and its influence but he outlined the history of the Baptist periodicals published in the state and gave an excellent history of their failures, mergers, and development into the present-day Baptist periodicals. Graves was a major force in this development and these papers were the organs by which the Landmark doctrine was spread more effectively than any other.

The Civil War of 1861–1865

One area which leaves a curious void in the historical development of Landmarkism is the American Civil War. At its heart this was a religious war. It was not just a moral war which pitted one side which was moral against the other which was not; rather, both sides claimed their cause was ordained by God. The Bible was quoted in support of the argument on both sides. In the decades leading up to the war the three largest Protestant denominations in America, the Baptists, Methodists, and Presbyterians, split over the issue of slavery. This gave birth to the Southern Baptist Convention and one would

---

12. Howell, *Terms of Sacramental Communion* and *The Evils of Infant Baptism*.

expect religious polemicists like the Landmarkers, especially Graves, to be very visible in the debate leading up to the war. Graves' wartime efforts in behalf of the South have been reported but hardly any notice of the defense of slavery, the condemnation of Northern churches, pastors, and politicians which came forth from the pages of the *Tennessee Baptist* has been considered. O. L. Hailey[13] in his biography of Graves stated flatly that Graves had no part in the great debate that tore the country apart.

Controversies Involving Landmarkers

There were several key controversies in which the Landmarkers were the driving force. The Graves-Howell controversy, the resultant challenge by Graves to unseat Howell as president of the Southern Baptist Convention, the controversy over mission boards, and the Whitsitt controversy have been widely reported. What is missing is a deeper look into miscellaneous unpublished sources, i.e., letters, diaries, and journals of the participants and observers of these events. These controversies were most widely discussed and circulated in the religious press of the day. Later discussions in theological journals have examined certain aspects of these controversies but much has been left unsaid.

Biographies of Major Landmarkers

Information regarding Graves' personal life is very limited, and most is supplied by O. L. Hailey, whose views and analysis of Graves are in many instances distorted by his relationship to Graves. (He was Graves' son-in-law.) However, the volume of what was written by Graves in periodicals, books, and sermons tests the resolve of the researcher who tries to read them all.

There has been little written on Pendleton's life other than short sketches or journal articles. Pendleton wrote an autobiographical work entitled *Reminiscences of a Long Life*.

J. M. Carroll (*Trail of Blood*) had little more than a few biographical sketches written about him. B. H. Carroll on the other hand was the subject of biographical and edited collections of his life and work by a variety of scholars.

---

13. Hailey, *J. R. Graves*.

Works on Landmarkism: Schools of Thought

A. T. Robertson took the Landmarkers and particularly Graves to task in a 1916 article accusing them of heresy.[14] The majority of Landmark works give no attention to this article by one of the preeminent Baptist scholars. Robertson was intimately involved in the Whitsitt affair and was professor of New Testament at Southern Baptist Theological Seminary during that period. It should be noted that O. L. Hailey was quick to spring to Graves' defense.[15]

An abundance of effort that has gone into the understanding of the factors, causes, and shapers of the Landmark movement and the influence it has had on the Southern Baptist Convention, but most stop short of making connection between the Landmark doctrines and many of the practices and beliefs of today's Southern Baptists. These connections may not be as direct as in the nineteenth century, but they are present nonetheless. Other than the lack of an easily discernible link between Landmarkism and today's doctrine and practice, two other factors may have resulted in the voids noted earlier. First, much of what was called Landmark doctrine in the nineteenth century has become known as the historical Baptist position. Second, most of the authors of these various works are Southern Baptists, and critiques of Landmarkers, particularly Graves, and their doctrines, are interpreted by many as an attack upon the Southern Baptist Convention itself. Therefore, I believe a more critical analysis could be made of doctrines and practices codified by the Landmarkers and more examination of previously unreported sources could fill in some of the voids thus shedding more light on the spread and influence of Landmarkism in the Southern Baptist Convention.

Structure of the Book

Chapter 2 lays the foundation for this work by looking at two men, J. R. Graves, and J. M. Pendleton, who were the leaders in establishing Landmark beliefs among Southern Baptists. Pendleton was more the professor and the pastor while Graves was the great polemicist and, particularly in his own eyes, the Baptist champion who was the defender of Baptist Church orthodoxy, history, and exclusivity against all the other denominations who were not, in his eyes, true churches of Christ. Two other men, the Carroll brothers, B. H. Carroll and J. M. Carroll, are examined in this chapter because they represent the progression of Landmarkism into the next generation after the deaths of Graves and Pendleton. The Carrolls made significant impact in the furtherance of

14. Robertson, "Heresy among Southern Baptists," 5–6.
15. Hailey, "Dr. Robertson's Reflections," 25.

Landmark doctrine and beliefs among Southern Baptists in somewhat different ways, B. H. through his involvement within education and the politics of the Southern Baptist Convention, and J. M. through his writing.

The focus of chapter 2 is on the theology of the four men mentioned above, some aspects of which have not been fully discussed previously, and the manner and extent to which their theology shaped Landmark beliefs. This chapter also brings out some theological differences between Graves and the other three men, an area that has not been discussed or in some cases has been misstated in certain aspects by other works. The examination of Graves' theology in certain areas raises some troubling questions, particularly the overriding question of why one with such views could be the Baptist champion in the eyes of so many.

Chapter 3 examines an integral piece of the Landmark claim for Baptist Church exclusivity, viz., the unbroken succession of Baptist churches from the time of Christ until the present day. Graves held this to be the key to identifying the true church and by his reckoning this key was held by no other church than the Baptist Church. This fundamental Landmark doctrine deeply influenced J. M. Carroll and his little book *The Trail of Blood* proved to have an enduring influence on generations of Southern Baptists. Many church historians and medieval scholars have refuted this theory. Chapter 3 draws heavily on existing work by competent scholars due in large part to the scarcity of original documents, translation difficulties, and accessibility of those documents. As in chapter 2, the focus is on the theology of the groups claimed to be the true church and the untenable nature of such claims considering their unorthodox theological doctrines. The fact that Baptists were ready to accept such groups as Baptist churches and as part of the line of succession of the true church despite their unorthodox beliefs is akin to the acceptance of Graves and his views. Many troubling beliefs could apparently be ignored to promote a view of Baptist Church exclusivity.

Chapter 4 investigates controversies spawned by the Landmarkers. The controversies featured attacks upon all who did not subscribe to their doctrines, practices, or views of Baptist Church history. It mattered not whether the ones holding different views were other denominations or other Southern Baptists, all who differed were targeted by the Landmarkers. In the early days Graves was the chief protagonist but his legacy and methods were apparent in later attacks by others upon those who diverged from the Landmark view. The denominational periodicals published by Graves were one of the chief organs for castigating those with different views and they continued to be used by his successors in that role well into the twentieth century. This chapter probes deeply into some of the early controversies through the examination of unpublished letters and notes of some of the participants. Going forward, later controversies which have largely been unconnected with Landmarkism are investigated and certain strains of Landmark doctrine and practice are exposed as undercurrents in many cases. The chilling effect which these controversies had on other Southern Baptists was felt for decades. Many who criticized the Landmark views were hounded out of their positions and were castigated openly in the religious press. This produced a cautionary reluctance on the part of many to disagree with the Landmark positions. This is developed for the reader in chapter 4.

Chapter 5 presents evidence for the transmission of Landmark beliefs throughout the twentieth century. This is a piece of the Landmark legacy which has not been studied or written on extensively. Many think that Landmarkism ceased to be a factor in the Southern Baptist Convention particularly when a number of churches with strong Landmark beliefs withdrew from the convention early in the twentieth century. However, that was not the case as chapter 5 goes on to demonstrate. Landmark and Landmarkism were terms that ceased to have meaning for most Southern Baptists, but as surveys conducted by the Southern Baptist Convention and my own surveys show, a significant number of Southern Baptists from pastors to college students hold some Landmark beliefs and, in the case of the college students, are not even familiar with the term Landmarkism. This chapter makes the case that for many within the Southern Baptist Convention, Landmark doctrines are simply Southern Baptist doctrines and beliefs.

2

Early Landmarkism
An Evaluation of Theology

An Evaluation of Theological Directions

SOME LIKE MORRIS ASHCRAFT say that "Landmarkism precipitated the greatest controversy in Southern Baptist life until the fundamentalist takeover eclipsed it."[1] But even the fundamentalist controversy/takeover within the Southern Baptist Convention had some roots in the Landmark movement as did other controversies that have arisen. This controversy, as well as other areas of Southern Baptist life today, was influenced by the Landmarkism of the nineteenth century although those influences are unrecognized by many today. These influences were not without some grounding in theology, and to a large extent some of that theological grounding came from the Landmarkers. The Landmark ecclesiology fostered an exclusive sectarian view of the local Baptist church and by extension the Southern Baptist Convention. This distinct ecclesiology is evident in the Landmark view of the succession of Baptist churches and the belief that Baptist churches are the only true church. This ecclesiology impacts views of soteriology and the sacraments. The Landmark view of the sacraments is reflected today in the closed communion practiced by some Baptist churches and a re-baptizing of new members, even those baptized by immersion upon profession of faith, but baptized in other than a Baptist church. In extreme cases this extends to those baptized by immersion upon profession of faith in other Baptist churches.

---

1. Tull, *High-Church Baptists in the South*, ix.

This "high churchism" of the Landmarkers was a denominational exclusivism that was highly sectarian in its ecclesiology. This exclusive ecclesiology manifested itself in a rejection of non-Baptist ministers since they affirmed that only Baptist ministers are true ministers of the gospel, and only baptism by immersion by an authentic minister of the gospel in a true (i.e., Baptist) church is true baptism. J. R. Graves, the father of Landmarkism, whose theology will be examined in more detail, wrote "that [by] treating the ministers of other denominations as the accredited ministers of the gospel, and receiving any of their official acts—*preaching* or *immersion*—as scriptural, we [would] proclaim louder than we can by words, that their societies are evangelical churches, and their teachings and practices orthodox as our own."[2] This was something Graves said Baptists did not want to do. Graves insisted that these other denominations are but "human societies" and represent nothing but "the expression of human *opinion*."[3] Landmarkers insisted that there was no invisible church and that the church was local, visible, independent, and democratic in its polity. No churches other than Baptist fit this description according to the Landmarkers. Finally, their ecclesiology was built around a doctrine of church succession that traced the existence of Baptist churches in an unbroken line back to the time of Christ. They held that Baptist churches "*alone* hold, and have alone ever held, and preserved the doctrine of the gospels in all ages since the ascension of Christ."[4]

According to Graves every religious society that claims to be a true church "must establish the fact of the existence of a similar people to themselves, holding and teaching similar doctrines and principles of Church polity during the Apostolic period and by the apostles recognized as Christians, and also from this period through succeeding centuries until the present."[5] By this he implies that the doctrines of the Landmarkers are historic and long-held Baptist doctrines. Many writers have taken the Landmark theology to task and shown rather convincingly that the Landmark positions were not historical Baptist doctrines but rather represented a departure from Baptist doctrine and practice. Rather than try to add to what has been established by competent writers in this regard, what follows is a look at some representative aspects of the theology of J. R Graves, J. M. Pendleton, and the Carroll brothers, B. H. Carroll and J. M. Carroll. Graves and

---

2. Graves, *Old Landmarkism*, 25–26. Graves highlighted his writing with italics, bold type, and all capital letters to make his points stand out. All such stylistic devices herein have been reduced to italics.

3. Ibid., 31 (emphasis in original).

4. Ibid., 25 (emphasis in original).

5. Graves, *Great Iron Wheel*, 21.

Pendleton were foundational in the formation of the Landmark movement and the Carrolls represent the next generation of Landmark thought and quite frankly the normalization and assimilation of some Landmark elements into the fabric of Southern Baptist life.

J. R. Graves—Representative Aspects of His Theology

James Robinson Graves, the father of the Landmark movement, was born in Chester, Vermont, on April 10, 1820. He was raised in a Congregationalist church but in 1835 he joined a Baptist church. In 1839 he moved to northern Ohio where he served as the principal of a small school. In 1841 he moved to Nicholasville, Kentucky, and assumed the position of headmaster of a school there. For all his positions in the field of education, Graves was largely self-educated and mastered several languages through self-study. In 1845 he accepted a job teaching in Nashville, Tennessee, and in July of that year joined the First Baptist Church of that city.[6] The pastor of First Baptist was R. B. C. Howell, an influential leader in the Southern Baptist Convention and editor of the *Baptist*. The *Baptist*, edited by R. B. C. Howell, was the original name of the *Tennessee Baptist* which was later taken over by J. R. Graves. The *Baptist* was a weekly newspaper published in Nashville by the Baptist General Association of Tennessee. The name was changed to the *Tennessee Baptist* in 1847.

Like all people Graves was to some extent a product of his environment and the religious environment on the frontier and in the new settlements of what was then called the southwest was one of a very competitive nature. The religious, secular, and cultural thought of the day was shaped by a rugged individualism and the pioneer spirit of those who had gone into the wilderness and carved out a life. This individualism marked political, secular, and religious ideas of the day. On the religious front the Second Great Awakening had produced great revivals of religion, particularly in Kentucky. This was a time of schism and conflict among the mainline denominations, and fragmentation of denominations into new denominations, all of which led to a competition for the hearts, minds, and membership of those in the frontier states. Much of this activity was centered in Kentucky and Tennessee and Graves found himself in the middle of this environment and sought to take his place as the champion of the Baptists. This highly sectarian, competitive environment, fed by the new revivalism, camp meetings, and a shortage of trained ministers, produced an environment wherein controversies flourished, and the older orthodoxy fell victim

6 Burnett, *Sketches of Tennessee's Pioneer Baptist Preachers*, 184–200.

to new measures. These influences undoubtedly shaped Graves to be the competitive, sectarian, combative, and yet in some ways winsome defender of what he believed to be Baptist (and thus true) orthodoxy.

Shortly after joining the First Baptist Church Graves accepted the pastorship of the Second Baptist Church of Nashville (November 15, 1846, according to a letter published in the pages of the *Baptist* on November 21, 1846). In that same issue of the *Baptist*, Howell introduced Graves as the assistant editor of that paper and called Graves "the indefatigable and successful pastor of the Second Church," and said that the editorial policy of the paper would be: "We shall still retain our [i.e., Howell's] supervision of the *Baptist*, and see that nothing finds its way into its columns that ought not to be there, and that what ought to be shall be published. And, since we do not desire to have credit for any thing we do not write, all articles of any importance hereafter written by us, will bear the signature of H. For the remainder our readers will look to our Assistant."[7]

This marked a major step forward in the advancement of Graves' views as he now had a forum other than the pulpit of the Second Baptist Church.[8] The denominational newspaper at this time was an important means of communicating doctrine, church news, and general news of the country to many people. As Tull says, the importance and influence of denominational papers grew. "Between the Civil War and the turn of the century the denominational newspaper was one of the most powerful instruments in forming denominational opinion."[9] Almost from the beginning Graves began to attack the validity of what he termed "alien immersions," the validity of Pedobaptist "societies" and indeed the validity of all non-Baptist churches, and the recognition of their ministers as ministers of Christ. Graves was brash and unrelenting in his attacks on those whose views differed from his own and he had a vehicle in what was arguably the most widely circulated and most successful denominational paper of the day to push forward those attacks.

In addition, in 1847, he created what would become a publishing empire by forming the Tennessee Publication Society, the constitution of which was later carried in the *Baptist*.[10] His publishing empire eventually grew strong enough to challenge the Southern Baptist Publication Society, which Graves contended was doctrinally impure. The publication houses under his control bore several names, e.g., Graves and Shankland; Graves,

7. *Baptist* (Nashville), 21 November 1846.

8. The *Baptist* had one thousand subscribers at the time and under the new name the *Tennessee Baptist* boasted 1,800 by the end of 1848 (see Baptist General Association of Tennessee, *Minutes*, 1849, 24).

9. Tull, *High-Church Baptists in the South*, 121.

10. *Baptist* (Nashville), 18 May 1848 (see appendix A).

Marks, and Company; and Southwestern Publishing House, and provided a point of direct influence with Southern Baptist pastors, churches, Sunday School classes, and laypeople.

The name of the *Baptist* was changed to the *Tennessee Baptist* in 1847 and in the June 29, 1848, issue Graves was listed as the editor, R. B. C. Howell's name dropped from the masthead, and Graves and Shankland listed as the sole publishers all without fanfare. (Graves and A. B. Shankland, his partner in the publishing house, served as president and vice president, respectively, of the Nashville Indian Mission Association formed March 25, 1846.) In addition to the regular editorials by Graves, two other features were included in the *Tennessee Baptist* in 1848. In the issue of February 3, 1848, a new feature, "The Querist," was introduced. The introductory notice read,

> We have concluded to devote a column of our paper each week, under the head of Querist, which column shall be devoted to the examination of such ecclesiastical and exegetical questions as may be propounded to us by our subscribers. We would not have our readers infer from this that we set ourselves up [as] . . . competent to pronounce upon any and every question, an "infallible opinion," or give accurate solution. We have no such vanity. An exchange of sentiments with our brethren is all we propose.[11]

Apparently, Graves wanted to answer questions that were not being posed or that others were reluctant to pose. Letters began to appear from one "Fidus," a mysterious figure who steadfastly refused to identify himself by any other means. The letters from Fidus, however, usually appeared in the regular columns of the paper, sometimes on the front page, and not in the Querist column. In the June 29, 1848, issue of the *Tennessee Baptist* there is a handwritten note on the primary source that reads, "Fidus is J. R. Graves, O. L. H. 7/27/14."[12] O. L. Hailey was Graves' son-in-law and biographer who published a biography of Graves in 1929. Hailey was the contributor of the original copies of the *Tennessee Baptist* that are housed in the library of the Southwestern Baptist Theological Seminary.

By these stratagems Graves was able to set forth his distinctive theology in one of the most influential media of the day, the weekly denominational newspaper. Although these doctrines are set forth in his voluminous works, they had been exposed to Southern Baptist church members, pastors, and seminary professors for years, in many cases, before the publication of many of his works. Many his writings were later incorporated into the literature of

---

11. *Tennessee Baptist* (Nashville), 3 February 1848.
12. *Tennessee Baptist* (Nashville), 29 June 1848.

the Southern Baptist Sunday School Board. A look at representative aspects of his theology follows.

Ecclesiology

In the introduction of the Querist column Graves shows his propensity for ecclesiology as he singles it out from the "exegetical questions." One could say that the doctrine of the church was the *sine qua non* of Graves' entire theology. He emphasized heavily the characteristics of the church as an institution to the neglect of the church as a body of believers. His emphasis on the place and the importance of the local church influenced all his theology.

Some of Graves' theology was undoubtedly shaped by his early association with R. B. C. Howell. Much of Howell's prominence in Southern Baptist life was owing to his strong opposition reflected in the pages of the *Baptist* against Pedobaptists and Campbellites.[13] While Graves was still a member of First Baptist Church in Nashville Howell was criticized by the *South Western Christian Advocate* in an article appearing in the *Baptist* for claiming that he had found the "true church of Christ and had found it in the Baptist church."[14] Howell's assertion that "John was the first who preached the gospel"[15] finds full expression in Graves' doctrine of the church.

The general assumption is that Graves' ecclesiology was formed gradually, taking full shape after the Civil War in the mid-1860s. That assumption probably stems from the fact that most of his books were published after the war, but his positions are seen taking shape much earlier as the editor of the *Tennessee Baptist*.

As early as 1848, writing under his pseudonym Fidus, he criticizes Rev. R. B. Burleson of Northern Alabama for favoring "open communion." Later in that same article he adds that each church should decide the matter. "The churches of Muscle Shoals cannot be dragooned into this doctrine [of open

---

13. Alexander Campbell was the founder of the Campbellites, or Disciples of Christ. He was a Baptist who took exception to the various boards and societies which were being formed. He considered the Missionary, Bible, Sunday School, and Tract Societies as the precursor to a national church. His views of ecclesiology and soteriology in particular led him to be disowned by the Baptists and he formed a new body, the Disciples of Christ. Campbell taught that one became a Christian by accepting the facts of the gospel, repenting, and submitting to baptism by immersion. He taught that Christ's sacrifice paid the penalty for sin but added that submission to baptism brought salvation to completion. He published a religious newspaper, the *Christian Baptist*, which he used to propagate his views, attract followers, and attack his foes. See Campbell, *Debate between Rev. A. Campbell and Rev. N. L. Rice*.

14. *Baptist* (Nashville), 25 July 1846.

15. *Baptist* (Nashville), 2 May 1846.

communion], nor can the advocates of primitive and apostolic practice be either terrified or cajoled into silence."[16] In just this one response we see Graves had already formed a very trenchant position toward close[17] communion, the autonomy and independence of the local church, and a hint of Baptist church succession. In November of that same year, again writing as Fidus, he states that "genuine Baptists in all ages re-baptized all they received into their membership and fellowship, from Rome or from any of her numerous daughters . . . they are all organizations, set up in opposition to the kingdom of Christ. I can't receive their acts."[18] Here already is the formation of a rejection of all non-Baptist baptisms, the assertion that all the churches that sprang from the Reformation are not true churches but organizations (societies is the word he later prefers), and the idea that all such churches, i.e., non-Baptist churches, are not part of the kingdom of Christ. His later formulation of these ideas in *Old Landmarkism: What Is It?* (1880) shows no different attitude. For example, he writes, "No organization on earth—unscriptural in these regards as every sound Baptist believes Campbellite and PedoBaptist societies to be—can be, or should be regarded as a church of Christ."[19] He adds near the end of the aforementioned column that "every member received into its [the local church's] fellowship be immersed by an authorized Bap. [sic] minister."[20] His emphasis on the "authorized administrator" thus surfaces early in his influential writings.

This question of an authorized administrator reappears in that same year. Fidus again writes "that the question [of valid baptism and therefore church membership] always did terminate on the validity of the administrator, for, a *properly organized church*, holding the proper doctrine, would always afford a *properly authorized administrator*. If a *church* is unscriptural, her *officers*, and their *acts* are also."[21] Notice the emphasis he places on organization and administration.

In the same issue Graves, as Fidus, also traces the Baptist family through the centuries based in large part on George Herbert Orchard's *Concise History of Foreign Baptists*. Graves in this article affirms that Baptists

---

16. *Tennessee Baptist* (Nashville), 6 July 1848.

17. Although the term has evolved into "closed" communion, the term used by the pastors, writers, and some theologians of the period was "close" communion as explained by Pendleton: "Communion is derived from the Latin word *communio* and close comes from *clausus* and means 'shut fast'" (*Tennessee Baptist* [Nashville], 5 June 1852).

18. *Tennessee Baptist* (Nashville), 16 November 1848.

19. Graves, *Old Landmarkism: What Is It?*, 151.

20. *Tennessee Baptist* (Nashville), 16 November 1848.

21. *Tennessee Baptist* (Nashville), 7 December 1848 (emphasis in original).

were known down through the centuries as: Novatians, Donatists, Phrygians, Galatians, Armenians, Paulicians, Paterines, Vaudois, Albigenses, Lollards, Waldenses, and Ana-baptists [*sic*]. This will be dealt with more fully in a succeeding chapter on Baptist successionism but the conclusion Graves draws from a very long article is that as these "Baptists" followed the rule (quoting Bullinger) that "they who by baptism are received into their churches ought not to have any communion with those called evangelical or any other whatsoever; for that our reformed churches are not true churches, no more than the churches of the Papists."[22] Graves adds, "Now this sentiment I endorse word and point. I do not regard any Pedobaptist church as a true church of Christ. . . . If such churches are not scripturally organized churches, why would we receive any one of their acts?"[23]

Regarding church government and proper officers of the church Graves wrote in 1850:

> There can be no such thing as a proper officer, unless one duly invested, by a legitimate government. Now how many forms of government did Christ institute for his church, one, or many? If He gave but one government, then some one and only one of the many now existing organizations must be that one—the only legitimate and proper government, and no ordinance is valid administered out of that one. If the government of the Primitive Church was republican, then is the Baptist church that one, being the only pure democratic government existing in the world. Now we care not how pious a man or minister may be, he must be a legitimate officer, or he has no authority to baptize, or to perform any official act, nor is any act he may perform official or valid.[24]

Here again Graves espouses the idea that the Baptist church is the only true church, but he also introduces the notion that the first church was democratic in its government, meaning it was republican, i.e., it was a republic with a democratic form of government, as the United States, and that is the only true form of church government. If a church is only local, then local self-government is one of its primary marks. This idea comes to the fore in 1853 in his attack upon Methodism with the interesting title *The Great Iron Wheel, or Republicanism Backwards and Christianity Reversed*. Graves was certainly influenced by his environment, but he had no qualms about projecting his present experience back into the New Testament and

---

22. *Tennessee Baptist* (Nashville), 7 December 1848.
23. Ibid.
24. *Tennessee Baptist* (Nashville), 7 February 1850.

thus establishing the biblical, christological, and apostolic foundation for what he determined to be the marks of the one true church.

One of his favorite illustrations of the kingdom and the churches of Christ was drawn from an analogy to the American Republic, the United States. He said often "that, by baptism, we become citizens of the kingdom of Christ, only because it introduces us into one of its constituents—a local church—just as we become a citizen of this Republic only by becoming a citizen of some one of its constituents—a State."[25] Besides the obvious theological problems Graves' analogy fails at several points. First, Christ is an absolute monarch over his church. Second, one does not become a citizen of the United States by first becoming a citizen of a state. The persons born in the United States or naturalized as citizens of the United States may then become citizens of any state they choose.

Later in 1850 Graves published a piece written by him that had been published in the *Southern Baptist Register for 1850*. It is worth including in its entirety here for it is the early foundation of much that is published later as definitive of Landmarkism.

> With the word of God before us we now lay down the *essential features*, without all of which no society can be justly entitled to be called a church of Christ.
>
> 1. It must be a *voluntary association*, of persons professing regeneration, and baptized upon that profession, and admitting no unregenerated person, adult or infant, to its ordinances, or fellowship.
> 2. It must have no temporal head as bishops, conferences or assemblies, and acknowledge no laws but those enacted by Christ and the apostles.
> 3. An *executive* body only, and its government, so far as men administer it *republican*, which was the government of the apostolic churches.
> 4. It must have preserved that form of doctrine, and the ordinances once delivered.
> 5. It must never have shed the blood of saints, or any human being for conscience sake.
> 6. One or more of such churches must have existed from the days of the apostles until now, for prophecy declares when

---

25. Graves, *Intercommunion*, 113, 161.

once set up this kingdom was never to be destroyed, and Christ said the gates of hell should not prevail against it.[26]

Following this Graves called a meeting of concerned Baptists at Cotton Grove, Tennessee, on June 24, 1851. Promoted through the *Tennessee Baptist* this meeting generated a great deal of interest throughout the South and many regard this as the official beginning of the Landmark movement. Graves posed five questions to those assembled at Cotton Grove, which he raised later that same month to the annual meeting of the Big Hatchie Association that met at Bolivar, Tennessee. These questions were adopted as a series of resolutions that became known as the Cotton Grove Resolutions and were adopted unanimously by the Big Hatchie Association. The resolutions were:

1. Can Baptists, consistently with their principles of the scriptures, recognize those societies not organized according to the pattern of the Jerusalem Church, but possessing different governments, different officers, a different class of members, different ordinances, doctrines, and practices, as churches of Christ?
2. Ought they to be called gospel churches, or churches in a religious sense?
3. Can we consistently recognize the ministers of such irregular and unscriptural bodies as gospel ministers?
4. Is it not virtually recognizing them as official ministers to invite them into our pulpits, or by any other act that would or could be construed into such a recognition?
5. Can we consistently address as brethren those professing Christianity who not only have not the doctrines of Christ and walk not according to his commandments, but are arrayed in direct and bitter opposition to them?[27]

These resolutions became the hallmarks of the Landmark movement as it came to be defined. Graves began to debate, through the pages of his newspaper, these issues with other denominations. In a letter to Joshua Soule, bishop of the Methodist Episcopal Church, South,[28] published in the

26. *Tennessee Baptist* (Nashville), 14 March 1850.
27. Graves, *Old Landmarkism*, xi–xii. It should be noted that Graves ran a series of articles in the *Tennessee Baptist* in December 1851 and January 1852 explaining and defending the five resolutions. (See appendix B for full text of the minutes of the Cotton Grove Meeting.)
28. The Methodist Episcopal Church, South, was formed as a separate denomination, as were the Baptist and Presbyterians in the South, over the issue of slavery. The

pages of the *Tennessee Baptist*, Graves says, "If the M. E. Church is a Church of Christ—a scriptural organization, Baptist Churches are not. One of them is an unscriptural and anti-christian organization.... Both are not—cannot be scriptural bodies—or Gospel Churches."[29] This letter was carried under the title "The Great Iron Wheel" which Graves published in book form in 1853. In the second installment Graves flatly told Bishop Soule that "the M. E. Church cannot justly be called a Church of Christ, 1st, because too young by 1747 years—being only 68 years old."[30] To Graves the Methodist church violated tenets number two and six of his piece written in 1850, and thus cannot under the Cotton Grove Resolutions be recognized as either a scriptural or true church, and no recognition can be granted to their ministers, nor could they even be addressed as brethren.

All of Graves' emphasis on the organization of the church produced a belief that the church was only a visible, local organization. Graves said, "Christ never set up but one kingdom, was never constituted King of but one kingdom, and his word recognized but one kingdom, and if this is visible, he has no invisible kingdom or church, and such a thing has no real existence."[31] Ideas of an invisible, universal church, Graves said, are "invisible nonsense." He asserted that the church is visible because all the terms used in Scripture for the church, such as kingdom, bride, church, body, wife, are visible and material things.[32] He adds, "The phrases 'Mount Sion,' 'the city of God,' and 'heavenly Jerusalem' denote the church of the New Testament.... It evidently can not mean an invisible church in heaven ... nor yet an invisible church of living Christians on the earth for such an institution does not exist."[33] This line of thinking necessarily excludes not

---

1844 General Conference voted to remove Bishop James Andrew from his bishopric unless he freed his slaves. The Southern delegates questioned the authority of the General Conference to carry out such an action. This dispute led the Methodists in the South to form a separate denomination, the Methodist Episcopal Church, South.

29. *Tennessee Baptist* (Nashville), 20 March 1852.

30. *Tennessee Baptist* (Nashville), 24 April 1852. Part of Graves' constant battle with the Methodist Episcopal Church, South, was a competition for members and growth. However, despite editorial attacks, debates supposedly won by Graves, and debates carried on in the pages of the religious papers of the day the Southern Baptists made no significant gains versus the Methodist Episcopal Church, South. Membership figures for 1845–1846 show the Methodists with 459,569 members and the Baptists with 365,346. By 1860 the figures were 757,205 and 650,000 respectively, an increase of approximately 298,000 and 285,000 respectively (see Baptist History and Heritage Society and Alexander Gross, *History of the Methodist Church, South*, Summers, *Confederate States Almanac*).

31. Graves, *Old Landmarkism*, 32.

32. Ibid.

33. Graves, *Work of Christ*, 240.

only the invisible church but the church universal, militant, and triumphant as well. His position is clear, "Christ never intimated that he had kingdoms numerous; one in heaven triumphant, and one on earth militant; one within the hearts of men, and one outward and visible. The invisible church and kingdom are myths . . . the locality of the church and kingdom of Christ is the earth and nowhere else."[34] The inevitable conclusion Graves reaches is that only Baptist churches make up the kingdom of God. Graves says as much when he writes, "This much will be admitted by all Baptists, that our churches are scriptural church organizations. If so, they alone constitute the visible kingdom of Christ."[35] He adds, "The kingdom of Christ is not composed of persons, but of churches."[36] Further, he says, "no one can enter the kingdom of Christ without becoming a member of some one of his visible churches."[37] When Christ says to Nicodemus in John 3:5 that "no one can enter the kingdom of God unless he is born of water and Spirit,"[38] Graves asserts, "It was of a visible earthly organization he spake—his church."[39]

As Graves sees it, the conclusive proof of his assertion that the church is only local is found in the exegesis of the Greek word *ekklesia*, which he says has but one possible meaning. It means simply a local organization. He adds, that in one hundred of the one hundred ten uses it refers only to a local, visible, organized church. He attributes the remaining ten uses to synecdoche "where a part is put for the whole, the singular for the plural, one for all."[40] He adds, "The irresistible conclusion from all this is that a religious organization that can not be assembled in one place and all its members act as a unit can not be a Scriptural *Ekklesia* or Church."[41]

As the kingdom cannot exist without being a local, visible, earthly organization, and since Graves believed the kingdom had existed since the time of John the Baptist, and since there was only one congregation at that time, the church composed the kingdom and the kingdom included the church.[42] The disciples became the church because they were "called out of the world by conversion and baptism [and] associated in a visible

---

34. Ibid., 287–88.

35. Ibid., 154.

36. Ibid., 267.

37. Ibid., 33.

38. Unless noted all references are to the *Holy Bible*, New International Version (Grand Rapids: Zondervan, 1984).

39. Graves, *Old Landmarkism*, 33.

40. Ibid., 38.

41. Graves, *New Great Iron Wheel*, 126–27.

42. Graves, *Intercommunion*, 153.

body according to the direction of Christ their only Head and King."[43] As the number of churches increased they composed the kingdom of God. But only those founded by Christ, in existence since the time of John the Baptist, and local, visible, and properly organized were considered true churches. Graves sums it up by stating, "Christ never set up on earth but one kingdom, which is a visible one, composed of his churches as constituencies."[44] For Graves, continuity of organization, a scriptural, democratic organization, constitutes the church, the kingdom, and such is found only in Baptist churches. In his own words, "If Christ has had witnessing Churches during all those ages, as he declared he would have, the Baptist churches are those bodies."[45]

The Trinity

As in his expressed doctrine of ecclesiology, much of what Graves related as Trinitarian doctrine first appeared in the pages of the *Tennessee Baptist*. However, his magnum opus was *The Work of Christ in the Covenant of Redemption, Developed in Seven Dispensations*, published in 1883. As in his earlier writings much of what is written is a compilation of earlier articles, debates, and queries answered in the pages of the denominational newspapers. In all his writings Graves always affirmed the eternal existence of the Trinity and the eternity of the Godhead. However, Graves denied the eternal Sonship of Christ and, in fact, the eternity of the designations Father, Son, and Holy Spirit. He said, "The terms Father, Son, and Holy Spirit are official and relative terms, and originated with the Covenant of Redemption, which is not eternal."[46] His position was that these designations are relevant only to the Trinity's actions in time and history which began at creation. His own words set forth his position clearly:

> Before the birth of creation there could have been no relationship existing as that of Father and Son, for these are terms of relationship, and imply order of being, and consequently demand time. If this be so, then evidently the phrases "Eternal Father, and Eternal Son" are inadmissible, since they involve a manifest contradiction. As certainly as the creator must exist before the thing created, the begetter must exist before the

---

43. Ibid.
44. Ibid., 20 (emphasis in original).
45. Graves, *Graves-Ditzler*, 1055.
46. Graves, *Work of Christ*, 35.

> begotten—Father before Son. And it is no less contradictious to say that Father and Son eternally self-existed in these relations.[47]
>
> "In the beginning was the Word." There must have been a point in time when the second Person was not manifested or known as the Word.[48]
>
> The several persons of the trinity, and the names Father and Son, by which these persons are revealed to us, are relative and official names, and therefore can not be qualified by the adjective eternal; since it would imply that a son could be as old as his father, for if always a son, then never begotten.[49]

Graves here, as pointed out earlier, often makes the mistake of reducing the complexities and mysteries of that which God has revealed in his Word to strictly literal human experience and univocal predication. Graves believed in a literal interpretation of Scripture to the extreme. In the closing pages of *The Work of Christ*, he wrote, "I have in this volume interpreted the Scriptures according to their literal sense, and I regard this as the only correct and safe principle of interpreting them. . . . Whoever may oppose this doctrine and the principle of a literal interpretation of the scriptures, will not the candid reader conclude with us that it was one of the Old Landmarks of the faith of the Apostolic Church."[50]

While not in any sense denying the eternality of the three Persons of the Trinity, Graves once again is at odds with much of orthodoxy. Augustus H. Strong, a Baptist theologian of note, says, "The Sonship of Christ is eternal . . . there never having been a time when the Son began to be, or when the Son did not exist as God with the Father."[51] John 1:18 is instructive in this matter the phraseology employed is that of the definite article with the present participle of the verb "to be" (*ho ōn*), i.e., "the (one) being in the bosom of the Father." This participial construction is not limited in point of time and what John expresses here is an eternal description. Charles Hodge says of this construction that the present tense of the verb preceded by the article expresses permanent being.[52] Some, like T. A. Patterson, maintain that Graves was only asserting a distinction between historical assumptions of authority and subjection as "recognized in the theological assumption

---

47. Ibid., 61.
48. Ibid., 62.
49. Ibid., 80–81.
50. Ibid., 556, 563.
51. Strong, *Systematic Theology*, 340.
52. Hodge, *Systematic Theology*, 473.

of first, second, and third persons—an impossibility with infinite, coequal beings . . . he was maintaining that a finite description of time must not be applied to an infinite community of eternal persons."[53] The various analyses of Graves' theology and its impact will be examined in more detail in chapter 5.

Christology

Many who have heretofore written about Graves' Christology have used phrases like: "Dr. Graves' position on the Person of Christ was in some respects peculiar."[54] "Christology is one of the most unsatisfactory aspects of Graves' theology."[55] "Dr. Graves held somewhat peculiar views of the twofold nature of the Lord Jesus."[56] An examination of Graves' views in the area of Christology show his views to be somewhat more than peculiar and unsatisfactory (this being one of the stronger words used).

Graves' teachings regarding the Trinity (above) suggest, although he did not explicitly say such, that there was a time when the Son did not exist. He is clear that the Second Person of the Trinity was eternal but his emphasis on restricting the names Father and Son to acts in time or immediately before time in the Covenant of Redemption produces the logical conclusion, as he did say, that these names cannot be used with the adjective "eternal."[57]

Regarding the two natures of Christ, Graves said, "We also see that the Person of the Son of God, being the Second Person of the Trinity is Divine, and only relatively human."[58] His position on the lack of a human soul in the God-man, Jesus Christ, stems from his interpretation of Old Testament theophanies. Referring to those theophanies he wrote, "No one will claim that there was a human soul in those bodies as well as the animating Divinity, and no more was there in their Great Archetype, the Son of Man,—the Christ."[59] He adds to his original error, "If in Christ was a union of two complete persons, a perfect man, soul and body, and a Divine Person, he would have been a Dual Being; and the Divine and human persons could have held intercourse with each other."[60] Graves, contrary to Scripture, adds, "So, in

53. Patterson, "Theology of J. R. Graves," 194–95.
54. Smith, "Critical Analysis," 19.
55. Patterson, "Theology of J. R. Graves," 323.
56. Hailey, *J. R. Graves*, 108.
57. Graves, *Work of Christ*, 61.
58. Ibid., 87.
59. Ibid., 91.
60. Ibid., 88.

the womb of the virgin, by the mysterious and joint agency of the First and Second Persons, he took upon himself our flesh . . . but the Person of that body was Divine."[61] It should be noted that Graves uses the term "person" as synonymous with soul in many instances.

A technique that Graves often used in debates with his opponents and which he incorporated into his writings was the use of syllogisms with faulty premises to reach his foregone conclusion.[62] To defend his assertion that Christ did not have a human soul he reasons as follows: "But if it be true that Christ subsisted in two persons [he means had two souls] as well as two natures here, the one human and the other divine, then it is evident that the former, being finite, must necessarily have been imperfect."[63] So rather than accept the clear word of the Scriptures and the historic doctrines of the church, which is understandable given his position on the church, he prefers to retreat into a form of Apollinarianism[64] with Arian[65] leanings in some elements of his Christology and his Trinitarian formulations.

Regarding the offices of Christ, Graves held that "Christ, though Lawful King, has not yet been Crowned King of kings. Many speak of Christ as now crowned and occupying his throne in heaven. So far from this being true, Christ, as messiah, has no throne in heaven, never had, and never will have."[66] This was not an isolated remark. Later in the same work he adds, "Christ has not yet been crowned, and . . . he is not reigning in heaven. And, as Messiah, will never reign there, but when he is crowned and reigns, it will be on the throne of his father David, which was an earthly throne."[67]

Graves also held to the kenosis[68] theory that in order to accomplish the work of redemption Christ had to divest himself of all vestiges of glory

---

61. Ibid., 91.

62. A syllogism is a formal argument or deduction that consists of a major premise, a minor premise, and a conclusion which follows from said premises. The premises are assumed to be known and lead to the conclusion.

63. Graves, *Work of Christ*, 121.

64. Apollinaris held that while in other men body, soul, and spirit coexist in unity (trichotomy), Christ possessed only a human body and soul. The Divine Logos had displaced the human spirit thus Christ was not fully human. Apollinaris was condemned by the first council of Constantinople (381).

65. Arius (who sparked the controversy that led to the council of Nicaea) held that there was a time when the Son was not. He said the Father was not always the Father for before the Son was begotten he could not have been a Father nor could the Son have been a son. Arius drew from this that there was a time when the Son was not, something Graves tries to avoid saying although he comes perilously close.

66. Graves, *Work of Christ*, 290.

67. Ibid., 415.

68. The term kenosis appeared in the middle of the nineteenth century as a new

and honor which would have been due a coequal member of the Godhead. He states specifically that "Christ emptied himself" of his glory and honor.[69]

The Atonement

Graves preferred to use the term "Covenant of Redemption" or "Covenant of Grace" to describe how God affected the salvation of men.[70] The parties of this covenant were the three Persons of the Godhead and according to Graves, as shown above; the titles of Father, Son, and Holy Spirit are relevant only to their respective actions in history. Consistent with that line of thinking Graves asserts that the Covenant required the Persons of the Trinity to assume new functions. The second Person of the Trinity covenanted to be the One who would live a life of obedience to the law and endure the curse of the law for mankind. Through his vicarious suffering he made propitiation for man and became the intercessor for man. Under the terms of the Covenant the Second Person thus came to be called the Son.[71]

Graves takes an Anselmian view of Christ's active obedience. He says that even granting that there was a perfect human person in Christ, "still this human side of Christ could not have fulfilled all righteousness by obeying the law perfectly for others; because . . . that human being, though sinless, owed a perfect obedience to the law for himself."[72] In words very similar to Anselm he adds, "The insulted dignity, the violated rights and just claims of the Divine Government, must be becomingly represented by some party in this Covenant."[73] On the other hand, he takes the view held by many before Anselm, the Ransom Theory which Anselm refutes in *Cur Deus Homo*. Graves wrote, "We are . . . consequently the slaves of sin and Satan, never to be released without a full ransom price."[74]

One of his more curious statements regarding the atonement says, "The shedding of the blood of Christ on Calvary was not the atonement . . . nor did he make, nor could he have made, an atonement on the cross, or on this earth . . . he must needs rise from the dead, and take his blood and

---

form of Christology whereby the God-man, not the Logos, "emptied" himself of, or laid aside the actual use of his divine attributes. Some forms of this theory have the incarnate Logos taking the place of the human soul.

69. Graves, *Dispensational Expositions*, 102.
70. Graves, *Work of Christ*, 67.
71. Ibid., 81–117.
72. Ibid., 119.
73. Ibid., 68.
74. Ibid., 112.

ascend to the right hand of God, before the true mercy seat on high, and there make atonement for his people."[75] Once again one sees that his literal reading of Scripture coupled with his dispensational theology and his view of the nature of Christ produces a strange theology that in the case at hand contradicts Christ's very words that it is finished, words spoken from the cross (cf. John 19:30).

His dispensational views also produced some odd statements regarding the application of redemption. He asserts, "Now, the blessing of his [Christ's] atonement, which is the fruit of adoption, viz., eternal redemption and glorification, no one has ever yet received, and no one will or can receive, until our Great High priest returns."[76] Graves formulates or explains this based on the following position:

> We are taught that nothing incomplete, imperfect or unglorified can enter or dwell in heaven. . . . The Scriptures also teach us that the dwellers in the presence of God are the recipients of *the fullness of joy*. . . . All such must be fully redeemed—perfected, glorified and satisfied. They can certainly look forward to no future change. . . . If these positions be correct, it is evident that Christians do not go to heaven when they die, for—saints, at their death are not fully redeemed. . . . All these—the most illustrious saints [those of Hebrews 11 and Revelation 6] that ever lived on this earth—had not ascended into heaven, but had for ages been impatiently waiting in a comparatively depressed state.[77]

He leans heavily on Peter's sermon at Pentecost wherein he says, "David did not ascend to heaven" (Acts 2:34). The conclusion he reaches is thus twofold. "No saint has yet ascended to heaven, and it is evident that no sinner has descended into hell."[78] His assumption is that all souls, both those of the sinner and the saint, are in Hades, which he defines simply as "unseen." The saints are in Paradise in a relative state of ease though unsatisfied and impatient while the sinners fare far worse. Graves calls this the "Middle Life," i.e., that which "Christ called Paradise" and "it is to paradise," he says, "that the souls of all the saved go now at death, where they will await the consummation of their complete salvation."[79] He adds, "While the souls of the righteous are retained in the custody of *hades*—the abode of spirits—they are subject to its laws and conditions . . . they are,

---

75. Ibid., 234.
76. Ibid., 234–35.
77. Graves, *Biblical Doctrine of the Middle Life*, 21, 26.
78. Ibid., 30.
79. Ibid., 61–62.

in a sense, captives, though 'prisoners of hope.'"[80] In another place Graves just blithely asserts the doctrine of purgatory, although he would call the Roman Catholic Church the fountain of all heresies and source of attacks upon the true church down through the ages. He says regarding paradise and hades, "That paradise, although a state of happiness, is not heaven itself, nor is hades hell itself, or purgatory, in which souls are purified of their sins by the fires of punishment. Hades is not purgatory, since no one can ever pass from it to the abode of the blest."[81] He never goes on to explain what he means by this, but a plain reading of what he says shows that souls in purgatory pass out of that place after purification although souls cannot pass out of Hades (which concept is a little mixed between his various writings but it is contrasted here with paradise). For a man who constantly affirms justification by faith alone, this whole idea of the purification (for which word we could substitute justification) of souls after death "by the fires of punishment," is dichotomous to the point of irrationality. After this purification, he holds that these purified souls can then pass out of purgatory into the abode of the blest.

Baptism

Integral to Graves' ecclesiology was his view of baptism as the exclusive province of the local Baptist church. He held that there were three essentials for a valid baptism. First was the mode—by immersion only. The second prerequisite was a proper administrator; and the third essential was a proper subject, a regenerate person, thus excluding infants. The first and third essentials will not be examined because these issues have filled untold pages and are beyond the scope of this work. However, the second essential goes right to the heart of Graves' ecclesiology and indeed forms the true essential for him. Valid baptism belonged exclusively to the authority of the local Baptist church, so much so that even baptism of a regenerate person by immersion was deemed invalid if performed outside a true, i.e., a Baptist, church. In his words:

> We learn from this Scripture [Acts 19:1–7]:
>
> 1. That persons may be immersed, and yet not have received the Christian immersion.
>
> 2. That they may be immersed by an administrator who had himself been immersed, and yet not obey Christ in the act.

---

80. Ibid., 54–55.
81. Graves, *Dispensational Expositions*, 228–29.

3. That persons may have been immersed, and satisfied with their baptism, and yet not have received Christian immersion or baptism.

4. That unless professing the proper qualifications, and professing the proper faith, an immersion by even a proper authority is null and void.[82]

Aside from the obvious exegetical assumptions he makes and the conclusions he draws from an isolated case, even if he is correct in his conclusions, he takes and extends his conclusion over the whole of church history. We see his assertions regarding proper administrators surfacing in various writings because he regards only the local, visible, Baptist church as a proper administrator. He writes, "If Paedo-baptist and Campbellite societies are not churches . . . the immersions of all those societies, not scriptural churches, are as null and void as their sprinklings would be."[83] "It is evident, therefore, that Baptist churches can in no way endorse or approve what Methodists call 'baptisms' though administered by immersion. Since it is not only administered by an organization that is not a church, and therefore has no authority, and by ministers unbaptized and unauthorized . . . Methodism is without Scriptural baptism."[84] "If no baptism be valid except administered by a duly ordained minister of Christ in a true Church of Christ, visible . . . let Presbyterians and the world decide if the baptisms of Luther, John Calvin, John Knox, or any one of the first Presbyterian ministers or members, were valid."[85] Of course, he adds "that John the Baptist was a duly called and qualified Christian minister, belonging to the Gospel, and not the Legal Dispensation. That he was both a member of Christ's church and officer of his kingdom. That he preached the Gospel, and his baptism was therefore as valid as those administered by the apostles."[86] It is essential for Graves' doctrine of church succession, which will be examined in more detail, that John the Baptist be "an authorized administrator." If the doctrine of the church is the *sine qua non* of Graves' theology, the question of the "authorized administrator of baptism" is *the sine qua non* of his doctrine of the church. The twin prongs of Graves' argument and the foundation of the Landmark case against "alien immersions" were that to be valid baptism must be administered by a true church, and second, valid baptism is necessary for the constitution of a true church. He will use this rather circular reasoning as

82. Graves, *Christian Baptism*, 7.
83. Graves, *Act of Christian Baptism*, 55–56.
84. Graves, *Graves-Ditzler*, 1039.
85. Graves, *Trilemma*, 46.
86. Graves, *Work of Christ*, 294–95.

the criterion for true Baptist churches down through the centuries even if they did not call themselves "Baptist churches." This will be dealt with more fully in chapter 3.

Anthropology

Graves denies that the penalty for sin was physical death because as he says, "Adam certainly did not die physically the day he violated the law." His assertion that Adam did not die that day is because, as he says, "the words of the law are not susceptible of this meaning . . . [because] if physical death is the penalty of sin, then in dying we pay all the debt we owe to violated law and the work of Christ was unnecessary."[87]

He is somewhat unclear on man's involvement in being the means by which sin came into the world. He says that "creation involved a finite or imperfect state of things, which as a secondary cause produced evil."[88] This certainly does not agree with God's summation of creation that it was all "very good." His view on the state of infants is quite clear. He holds that all infants "Jew or Gentile, Christian or Heathen" are recipients of God's grace. He says, "All infants . . . dying in infancy, not having sinned after the similitude of Adam's transgression, have been made special recipients by the grace of Christ . . . grace must compensate in every infant that dies, [for] the native injury it received from the first Adam."[89] His view of Scripture and his overblown literal reading of the text are seen in his conclusion: "David's infant was saved; and, if his, therefore all infants."[90]

Much of Graves' theology was guided by an anthropocentric rather than a theocentric understanding of Scripture. As was mentioned earlier Graves was a product of the rugged individualism which marked the westward expansion of the nation. This individualism was marked by the belief in a person's ability to take religious matters into their own hands and to formulate their beliefs based on their own instinct, literal reading of the text, and private opinion. Theological reflection disappeared in the face of itinerant revivalism and the self-evident truths of individual interpretation. James Patterson has addressed this synthesis between Graves' individualism and the Landmark ecclesiology. Patterson says, "Graves repeatedly integrated the tenets of individualism and republicanism with his Landmarkism."[91] In

---

87. Ibid., 68.
88. Ibid., 60.
89. Ibid., 139.
90. Ibid.
91. Patterson, "J. R. Graves Synthesis," 12.

defending the superiority of Baptist polity, "Graves did not manifestly appeal to scriptural arguments but rather to the assumed compatibility of his ecclesiology with republicanism and individual rights."[92]

Eschatology

Graves was a premillennial dispensationalist at a time when that designation was relatively unknown or at the very least in its infancy.[93] John Nelson Darby completed his *Synopsis of the Books of the Bible* (5 vols.) between the years 1857–1867. This exposition Oswald T. Allis calls a "great treasure-house of Dispensational teaching."[94] This was certainly early enough for Graves to be influenced by Darby but there is no reference to any such reliance in any of Graves' works. However, two things stand out as essential factors in dispensationalism both of which find emphasis in Graves' theology—the distinction between Israel and the church and the hermeneutical principle of literal interpretation. Graves' interpretation of the Scriptures in their literal sense as the only safe and reliable method of interpretation has been noted above. His view of Israel and the church very clearly shows he regarded the church as distinct in nature, time, and organization from Israel.

Graves says concerning the church in the Old Testament, "If it is asked, 'Why not the kingdom of heaven and the church . . . before the days of John the Baptist?' I answer, For the best of reasons: neither existed before."[95] He adds, "The good olive tree [Romans 11] does not represent the literal family of Abraham or the Jewish nation . . . nor is it true that the Gentiles are ever to be grafted into it." Of course Graves' rejection of the universal

---

92. Ibid.

93. To define premillennial dispensationalist, one must look to the latinized word millennium which means a thousand years and is taken from the six occurrences of the Greek *chilia etn* in Revelation 20:1–7. Premillennialists hold that this age and the eternal state are separated by a thousand-year reign of Christ on the earth. This thousand-year reign will begin with Christ's return and will be distinguished by the final rebellion of Revelation 20:7–9. Thus, a premillenialist believes that Christ's return will happen before the thousand-year reign begins. The premillennial view was fostered initially by C. I. Scofield and his *Scofield Reference Bible*, originally published in 1909, and the Dallas Theological Seminary, founded in 1924 by Lewis Sperry Chafer. Foundational to the work of Scofield and Chafer were the writings of John Nelson Darby (1800–1882), often called the father of dispensationalism. Darby's key works were translated into English in the period 1857–1867 and he made lecture tours of America between 1870–1874. Graves published his book *The Work of Christ in the Covenant of Redemption, Developed in Seven Dispensations* in 1883.

94. Allis, *Prophecy and the Church*, 13–14.

95. Graves, *Work of Christ*, 272.

church because "the churches of Christ are each complete and independent bodies,"[96] and his assertion that in the first week of Christ's ministry he established a visible church and during his ministry there was but one church and that church was inaugurated by John the Baptist and was constituted of the baptized disciples which Christ received from John,[97] leaves no room for any continuity between the church of the Old Testament and the church of the New Testament. Graves contended that the former did not exist. He says that the "oft quoted passages afford no evidence that the church and Kingdom of Christ and the Jewish Kingdom before Christ, were one and the same, but contrariwise."[98]

Graves' dispensational premillennialism and his literal reading of the Scripture also produced some strange expressions of the intermediate and final state of Christians. It is of note, also, that he calls the doctrine of the premillennial coming of Christ "one of the old landmarks of primitive Christianity and should be received and held fast by all Christians of this age. Christians of all ages have held that the world would enjoy a thousand years of peace and happiness. . . . No one has ever questioned that such a glorious Age is clearly foretold by sacred writers in both Covenants."[99]

In his dispensational interpretations of the parables of the Lord he ends up with several classes or states of Christians, several examples of which follow:

> There will be millions saved during the millennial age, but these will not constitute the Bride of Christ . . . but, with the saved nations, will constitute the subjects over whom Christ and his Bride will reign for the thousand years.[100]

> All Christians are loved by Christ, and will be saved and rewarded according to what they have done and suffered for Him, but will not constitute His bride.[101]

> These [144,000 of Revelation 14] represent the comparatively few "choice ones" of the earth . . . and these . . . alone, will be honored with being made the Lamb's wife.

> [They were honored because] they were virgins. They had, while living here, kept themselves pure and chaste—intact from the

---

96. Graves, *Intercommunion*, 272.
97. Graves, *Work of Christ*, 264.
98. Ibid., 282.
99. Ibid., 313, 405.
100. Ibid., 461.
101. Graves, *Dispensational Expositions*, 251.

> sinful and demoralizing pleasures of the world [e.g.] the ballroom, the opera and the theater. [Additionally] they obeyed, from the heart, all His commandments.[102]

> John has shown [he quotes Revelation 7:9–17] a countless multitude of palm-bearers of all nations, who were Christians; but they were no part of the bride; nor were they honored, or even blessed, with even an invitation to the marriage supper, and yet they were saved.[103]

> These five unwise virgins were not enemies of Christ. . . . All that is said of them implies that they represent Christians as certainly as the wise ones. The door was shut, not of friendship certainly, or of love, but of a present blessing and enjoyment—i.e. participation as guests in the wedding supper. [Christ] will not close the door of salvation against them, but only the door of a present distinguished honor and blessing.[104]

> When He comes to receive His "elect ones" to Himself, the unfaithful and unwatchful will be "left" to suffer with "hypocrites and unbelievers" those terrible years of . . . the great tribulation. How sad to think the large proportion of Christians will lose the highest honors, and only through the greatest tribulation will enter the Kingdom.[105]

> Since he was the lord's own servant [the parable of the talents], as were the other servants, like them he represented Christians, but as a slothful servant he represented slothful ones . . . therefore, [he] deserved to be sorely chastened [and] learn obedience through suffering, which, in his case, was spoken of as "outer darkness."[106]

Graves through these interpretations has set forth at least three classes of Christians, the bride of Christ, those who are not the bride but worthy of attending the wedding supper, and those who are unworthy of attending. In addition, he speaks of entering the kingdom through the great tribulation although his adamant position stated over and over is the kingdom is the sum of the properly organized visible churches.

---

102. Ibid., 252–53.
103. Ibid., 254.
104. Ibid., 256, 260, 263.
105. Ibid., 264–65.
106. Ibid., 276.

Graves' Key Principles

Despite what has preceded regarding the odd, peculiar, and outright heretical nature of some of Graves' theology, he was in many regards within the mainstream of Christian orthodoxy and particularly Baptist orthodoxy. He constantly advocated and defended what he considered to be any form of attack upon salvation by faith alone. His own confession, his firm avowal of and illustrations of salvation by grace through faith alone punctuated his debates, his writings, and his preaching. For Graves this rose above all other considerations—the grace of God as the foundation of and faith in Christ as the only means of justification.

His writings, debates, and sermons were filled with repeated themes. One of the doctrines he reiterated constantly in the pages of his newspapers was, one Lord, one faith, one Immersion (as he phrased it) (Eph 4:5). He always said that the Word of God and the Spirit of God are the agents in regeneration. The exercise of the grace of faith and repentance, he said, "no one could exercise without the influence of the Holy Spirit."[107] He advocated the perseverance of the saints because he said, by faith we are indissolubly united to Christ and this is what secures our salvation. Many of these formulations are quite Calvinistic, although Graves would have recoiled at any such suggestion. Even given the errors into which his over-literal interpretation led him, he always maintained that the Bible, and the Bible alone, was the sole rule of faith and practice.

It would not be going too far to say that Graves saw himself as the great prophet of God sent to reclaim those who had wandered into false doctrine by proclaiming to them the truth of God's Word. He looked upon the peculiar mission of his editorial work, as the leader in proclaiming Baptist policy, "to fulfill our peculiar mission—which is to be the witness of Christ's truth against every system of error, and those who originate or advocate them, and above all, by no act to countenance, recognize, aid or abet them who teach error, or to confirm those who are in error."[108]

J. M. Pendleton—Representative Aspects of His Theology

James Madison Pendleton was born in Virginia, November 20, 1811. His family moved to Kentucky when he was just a baby and there he grew up. In 1829 he made confession of an experience of grace and was baptized at the Bethel Baptist Church in Christian County, Kentucky. That same church

---

107. Graves, *Old Landmarkism*, 66.
108. Hailey, *J. R. Graves*, 58.

licensed him to preach in 1830 and after being ordained in 1833 served four years as the pastor of the Bethel Baptist Church and the Hopkinsville Baptist Church. He was called to the Bowling Green Baptist church in 1837 and remained there for twenty years.[109] It was in Bowling Green that he met J. R. Graves.

O. L. Hailey gives the following account of Graves' and Pendleton's first meeting:

> Graves went to Bowling Green to preach at Pendleton's church. On finding that Pendleton was accustomed to receiving alien immersions Graves was ready to return at once to Nashville for he said, "a visiting minister should not preach from the pulpit of a pastor doctrines contrary to those held by that pastor." Pendleton persuaded Graves to stay because he had "never given the matter of alien immersion a thorough study and shall be glad to hear you preach on that subject." Pendleton subsequently agreed with Graves and Graves asked Pendleton to write a tract "that will set forth the differences between Baptists and Pedo-Baptists, showing why we cannot consistently fellowship with Pedo-Baptists as regular churches of Jesus Christ, nor receive their immersion, nor recognize their ministers as scripturally ordained ministers of the gospel."[110]

To say the least, this is a very specific list for one's own "thorough study." The result of Pendleton's work was *An Old Landmark Re-set*, which proved to be the namesake of the Landmark movement. James E. Tull says, this work caused great excitement "throughout the Southern Baptist Convention and put the issue in the center of denominational discussion. At least 40,000 copies of this tract were distributed."[111]

Pendleton, however, did study theology. He was a professor of theology holding the first chair in that department at Union University in Murfreesboro, Tennessee, and was an accomplished writer and preacher. What follows is an analysis of Pendleton's theology, the extent to which it shaped the Landmark movement, the agreement and departure from what Graves affirmed, and differing accounts of his positions than what has been attributed to him by others. As far as practical the same order will be followed as was seen above in the analysis of Graves' theological positions.

---

109. Burnett, *Sketches of Tennessee's Pioneer Baptist Preachers*, 400–402.
110. Hailey, *J. R. Graves*, 76–77. (Graves and Pendleton met in 1852.)
111. Tull, *High-Church Baptists in the South*, 4.

Ecclesiology

Whereas Graves said the term *ekklesia* has but one possible meaning and that meaning was simply a local congregation, Pendleton would not go that far. He said, "It is usually . . . employed to designate a particular congregation of saints or the redeemed in the aggregate. It is used in the latter sense in several passages, as, for example . . . Eph. v. 25–27. In these places and in several others it would be absurd to define the term 'church' as meaning a particular congregation of Christians meeting in one place for the worship of God."[112] This may accord with Graves' explanation that the word is often used as synecdoche,[113] but Graves added, "A Religious organization that can not be assembled in one place and all its members act as a unit can not be a Scriptural *Ekklesia* or Church."[114] Pendleton agreed that the majority of instances of the use of the term "church" in the New Testament denote a local assembly, but when he uses certain examples as "the church at Jerusalem" he neglects to consider that the thousands of believers in Jerusalem had no place to assemble in one place as a local assembly. It is beyond conception that the church at Jerusalem could meet "in one place and all its members act as a unit."

Pendleton defined the church as follows:

> A church is a congregation of Christ's baptized disciples, acknowledging him as their Head, relying on his atoning sacrifice for justification before God, depending on the Holy Spirit for sanctification, united in the belief of the gospel, agreeing to maintain its ordinances and obey its precepts, meeting together for worship, and co-operating for the extension of Christ's kingdom in the world.[115]

This definition is clear and theologically sound and avoids the extremes to which Graves was prone. The question that arises is simply, how did Pendleton and Graves cooperate, work together, defend Landmarkism, and generally shape Southern Baptist life at least in the southwest during the nineteenth century? This is a question which will arise more than once as Pendleton's theology is examined. The first explanation which is offered up regards the date of publication of Pendleton's *Christian Doctrines* from which the above quotes are taken. This was first published in 1878, seventeen years

---

112. Pendleton, *Christian Doctrines*, 329.

113. Synecdoche is a figure of speech whereby the part is understood for the whole or the whole is for the part.

114. Graves, *New Great Iron Wheel*, 126–27.

115. Pendleton, *Christian Doctrines*, 330.

after Pendleton and Graves parted company in the early years of the Civil War. Did Pendleton's position change? Did he moderate some positions after he was in a sense out from under the influence of Graves? Did he see the damage that the Landmark controversies caused to the denomination and thus abandon controversial, sectarian, high-church positions? To answer these questions Pendleton's writings, sermons, editorials, and articles will be examined during his association with Graves, i.e., when Pendleton was in Kentucky and Tennessee and afterward when he moved to Pennsylvania.

Pendleton, in fact, seems to be somewhat of a puzzle to many. The generally accepted view of Pendleton can be summarized with a few examples. Bob Compton says that Pendleton "accepted the idea of the universal church."[116] According to Tull, Pendleton never relinquished the idea of the universal church, refused to subscribe to the theory of church succession, and thought the theory of non-intercommunion was trivial.[117] Walter Shurden wrote, "Pendleton disagreed with Graves at this point [the church was visible and local only and not universal or invisible]."[118]

Pendleton, however, in his book *Landmarkism, Liberalism and the Invisible Church,* includes an essay written by J. N. Hall, "Baptists and the Nature of the Church, The New Issue. The Invisible Church Idea." The important points Hall sets forth are:

> For our part we deny this whole "invisible, universal church" idea. There is but one sort of church in the New Testament; and that is a local and visible church. . . . There is not a passage in the Bible where the word "church" is so used as to embrace all the saved . . . no inspired writer ever makes mention of such a church. . . . This "invisible church" cannot perform any of the functions of a church. . . . There are not two sorts of churches of Christ—one big, invisible church and the other, little, visible churches.[119]

Hall's reasoning like much of Graves' was due to an over-literal rendering of the words of the text. Hall's position was that invisible preachers couldn't preach, nor could baptism be administered by invisible administrators. However, we need not assume that Pendleton merely approves of Hall's thesis. Pendleton wrote earlier in that same work, "There is no universal visible church; and if the universal invisible church, composed of all the

---

116. Compton, "J. M. Pendleton," 56.
117. Tull, *High-Church Baptists in the South,* 44.
118. Shurden, *Not a Silent People,* 76.
119. Pendleton, *Landmarkism,* 68–71.

saved, has what Dr. E. calls 'form,' it is impossible to know what it is. We have no idea of 'form' apart from visibility."[120]

However, Pendleton was not consistent in his use of terms and/or his doctrine. In two sermons printed in the *Tennessee Baptist* in 1855 and 1856 Pendleton speaks of the members of "the church triumphant in heaven" as distinguished from the "visible Church of Christ on earth."[121] This is in direct contradiction to Graves' assertion that Christ "has no invisible kingdom or church, and such a thing has no real existence."[122] This position is also different from Pendleton's own assertions above. Later, after moving to Pennsylvania, Pendleton preached a sermon entitled "An Unfaithful Church in Danger of Extinction." From his notes, he writes, "Local churches may lose their visibility [but] the church universal will never become extinct."[123]

Tull also asserts that Pendleton refused to subscribe to the theory of church succession.[124] Pendleton certainly held that John the Baptist was "the first Baptist preacher."[125] In his works *Landmarkism, Liberalism, and the Invisible Church* and *Church Manual, Designed for the Use of Baptist Churches*, Pendleton included articles by Graves and affirmed his own belief in church succession.[126] It is possible that one could reach the conclusion that Pendleton did not ascribe to the theory of church succession by taking his words from a letter to the *Religious Herald* out of context. The editor of the *Religious Herald* asked Pendleton to set forth his views concerning the rebaptism, ordination, and state of those baptized by one Dr. Weaver, a pastor of a Baptist church in Louisville, Kentucky, who was baptized privately by James P. Boyce, the first president of the Southern Baptist Seminary at Louisville. Weaver had been immersed by a Methodist minister and it was on that basis that he was admitted into the Baptist church. The issue was that of alien immersion not church succession. Pendleton wrote, "I simply assume the incompetency of an unbaptized man to administer baptism."[127] The invalidity of Weaver's baptism rendered him an unqualified administrator as Pendleton explained: "I have seen no account of Dr. Weaver's ordination. The point made by Dr. Jeter is unquestionably a good one—namely,

---

120. Ibid., 29.
121. *Tennessee Baptist* (Nashville), 22 December 1855, 27 September 1856.
122. Graves, *Old Landmarkism:*, 32.
123. Pendleton, "An Unfaithful Church in Danger of Extinction," handwritten sermon notes, Uplands, PA (14 December 1876).
124. Tull, *High-Church Baptists in the South*, 44.
125. *Tennessee Baptist* (Nashville), 5 June 1852.
126. See Pendleton, *Landmarkism*, 41–46, and Pendleton, *Church Manual*, 91–97.
127. *Religious Herald* (Richmond, VA), 18 September 1879.

that an ordination, so called, before baptism is null and void. . . . There can be no scriptural ordination without church membership, and no church membership without baptism."[128] Pendleton's conclusion included the following words: "There needs to be no discussion of the doctrine of 'church succession.' Let that be, for the time at least, held in abeyance. From this day let all brethren discourage 'irregular baptisms.'"[129] The issue was not church succession. His point was simply that if there were no irregular baptisms there would be no opportunities for such questions to arise, as in the Weaver case, of the status of those baptized by Weaver before his "regular baptism."

Pendleton's advice regarding those baptized by Weaver before his own baptism at the hands of a Baptist minister and thus before his true ordination reveals his stance on the authority of the local church. He said in that regard, "What is to become of those members of our churches who have been immersed by Pedobaptists? The churches will do as they have done—just as they please. Their authority, under Christ, is supreme. . . . If the churches prefer that such members shall remain undisturbed, so it will be. The state of things will remain as it is, and just as it has been. But, for the future, let all encourage such baptisms as all believe to be valid, and to which none, therefore, can object."[130] To say the least he is inconsistent in the rejection of Weaver's ordination and baptism while holding that the local church could accept those baptized by Weaver as acceptable.

However, regardless of Tull's conclusions and Pendleton's attempts to avoid the question, Pendleton's affirmations regarding proper baptisms, i.e., those performed by ordained Baptist ministers who themselves were baptized by similarly qualified men, lies at the heart of church succession theory. A letter to the editor of the *Religious Herald* pointed out this fact. The writer (W.A.M.) wrote, "Dr. P., in order to know he has a valid baptism for himself, or any of his brethren, must be able to trace a line of converted, baptized, and ordained men back to the time of the apostles, and be careful, then, to see that Judas Iscariot—'one of the twelve,' but 'a devil.'—is not at their head."[131]

Tull also asserted that Pendleton thought the agitation over intercommunion was trivial and unimportant.[132] Pendleton's own words demonstrate an attitude quite to the contrary. In a letter to Graves published in the *Tennessee Baptist* Pendleton wrote, "You remember, brother G., what you said

128. Ibid.
129. Ibid.
130. Ibid.
131. *Religious Herald* (Richmond, VA), 23 October 1879.
132. Tull, *History of Southern Baptist Landmarkism*, 259–60.

of communion. You insisted that the 'Discipline' favors 'close communion.' ... Hence my reply, in which I maintained your position."[133] Later in the same letter and more pointedly he added, "I now say that what is called 'open communion,' I care not what denomination is a 'humbug.'"[134] Pendleton said the Lord's Supper must be restricted to the churches because it is a church ordinance. "Baptist dare not commune with Pedobaptists, because Pedobaptist societies are not gospel Churches. . . . If Baptists commune with Pedobaptists, they must admit that the societies of the latter are Gospel churches—an admission which no consistent Baptist ever has made, or ever will make."[135] Additionally, Pendleton asserts that even among Baptist churches it should not "be forgotten that every church is an independent body. This fact settles forever the question that intercommunion between members of Baptist churches is based on courtesy and not on right."[136] None of these assertions sound trivial or unimportant given the language Pendleton uses to set forth his case. However, it must be noted that the notes of a sermon preached in 1876 contain not even the slightest mention of close communion even under the subheading of unworthy partakers.[137]

Underlying the debate over close communion was the autonomy and authority of the local church. Pendleton, as Graves, held that the true form of church government was and is democratic. He says, "Every local christian [sic] congregation is a Democracy."[138] (It is interesting and revealing that he would capitalize "Democracy" and not "Christian" in his sentence.) Such a theory of church government makes every church independent of every other church. Pendleton adds, "And this form of government is in accordance with the New Testament—Christianity has never made *cyphers* of the people. It has never exalted the ministry to an irresponsible superiority above the laity. It takes Methodism and Romanism to do this. Whatever things are wrong among Baptists, their form of church government is certainly right."[139] "Baptists glory in their form of church government—which recognizes every church as a little republic in itself."[140]

---

133. *Tennessee Baptist* (Nashville), 5 June 1852.

134. Ibid.

135. *Tennessee Baptist* (Nashville), 30 July 1859.

136. Pendleton, *Three Reasons*, 209.

137. Pendleton, "The Lord's Supper," handwritten sermon notes, Uplands, PA (29 March 1876).

138. *Tennessee Baptist* (Nashville), 19 July 1856.

139. Ibid.

140. Pendleton, *Baptist Church Manual*, 43.

This church government was congregational, as Graves also affirmed; it was the "form of government in the first church in Jerusalem." Pendleton wrote, "I am a Baptist because Baptists adopt the form of church government recognized in the New Testament—that is to say, the congregational form of government."[141] He added, "Congregationalism . . . distinctly recognizes these truths:

1. That the governmental power is in the hands of the people . . .
2. The right of a majority of the members of a church to rule . . .
3. That the power of a church cannot be transferred or alienated, and that church action is final . . ."[142]

"[This] view of church government given in the preceding pages I sincerely believe accords with the teachings of the New Testament," he concluded.[143]

Pendleton's view of church government seemed to remain consistent. As late as 1881 he said in a sermon, "Christianity teaches the great republican truth that power belongs to the people, that it can never be rightfully alienated from them in state or church."[144]

Although Pendleton's expression of the doctrine of the church was more theologically sound and less polemical than Graves', one finds that the bulk of his published writing (in the form of editorials, responses to letters to the editor, etc.), which by Pendleton's own estimate exceeded eight hundred articles)[145] was with few exceptions in lock step with Graves and not markedly different as some have proposed.

Christology

When Graves began his work *The Work of Christ in the Covenant of Redemption, Developed in Seven Dispensations* (published in 1883) wherein he denied that Christ possessed a human soul, one must ask, was he aware of and had he read Pendleton's *Christian Doctrines, A Compendium of Theology* (published first in 1878)? In *Christian Doctrines* Pendleton condemns those who say Christ did not have a human soul. He writes, "The other false

---

141. Pendleton, *Three Reasons*, 148.

142. Ibid., 153.

143. Ibid., 170.

144. Pendleton, "The Kingdom Set Up by the God of Heaven," handwritten sermon notes, Uplands, PA (13 July 1881).

145. *Baptist* (Nashville), 13 July 1861.

view, which also deserves most decided condemnation is, that Christ had no human soul. It is supposed by the advocates of this theory that the Word in becoming flesh took a human body only into union with himself."[146] In refutation of such belief he says (contra Graves), "If Jesus Christ did not possess a soul as well as a body, he was not a man. The union of a body with his divine nature would not make him a man. There must be the union of a human body and a human soul to constitute Jesus a man, and then there must be the union of his humanity with his divinity to constitute him the Christ."[147] It would appear that Graves developed his aberrant theological positions in the twenty years after he and Pendleton parted company. He wrote in an editorial on the occasion of Pendleton's departure from his position as associate editor, "*We are not aware that we differ touching any matter of religious faith and practice*, though for several years before an editor or contributor he was a strong opposer [sic] of Old Landmarkism when we were its sole public advocate."[148]

These matters would have included Pendleton's affirmations published in the pages of the *Tennessee Baptist*, e.g., "Jesus Christ possesses a compound nature. . . . He was truly and properly man."[149] Even after their separation Graves published an article by Pendleton which addressed much that had "been published in The Baptist in regard to the person and sufferings of Christ."[150] Interestingly enough, Pendleton's answer is a long (almost two-column) quotation from Calvin's *Institutes* (bk. 2, ch. 14). Key in that quotation to the present topic are the words, "For we assert, such a connection and union of the divinity with the humanity, that each nature retains its properties entire, and yet both together constitute one Christ."[151] During the time period represented (1852–1861) there may have been no difference in their theology but it is certain that later reflection and/or the codification of what was meant by certain terms produced a marked difference in the Christology of Graves and Pendleton. Pendleton's assertion that views which held that Christ had no human soul deserved condemnation would have to include, one would assume, the views of his old friend Graves.

Although, as was pointed out, Graves did not say that the Second Person of the Trinity was not eternal, he did affirm that the adjective "eternal" should not be used in conjunction with the names Father and Son.

---

146. Pendleton, *Christian Doctrines*, 201.
147. Ibid., 203.
148. *Baptist* (Nashville), 13 July 1861 (emphasis in original).
149. *Tennessee Baptist* (Nashville), 31 March 1855.
150. *Baptist* (Memphis), 30 October 1869.
151. Ibid. (emphasis added).

Pendleton took a contrary view asserting, "When it is said in Psalm 90:2, 'From everlasting to everlasting thou art God,' it is universally understood that God has existed from eternity. Why then, do not the words 'from everlasting,' when applied to the Lord Jesus mean the same thing? They must have the same meaning."[152] He also affirmed, "The only-begotten Son of God dwelt in the bosom of the Father from eternity."[153]

The Atonement

Pendleton is quite clear regarding the atonement and Christ's sacrifice, its necessity and efficacy. He writes, "Jesus certainly died to make an atonement for sin.... His agonies were atoning agonies. His blood was expiatory blood. The atonement of Christ furnishes the only reason why God can forgive sins."[154] Again we find him at odds with Graves' assertion that Christ did not make atonement on the cross. Pendleton said, "He [Christ] bore the awful pressure of the burden till the work of atonement was completed. Then he died."[155]

For Pendleton, a correct view of the Person of Christ was essential for a correct understanding of the atonement. Those who deny the necessity of the atonement and/or confine all the consequences of sin to this present life do so because they have a faulty view of the Person of Christ. The errors of the Unitarians and of Beecherism[156] were infecting all denominations because as Pendleton said, "All these notions grow out of false views of the divine character . . . the deification of the humanity of Christ . . . a view of the Fatherhood of God separated from the atonement."[157] Pendleton adds in this regard, "The N.T. doctrine of the Fatherhood of God is the doctrine of spiritual paternity. Men are God's children not because he has created them but because he has regenerated and adopted them. [It] is not through the first Adam, but through the second, the Lord of heaven.

---

152. Ibid., 81.
153. Ibid., 198.
154. *Tennessee Baptist* (Nashville), 31 March 1855.
155. Pendleton, "Three Prominent Gospel Facts," handwritten sermon notes, Uplands, PA (4 February 1876).
156. Beecherism (after Henry Ward Beecher) held that abstractly considered, all churches are equally good or bad. One is a Christian not because of what he believes but how he lives. Beecherism did not recognize the two distinct natures of Christ and argued that his sufferings were infinite. Due to a denial of the Trinity, Beecherism did not accept the Incarnation. It also misrepresented the doctrine of regeneration (see Brownson, *Works*, 3:460–84).
157 Pendleton, "The Fatherhood of God in Relation to the Atonement of Christ," handwritten sermon notes, Uplands, PA (27 September 1876).

Union with Christ creates brotherhood and brotherhood in Christ establishes Fatherhood in God."[158]

As to the necessity of the atonement, Pendleton addresses the perversion of grace with works and the perversion of God's goodness, which confuses toleration with love. "Some say," he writes, "if we cannot be saved without repentance, faith, and holiness of life, there must be merit in these things, and we may safely rely on this merit. These works are made to take the place of grace and the gospel of the grace of God is perverted.... Some say if God is love he is too good to punish his creatures though they are guilty of disobedience. They appeal to the parental character of God. I meet them on their own ground. Is it a proof of the goodness of any father that he does not punish his disobedient children?"[159] The moving cause of the atonement Pendleton finds in God's grace. "It was not the death of Christ that originated grace within the bosom of God, but it was the grace already there that led to his death."[160]

Although Pendleton was a fairly consistent Calvinist in his theological views, we do see some equivocation on the doctrine of limited atonement. He says regarding that, "The epithets *limited* and *unlimited* are not very happily chosen in their application to the atonement of Christ. All will admit that it is limited in the sense that fallen angels are excluded from its provisions, but some think it limited to a part of the human race. I hesitate not to say that it is unlimited so far as human beings are concerned. This is the only valid reason for preaching the gospel to all men."[161] (This view totally ignores the most valid reason, i.e., the command of the Lord Jesus Christ.)

Baptism

Whatever the differences that may have existed in the theological positions of Graves and Pendleton in other areas one could say they were in lockstep in their view of baptism. The doctrine of baptism is central to Pendleton's view of ecclesiology. As he writes in the introduction to the chapter on baptism in *Christian Doctrines*, "If ... a church is a congregation of Christ's baptized disciples then we must consider two important questions, What

---

158. Ibid.

159. Pendleton, "Perverting the Words of God," handwritten sermon notes, Uplands, PA (14 July 1876).

160. Pendleton, "Christ Tasting Death," handwritten sermon notes, Uplands, PA (26 July 1882).

161. Ibid. (emphasis in original).

is baptism? And Who are to be baptized?"[162] These questions take up the mode and subjects of baptism, which, as stated earlier, are beyond the scope of this work but Pendleton's view of baptism encompassed much more than a justification of immersion as the only legitimate means and regenerate believers as the only fit subjects.

Pendleton's dogmatic assertions as to the mode and subjects of baptism spilled over into the definition of what constitutes a true church, true gospel preachers, and recognition of same. Notice how he builds this case:

> Baptism is essential to the existence of a visible church—it is the means of initiation into it, and that all legitimate authority to preach the gospel must come through a visible church of Christ. But then Dr. Hill thinks those societies which recognize *sprinkling and pouring* as baptism are gospel churches. Here we are poles asunder.... I submit that whatever affects the materials of which a gospel church is composed, and substitutes something else for the Scriptural method of initiation into it, is "material" and "fundamental." What are the materials of a gospel church? All Baptists say, baptized believers.... Again, what is the action of baptism? All Baptists say immersion. But Pedobaptists have substituted sprinkling and pouring for it.... Is not the abolition of that act "fundamental disorder?" ... If Pedobaptist Societies are not gospel churches—and they cannot be if in "fundamental disorder"—then Pedobaptist preachers are not gospel ministers.... Pedobaptist Societies not being gospel churches, their preachers are not gospel ministers.[163]

What constitutes baptism is at the root of the Landmark movement and the high-church mentality that marked the era. Pendleton seemed to take some small amount of pride in the high-church accusations leveled against the Southern Baptists. "If it be 'high churchism' to believe that there can be no gospel ministry without gospel churches, and no gospel churches without gospel baptism, and no gospel baptism without immersion—the Review will advocate 'high churchism.' Baptists to lay consistent claim to ecclesiastical existence must be what you call 'high churchmen'—must be Old Landmark men."[164] The ecclesiastical existence of Baptist churches depends on holding Landmark tenets! Pendleton adds, "Dr. Hill admits that

---

162. Pendleton, *Christian Doctrines*, 342.
163. *Tennessee Baptist* (Nashville), 16 December, 1854 (emphasis in original).
164. *Tennessee Baptist* (Nashville), 14 April 1855.

the question, What is baptism? enters essentially into the Old Landmark controversy. This I have ever insisted upon."[165]

For Pendleton the purity of baptism as to the subjects and the mode was essential to the purity of the church. He emphatically states this, "Reason second, I am a Baptist because Baptists consider the immersion in water, of a believer, essential to baptism—so essential that there is no baptism without it."[166] With such words it is not difficult to see the importance of church succession, pulpit affiliation, recognition of the ministers of other denominations, and the problems that result in the Landmark doctrine with the ordination of unimmersed ministers and ministers immersed by one who was not himself immersed. Brief illustrations above of Pendleton's ensnarement in such issues are merely illustrative of the conundrums in which one may become trapped if rigidly holding to the Landmark doctrines. When the doctrine of the church ties the purity of the church and the government of the church to the fact that all the members of said church are immersed believers, what is the result when these same believers are rebaptized once, twice, or even three times because by their own admission they were not regenerate believers when they were previously baptized? Pendleton recognized that "all the baptized are not pardoned"[167] but he failed to extend the consequences of that into church government and the assertion of the purity of the Baptist church as opposed to other societies which he called not true churches.

Baptism is the linchpin which held together the Landmark theology and to a certain extent all Baptist theology, an assertion that will be examined more fully in following chapters. For Pendleton and Graves, and all who held to their view of ecclesiology, it was essential. Irrespective of other differences in the theology of the two, when it came to baptism and its essential place in Landmark doctrine and practice they were assuredly of one mind.

Anthropology

Pendleton believed that man was created male and female as free moral agents "capable of retaining their primitive integrity," and yet conversely "capable of sinning and falling from that exalted position."[168] This affected

165. Ibid.
166. Pendleton, *Three Reasons*, 82.
167. J. M. Pendleton, "Repentance and Baptism," handwritten sermon notes, Uplands, PA (17 March 1882).
168. *Tennessee Baptist* (Nashville), 1 September 1855.

man's disposition and inclination toward sin. He held that man was depraved and always inclined to sin. He wrote, "The will of every being necessarily partakes of the nature of that being. A depraved being in the exercise of his will always gives indications of depravity."[169]

Pendleton held a trichotomous view of man's constitution and his relationship to God. He was aware that there was a certain lack of precision in the scriptural use of these terms body, soul, and spirit when describing man and his various relations, particularly to God. He also says that "as far as the element of the pneuma is concerned, [it] is almost entirely in abeyance throughout the Old Testament . . . but it is equally true that in the New Testament it is recognized only in the Epistles of Paul . . . [and] the Savior evidently used the term psyche or soul to denote not only the living principle, but the pneuma or spirit."[170] However, in spite of this recognition, Pendleton quotes approvingly from G. D. Boardman and a series of articles which appeared in the *Baptist Quarterly*:

> The scriptural anthropology, as we conceive is this: Man consists of *soma*, *psyche*, and *pneuma*—body, life or living principle, and spirit. It is the union of these three which makes up the wonderful thing which we call a human being. It is not the body alone, nor the living principle alone, nor the spirit alone which makes the man; but it is the union of the three. Herein lies our defense of the term anthropology, which in this discussion we use in its strictly literal primitive sense. We do not affirm that this threefold distinction which we have indicated is always observed in Holy Scripture. But we do affirm that it is observed with sufficient frequency and emphasis to demand from us formal recognition of it. Neither do we pretend to discriminate with absolute accuracy between these several parts or aspects of man's nature.[171]

Absolute accuracy seems to be the casualty as Pendleton again approving of Boardman draws some conclusions from this threefold nature of man. He says, "God is not said to be the Father of our bodies or of our souls; of these he is only the maker and framer. But he is said to be the Father of our spirits. It is not our bodies, or our souls, but our spirits which are the offspring of God. The animal has a psyche, a soul, as well as man."[172] Pendleton uses this division between soul and spirit to explain the parable

169. Ibid.
170. *Baptist* (Memphis), 1 February 1868.
171. Ibid.
172. Ibid.

of the sower. The seed that sprang up quickly but later withered fell only on the soul, he says, and did not penetrate to the spirit. "The work was confined only to the animal, psychical part of his being."[173]

Interestingly, it was Pendleton's defense of the Negro as possessing in all respects the same constituent parts as other men which opened the rift between him and the overwhelming majority of Landmarkers and Southern Baptists. This also led to his relocation to the North in the early part of the Civil War. Long before the Civil War, Pendleton notes in his journal that the subject of slavery was raised at the Home Mission Society meeting in 1844. He recorded that Richard Fuller made an impressive defense of slavery at the meeting, saying, "There must be a new Bible before it could be proved that slavery is a sin."[174] In the lead-up to the war the religious papers of the South were filled with articles asserting the inferiority of the Negro and many asserted that this was due to the lack of a soul and/or the curse of Ham. To cite just two of the many examples: "[It is] high heaven's decree, that the two races shall be unequal, that the sons of Ham shall serve in the tents of Shem . . . as foreordained by the omnipotent fashioner of the globe."[175] "The black race cannot be prepared during a whole lifetime to take charge of families, or perform the duties of citizens."[176]

Pendleton stood firmly opposed to such rhetoric. His attempts to temper and refute such talk eventually led to his relocation to Pennsylvania in the early part of the Civil War. As that crisis precipitated he wrote, "I feel a supreme contempt for the atrocious prejudice which makes *birthplace* the chief element in calculating merit or demerit."[177] After the war in correspondence with R. L. Breckinridge, discussing the war and God's judgment, Breckinridge wrote, "God has shown by his providence . . . that he abhorred that entire perversion of his Holy Word, upon which the Religious Preachers of the South, led their flocks to the brink of destruction."[178] Victory in a bitterly fought Civil War with brother pitted against brother and son against father was perceived as the arbiter of theological differences.

---

173. Ibid.
174. Pendleton, "Journal of James Madison Pendleton, 1844, entry for April 26."
175. *Tennessee Baptist* (Nashville), 3 January 1852.
176. *Tennessee Baptist* (Nashville), 26 January 1861.
177. *Tennessee Baptist* (Nashville), 23 March 1861 (emphasis in original).
178. R. L. Breckinridge to J. M. Pendleton, 5 February 1886.

Eschatology

Pendleton's view of the intermediate state of man and the end times was quite different from Graves. He rejected the view that the soul sleeps or is unconscious from death to the resurrection. Contrary to Graves, he specifically refuted the theory (which he admitted was held by many theologians) "that the redeemed will not enter into heaven till after the judgment."[179] He wrote that these theologians argue that Paradise will be the abode of the saints until the resurrection, a view specifically set forth by Graves. "Many theologians entertain this opinion. [That the soul goes to Paradise to abide till the resurrection.] They think that the redeemed will not enter into heaven till after the judgment. This is by no means a satisfactory theory."[180] This entire line of argument could well be interpreted to be aimed directly at Graves. Pendleton's considered opinion in the matter after reviewing Scripture was simply, "There is in the term paradise, as used in the New Testament, nothing that requires us to believe it a place distinct from heaven."[181] Views which present Paradise as a place distinct from heaven meet with "insuperable objections."[182] "Paradise is heaven."[183] For Pendleton, "Absent from the body—present with the Lord" (2 Cor 5:8) means "the glorious presence of the Lord is doubtless referred to, and this is enjoyed only in heaven."[184]

Pendleton asserts that in eternity, "Every man stands on the basis of his 'pure individuality.'"[185] He contrasts this with nations who are punished in this lifetime for their sins. The judgment of God will fall upon ungodly nations. The impenitent sinner on the other hand may well live and work often unmolested but "finally will suffer a self-procured damnation. The wages of sin is death. The sinner labors in the service of sin until the close of his short day of probation and then receives his wages."[186]

Pendleton was an amillennialist, the widely held eschatological view before Darby's premillennial dispensationalism, which Graves embraced in his own work, *The Work of Christ in the Covenant of Redemption*, as noted in the discussion of his views. Pendleton asserted, "There will be a resurrection

---

179. Pendleton, *Christian Doctrines*, 374.
180. Ibid.
181. Ibid., 375.
182. Ibid.
183. J. M. Pendleton, "The Prayer of the Penitent Robber Answered," handwritten sermon notes, Uplands, PA (1 March 1876).
184. Pendleton, *Christian Doctrines*, 376.
185. *Tennessee Baptist* (Nashville), 1 January 1855.
186. *Tennessee Baptist* (Nashville), 1 September 1855.

of the just and the unjust, and with my view of the Scriptures the two classes will rise at the same time."[187] This is at variance with the dispensational views set forth by Graves.

Contrary to Graves' assertion that there will be millions saved in the millennium who will not be the bride of Christ, Pendleton says, "Those whom the Father gives the Son are predestinated to be conformed to the image of the Son, Rom. 8:28, and this election to salvation is proved by their calling or regeneration. They are to constitute the bride, the Lamb's wife."[188]

Other Issues

Pendleton was not the literalist that Graves was when it came to the Scripture. In reference to Revelation he said, "It is to be remembered that the book of Revelation abounds in figurative language."[189] Pendleton affirmed, "All Scripture is given by God. The Bible is not of human origin. . . . By the inspiration of the Bible I mean that the writers of the Old and New Testament were so directed and immediately under the influence of the Holy Spirit, that God himself spoke through them to the world. . . . The sacred writers were infallibly preserved from error."[190]

In other matters, after the war, Pendleton did not endear himself to many in the South largely because he rejected the rhetoric that continued to flow from the religious papers of the South regarding the inferiority of the Negro and his inability to cope with freedom. In an article published in the *New York Examiner* and reprinted in the *Baptist* Pendleton took on the noted Harvard professor Louis Agassiz.[191] Pendleton quoted Agassiz in context as saying, "The negro . . . has not been endowed by God with the same volume of brain as the white man. . . . He is an inferior animal to the white man. . . . There is not a bone in the negro's body relatively of the same shape, size, articulation, or chemically of the same composition as that of the white man's. . . . Even the negro's blood is chemically different from

---

187. J. M. Pendleton, "Union with Christ and the Blessings Resulting There From," handwritten sermon notes, Uplands, PA (8 February 1876).

188. J. M. Pendleton, "Christ's Prayer for Those Given Him by the Father," handwritten sermon notes, Uplands, PA (11 April 1876).

189. Pendleton, *Christian Doctrines*, 381.

190. *Tennessee Baptist* (Nashville), 6 September 1856.

191. Louis Agassiz (1807–1873) was a noted paleontologist, glaciologist, and geologist famous for his theories of ice ages and rejection of Darwinian evolution. It is claimed he was not a racist although not all support such a view. See Gould, *Panda's Thumb*.

that which courses in the veins of the white man."[192] Agassiz believed the different races were created in different locales and that the Genesis account spoke only of the white race. Pendleton, ever the theologian, takes Agassiz to task on this account. "His [Agassiz's] theory requires different creations, and he does not believe that the whole human race has descended from one pair. I give Prof. Agassiz all the honor due him in his legitimate explorations in the wide realm of nature; but when he attempts to make the science of ethnology teach something in conflict with the Bible, I demur."[193] After many arguments, Pendleton rests his case on the doctrine of redemption. He says he is familiar with Agassiz's reverence for God and respect for the Bible, but he adds, "What avails this while he cherishes a theory which, in its far-reaching implications, unsettles the foundation of human redemption . . . the ultimate analysis of the scriptural view of sin and salvation must be sought in the unity of the race of Adam."[194]

Many of the religious papers of the South castigated Pendleton. One even carried a poem to the memory of his son John Pendleton who fought for the Confederacy and died in battle. The poem portrayed Pendleton as a monster who desired that his son die in the first battle of the war because he would dare to oppose his father and fight for the South. Pendleton wrote of this, "The charge against me will not be believed after I am dead; for the grave is a wonderful extinguisher of prejudice and animosity. But how discreditable to human nature, that a slandered man has to go into the grave to find protection from the shafts of calumny!"[195]

The Baptist carried an article by Pendleton entitled "Masonry Run Mad" in 1869 and it released another storm of letter writing and editorializing throughout most of that year. Pendleton thought Christians had no place in a Masonic lodge. He summed it up, "If men of the world wish to join Masonic Lodges, I have nothing to say. I do say, however, that when Christians join them they discredit Christianity."[196] This debate was carried on from January to July 1869 in the pages of the *Baptist*.

These issues although not directly related to theology were answered by Pendleton on theological grounds. If Graves was the polemicist, Pendleton was the theologian. It is worth noting that both these issues, the unity of the race and Masonry, would both bubble over later in Southern

192. *Baptist* (Memphis), 25 June 1868.
193. Ibid.
194. Ibid.
195. *Baptist* (Memphis), 10 August 1867.
196. *Baptist* (Memphis), 9 January 1869.

Baptist life and Landmark influences would be evident in the controversies which followed.

Although Graves wrote on the occasion of Pendleton's leaving the staff of the *Tennessee Baptist*, "*We are not aware that we differ touching any matter of religious faith and practice . . . ,*"[197] they differed on a number of theological issues, as these examples demonstrate. Other writers have attributed to Pendleton positions he did not hold or did not hold with the unwavering solidity they intimated. The examples above are prime examples of such. In fact, it was on the points of church succession, intercommunion, and the refusal to recognize non-Baptist churches and ministers that the words of Graves ring true. In other matters Pendleton differed greatly with Graves and often directly refuted the positions held by Graves. That being the case, wherein, one asks, lies their long association and mutual affection. Quite simply it was the Baptist doctrine of baptism and the Landmark doctrines associated with it. As Graves said, Pendleton was for a number of years "a strong opposer of Old Landmarkism when we were its sole public advocate."[198] Swayed by Graves, Pendleton became the theological base, advocate, and codifier of Landmarkism. This bound them together even though their theology was markedly different in so many areas. In the simplest terms, a baptistic doctrine of baptism and a highly sectarian view of the Baptist church as the only true church met Graves' definition as "not [differing] touching any matter of religious faith and practice."

The Carroll Brothers—
Representative Aspects of Theology

The Carroll brothers, J. M. Carroll (1852–1931) and B. H. Carroll (1843–1914), represent the next phase in the development of Landmarkism. They were younger contemporaries of Graves and Pendleton and they are examined here because they represent the forward movement of the Landmark movement and because both men were very influential, in different ways, in establishing Landmarkism as one of the defining influences in Southern Baptist belief and practice.

---

197. *Tennessee Baptist* (Nashville), 13 July 1861 (emphasis in original).
198. Ibid.

Benajah Harvey Carroll

Benajah Harvey Carroll was born in Mississippi December 27, 1843. His father moved the family to Arkansas in 1848 and then to Texas in 1858. Although like Pendleton he was opposed to the secession of the Southern states, when the Civil War began he enlisted in the Confederate army. He was wounded during the war. His conversion took place in 1865 and he was called to the ministry in 1869. He was called as the assistant pastor of the First Baptist Church, Waco, Texas, in 1870 and became pastor of that church, where he served for thirty years, in 1871. Although he never attended a theological seminary, he taught theology and Bible at Baylor University in Waco from 1872–1905. He organized the Baylor Theological Seminary in 1905 and led in the founding of Southwestern Baptist Theological Seminary. In March 1908 he became president of Southwestern Baptist Theological Seminary where he served until his death. He published thirty-three volumes, the most notable of which was *An Interpretation of the English Bible* in seventeen volumes. His work shaped the theology of Southwestern throughout the early years of that institution.[199]

Ecclesiology

Baptist historian Leon McBeth wrote of Carroll, "I will affirm that there is a Baptist tradition of the Southwest and that it centers in Texas; that this tradition emerged around the turn of the present century; that Southwestern Baptist Theological Seminary is its major institutional expression . . . I will nominate B. H. Carroll as the primary architect of the new tradition."[200] The question that arises is simply: Is that new tradition an offshoot of Landmarkism? According to McBeth, "Carroll read several works of J. R. Graves . . . and no doubt absorbed some of his emphases, including the Landmark view of successionism in Baptist history, namely, that our denomination was formed by Jesus Christ, named for John the Baptist, and that Baptist churches have existed by unbroken succession from the New Testament to the present. . . . Carroll had no sympathy for any view of Baptist history

---

199. See Lefever, *Fighting the Good Fight*, and Cranfill, *Sermons and Life Sketch of B. H. Carroll*. It should be noted that most of Carroll's works are posthumous compilations by J. W. Crowder, Carroll's student and assistant. Crowder wrote, "Let it be understood once and for all that my relation to this work was and is Dr. Carroll's own arrangement, whether wise or unwise. I was with him for nine years, four as a student and five years as his assistant. . . . Suffice it to say that the work pleased him and that he made provision in his will for the part I was to play in the matter." Crowder, *Dr. B. H. Carroll*, 168.

200. McBeth, "Texas Tradition," 38.

that left any gaps between the banks of the Jordan and the banks of the Brazos."[201]

In fact, he quotes approvingly Graves' questionable interpretation of Matthew 11:11. Many interpret Jesus' words there as meaning John the Baptist belonged to the Old Testament dispensation. Carroll uses Graves' explanation of the passage in question in *The Seven Dispensations* wherein Graves says the Greek word *mikros* is an adverb modifying the verb "is." He thus renders the text: "he that is *later* in the kingdom is greater than John." This is an obvious case of eisegesis to defend one's doctrine rather than taking the doctrine from the text.[202] Carroll's view of this is expressed by his support of Graves' explanation, "If *mikros* were nowhere else in the whole range of Greek literature used adverbially, it evidently is here. The facts compel us to read it."[203] This type of eisegesis and interpretation will play a key part in Baptist history and the controversies spawned by the Landmarkers, which will be discussed in chapter 4. According to McBeth, Carroll used Pendleton's *Church Manual, Designed for the Use of Baptist Churches* for years in his ecclesiology classes at both Baylor and Southwestern Seminary.

Like Graves and Pendleton, Carroll affirmed, "We believe that the church, with all that pertains to it, is strictly a New Testament institution."[204] He presses this point, "The New Testament is the law of Christianity. All the New Testament is the law of Christianity. The New Testament is all the law of Christianity."[205] He holds that this has ever been proclaimed throughout history, through banishment, dungeons, fire, and martyrdom this voice has been heard, "a Baptist voice."[206] This church has been in existence since Christ established it. "Christ himself appointed its Apostles and its first seventy elders."[207] (He apparently has in mind the seventy who were sent out in Luke 10.) He cites John 4:1 to prove "Jesus made disciples before he baptized them," even though John 4:2 says clearly that Jesus baptized no one.[208] In his *Interpretation of the English Bible* he corrects, or his redactor corrects, his

---

201. Ibid., 42. (The Brazos River flows through Waco, Texas.)

202. The Baptist New Testament scholar A. T. Robertson says the phrase *ho mikroteros* is best translated by the Authorized Version, "he that is least." He adds, "The article with the comparative is a growing idiom in the vernacular *Koiné* for the superlative." Robertson, *Grammar of the Greek New Testament*, 668.

203. Carroll, *Interpretation of the English Bible*, 132.

204. Carroll, *Baptists and Their Doctrines*, 11.

205. Ibid., 13.

206. Ibid., 14.

207. Ibid., 11.

208. Ibid., 22.

statement regarding the baptizing "which Jesus did when he also (through his disciples) baptized."[209]

Like Graves and Pendleton, his ideas of church government were based largely on the American political experience. He says the church is "a federation, like the United States."[210] "The church is a pure democracy. Indeed, it is the only one in the world. There is no disbarment of franchise on account of race, education, wealth, age, or sex."[211] Later events would prove this to be far from the truth in many Baptist churches of the South.

Carroll also argued against the idea of a universal church. He believed that only when all those called of the Lord were glorified would that assembly be considered a church. "The only *existing* representation or type of the *ecclesia in glory* is the particular assembly on earth."[212] He expanded that definition by saying, "The term ecclesia cannot be rationally applied to all denominations collectively, nor to all living professors of religion, nor to all living believers collectively. In no sense are any such unassembled aggregates an ecclesia. None of them constitutes the flock, bride, temple, body, or house of God, either as a type of time or a reality of eternity. These terms belong exclusively either to the particular assembly now or the general assembly hereafter."[213] In all these assertions one sees little difference from Graves. Where Carroll does soften his approach versus that of Graves is in the rhetoric he uses. He asks the question should Baptist brethren be disfellowshipped for holding to the doctrine of an invisible, universal church? Carroll answers that in the negative but adds, "I honestly and strongly hold that even on this point his theory is erroneous and tends practically to great harm . . . the theory of the co-existence, side by side, on earth of two churches of Christ, one formal and visible, the other real, invisible and spiritual . . . is exceedingly mischievous and so confusing that every believer of it becomes muddled in running the lines of separation."[214] He himself becomes a little muddled when commenting on 1 Peter 2:4 he says, "The spiritual house of which Peter speaks is unquestionably the church."[215]

Carroll seems to mix his own thinking and use of illustrations when he tries to describe the honor due to Christ's church. He says, "Had I lived in the days of Moses I would have given honor to the tabernacle—in the

---

209. Carroll, *Interpretation of the English Bible*, 10:233.
210. Carroll, *Baptists and Their Doctrines*, 28.
211. Ibid., 31.
212. Ibid., 44 (emphasis in original).
213. Ibid., 44–45.
214. Ibid., 59.
215. Carroll, *Interpretation of the English Bible*, 11:17.

days of Solomon to the Temple alone."[216] Does he really mean that he would honor the temple alone and not the God who was worshipped there? One would think not, but, as with Graves, when these arguments are pushed too far the conclusions become questionable.

The question of close communion seemed to be quite settled in Carroll's mind. He wrote, "There is no more convincing argument against open communion of any kind. No open communion argument can stand before the declaration, 'It is *the Lord's table . . .*' No matter what anybody says, we should stick to the doctrine that Christ placed that table in his church, not for them to say who shall come, but for God to say who shall come. One has to be inside the church before he is entitled to sit at the Lord's table."[217] It is clear from the examples preceding his statement that Methodists, Presbyterians, and others are not "inside the church."

Theological Influence

What we see in B. H. Carroll, a paragon of Baptist history, education, seminary development, and influential member of the Southern Baptist Convention, is an affirmation of a continued dissemination of the distinctive Landmark doctrines of ecclesiology and the high-church attitude that was characteristic of the Landmarkers.

He was to play a pivotal role in the Whitsitt controversy (see chapter 4). This controversy was to have at its nucleus the very high-church position affirmed by Carroll. His influence went far beyond that controversy. His instrumentality in the formation of Southwestern Baptist Seminary could be tied to the weakness he saw in Southern Baptist Seminary as evidenced by the Whitsitt affair. His legacy, Southwestern Seminary, is the center of what Leon McBeth called the Texas Baptist tradition. It was and, it will be argued later, is in some respects a tradition that argues for an unbroken succession of Baptist churches and a Baptist church exclusiveness that seeks to discount or diminish other "so-called churches."

James Milton Carroll

J. M. Carroll was the younger brother of B. H. Carroll. He was born while the family lived in Arkansas and was six years old when they moved to Texas. Due to the outbreak of the Civil War he did not receive a proper education as

---

216. Carroll, *Baptists and Their Doctrines*, 59.
217. Carroll, *Interpretation of the English Bible*, 8:180.

a young man. However, he entered Baylor University when he was twenty-one years of age although as his biographer said, he could "not have entered the seventh grade of a public school today."[218] Carroll had a great capacity for learning and in the space of five years completed the equivalent of a Master of Arts degree. Upon graduation he served as pastor of two churches at Oakland and Anderson, Texas. It was in that same period that he began work as corresponding secretary of the Sunday School Convention of Texas. He was involved with denominational work for the remainder of his life. He raised extremely large amounts of money for the Baptist schools and mission enterprises in Texas. By some estimates he raised over eight hundred thousand dollars for denominational work of Southern Baptists in Texas. He served a short time as president of Oklahoma Baptist University and served as president of Howard Payne College. His single greatest achievement was the planning and building of San Marcos Baptist Academy in west Texas.[219]

One of Carroll's obituaries noted, "He was pre-eminent in the field of history . . . [a] writer and lecturer on Baptist history."[220] The article noted that he had just been invited to be part of the faculty at Southwestern Seminary and that his considerable library "containing the most complete collection in existence of source material on Texas Baptist history was given to the Seminary."[221]

Ecclesiology

Although Carroll's published material and views of theology are almost nonexistent and certainly minuscule in comparison to his brother, Pendleton, or Graves, the far-reaching impact of what he did write has shaped Southern Baptist views of ecclesiology as much or more than the other three men combined. Carroll's *Trail of Blood*,[222] which will be analyzed in some detail in the next chapter, is still in print and has been read by literally millions of Southern Baptists and has been absorbed into the genetic code of

218. Graham, ed., *Baptist Biography*, 46.
219. Ibid., 45–49.
220. *Baptist Messenger* (Oklahoma City), 15 January 1931, 1.
221. Ibid. A most curious quote at the end of the referenced article may reveal some of the simmering discontent in the aftermath of the Civil War and the manifestation of racial bigotry that would yet surface in the Southern Baptist Convention. The article concluded with these very curious words, "Above all he was a white-souled Christian who gave his best, first, and last, to the Kingdom of God." Of course, this reference could be to the sinless nature of Carroll's soul as cleansed by the blood of Christ, etc., but it seems an odd way to phrase such.
222. Carroll, *Trail of Blood*.

Southern Baptist life. This work by the "pre-eminent Baptist historian" is rejected today by every reputable Baptist historian but the views of Baptist church succession set forth in it still influence a disproportionate number of Southern Baptists. This will be examined in a later chapter.

Carroll's thesis in *The Trail of Blood* was that whatever names these various groups bore throughout history they all bore the name "Ana-Baptists" which was later shortened to Baptists. He asserted these churches held the same fundamental doctrines all through this long and bloody history. Carroll's ecclesiology can best be summed up with his own list of these ten fundamental doctrines:

1. A spiritual Church. Christ its founder, its only head and law giver.
2. Its ordinances, only two, Baptism and the Lord's Supper. They are typical and memorial, not saving.
3. Its officers only two, bishops or pastors and deacons; the servants of the church.
4. Its Government, a pure Democracy, and that executive only, never legislative.
5. Its laws and doctrines. The New Testament and that only.
6. Its members. Believers only, they saved by grace, not works, through the regenerating power of the Holy Spirit.
7. Its requirements. Believers on entering the church to be baptized, that by immersion, then obedience and loyalty to all New Testament laws.
8. The various churches—separate and independent in their execution of laws and discipline and in their responsibilities to God—but cooperative in work.
9. Complete separation of Church and State.
10. Absolute Religious Liberty for all.[223]

Carroll tried for many years, without success, to have *The Trail of Blood* published. The fallout over the resignation of W. H. Whitsitt, president of Southern Baptist Theological Seminary in Louisville, Kentucky, which was brought about by Landmark forces over the issue of Baptist church succession, had been kept alive by B. H. Carroll. J. M. Carroll's work two decades later may not have been received well by many in the Southern Baptist academic community. Carroll wrote to E. P. Alldredge, at the time the secretary of the Department of Survey Statistics for the Southern

---

223. Ibid., 56.

Baptist Sunday School Board, who was also serving as the book editor for the Sunday School Board, I. J. Van Ness having vacated that position. Apparently Carroll was unaware at the time of his writing that John L. Hill had taken over that position in June 1922.[224] In the letter Carroll says that he has doubts that "Dr. Van Ness would be willing to give the matter [he refers to the matter of publishing *The Trail of Blood*] a second consideration."[225] "However," he adds, "it's my purpose to again go carefully over the whole matter again before submitting the matter for publication. The only man who has yet seen fit to severely criticise [sic] the lectures was an Episcopal preacher.... He only heard one of the 4 [lectures]. And his criticisms were about all answered in the other 3."[226] "The Title of the mss. is 'The Trail of Blood.' All who have examined it congratulate me on the title."[227]

Carroll had no success in getting his book published. But J. W. Porter attended Carroll's lectures and was so impressed he asked Carroll for permission to publish the book. Carroll died in 1931 shortly before the book was published.[228] The little book that no one would publish is still in print and has sold over two million copies—more than all the books of Graves and Pendleton combined and its impact has been far wider in its reach.

Theological Influence

It is hard to overemphasize the theological impact of Carroll's one notable published work. This little book has influenced three generations of Southern Baptists. It has been presented as accurate and reliable Baptist church history, and, despite the instruction and presentation of historically reliable documentation to the contrary by many seminary professors and professors of church history at many Baptist colleges and universities, it continues to make its presence felt in the beliefs of Southern Baptists. Although, as will be presented later, one could not find a professor of church history today who openly teaches or espouses such a view, it is still a belief held by even the newest generation of Southern Baptists (see chapter 5). There is no reasonable explanation other than the influence of the Landmarkers and, in the case of Baptist church succession, J. M. Carroll.

---

224. Keegan, "Introduction to E. P. Alldredge Papers."
225. J. M. Carroll to E. P. Alldredge, 17 July 1922.
226. Ibid.
227. Ibid.
228. Carroll, *Trail of Blood*, 1.

Conclusion

This evaluation of the theological positions of J. R. Graves, J. M. Pendleton, B. H. Carroll, and J. M. Carroll has highlighted some notable differences, particularly between Graves and the other three. Graves' own words notwithstanding, there are marked differences in his theology and that of Pendleton. The Carrolls were of a mind with Pendleton, and B. H. Carroll used his books as texts for years at Southwestern Seminary. The question that stands over this is simply: Why would Graves be a champion for such men? How can they overlook what some called his peculiar positions?

The answer must be found in his ecclesiology and his positions on baptism, the authorized administrator of baptism, and the high-church exclusiveness he formulated for the Baptist Church from these positions. These men and many other Baptists were not immune to the cultural, social, and religious forces that drove Graves. They accepted his positions because they validated the Baptist Church as the one true church and separated them from other denominations, or societies as they preferred to call them. The Landmarks driven deep into the genetic code of Baptist life by Graves and his associates were the critical issues. One could overlook or explain away odd theological positions if these key doctrines, which validated, galvanized, and inspired the Baptists, were correct and championed unswervingly. This same pattern, the same turning of a blind eye to key issues, will be repeated through many Landmark controversies in the nineteenth century, the twentieth century, and even to the present day through denominational leaders, denominational papers, and the Landmark DNA which became an unseen part of Baptist life—an unseen but nevertheless real and vital part of much of Baptist life and belief in a surprising number of Southern Baptists.

3

An Evaluation of Baptist Church Succession

Evaluating the Claims of Baptist Church Succession

CENTRAL TO THE LANDMARKERS' doctrine of Baptist Church exclusivism was the formulation of an unbroken line of Baptist Church succession from the time of Christ to the present. Although W. Morgan Patterson attributes to J. R. Graves "more than any other individual . . . the wide acceptance of Baptist succession as orthodoxy among Southern Baptists,"[1] it must be said that J. M. Carroll's *Trail of Blood* has had a more far-reaching and lasting influence and remains the most widely circulated piece of literature espousing the view of an unbroken succession of Baptist Churches. Graves regarded the persecution of believers by the established church as the sure sign by which to identify Baptists down through the ages. In the introductory essay to Orchard's *History of Foreign Baptists*, Graves said, "The clearest and most satisfactory proof [that] . . . successions of Baptist communities have come down to us from the apostles, [is that they are] all striped and scarred and blood covered."[2] He later used the phrase, picked up by Carroll, "trail of blood."[3] It is in Carroll's work by that name that the line of Baptist Church succession primarily set forth by Orchard's *History of Foreign Baptists*, and spread through Graves' republication of that work in 1855, has been disseminated far beyond the thousands of copies of Orchard's work which Graves printed. Over two million four hundred thousand copies of *The Trail*

---

1. Patterson, *Baptist Successionism*, 26.
2. Orchard, *Concise History of Foreign Baptists*, xviii.
3. Graves, *Trilemma*, 119.

of Blood have been published and distributed and it remains the most widely circulated writing on Baptist Church succession.

Graves held that the doctrine of an unbroken succession of Baptist churches was necessary to identify the true church. This thought was central to the Landmark ecclesiology. Baptist succession finds continuity not in a chain of apostolic succession but in a continuity of organization. The succession of true churches assures a continuity of pastors. In the words of Graves, "Christ, in the very 'days of John the Baptist,' did establish a visible kingdom on earth . . . if his *kingdom* has stood unchanged, and will to the end, he must always have had true and uncorrupted churches, since his kingdom can not exist without true churches."[4] Of course, for Graves the definition of true churches was Baptist churches and his mission was to establish the "Old Landmarks" which he interpreted to mean "those principles which all true Baptists, in all ages, have professed to believe."[5] It is the purpose of this chapter to examine these "principles" held by these so-called "true Baptists" down through the centuries. Carroll stated that he had discovered an unbroken chain of true churches across the centuries. Since there is a great commonality between his chain and the groups that Graves set forth as Baptist churches down through the ages, Carroll's chart (see appendix C) will be used to identify the groups whose theology will be investigated to ascertain what the principles were which these "true Baptists, in all ages, have professed to believe."

It should be said that this is not an in-depth refutation of Baptist church succession. (That topic has been addressed by capable authors for over one hundred years.) W. H. Whitsitt, *A Question in Baptist History* (1896), presents an anti-successionist view that places the beginnings of Baptists in the seventeenth century. This was a source of great controversy with the Landmarkers and eventually led to Whitsett's resignation at Southern Seminary. (This will be addressed in more detail in chapter 4.) A. H. Newman, *A History of Anti-Pedobaptism: From the Rise of Pedobaptism to A. D. 1609* (1896), a famous Baptist historian, refutes successionist theory, while Winthrop S. Hudson, "Baptists Were Not Anabaptists," *Chronicle* (1953), makes a solid case that Baptists grew out of Protestantism not Anabaptism. W. Morgan Patterson, *Baptist Successionism: A Critical View* (1969), offers an effective critique of Thomas Crosby's Anabaptist connection,[6] and James

---

4. Graves, *Old Landmarkism*, 122–23 (emphasis in original).

5. Ibid., xiv.

6. Thomas Crosby (1683–1751) wrote *The History of the English Baptists* (1783) in which he argued that the New Testament Church practiced believer's baptism and infant baptism was a much later introduction that could not be traced back to the apostolic age. He did not try to establish Baptist Churches back to the apostolic age but

E. McGoldrick, *Baptist Successionism: A Crucial Question in Baptist History* (1994), explores the orthodoxy of the groups Carroll claimed as Baptists in *The Trail of Blood*. Rather than revisit what has been said before, the goal in this chapter is to highlight some of the theological positions of those who were hailed as Baptists down through the ages. These views will be compared with the representative views of Graves, Pendleton, and Carroll delineated in chapter 2.

According to Carroll's chart the Baptist churches declared non-fellowship with what he calls the "irregular churches" in the year AD 251. This was over the issue of infant baptism and baptismal salvation and he says that the Baptists thus received their first and oldest nickname Ana-Baptists.[7] With some overlap of various groups (obviously necessary to maintain an unbroken line) the groups Carroll lists in roughly chronological order are: Montanists, Novatians, Paterins, Cathari, Donatists, Paulicians, Arnoldists, Henricians, Albigenses, Waldenses, Ana-Baptists, and Baptists when in the sixteenth century the "Ana" was dropped from their name.[8] Carroll thus sets down the views inculcated by Graves, largely based on Orchard's work, but views which had managed to make their way into the mainstream of Baptist life even before Carroll's work was published. A quote by George B. Taylor, reproduced by Willis Jarrell, is representative of these views.

> Baptist principles and Baptist practices have existed in all ages from the Reformation back to apostolic times. I humbly claim that we originated not at the Reformation, nor in the dark ages, nor in any century after the Apostles, but our marching orders are the commission and that the first Baptist church was the church at Jerusalem.[9]

Taylor was not the only one to express such views. When Carroll says that he "had discovered an unbroken chain of true churches across the centuries," it must be said that his "discoveries" were made in the pages of works before his own. *The Trail of Blood* is a recapitulation of much that had been chronicled by other writers, edited into a manageable little booklet that could be presented in a series of lectures the layperson could grasp. The average layperson who had neither the time nor educational background to read Orchard's book or other Baptist succession proponents like Thomas Crosby or David Benedict could read Carroll's little book. A brief look at

---

did define the Anabaptists as the ones from whom the English Baptists were descended.

7. J. M. Carroll, *Trail of Blood*, chart (see appendix C).

8. Ibid. It should be noted that the spelling of the names of some of these groups varies from author to author.

9. Willis Anselm Jarrel, *Baptist Perpetuity*, 38–39.

Carroll's sources and church succession works which were published before *The Trail of Blood* follows.

A Brief History of Baptist Church Succession

The idea of an unbroken line of "true churches" stretching back to the time of Christ did not originate with Carroll, Graves, or the Landmarkers. It was, however, exactly what Graves used to promote the Landmark view of Baptist Church exclusivity and the weapon he wielded against other denominations since none of them could or would make the same kind of claims.

A Summary of Works Claiming Baptist Church Succession

Long before Carroll published his little book, which was more of a condensation of what had been written by others, a succession of authors had written works claiming to see Baptists in nearly every century and in various dissenting groups. As early as 1790 Robert Robinson published *The History of Baptism*.[10] This work claimed many of the sects, which dissented from the church, as Baptists. This was regarded as a significant work to prove church succession as witnessed by Graves' reprinting of the original. It is interesting that in the introduction Graves made the disclaimer that he would be "assuming to [himself] the privilege to add such foot-notes as in my judgment I think the claims of truth demand."[11] Robinson claimed Manicheans, Bogomils, Paulicians, and Donatists as Baptists. He says, "The Donatists were Trinitarian Anabaptists."[12] The tenor of his ideas is reflected in the heading for one of his later sections: "All Baptists However Diversified Agree in Holding What Are Called Anabaptistical Errors."[13] In other words, Baptists, as shown in his work, may have been known by a variety of names over the years but certain baptistic principles could be found in those groups.

Jonathan Davis wrote *History of the Welsh Baptists* in which he claimed that the Welsh Baptists were the seed of Gomer, eldest son of Japheth, eldest son of Noah, and that they landed in Britain about three hundred years after the flood.[14] He holds to the theory that Baptists did not spring from the Reformation as they have a heritage that precedes all other denominations.

10. Robinson, *History of Baptism*.
11. Ibid., xvii.
12. Ibid., 279.
13. Ibid., 593.
14. Davis, *History of Welsh Baptists*, 18–19.

He says, "It is a fact that cannot be controverted, that there were Baptists here at the commencement of the Reformation."[15] He makes the case that Baptists were martyred in large numbers and this is the testimony of their faith and their beliefs.

Two massive works, Orchard's *Concise History of Foreign Baptists* referenced above and Mosheim's *Ecclesiastical History*, were widely referenced by Carroll. Mosheim's work is far more objective and excels in scholarship. Written in 1726 it was translated into English by J. Murdock in 1841 and Archibald MacLaine in 1842. Many of the authors after this date quoted extensively from these two works, although Orchard was more useful to the Landmark cause. In the introduction to Orchard's work, republished by Graves, he praised church history but added that none had been written for seventeen hundred years because those which had been written covered the years 300 to 1600 only by telling the story of "the scarlet harlot riding on the beast with seven heads and ten horns . . . drunk with the blood of saints." Graves added, "It is high time for the history of the Church of Christ to be written . . . the world has quite long enough wondered after the Beast, and the Church of Christ left in the obscurity of the wilderness."[16] Orchard drew on Mosheim's work to chart groups that dissented from the Roman Catholic Church and rejected infant baptism. These groups included the Montanists, Novatians, Donatists, and others. He connected these groups with the Baptist church. This was the unbroken succession of true churches leading to the Baptist denomination in England and later America.

One who took a more measured approach was David Benedict. He wrote, "I shall not attempt to trace a continuous line of churches as we can for a few centuries past in Europe and America. This is a kind of succession to which we have never laid claim; and, of course, we make no effort to prove it."[17] He makes no claim to prove an unbroken line of churches, however, he lists the Montanists, Novatians, Paulicians, Paterines, Waldenses, Albigenses, Henricians, Arnoldists, and Cathari without condemning them. He takes an approach that says we can't know for sure. Another conservative approach was that taken by John Cramp. He wrote, "I am not disposed to regard any persons as primitive Baptists unless they practiced the baptism of believers; their rejection of infant baptism will not warrant the imposition of that worthy name on them. Mr. Orchard's 'History of Foreign Baptists,' and other works of a similar kind, have now and then fallen into error."[18]

---

15. Ibid., 19.
16. Orchard, *History of Foreign Baptists*, ix, xi.
17. Benedict, *General History of the Baptist Denomination*, 51.
18. Cramp, *Baptist History*, 69.

Even with his cautious approach the very title of Cramp's work says that Baptists stretch from the foundation of the Christian Church forward. It must be said that many of the groups claimed by other writers did practice what was called believers' baptism and thus would meet Cramp's limited definition of a true Baptist.

Two other key works by D. B. Ray and Henry Vedder went much further in establishing Baptist succession. Ray's work relied on much that Graves had published in the religious press and made the case, unapologetically, for Baptist church succession. He wrote, "It is no new doctrine among Baptists to claim the succession of the churches of Jesus Christ."[19] He said a succession of the Novatians had continued down to the Reformation and claimed that Albigenses, Henricians, Petrobrussians, Paterines, and Cathari were actually all Waldenses by different names.[20] He links these groups with the Waldenses and the key is the mode of baptism. In his view of history, the Waldensian period lasted 1260 years to coincide with the 1260 years of Revelation 12:6 as he interpreted that passage. He lists the Waldensian period as beginning between AD 275–325. His analysis of these groups is clear. He states, "I am fully satisfied that the Waldensian period of the church, during her retirement in the wilderness, is the purest part of her history since the apostolic age."[21]

Vedder claimed the "Novatians were the earliest Anabaptists."[22] Vedder quite tellingly gives the criteria by which these dissident groups were to be judged as Baptists and thus the true church. "Any body of Christians that holds to the supremacy of the Scriptures, a church of the regenerate only, and believers' baptism, is fundamentally one with the Baptist churches of today, whatever else it may add to or omit from its statement of beliefs."[23] A careful study of these dissident groups will show that they had almost nothing in common with modern day Baptists other than in most cases the mode of baptism, church polity, or dissent from the Catholic Church.

One other work of interest is J. A. Shackleford's *Compendium of Baptist History*.[24] Shackleford draws on Mosheim and Orchard but is thoroughly Landmark in his view of church succession. He says of the Waldenses "that these were Baptist churches there can be no doubt."[25] He adds, Baptists re-

---

19. Ray, *Baptist Succession*, 17.
20. Ibid., 113.
21. Ibid., 336–38.
22. Vedder, *Short History of the Baptists*, 64.
23. Ibid., 115.
24. Shackleford, *Compendium of Baptist History*.
25. Ibid., 118.

pudiate the insinuation "that their churches are a branch of the church of Christ, but claim that their's [sic] are the true churches."²⁶ Regarding other denominations he said, "We do not recognize these reforms [churches that sprang from the Catholic Church in the Reformation] as true churches."²⁷ Of particular interest in Shackleford's work is the chart he constructed to trace the history of the true church by its various names through the ages. This will be examined in more detail when Carroll's sources are investigated.

J. R. Graves' Support of Baptist Succession

J. R. Graves was the first to widely publicize and popularize the notion that Baptist churches (true churches in his estimation) could be traced in an unbroken line back to John the Baptist and the church Jesus established. He did not originate the idea as evidenced above but he spread the idea among Southern Baptists and made it foundational for the Landmark ecclesiology. As he said, "My position is that Christ, in the very days of John the Baptist, did establish a visible kingdom on earth, and that this kingdom has never yet been 'broken in pieces' . . . therefore, if his kingdom has stood unchanged, and will to the end, he must have always have had true and uncorrupted churches."²⁸

Graves leaned heavily on Orchard's *History of the Baptists* and Robinson's *History of Baptism*. He reprinted both works and wrote an introduction to each. In *The Trilemma*, he claims the Baptist denomination to be the only one established by Christ as His visible church and refers the reader who wished to be satisfied with his claims to read, after the New Testament, Orchard's and Robinson's works.²⁹ He insisted that the descent of the Baptist churches of America extended "back to the apostles' time."³⁰ Standing over the various groups claimed as Baptists through the ages were, in Graves' definition, the Anabaptists. As he explained, "The genuine Anabaptists . . . were the only 'salt of the earth,' and the 'light of the world,' during the 1600 years that preceded the Reformation."³¹

The widest dissemination of Baptist succession views in Graves' day, however, was in the *Tennessee Baptist*. For example, in November and December of 1848, Graves, under his pseudonym "Fidus," contends with

26. Ibid., 282.
27. Ibid., 283.
28. Graves, *Old Landmarkism*, 122–23.
29. Graves, *Trilemma*, 138n.
30. Ibid., 124.
31. Ibid., 127.

J. L. Waller of the *Western Review* over the issue of authorized administrators of baptism. Throughout the series of articles Graves leans heavily on Baptist church succession and refers to Orchard, Mosheim, and others to support his position. He traces the Baptist line of succession through Novatians, Donatists, Phrygians, Paterines, Vaudois, Albigenses, Waldenses, and Ana-baptists.[32] The exclusivity of Baptist churches is noted over and over, particularly in articles on church government and baptism. The argument was always the same, i.e., only the Baptist church can trace an unbroken line of true churches back to the first church in Jerusalem. Graves wrote, "Protestant Historians frankly admit that Baptist churches are the only religious communities that have stood since the Apostles."[33] It must be remembered that when Graves says "protestant" he means churches which came out of the Protestant Reformation which would not include Baptist churches in his view of an unbroken succession of Baptist churches. It is interesting that Graves published a letter from G. H. Orchard wherein Orchard promised to write several articles for the *Tennessee Baptist* including excerpts from his book showing "that the despised Anabaptists have been God's servants throughout time . . . a negation of infant baptism through the early churches . . . [and] strict communion in all the churches."[34] Many of these were produced in serial form but the American Civil War brought an end to the *Tennessee Baptist* and soon occupied the pages of the paper with other concerns.

Support by Other Landmarkers

J. R. Graves was not the only Landmarker to vigorously support the idea of Baptist church succession. Before Carroll's book was published other Landmarkers were on record as supporting and offering up their own views of an unbroken line of Baptist churches stretching back to the first century. James E. Tull said, "The church succession theory perhaps derives its chief importance from the fact that it is a compact summary of the Landmark faith."[35] This Landmark view of church history was propagated throughout the Southern Baptist Convention by key figures within the denomination and served, as Graves often used it in debates, to separate Baptists from other denominations in an exclusive and at times dismissive way.

One of the most powerful Baptist figures of the late nineteenth century and early twentieth century was B. H. Carroll, a younger contemporary of

32. *Tennessee Baptist* (Nashville), 7 December 1848.
33. *Tennessee Baptist* (Nashville), 23 March 1861.
34. *Tennessee Baptist* (Nashville), 9 August 1856.
35. Tull, *History of Southern Baptist Landmarkism*, 187.

Graves (see chapter 2). Carroll held to the doctrine of Baptist church succession and rejected alien immersion. Carroll was instrumental in securing the resignation of W. H. Whitsitt, the president of Southern Baptist Theological Seminary, because Whitsitt had published a work repudiating the Baptist successionist view. This controversy will be covered in detail in chapter 4. Carroll was a powerful figure within the Southern Baptist Convention, a member of the Southern Baptist Seminary board of trustees, the founder of Southwestern Baptist Seminary and his support of the Landmark view of history exerted a great influence in the beliefs of rank and file Southern Baptists.

Another influential Southern Baptist who held church succession views was E. E. Folk, editor of the *Baptist and Reflector* for twenty-nine years. Folk was not insistent that Baptists could be traced in an unbroken line through the ages, but he did say, "You cannot put your finger upon any year this side of the Apostles and say that the Baptists originated then. The only place you can look for their origin is in the New Testament. It was then they started."[36] Folk says that despite the difficulties of tracing this line of succession it is clear that "down through the ages there have been people holding essential Baptist principles."[37] The groups he listed were: the Novatianists, Donatists, Cathari, Paulicians, Vaudois, Petrobrussians, Henricians, Albigenses, Waldenses, Anabaptists, and the Mennonites.[38]

E. Y. Mullins, president of Southern Baptist Theological Seminary for almost thirty years, displays the deference that many had to pay to the belief of Baptist church succession. He succeeded W. H. Whitsitt at the seminary. Mullins wrote, "Many of the parties of the middle ages and others which have frequently been claimed as in all particulars conforming to modern Baptist churches, and therefore in the line of succession, have varied to a greater or less extent from present day Baptist doctrines. This has been my objection to some of the histories which have been printed heretofore, they have proved too much."[39] However, given the opposition which Whitsitt encountered, Mullins was quick to add, "There were divergencies [sic] and variations [in these different groups], but . . .Baptists have always allowed a certain degree of latitude in belief without necessisarily [sic] ceasing to be classified in a general way among Baptists."[40]

Graves drew from early works, primarily Orchard. However, after decades in which the Landmark theory of Baptist church succession was

36. Folk, notes from a speech delivered in 1916.
37. Ibid.
38. Ibid.
39. E. Y. Mullins to John T. Christian, 12 July 1918.
40. Ibid.

published and defended, the succession of Baptist churches was set forth to varying degrees by influential Southern Baptists throughout the late nineteenth and early twentieth century.

J. M. Carroll's Enduring Contribution to Baptist Church Succession

As the preceding sections have shown, Baptist church succession was one view of Baptist history which was promoted by certain authors and seized upon by the Landmarkers as the key to their claims of Baptist church exclusivity and a rejection of other churches as mere "societies" and thus not true churches of Christ. As has also been shown, there was no unanimity of opinion or historical work regarding exactly which groups were true Baptists, their names, dates, and in many cases their doctrines. Some like W. A. Jarrel preferred to speak of a Baptist perpetuity, i.e., a succession of true doctrine which was preserved from New Testament times to the churches of the Southern Baptist Convention.[41] In spite of the number of works promoting a successionist view of Baptist history, other works that presented a less absolute view of an unbroken line of Baptist churches, and others like Whitsitt's work which refuted such views, it can be said that the average member of the typical Southern Baptist church had neither the patience to carefully study the hundreds of pages of claims and sometimes conflicting accounts of history nor a knowledge of ancient and medieval history necessary to make a careful reading of all the books and materials available. This is precisely the void that Carroll's little book *The Trail of Blood* filled.

This little book of fifty-six pages, it could better be called a pamphlet, was assembled from lectures given by Carroll promoting the Landmark succession theory. He drew on a number of sources but claimed that he had discovered an unbroken line of true churches across the centuries. He illustrated his claim with a chart which he used in his lectures, his pamphlet being the written commentary on the chart. This could easily be read in one sitting and the scholarly tone, copious references, and the chart presented a mass of seemingly scholarly proof, particularly for those who had no knowledge of church history. The fact that this book has enjoyed a circulation far greater than all the other works on church succession combined, and that it remains in publication today, and still sells at a respectable rate each year bears testimony to its effectiveness and popularity. An analysis and critique of Carroll's work follows.

---

41. Jarrel, *Baptist Perpetuity*.

An Analysis and Critique of J. M. Carroll's *The Trail of Blood*

Many church historians have recognized, for the reasons stated above, the impact of Carroll's work. James McGoldrick said, "The popularity of the successionist view has been enhanced enormously by . . . *The Trail of Blood*."[42] Carroll's stated objective in publishing that book was explained in the full title: *The Trail of Blood: Following the Christians Down through the Centuries from the Days of Christ to the Present Time, or, The History of Baptist Churches from the Time of Christ, Their Founder, to the Present Day.* It is quite clear from the title that Carroll equates Christians with Baptists and names Jesus Christ as the founder of the Baptist church which had its origin in the days of Christ. What is not explicitly stated but is assumed and is the true reason for this publication is simply that other churches and denominations, having their origin centuries later, are not the church Christ founded and hence not the true church. Since Carroll's book was, as shown above, the primary source for Southern Baptists' beliefs regarding the history and founding of the Baptist church, it is necessary to evaluate his thesis, sources, and presentation.

History and Development of Carroll's Work

It is not altogether clear why Carroll began his lecture series on Baptist church succession. Those lectures were the foundation of *The Trail of Blood*. What is clear is the difficulty which he encountered in getting his work published (see chapter 2.) It is also abundantly clear that his brother B. H. Carroll was instrumental in the removal of W. H. Whitsitt as president of Southern Baptist Theological Seminary because Whitsitt had published a view of Baptist history that was diametrically opposed to the Landmark view. B. H. Carroll was solidly in the Landmark camp and his brother J. M. was as well. It seems that J. M. Carroll saw the need, as increasingly church history scholars criticized the Landmark view to inculcate that view in the average Southern Baptist by visiting churches and giving his lectures in a week of nightly meetings. These meetings grew in notoriety and were attended by those who belonged to other denominations as witnessed by Carroll's reference to an Episcopal minister who attended some of his lectures.[43] The meetings were vastly popular with Southern Baptists because of the claim presented by one heralded as a Baptist historian (for his work *A History of Texas Baptists*), supposedly based on an

---

42. McGoldrick, *Baptist Successionism*, 1.
43. J. M. Carroll to E. P. Alldredge 17 July 1922.

exhaustive study of church history, that established the Baptist church as the only church with roots in the first century and the only one descended from the church Jesus established.

According to Carroll's own testimony he had always been interested in church history and, as he relates, "when [he] was just a boy, [he] saw the many denominations and wondered which was the church the Lord Jesus founded."[44] However, by his own admission, he could not find the historical documents of the Baptists. This led him to conclude that the documents had perished along with the Baptists who had been martyred by the Catholic Church among others.[45] He found these dissident groups, which others had called the true church or Baptists, in the pages of Orchard, Benedict, Ray, Graves, and others. It was said that Carroll in the course of his search amassed a great library that was later donated to Southwestern Baptist Seminary in Fort Worth, Texas, where his brother B. H. Carroll served as president.[46] It is next that these sources and Carroll's use of them should be considered.

Analysis and Critique of Carroll's Sources

The Trail of Blood boasts a copious bibliography. There are seventy-five entries (eliminating duplications). However, when one comes to the actual text there are only eighteen references from a total of eleven works in a work of fifty-six pages (five of these occur in one reference and two referenced works are not listed in the bibliography). Of these eleven works, ten are discussed above. The *Schaff-Herzog Encyclopedia* Carroll cites only in a general way to confirm that persecution of various groups did take place. Carroll did not rely on Schaff's eight-volume church history as there is the greatest discrepancy between the dates Schaff gives for the various dissident groups and those given by Carroll.

The sources from which Carroll did draw, as witnessed by his sparse references within the book, were supportive of and in general agreement with the idea of a succession of Baptist churches. Mosheim's *Ecclesiastical History* would be the exception, but his documentation of the persecution suffered by the various groups in opposition to Rome was evidence enough to support Carroll's thesis. References to Mosheim would have added credibility in that day. Carroll produced a condensed summary of much that had been written regarding the succession of Baptist churches. His methodology was to affirm Baptist principles and then point to groups throughout history

---

44. Carroll, *Trail of Blood*, 2.
45. Ibid., 2–3.
46. Ibid., 2.

who held in some form to some of those principles. This he did without regard to other practices of the various groups which may have put them at variance with the historic confessions of the Church.

Of particular interest among Carroll's sources was J. A. Shackleford's *Compendium of Baptist History*. Shackleford is not well-known. He was a Baptist, but little is known of his ministry or life. He does not appear in the histories of the Tennessee, Alabama, Kentucky, Arkansas, Texas, or Georgia Baptists.[47] What is striking is that Shackleford's work which was completed in 1891 and published in 1892 was not his original intent. He merely set out to prepare a chart which would give one, as he said, "a bird's eye view of Baptist History, with its relations to the Catholic hierarchy, and the branches of the Romish church."[48] As he gathered the material for his research he amassed such a quantity of historical information that he felt a larger work was required. What is of interest, however, is the fact that Carroll's chart in *The Trail of Blood* looks amazingly similar to Shackleford's, published thirty years earlier. Shackleford's chart is in a vertical format while Carroll's is horizontal, but the design and layout are nearly identical. Carroll adopted the same red and black circles Shackleford used and there are forty-three identical dates, countries, and groups in precisely the same order, duration, and location. To even the casual observer it is clear Carroll has used Shackleford's work and claimed it as his own. This was not mentioned by Carroll's contemporaries or others. One must ask, was this because of the power of Carroll's brother, B. H. Carroll, the fallout from the Whitsitt controversy, and/or the wide acceptance of the Landmark view of Baptist church succession among Southern Baptists? What is clear is that Shackleford's work is not found in the libraries of many Southern Baptist colleges, universities, and seminaries while Carroll's work is the most widely circulated piece of Baptist succession literature in history.

The Enduring Nature of Carroll's Work

One must ask, what is it about *The Trail of Blood* which has led to its longevity and wide distribution? First, the great controversy over the research by W. H. Whitsitt (mentioned above and detailed in chapter 4) stirred many Southern Baptists to question the historicity of the Landmark claims. It was necessary to still these doubts because the succession of Baptist churches

---

47. The particulars of Shackleford's life and ministry could well provide the material for further research and other work in this area as there seems to be some question of the originality of Carroll's work in view of what Shackleford produced.

48. Shackleford, *Compendium of Baptist History*, 9.

stood at the heart of Landmark rejection of other denominations and churches as true churches of Christ. This is seen in the number of works published around the time of Whitsitt's resignation which support the Landmark view. Whether or not B. H. Carroll played a role in encouraging his brother to begin his lecture series which would ultimately become *The Trail of Blood* is unknown but given his role in the Whitsitt affair it is a definite possibility.

As outlined in chapter 2, Carroll had no success in getting the Southern Baptist Convention to publish his book. This was due in large part to the number of former Whitsitt colleagues and students who filled different roles within the convention. However, J. W. Porter, pastor of First Baptist Church, Lexington, Kentucky, attended one of Carroll's lectures and was so impressed that he asked Carroll for permission to publish the lectures. Carroll agreed and wrote out the lectures which Porter then published.[49] The entire first edition quickly sold out.

The second edition of the book was published by Ashland Avenue Baptist Church, Lexington, Kentucky. Ashland Avenue Baptist Church was organized by J. W. Porter and the charter membership included thirty members of the First Baptist Church who formed the new church. Eleven months after its formation in January 1916 Clarence Walker was called as the pastor of the Ashland Avenue church. The first tent meeting of the new church was conducted by Porter and Walker in 1917.[50]

It was Walker and Ashland Avenue Baptist Church who took up the publication and distribution of *The Trail of Blood* with the second edition in 1931 and have continued to do so to the present day. Clarence Walker was solidly in the Landmark camp and held to the succession of Baptist churches as the true church throughout the ages from the time of Christ. Walker wrote an introduction to the second edition and quoted approvingly Carroll's "marks" of the true church and the fact that the true church could be traced by their martyrdom down through the ages as they dissented from the church at Rome.[51] But it was through Walker's promotional efforts that the book began to be circulated and popularized.

In July 1922 Walker began publication of the *Ashland Avenue Baptist*. Like Graves' *Tennessee Baptist* it was a weekly digest of sermons, doctrinal topics, church news, advertisements, and other news. By 1936 it had a circulation of nineteen hundred subscribers and by 1986 had over sixty-six

---

49. Carroll, *Trail of Blood*, 1.

50. Ashland Avenue Baptist Church, Seventieth Anniversary Historical Statistics, January 30, 1986.

51. See Carroll, *Trail of Blood*, 1–5.

thousand subscribers, far more than Graves ever reached.[52] Walker like Graves took on challengers to the Landmark view of church history. As late as 1953 Walker took on the Catholic paper, the *Register*, Denver, Colorado, that published an article entitled "Baptist Don't Go Back to Christ."[53] Notably, his refutations are largely quotes from Carroll's book. The article and those editions of the paper included appeals to his readers to help circulate *The Trail of Blood*. Walker states within one article that over three hundred thousand copies of *The Trail of Blood* have been distributed.[54]

In fact, it was the Baptist press in various periodicals and weekly newspapers which promoted Carroll's book to many Southern Baptists. This coupled with the low cost of the book, which was more like a pamphlet, served to make this view of church history the dominant view of church members in the Landmark belt in the Southwest. The annual printing of eight thousand copies by the publisher over eighty years after its first publication testifies to the reach and impact of Carroll's work. What must be answered is simply, who are the groups claimed to be the true church, i.e., Baptist churches, throughout history, what did they believe, and are those beliefs compatible with beliefs held by Southern Baptists and the historic confessions of the Church? Those questions are addressed in the following section.

Review of Groups Claimed as Baptists by the Landmarkers

Carroll's chart and his narrative are filled with many dates, the duration of certain groups, and events which differ widely from many respected historians. No effort is made to compare these discrepancies or reconcile them. All the dates and references noted are all Carroll's unless otherwise noted. For example, Carroll notes that the first nickname given to Baptist churches was "Christians" and the next beginning in 251 was "Ana-Baptists."[55] He puts this title Ana-Baptist over all the various groups named until the seventeenth century when they came to be known only as Baptists.

Given the antiquity and scarcity of the primary sources the examination of the doctrines of these various groups will rely heavily on the work of other scholars which contain translations of primary sources. These sources

---

52. Ashland Avenue Baptist Church, Seventieth Anniversary Historical Statistics, January 30, 1986.

53. Walker, "The Trail of Blood: True or False? Dr. Carroll's Statements Called in Question, Pastor Walker Answers ...," *Ashland Avenue Baptist*, March 6, 1953, 1.

54. Ibid.

55. Carroll, *Trail of Blood*, chart.

are not only quite limited but, in some cases, the only extant sources are hostile ones. No attempt is made to examine every doctrine of the various groups but only those which would cause them to stand out as "Baptists" in the Landmark view. After looking at the appeal of these various groups each will be examined to compare certain of their beliefs with the historic confessions of the church and historic Baptist doctrines. The groups claimed by Carroll and examined in his chronology are: Montanists, Novatians, Paterins, Cathari, Donatists, Paulicians, Arnoldists, Henricians, Albigenses, Waldenses, and Anabaptists.

The Appeal of These Groups to the Landmarkers

Carroll's approach in identifying the true church was to set forth the marks of the true church and from there to show how the different groups in his history satisfied those requirements. It must be said that he was not consistent in his application of all ten marks but the key marks for inclusion were rejection of infant baptism, believers' baptism by immersion, democratic (congregational) church government, and a complete separation of church and state.

According to Carroll, the true Baptist principles were preserved by the Montanists in the third to the fifth centuries.[56] Montanism accepted the basic tenets of Christianity, accepted the deity of Christ, but affirmed the continuing validity of prophetic utterances. It seems the only qualification for the clergy in the mind of Montanus, the founder, was being endowed by the Holy Spirit to have these ecstatic utterances.

James McGoldrick says that advocates of Baptist successionism are almost unanimous in their praise of Montanism as "the initial baptistic effort to preserve the purity of apostolic teaching."[57] Concerning ecclesiology the Montanists "disapproved of an organized Church hierarchy."[58] This would stand them in good stead with the Landmarkers for they had the correct organization, i.e., no church hierarchy but rather a local church autonomy, and the obvious conclusion was that this was the correct organization because it was so near the first church in Jerusalem chronologically. Or to put it in the words of J. R. Graves, "a properly organized church ... would always afford a properly authorized administrator."[59]

---

56. Ibid.
57. McGoldrick, *Baptist Successionism*, 10.
58. Runciman, *Medieval Manichee*, 182.
59. *Tennessee Baptist* (Nashville), 7 December 1848.

According to Carroll the Novatians joined with the Montanists as preservers of true Baptist doctrine in the fourth century.[60] Orchard proposed in his work to prove a succession from the Novatians to the Baptists of the eighteenth century. However, at the beginning of his account he states, "There was no difference in point of doctrine between the Novations and other Christians."[61] "The Novations . . . contended that the sacrament (baptism) could not be administered rightly in the Catholic Church because it had become corrupt. In other words [words Graves would approve], a baptism could not be valid if it were performed by an unworthy clergyman."[62] This is in lockstep with Graves', Pendleton's, and the Landmarkers' assertion that if a church is unscriptural her officers and her acts are as well. In addition, the Novations met the basic test of being a Baptist church, i.e., they opposed Rome and were often persecuted for doing so. Graves' declares that *"the Baptists in the east were called Novations [sic]."*[63]

Carroll lists the Paterins as the carrier of true Baptist doctrine from the fourth to the sixth centuries.[64] Graves gives the following account of the Paterins: "The Paterines [sic] a Christian people, filled Italy, and subsequently flooded all Europe—They accounted the Pedo-baptist church, *Antichristians*, contemned [sic] all clerical authority and orders. They immersed penitents and *re-immersed all those who had been baptized in other communities.*"[65] The Paterins opposition to imperial interference in church affairs and a belief that they were the only true church would endear them to the Landmarkers.

Carroll lists the Paulicians in his chart as an overarching group for about five centuries and under the Paulicians he has listed the Cathari. The Cathari opposed the doctrines and customs of the established church and called the adherents of it Romanists. They held that there were two churches one of the wicked and one of the righteous. Of course, they themselves constituted the righteous and true church and there was no possibility of

---

60. Carroll, *Trail of Blood*, chart. It is interesting that Carroll gives a date of 251 as the time when non-fellowship was first declared between the true churches and the irregular churches. That was the date of Novatian's clash with Cornelius the bishop of Rome which resulted in a schism over the Christians who had lapsed during the Decian persecution.

61. Orchard, *Concise History of Foreign Baptists*, 54.

62. McGoldrick, *Baptist Successionism*, 19.

63. *Tennessee Baptist* (Nashville), 7 December 1848 (emphasis in original).

64. Carroll, *Trail of Blood*, chart. Note: there are several different spellings for Paterenes.

65. *Tennessee Baptist* (Nashville), 7 December 1848 (emphasis in original).

salvation outside of their church.⁶⁶ The Cathari met the Landmarkers' test for being separate from the established Roman church, being persecuted for their faith, and believing that they were the one embodiment of the true church. This was enough for them to be true Baptists and part of the unbroken succession of Baptist (true) churches.

Carroll attributes to the Donatists the honor of preserving true Baptist doctrine in the fifth through the ninth centuries.⁶⁷ Graves says of the Donatists that they "were good Ana-Baptists who seceded from the old church of Africa on account of *corrupt practices*. They denied the *validity of baptism* as administered by *the church of Rome*, which was by *immersion*, and *rebaptized* all who left that church to unite with them."⁶⁸ The distinguishing marks of Donatist theology for the Landmarkers would have been their repudiation of the link between church and state that Constantine had begun to establish. Their core tenet declared that clergy who had lapsed during the persecution were unworthy priests and more importantly all their actions, especially the administration of the sacraments and the ordination of other priests, were improper.⁶⁹ They were the "High Churchmen of the fifth century" and insisted on pure church-membership and rejected unworthy ministers. One of their most prominent characteristics was the "baptizing anew those that had already been baptized, whether in infancy or not, by those whom they regarded as unworthy."⁷⁰ This alone would have endeared them to the Landmark Baptists.

Carroll in his chart considers the Paulicians a key link in the succession of Baptist churches. They are the group that fills in all the blanks for five centuries when another group cannot be found to fill the void. The doctrines of the Paulicians included an ecclesiology that considered their church as the only true church and regarded the Roman, Greek, and Armenian churches "as absolutely evil and Satanic, and on every occasion to be denounced in the bitterest way."⁷¹ They said that those who perverted Christ's ordinance (by baptizing infants) are "utterly evil and full of the deceit of demons."⁷² What we see in this group are people who claimed to be the orthodox defenders and preservers of the Christian faith, the only true church, and one bitterly

66. Ibid., 475.
67. Carroll, *Trail of Blood*, chart.
68. *Tennessee Baptist* (Nashville), 7 December 1848 (emphasis in original). It is probable that Graves meant sprinkling here, but the quote is as it appeared in the original.
69. Wright, "Donatists in North Africa," 202–3.
70. Newman, *Manual of Church History*, 208–10.
71. Ibid., 382.
72. Ibid.

opposed to the established churches that had apostatized. They denied the validity of baptism performed by the Roman and Orthodox churches and refused to recognize their clergy. In addition, they held that the Lord's Supper could only be properly observed within the Paulician churches. If all that sounds quite similar to the Landmark position it is little wonder that the Landmarkers have no problem accepting the Paulicians in the line of succession of "true churches" and in fact use them, as does Carroll, as one of the anchors of Baptist orthodoxy. When you add the fact that they suffered great persecution at the hands of the established church you have the perfect historical definition of the true church according to the Landmarkers.

The things that endeared the Arnoldists to the Landmarkers were their opposition to the Roman Catholic Church, their rejection of ministers who were not orthodox according to their standards, and a rejection of infant baptism.[73] The idea advanced by some that the Arnoldists practiced believer's baptism would, of course, further validate their status as the true church among the Landmarkers. Arnold met the final test of the Landmarkers dying a martyr of the "true church" at the hands of the established Roman Catholic Church. "After his corpse had been reduced to ashes in the fire, it was scattered on the Tiber."[74]

Carroll says that the Henricians carried on the true church in the thirteenth century. Henry of Lausanne for whom this movement is named had been a Benedictine monk and the primary information about him and the Henricians came from the "registers of the bishops of LeMans, the works of St. Bernard of Clairvaux, and a letter from a monk named William."[75] Cathcart's *Baptist Encyclopædia* says that Henry "was a Bible Christian is absolutely certain and that his followers rejected infant baptism is the testimony of St. Bernard and of all other writers who have taken notice of the Henricians."[76]

Carroll gives the Albigenses the title of upholders of true Baptist doctrine in the fourteenth century. The Albigenses have a special place in the hearts of the Landmark proponents of Baptist church successionism. This is due, no doubt, in large part from the profuse praise heaped upon them by Orchard. He called them, along with the Cathari, the two witnesses of Revelation 11:3–4.[77] The Albigenses were essentially Cathars that flourished in southern France, beginning in the region of Albi. The Albigenses met the essential test of the Landmarkers, i.e., being opposed to the Roman church,

---

73. Peters, *Heresy and Authority*, 179.
74. Ibid., 180.
75. Ibid., 50.
76. Cathcart, *Baptist Encyclopedia*, s.v. "Henricians."
77. Orchard, *Concise History of Foreign Baptists*, 161.

suffering intense persecution for their beliefs, and considering themselves as the only true church. They are accorded a special place in the history of the "true church" as set down by the Landmark historians. As Carroll affirms in his chart these names, e.g., Albigenses, are just nicknames for Baptists. Cathcart says that "throughout the nine hundred years of their heroic suffering and astonishing successes, they have always shown supreme regard for the Word of God."[78]

Carroll's chart shows the Waldenses as the guardians of true Baptist doctrine from the fourteenth to the eighteenth centuries. The Waldenses, also known as Waldensians, derived their name from a corruption of the name of their founder Valdès, sometimes called Waldo; they also were called Vaudois, the Poor Lombards, and other corruptions of Valdès. Graves referred to them as the Vaudois and claimed that they numbered "tens of thousands in the neighborhood of the Pyrennes [sic]." He added that they "as Baptists immersed all they received into their churches on a profession of faith, and re-immersed those who joined from other communities."[79] In a very long article, which Graves ran in the *Tennessee Baptist*, entitled "Were the Waldenses Baptists or Pedo-Baptists?" and signed by J. L. W. (probably J. L. Waller, as the article was a reprint from the *Western Baptist Review*, edited by Waller) closes with these words, "It is certain that they were Baptists."[80]

The Landmarkers were always trying to claim that Baptists had no heritage flowing from the Protestant churches and as Graves often cited, the Anabaptists were separate from and even preceded the Reformation. The problem in identifying the beliefs of the Anabaptists arises from the fact that the very term Anabaptist did not encompass a single united religious body with a single confession of faith. Graves approvingly quotes Heinrich Bullinger's summary of the Anabaptists:

> The Ana-baptists think themselves to be the *only true church of Christ*, and acceptable to God; and teach that they who by baptism are received into their churches ought not to have *any communion* with [those called] evangelical *or any other* whatsoever;

---

78. Cathcart, *Baptist Encyclopedia*, 597–98.
79. *Tennessee Baptist* (Nashville), 7 December 1848.
80. *Tennessee Baptist* (Nashville), 9 May 1849. (According to Tull, Graves was probably influenced by Waller's writings in developing his theory of church succession. Waller also put forth views that rejected all churches other than Baptist churches because they had received their baptism from the Roman Catholic Church. See Tull, *High Church Baptists in the South*, 54, 57.)

for that our (reformed) churches are not *true churches*, no more than the churches of the Papists.[81]

Carroll says by the end of the sixteenth century, "The hated Ana-Baptists (called Baptists today), in spite of all prior persecutions, and in spite of the awful fact that fifty million had already died martyr deaths, they still existed in great numbers."[82] Graves calls "the true Anabaptists . . . the only 'salt of the earth,' and the 'light of the world,' during the 1600 years that preceded the Reformation."[83]

The Anabaptists focused on the *ekklesia*. Like Graves, Carroll, and other Landmarkers they rejected the idea of an invisible church. "For the Anabaptists nothing could be farther from the truth [than the idea of an invisible church]. . . . *Theirs was always a visible church*."[84] There is a widespread consensus among scholars that Anabaptism concurred with the Reformers on the major points of doctrine differing only on baptism, the church, or the place of the Christian in society and government. The Landmarkers would protest that the Anabaptists were not part of the Reformation but were and have been in existence through the long ages of the church and are no part of Protestantism. The very differences from the Reformers, viz., rejection of infant baptism, rebaptism of those baptized in infancy, church polity, and the complete separation of church and state would qualify them as the true church and thus Baptist churches in the assessment of the Landmarkers and indeed this is witnessed in Carroll's comments that this is the name by which all true churches were known whatever other name may have attached to them.

These "marks" borne by these various groups qualified them as the true church and thus Baptist churches. This was the basis for the Landmark claims initiated by Graves and popularized by Carroll. For the average Baptist layperson Carroll's work was short enough and dealt with matters of history about which they generally had no knowledge thus producing an authority which verified the Landmark view of history and a view of Southern Baptist exclusivism that most were eager to embrace. There is, however, more to be said about these groups through which the Baptist heritage is traced.

---

81. *Tennessee Baptist* (Nashville), 7 December 1848 (emphasis in original).

82. Carroll, *Trail of Blood*, 35. The number of fifty million is from Ray, *Hand-Book of Baptist History*.

83. Graves, *Trilemma*, 127.

84. Friedmann, *Theology of Anabaptism*, 117 (emphasis in original).

Conclusion

These eleven groups through which the true church was preserved down through the ages, according to Graves, Pendleton, Carroll, and many Southern Baptists, and only these groups they would insist, have held to true Baptist principles, and maintained an unbroken succession of Baptist churches from the first Baptist church in Jerusalem. The question must be asked, however, what it is about these groups that led Orchard, later Graves and Pendleton, and finally Carroll, the systematizer of this belief, to accept and defend these as the true church and the only true church down through the centuries?

First, in the minds of the Landmarkers and indeed in the minds of most Baptists today would be the rejection of infant baptism exhibited by the Arnoldists and the Henricians, as well as the insistence of the Donatists that all who were baptized in infancy be re-baptized. In addition, the baptism of the Cathars could be styled believer's baptism. It could be argued that the Waldenses also rejected infant baptism although as noted above that was not universal among the Waldenses. The Anabaptists held a special place in the Landmark view of Baptist Church succession standing as the banner over all these groups (as Carroll has them in his chart) as the supreme rejecters of infant baptism and the ones who were martyred by the millions, according to their version of history, rather than compromise their views of believer's baptism.

Second, one of the key tenets of the Landmarkers was the view that acts not performed by ministers of a properly organized church (a Baptist church in their view) were invalid even if performed in the proper manner and mode. They would have heartily agreed with the Novatians, the Donatists, and Arnoldists who held the same view, i.e., a rejection of ministers who were unworthy, meaning ministers outside their belief system, and all their acts.

Third, a common thread among these groups was the rejection of the organized church, as expressed by the Montanists, and the belief explicitly claimed by some, such as the Paulicians and the Cathari, that they alone were the only true church. This is pure Landmarkism.

These views would be embraced by the Landmarkers and they would certainly qualify these groups as true churches, meaning Baptist churches in Landmark terminology. However, among these same groups are many such as the Paterins, Paulicians, Albigenses, and Cathars who were consistent dualists. The aberrant Christology of these groups was varied but managed to cover most of the significant historical christological heresies from the docetism of the Paterins and the Cathars, to the adoptionist

Christology of the Paulicians, and the denial of Christ's full humanity and a failure to recognize the eternal and essential deity of Christ by various groups. This combined with the Henricians rejection of original sin and a Pelagian view of salvation, the acceptance of things like infant baptism, baptismal regeneration, a rejection of water baptism in favor of spiritual baptism, and the assertion that John the Baptist was one of the chief demons has to raise questions as to why these groups would ever be considered the succession of the one true church, which in Landmark terminology would mean a Baptist church.

To answer this question, one must remember that the Landmark position was that although certain long periods of apostasy were evident in the history of the church there were certain churches that never apostatized, churches which were always true churches. These true churches withdrew from the apostate church and suffered persecution as a result. This "trail of blood" marked the history of the true churches, i.e., Baptist churches, by whatever name. This position was established before any critical research had been done but was the foundation of the Landmark system. James Tull notes that "however sectarian some Baptists may have been in certain periods of their history, few Baptists before Landmarkism had claimed that there were no churches except Baptist churches."[85] Graves had formulated a position of Baptist church succession but had no historical grounding for his position. Then he discovered Orchard's work and found "historical scholarship" that proved exactly what he needed—highly sectarian groups that embraced at least one of the true marks of the church, as he saw it, and seeing what was needed to establish the truth of Landmark assertions it was possible to turn a blind eye to the doctrinal errors of the groups he unabashedly identified as the "true church."

Albert Henry Newman wrote concerning some of these groups mentioned above: "While we admire the zeal for pure membership, the fidelity to conviction, and the heroic self-denial of the schismatic parties of the early Christian centuries, we cannot fail to see [in the established church] with all its errors and corruptions, more of the Spirit of Christ and a nearer approach to apostolic doctrine and practice than in Montanism, Novatianism, or Donatism."[86] The same may be said of the Paterins, Cathari, Paulicians, Arnoldists, Henricians, Albigenses, Waldenses, and many of the Ana-Baptists who can in no way be identified with the true church or any true Baptist church. It is on this shaky foundation, popularized by Carroll,

---

85. Tull, *High-Church Baptists in the South*, 57.
86. Newman, *History of Anti-Pedobaptism*, 27–28.

that the Landmark doctrine of Baptist church exclusivism from the time of Christ to the present day rests.

4

Controversies Generated by Landmarkers

A Taste for Controversy

IN A LETTER OF March 5, 1859, to his parents, Basil Manly Jr. wrote, "I see Graves comes out again with [the] most flagitious charges against E. P. Walton. If I were Walton, I should sue him for libel, before I was a day older, i.e., provided of course the charges were untrue as I suppose they are. There is no use in trying to keep terms with that man Graves."[1] This sentiment is the legacy of the Landmark movement in its early days.

As noted in earlier chapters, the *Tennessee Baptist* and later the *Baptist* were organs for the propagation of theological views, historical theology, church polity, organizational strategies for conventions and boards, and attacks against all who disagreed. Graves' position was quite simply that contending for the faith is "an *imperative* and *all-important* Christian duty."[2] One of the controversies which will be examined in this chapter erupted between R. B. C. Howell, pastor of the First Baptist Church in Nashville, Tennessee, and J. R. Graves. This running dispute, charges, and trial lasted the better part of three years. The church pressed charges against all the

---

1. Basil Manly Jr. to Basil and Sarah Manly, 5 March 1859. Basil Manly Jr. was a prominent Southern Baptist and son of Basil Manly Sr., who was instrumental in the formation of the Southern Baptist Convention. Manly Jr. joined the faculty of Southern Baptist Theological Seminary in 1859.

2. *Tennessee Baptist* (Nashville), 10 September 1853 (emphasis in original). The *Tennessee Baptist* was said to have the "largest circulation of any Baptist paper in the world" (Cathcart, *Baptist Encyclopedia*, 467). Both Cathcart and Albert Wardin (*Tennessee Baptists*, 163.) give circulation figures for 1860 of 13,000 subscribers. Graves, however, cites a circulation of "almost 15,000" (*Tennessee Baptist*, 7 January 1860).

Landmark members of the church and in Manly's letter of March 5, 1859, he makes mention of the fact. "You see that Dayton and Scovel, and Shankland and the rest have been excluded also. What a howl the Tenn. Bap. will raise about that."[3] Manly was familiar with the tactics of the Landmarkers and knew what to expect. As we will see when we examine that case, he was correct in his assessment.

The history of the Landmark movement has been marked by such "howling" as well as schisms, personal attacks, takeovers, attacks on convention boards, attacks on seminaries, and all that within what they considered to be the true church. Their attacks on Pedobaptists were relentless and they were joined in these attacks by some of the very members of the Southern Baptist Convention who were the target of their most intense campaigns. These overt attacks seemed to die out after the Civil War but as James Tull said, "There is considerable evidence . . . that Landmark ideology prevailed in much of the Convention and, indeed, endures until the present day."[4] John Steely summarized the Landmark movement by saying:

> The story of the Landmark movement in the Southern Baptist Convention may be told in three parts. First, it was a tendency toward high-church exclusiveness, appearing in the Convention under the influence of J. R. Graves. . . . Second, it was a schism in the Baptist fellowship about the close of that century, ostensibly over the methods of missionary work but actually due to a radical disagreement in the field of ecclesiology. Third, it is a flourishing force in the convention in the mid-twentieth century, evidenced in currents of thought, patterns of preaching, and organizational principles.[5]

Controversies are nothing new among Baptists. John Goodwin, the celebrated pastor of a London separatist congregation, in a spate of letter writing, editorializing, and exchange of tracts bitterly condemned the Baptists. (The methods and the attacks call to mind Graves and the Landmarkers.) Goodwin said of the Baptists:

> [They are] heady, rash, fierce, despisers of others, self-conceited, arrogant, quarrelsome, clamorous, captious, vain boasters, unjust defamers of men dissenting in judgment from them. [He attributed these "unchristian qualities" to] the simple conceit

---

3. Basil Manly Jr. to Basil and Sarah Manly, March 5, 1859.
4. Tull, *High-Church Baptists in the South*, 92.
5. Steely, "Landmark Movement," 134.

that you are, by means of your new Baptisme, gotten nearer to God and deeper in his favour than other men.[6]

The Landmark movement, like the Puritans and Separatists in England at the time of the English Revolution, experienced some of its most overt influence in a period of history in the United States that was characterized by intense political as well as religious rivalry. The political conflict during the 1850s intensified until it resulted in Civil War. The slavery question was the driving force behind this conflict and the churches for the most part aligned themselves geographically on the slavery question. The pulpits on both sides thundered with the most condemnatory rhetoric aimed at the other side and this readily found its way into the religious newspapers as has been noted above. All denominations engaged in this debate, a debate often marked by slander, misinformation, and misstatement, in a battle for members, readership, subscriptions, and influence. One observer noted, "Theological champions meet with burnished swords and cut and hew each other to the wondrous gratification of their respective partisans, who gather in hundreds for successive weeks to these scenes of religious combat."[7] Very few had such a taste for these polemics as Graves and few could stand up under his withering and sustained attacks. In the supercharged atmosphere of the times he emerged as the Baptist champion to many. He also won many to the Baptist cause, but he caused as much dissension within the Baptist ranks as he did among their opponents. He spearheaded many controversies, and even after his death, the roots of Landmark controversy remain with the Southern Baptist Convention.

Some of the notable controversies will be briefly examined. Following those will be a survey of Landmark influence and ideology within the Southern Baptist Convention on a variety of issues, which although not rising to the level of the controversies of the mid-nineteenth century are nonetheless notable events in the history of Southern Baptists.

Attacks on Other Denominations

The Landmark position toward other denominations was clearly articulated by J. R. Graves. "No organization on earth [as] unscriptural . . . as every Baptist believes Campbellite and PedoBaptist societies to be . . . should be

---

6. Ballamie, *Leper Cleansed* (1657), 31; quoted in McGregor and Reay, *Radical Religion*, 42.

7. *Tennessee Baptist* (Nashville), 26 August 1851.

regarded as a church of Christ."[8] "They are all organizations, set up in opposition to the kingdom of Christ."[9] Landmarkers considered Baptist churches to be the only true churches. This high-church mentality as James Tull called it was reflective of other traditions. The Roman Catholic Church claimed to be the only true church and held there was no salvation outside that church. Other denominations claimed they were the true church because of apostolic origins, apostolic order, or more closely following the New Testament pattern. Landmarkism sought to destroy the claims of the other denominations. The Landmarkers insisted that a chain of Baptist churches in unbroken succession could be traced back to apostolic times, indeed to the first church in Jerusalem which they said was a Baptist church. Also, by asserting that all the various groups in the chain of succession held all the fundamental doctrines and practices of the first church in Jerusalem, they sought to establish a high church that was unchallengeable and unassailable by the claims of other denominations.

The appeal of the Landmark system was its embrace and defense of traditional Baptist principles. Landmarkism arose in the mid-nineteenth century, a time that was marked by several high-church movements. From the Campbellites to the Mormons almost every denomination made some claim to be the true church because of apostolic origins, restoration of the true gospel, or restoration of the true pattern of New Testament church polity and practice. Graves thrived on conflict and his attacks on other denominations and their claims endeared him to many Baptists. His attitude toward other Protestant churches was summed up in his famous debate with Jacob Ditzler: "No Protestant body claims an existence prior to the year 1500, except as they existed in the fruitful womb of the mother of Harlots [the Roman Catholic Church]."[10] "If Christ has had witnessing Churches during all these ages, as he declared he would have, then Baptist Churches are those bodies."[11] Graves saw himself as the defender of the true faith, the lone Elijah on Mt. Carmel against all the false prophets. He wrote, "The valley of the Mississippi is destined to be the great battle ground ... that a general conflict is to take place here, we have for the past five years predicted. In the Valley of the Mississippi, the lines are *now drawing* for a deadly conflict between true Christianity, and antichristian Popery."[12] What he meant by Popery is clear. In the same article he states, "The principles of

8. Graves, *Old Landmarkism*, 151.
9. *Tennessee Baptist* (Nashville), 16 November 1848.
10. Graves, *Graves-Ditzler*, 1051.
11. Ibid., 1055.
12. *Tennessee Baptist* (Nashville), 25 February 1854 (emphasis in original).

Romanism are incorporated into the creeds of the different sects, which are only extrescences [sic] (extensions) of the Roman apostacy [sic], and that to be consistent, these sects must of necessity go back to the bosom of their mother."[13] For Graves, his task was clear and he rallied a great number of Southern Baptists and enlisted them in this great struggle.

Attacks on the Campbellites (Disciples of Christ)

Graves first achieved fame as a formidable debater and defender of Baptist doctrine in a written debate carried on with Alexander Campbell. Campbell was the publisher of the *Millennial Harbinger*, a competitor of the *Tennessee Baptist*.

"In 1816 Campbell preached his famous 'Sermon on the Law' before the Redstone Baptist Association. In this message he exalted the authority of the New Testament over that of the Old."[14] Campbell held that essential Christianity was belief in one fact, viz., that Jesus is the Christ and submission to one institution, immersion.[15] It is also worth noting that Campbell articulated an opposition to missionary societies (a later controversy which involved the Landmarkers). He wrote, "Our objections to the missionary plan originated from the conviction that it is unauthorised [sic] in the New Testament, and that in many instances, it is a system of iniquitous peculation and speculation."[16] In words, which would sound familiar in later arguments, he wrote of the church:

> The societies, called churches, constituted and set in order by those Ministers of the New Testament, were of such as received and acknowledged Jesus, as Lord Messiah, the Savior of the world; and had put themselves under his guidance. The *only* Bond of Union among them, was faith in him, and submission to his will. No subscription to abstract propositions framed by Synods no decrees of Councils sanctioned by Kings; no rules of practice commanded by ecclesiastical courts were imposed on them as terms of admission into, or of continuance in this *holy brotherhood*.[17]

---

13. Ibid.
14. Tull, *Shapers of Baptist Thought*, 104.
15. Ibid., 110.
16. *Christian Baptist* (Buffalo Creek, VA), 4 July 1823.
17. Ibid. (emphasis in original).

As James Tull explained, the Campbellite controversy brought a new and intense scrutiny on the whole issue of baptism. The validity of Campbellite and Pedobaptist immersions was the issue. The older view held that Campbellite baptisms were valid because they were performed by immersion. The newer view held that not only the person being baptized, but also the administrator, must have been immersed for the baptism to be valid. The debate centered on whether it was essential for the administrator to have been immersed. But even if it was deemed essential for the administrator to have been immersed it was still possible for a Pedobaptist minister to have been immersed upon conversion and thus immersions performed by him would be valid baptisms. To address this eventuality the theory of baptismal succession was introduced. This only left one problem—Campbellite ministers who were in a line of baptismal succession. To solve this problem the theory was put forth that baptism could only be performed by a Baptist minister in good standing within the denomination.[18] Graves and the Landmarkers did not invent this view but he was quick to seize upon it and combine this with his view of church succession to deny the validity of any baptism, even by immersion, if it was not administered in a Baptist church.

Graves threw down the gauntlet to the Campbellites in the pages of the *Tennessee Baptist* on May 15, 1852. (He issued similar challenges to the Roman Catholics, Presbyterians, Jews, Methodists, and Episcopalians.) He offered a one hundred–dollar "premium" for anyone who could meet his challenge. His challenge: "To Campbellites. $100 for reason or revelation, to prove that no person can be pardoned, regenerated, justified or saved in heaven, unless immersed in water . . . as taught by Mr. Campbell."[19]

In reply to Graves, Alexander Campbell sent a rather long letter to the *Tennessee Baptist* which was published on May 6, 1854. The letter itself is undated so it is unknown exactly when Campbell replied, although he said he had no personal acquaintance with Graves or where he lived. He opened his letter with that explanation and added, "I have heard of him as a stout 'accuser of the brethren' and as a distinguished braggart."[20] Campbell delineates his doctrine with what he believes to be scriptural proof, as Graves' challenge requested. He summarizes: "The original cause is *grace*. The meritorious cause is *blood*. The instrumental causes are *faith, repentance, baptism*, all expressed and perfected in the last act."[21] The remainder of the letter was highly critical of Graves, e.g., "I have not time or inclination

18. For a full discussion of this, see Tull, *High-Church Baptists in the South*, 71–73.
19. *Tennessee Baptist* (Nashville), 15 May 1852.
20. *Tennessee Baptist* (Nashville), 6 May 1854.
21. Ibid. (emphasis in original).

to expose the flimsy sophistry in which he veils himself. I will not say thy money go to heaven with thee, neighbor Graves, for I perceive you have passed the Rubicon. I sympathize with the young man.... I can candidly say that I am sorry to see him playing such pranks as might make angels weep, and in which gentlemen, scholars, and Christians can see much to regret and nothing to admire."[22]

After such words the battle was joined and Graves never tired of reminding the Campbellites that they were no church of Christ. The exchange between Graves and Campbell was carried in the pages of the *Tennessee Baptist* throughout 1854. Graves collected these exchanges in book form (as he did many of his newspaper series, letters, and debates) publishing in that same year, *Campbell and Campbellism Exposed: A Series of Replies to A. Campbell's Articles in the Millennial Harbinger*. Later Graves said of Campbellism, "[It is] the most pernicious and deadly heresy ever propagated under the name of Christianity."[23] Alexander Campbell died in 1866 without the debate reaching any final resolution. However, typical of Graves' attitude toward the Campbellites, and indicative of the long-standing animosity between the parties, was his response to a letter protesting his characterizations of the Disciples of Christ posted in the *Baptist* in 1868. The letter objected to being called Campbellites instead of Christians, the Christian Church, or Disciples of Christ. To this Graves responded, "The Christian Church is a religious society, scripturally organized, holding the doctrines and administering the ordinances as Christ delivered them to his apostles. I cannot by pen or lip declare to the world that your Society in this city is such." He adds, "If yours is the Christian Church, then the Baptist Church, nor any other religious society in this city, or in this world, is a Christian Church. What I have urged against the appellative of Christian Church, weighs as conclusively against that of 'The Disciples of Christ.' If your religious brethren are truly *the* Disciples of Christ, all other professed Christians holding different doctrines are the disciples of men."[24]

Graves was reacting to what he saw as a sacramental interpretation of baptism and the problem the earlier hard-line Baptists had with the Campbellites. They met the loose definition of baptismal succession and that could not stand among the highly exclusive, sectarian elements within the Baptist denomination. This reaction and ongoing attack against the Campbellites encouraged many Baptists to regard baptism increasingly as a mere symbol,

---

22. Ibid.

23. *Tennessee Baptist* (Nashville), 17 March 1855.

24. *Baptist* (Memphis), 19 December 1868 (emphasis in original). Although Graves offered a list of excuses, his answer to the letter in question came five months later.

an adverse consequence of the attacks to preserve the integrity of baptism and the church as viewed by the Landmarkers.

Attacks on the Methodists

The Methodist Episcopal Church, South, grew from 460,000 members in 1844 to 757,205 by 1860. Much of that growth took place in Kentucky and Tennessee.[25] In the same period the Southern Baptist Churches grew in membership from 365,436 to 650,000.[26] These two denominations dominated the growth and spread of churches on the frontier and consequently were often at odds as they competed for members, with each asserting that their own doctrine was true biblical doctrine. These debates were carried on in the various denominational weekly newspapers, in person, and sometimes in absentia. Orren L. Hailey, Graves' son-in-law, and biographer, even attributes to the Methodists the "circumstances which led to what is known as his landmark view."[27] In a defense of Graves and by way of explanation of how he came to his Landmark views Hailey wrote:

> It should be remembered that as editor of *The Tennessee Baptist*, he was surrounded by the central power of Southern Methodism. Bishop Soule had his headquarters in Nashville. The great Book Concern with its book editor, Dr. Summers, its secretaries and agents, was located there. The only Methodist paper in the South, at that time, with the talented and virulent editor, Dr. McFerrin, was a power whose chief aim seemed to be to break down the Baptist paper, and damage or exterminate that people throughout the South.[28]

This view of Graves presents him as the beleaguered champion of Baptists who would fight against all odds. Graves and the *Tennessee Baptist* were sued on one occasion by a Methodist minister for libel and lost a judgment of seven thousand five hundred dollars, a judgment that was subsequently upheld by the Tennessee Supreme Court.[29] Rather than deterring him such events only served to solidify the view which Graves had of himself as the

---

25. Gross, *History of the Methodist Episcopal Church, South*, and Summers, *Confederate States Almanac*, 16.
26. Baptist History and Heritage Society.
27. Hailey, *J. R. Graves*, 53.
28. Ibid.
29. Ibid., 1–2.

lone warrior for the Baptist cause and it certainly influenced the way in which he fiercely waded into the conflict.

It must be said that the conflicts with the Methodists preceded Graves and the Landmarkers. R. B. C. Howell, pastor of First Baptist Church in Nashville, Tennessee, and editor of the *Baptist* was engaged in a debate with the *South Western Christian Advocate* in the pages of the *Baptist* before Graves arrived.[30] Howell wrote, "We regret to see the *South Western Christian Advocate* returning to its old spirit of hostility against Baptists."[31] The editorial in the *Advocate* asked, "If there be a true church of Christ . . . and it is found in connection with the Baptist Church . . . which one of the so called Baptist Churches is the true one. Is it [the] . . . Particular . . . Calvinistical [*sic*] . . . Predestinarian . . . Freewills . . . Regular . . . Separate . . . Missionary . . . Anti-Missionary . . . Reformed . . . Seventh Day . . . or the Christian Baptists?"[32] To this Howell responded by asking which of the sects of the Methodist Church were to be regarded as the true church, the Wesleyans, Whitfield Methodists, Episcopals, Protestant, Radical, Abolition, Pew, Anti-Pew Methodists, or the Methodist Church North or the Methodist Church South.[33] Thus the argument was joined early and the ground was set for the Landmarkers to carry out their attacks.

The attacks of Graves upon all "Pedobaptist societies" regularly filled the pages of the *Tennessee Baptist*. This did not go unchallenged by the *Nashville Christian Advocate* the chief organ of the Methodist Episcopal Church, South, at the time. In the issue of October 18, 1850, they printed the following:

> There are in this city [Nashville] five Methodist pastors, two Presbyterians, one "Christian Baptist," one Episcoplaian [*sic*], and one "Old Side Baptist." Now, if the editor of the Baptist [Graves] can procure a certificate from any two of the above—named pastors, that he is of sufficient importance, and his standing and course as a gentleman, a minister of the gospel, and as an editor entitle him to respectful notice in the columns of a Christian

---

30. Circulation figures for the two papers are somewhat revealing. In 1845 the *South Western Christian Advocate* had a circulation of 7,000 subscribers. The *Baptist* in 1846 had only 1,000 subscribers. Although by 1851 under Graves' leadership the *Baptist* had increased its subscriptions to 5,000, the *South Western Christian Advocate* by 1851 had increased to over 14,000 subscribers. The question must be asked if Graves' animosity toward the Methodists was purely doctrinal or was it influenced by a professional jealousy as a newspaper editor (see Wardin, *Tennessee Baptists*).

31. *Baptist* (Nashville), 25 July 1846.

32. Ibid.

33. Ibid.

paper, and will justify any one who has self-respect to controvert with him, we will promise to notice him occasionally.[34]

Thus began a long series of debates, editorial sniping, books, and tracts designed to discredit the views of the other side. Graves led the way for the Landmarkers essentially taking on all comers from the Methodist camp. Other Landmark Baptists joined in the fray, but Graves was the one who led the charge.

In August 1851, Graves engaged in an eight-day debate with Mr. Fly of the Methodist Church. This debate in Quincy, Tennessee, drew a crowd of two thousand five hundred spectators on the fifth day of the debate.[35] The full proceedings of the debate were carried in the pages of the *Tennessee Baptist*. Graves' central tenet upon which he hammered mercilessly was that "Christ had given us a pattern for the formation of churches, in the Testament."[36] He highlighted that this pattern specified the government, officers, membership, ordinances, and doctrines. His conclusion in the debate was: "If, therefore, we find Christian bodies differing, we may know they are not fashioned after this infallible pattern . . . [and] these conflicting branches *were not* the Church of Christ."[37] He lumped into this conflicting mass of churches Methodists, Presbyterians, Episcopalians, Catholics, and Mormons. In one of his final arguments Graves brings to the fore an argument he would constantly set forth and which he later included in the title of one of his books against Methodism—"republicanism" (*The Great Iron Wheel, or, Republicanism Backwards and Christianity Reversed*). He simply concludes that it can be shown that Christ gave the government of his church into the hands of the people and a government in which the people rule is "republican." This doctrine was one of "Six Fundamental Doctrines of Baptist Churches" which were a regular feature in both the *Tennessee Baptist* and the *Baptist* when Graves was editor. Doctrine number six stated:

> All religious societies having *legislative powers* and *clerical* or *aristocratical* governments (i.e., in the hands of the clergy, or a few, as a session) are anti-scriptural and anti-republican tyrannies which no christian [sic] can lawfully countenance, or *republican freemen* ought to support: consequently all the acts and ordinances of such irregular bodies are *illegal*, and ought not to be received by us; nor should such societies be, in any way,

---

34. Quoted in the *Tennessee Baptist* (Nashville), 16 November 1850.
35. *Tennessee Baptist* (Nashville), 8 August 1851.
36. *Tennessee Baptist* (Nashville), 30 August 1851.
37. Ibid. (emphasis in original).

recognized as scriptural churches or their preachers as official ministers of the gospel.[38]

This being the case he concludes that "the Methodist Church is unscriptural."[39] The coverage in the *Tennessee Baptist* concluded the report of the debate with the self-serving assessment: "Never before did Baptist principles triumph more gloriously. It truly has been a one-sided business."[40]

On March 20, 1852, the *Tennessee Baptist* began carrying a series of thirteen letters addressed to Bishop Joshua Soule, bishop of the Methodist Episcopal Church, South, under the heading "The Great Iron Wheel."[41] These letters and exchanges ran through August 1853. A rather long excerpt from this first letter (a letter only by Graves' definition, as this was published and distributed across the South) sets forth the tone of the whole affair instigated by Graves.

> But alas sir, how soul crushing would be the thought that you have exhausted the whole of life, and hazarded all those dangers and underwent all those toils to advance the interests of an organization, not instituted by Jesus Christ, or authorized by his word—but a mere human, man devised system—a rival fold, whose very being and advancement is hostile to, and subversive of the Church and Kingdom Christ set up and designed to fill the world! What an awful thought for an aged minister about to die, that he has spent his long life and exhausted all his mighty powers of mind and body in opposing the Kingdom of Christ, and directing those seeking to enter it, into a rival organization, which becoming universal, would blot out the doctrines, constitution and very being of Christ's church from the world![42]

Graves' initial attacks in the spring of 1852 also drew responses from other Methodists. A letter in the *Nashville Christian Advocate* on April 22, 1852, written by J. S. Scobee, a Methodist minister, attacked Graves. He accused Graves of "egotistical bigotry, reckless and untruthful assertions, and sectarian fanaticism."[43]

---

38. For one of the many examples, see the *Tennessee Baptist* (Nashville), 10 December 1859 (emphasis in original).

39. *Tennessee Baptist* (Nashville), 30 August 1851.

40. Ibid.

41. A number of Graves' books were first serialized in the pages of the *Tennessee Baptist* before they were collected, edited, and published. Other examples include *Graves-Ditzler*, *Work of Christ*, and *Trilemma*.

42. *Tennessee Baptist* (Nashville), 20 March 1852.

43. Quoted in the *Tennessee Baptist* (Nashville), 15 May 1852.

Scobee's letter was answered by a fourteen-member committee from J. M. Pendleton's church. It is interesting, in view of Graves' style in the instigation of this controversy, that the committee asserted, "If the statements in the letter before us were true, we do not see how a christian [sic] spirit could have prompted their publication. What good would, in that event, have resulted from the publication?"[44] The irony of that statement in view of Graves' comments is quite palpable.

Scobee claimed in the letter that the Baptists led by Graves put forth a proposition to the church that they "should pray for the death of those who were opposed to their meeting, and as brother Randolph [another Methodist minister] was the leading man . . . of course their prayers were especially directed for his departure."[45] The fourteen signatories of the letter explicitly denied that the church resolved to pray for the death of Mr. Randolph.

Even though the letter explicitly defended Graves, it also quoted Pendleton as saying, "The Methodist church government was the most tyrannical in the religious world, so far as he knew, except the Roman Catholic."[46] However, it is to be noted that confronted with the question of whether or not he would defend everything that Graves said about other denominations Pendleton responded, "That is a very singular question." This was followed by an assertion that to endorse "every sentence and phrase that another uses in four weeks [of] ardent extemporaneous preaching, is intensely nonsensical."[47] Even at this date there is some reluctance on the part of Pendleton to join Graves in every facet of his virulent attacks on other denominations.

Graves continued his attacks upon the Methodist Church. In October 1852 a three-column letter contained the following: "Let it be distinctly noticed that it was not necessary for one to be a *christian* [sic] to be a Methodist."[48] However, it was never Graves' position that members of these "societies" were all unchristian. He maintained that there were in fact Christians in these societies that claimed to be churches. Pendleton joined in that assessment. He wrote, "Baptists very cheerfully consent to the doctrine that there are Christians outside of Baptist churches; but they are outside of New Testament churches whenever that is the case. It is their duty to come into New Testament churches and not the duty of New Testament churches [i.e., Baptist churches] to go out to them."[49] This kind of criticism centered upon

44. *Tennessee Baptist* (Nashville), 15 May 1852.
45. Ibid.
46. Ibid.
47. Ibid.
48. *Tennessee Baptist* (Nashville), 30 October 1852 (emphasis in original).
49. J. M. Pendleton, *Landmarkism, Liberalism, and the Invisible Church*, 73.

the fact that these so-called churches admitted unregenerate people into their membership (e.g., infants) and the regenerate who happened to be members of these societies were unbaptized, having been baptized improperly or by an unbaptized administrator. In the same letter by Graves, noted above, he had advice for these Christians who were outside the true church. "Let Christian Methodists consider well the fact, they are supporting with all their talents and influence a system which they have been taught to look upon as a veritable *Church* of Christ, but which in fact is a *human system*, devised, and set on foot, and directed, by *unconverted* or *unregenerate* men!"[50] He adds, "They are not following Christ while they enter the folds and follow the teachings of John Wesley."[51] Later in the great Graves-Ditzler debate Graves issues a similar remonstrance to the Christian Methodists. "I have now discharged my duty to the thousands of deceived Christians in Methodist Societies. . . . The societies of which they are members are not churches, and they are, therefore, unbaptized!"[52]

J. M. Pendleton regarded Graves' critique of Methodism as highly effective. When a letter to the editor was published in the *Tennessee Baptist* lamenting the appointment of messengers in the Oregon association to sister churches such as the Methodists, Pendleton responded that they need a few "copies of the Tennessee Baptist."[53] As the tensions in the country escalated leading up to the Civil War, Pendleton noted in the *Tennessee Baptist* that a copy of *The Great Iron Wheel* was burned in Montgomery, Alabama, presumably because some construed parts of it to be offensive to slaveholders. Pendleton asked in his editorial, "Why was this? Is there anything in the Iron Wheel offensive to slaveholders? Why were not the former anti-slavery editions of the Methodist Discipline burned?"[54] It is true that Pendleton did not fancy book burning, for as he said, "[they] might be induced in certain circumstances to burn authors as well as their books."[55] His assessment was to the effect that the one who furnished *The Iron Wheel* for the flames was "anti-Landmark" and "a compromising Baptist."[56]

After the Civil War, Graves continued to set forth, in the pages of the *Baptist*, his opposition to the Methodist Church. In 1876 he published *The*

---

50. Ibid. (emphasis in original).

51. Ibid.

52. Graves, *Graves-Ditzler*, 1005. This debate was between Graves and Jacob Ditzler, a Methodist and a professional debater, in Carrollton, Missouri, in 1875.

53. *Tennessee Baptist* (Nashville), 11 July 1857.

54. *Tennessee Baptist* (Nashville), 17 March 1860.

55. Ibid.

56. Ibid.

Graves-Ditzler Debate which recapitulated the full details of what Baptists took to be a stunning victory for the Baptist cause. The critiques of Methodism in the later years of his publishing and editorializing remained unchanged from the representative samples examined here.

Attacks on the Presbyterians

The Landmark attack upon the Presbyterians centered primarily on the issue of church polity and baptism. Graves included the Presbyterians in his offers of one hundred dollars for anyone who could provide scriptural proof for what he listed as Presbyterian doctrines.[57] However, his most effective critique of Presbyterianism and, if not, all Protestantism was presented in *The Trilemma, or, Death by Three Horns*.[58] Seizing on an issue, which had come before the General Assembly[59] regarding the validity of Roman Catholic baptisms, Graves was able to draw a net around Presbyterians and indeed all Protestants from which he saw no way of escape.

Graves bases his case on a couple of assumptions. No organization except a true Church of Christ (visible) can administer scriptural baptism. Conversely, if the baptism is considered to be scriptural and valid the organization administering it must be a true Church of Christ. With these baseline assumptions one must conclude that a pronouncement that the baptisms of the Roman Catholic Church are valid necessarily means the Roman Catholic Church is a true Church of Christ.[60] In Graves' own words and emphasis we see the importance in which he holds this:

---

57. *Tennessee Baptist* (Nashville), 15 May 1852.

58. Graves, *Trilemma*. Trilemma was a word coined by Graves in 1860 during his debates and editorials against other denominations. In his own words, "Trilemma is not in the dictionary. When one is pinned between two difficulties, we say he is in a di-lemma [*sic*]. When he is pinned between two difficulties and pierced by a third, may we not say he is in a tri-lemma?"

59. Graves said the issue had been before the Presbyterian General Assembly no less than three times in the last few years. Indeed, the issue was an item of discussion at the General Assembly of 1790, 1835, 1845, and 1854 as Graves points out. This question of the validity of certain baptisms was studied as late as 1981 in the Reformed Presbyterian Church Evangelical Synod, 1977 in the Presbyterian Church in America, and 1987 in the Presbyterian Church in America (source: Presbyterian Church in America Historical Center, St. Louis, MO).

60. Graves, *Trilemma*, 12–13. (It should be noted that this is a thorny problem and remains an item of discussion among Presbyteries and the General Assemblies of many Presbyterian denominations. Graves, to his credit, recognized the difficulty presented by this issue.)

That No organization but a True Church of Christ, visible, can administer Scriptural Baptism. Conversely, if the baptism is considered scriptural and valid, the society administering it must be acknowledged and treated as a True Church of Christ, visible. Now all can see if the baptisms of the Church of Rome are pronounced scriptural and valid, then the Church of Rome must be admitted to be a *true church* of Christ, visible.[61]

Based on this trilemma, Graves attacks the baptisms of the Reformers, Calvin, Luther, Zwingli, and Knox. He reasons that they were never baptized if the Roman Church was unscriptural or they were excommunicated by a true church. In either case, their ministries were invalid and thus the churches they formed were also invalid and not true churches. In the *Trilemma* Graves reports the conclusions of the Presbyterian Church of America General Assemblies of 1790, 1829, 1835, and the New School Presbyterian General Assembly of 1854.[62] He gives details of the proceedings gathered from the reports carried in the various religious papers of the day. (He cites the *Western Baptist Review*, the *New York Observer*, and the *New York Daily Times*.) All the various assemblies were unanimous in their assertion that the Roman Catholic Church was no true church and that her doctrines were hopelessly corrupt. This, in Graves' mind, entangled Presbyterians in an irresolvable dilemma or in his words a trilemma.

If the General Assembly decided that the baptisms of the Church of Rome were valid they thereby asserted that it was a true church and they would be guilty of schism, excommunicated, and all their ministers unordained. If on the other hand the General Assembly decided that the baptisms of the Roman Church were invalid, all the ministers of the Presbyterian Church are unbaptized and thus all the baptisms they have administered through the years are invalid and they are thus no true church of Christ. The trilemma, Graves said, was the "inability to decide whether its own ministers are baptized, or have authority to baptize, and, consequently, whether their societies are visible Churches of Christ!"[63]

The inevitable conclusion of this for Graves was clear: "*No Presbyterian or Pedobaptist can have a reasonable assurance that he has been truly baptized.*"[64] He set forth a number of challenges to the Presbyterians:

---

61. Ibid. (emphasis in original).

62. A schism took place within the Presbyterian Church in 1837 and the Old School Presbyterians and New School Presbyterians were the result. See Smith, *Studies in Southern Presbyterian Theology*.

63. Graves, *Trilemma*, 72.

64. Ibid., 26 (emphasis in original).

CONTROVERSIES GENERATED BY LANDMARKERS 105

> Can not Presbyterian ministers, with all their boasted learning, decide among themselves whether they have received Christian baptism? Can they not tell the world, when convened in their great Assembly, whether they be duly ordained and baptized ministers of Christ or not? Can they tell the world whether their societies are visible Churches of Christ?[65]

Graves continued to press his attack on the question with which the Presbyterians struggled.

> The Old School General Assembly of the Presbyterian Church in the United States . . . decided that no baptism was valid except administered by a regular ordained minister in the true Church of God, visible; that the Romish Church was not the Church of God at all, and that, therefore, baptism administered within its pales and by its priesthood was no baptism! Then, according to Presbyterian principles, John Calvin, Theodore Beza, John Knox, and their contemporary Reformers, all of whom were baptized by Papists, had no Christian baptism.[66]

For Graves, this broke the chain of baptismal succession and produced unbaptized, unordained ministers who were in fact no gospel ministers at all. He is very clear about the duty required of all true Baptists.

> Baptists need not be reminded of their duty in this case. Shall we be so kind as to step in and decide this matter for Presbyterians and Pedobaptists? Shall we, by our *acts*, say to them, and to the world that is watching us, we regard those men baptized and duly-ordained ministers in true Churches of Christ? Do we believe they have received valid baptism? Do we believe that their societies, originated and set up, not by the God of heaven, built, not by Christ, but by Luther, and Calvin, and Wesley, are Scriptural Churches, or Christian Churches in any sense? Baptists do not. No intelligent and true Baptist can.[67]

Graves' argument regarding the validity of the regeneration and baptism of men such as Wesley, Luther, Calvin, and Knox may have met with approval from many Southern Baptists who saw themselves engaged with a struggle against these other denominations, but his argument rested on a weak and tenuous footing. As was shown in chapter 3 the Landmark claim that their own baptisms rested on an unbroken succession of churches

---

65. Ibid., 72.
66. Ibid., 51.
67. Ibid., 77 (emphasis in original).

which stretched back to Christ was nothing other than a revisionist if not a fanciful interpretation of history.

In addition to a prejudiced view of history revised to draw a foregone conclusion, Graves makes the mistake of assuming that organizational succession necessarily results in doctrinal succession. This stands out clearly in the discussion of Graves' own theology (chapter 2). The high-church view set forth by the Landmarkers and the attacks on other denominations clearly shown in the examples above epitomize the Landmark position that there is only one true church and that is the Baptist church. This type of sectarian exclusivity is precisely that which Paul condemns in 1 Corinthians 3. "When one says, 'I follow Paul,' and another, 'I follow Apollos,' are you not mere men? What, after all, is Apollos? And what is Paul?" (1 Cor 3:4–5a) The kind of extreme, sectarian, exclusivity advocated by Graves obscures the unity of the church and given its own full rein would destroy the church but the glorious Head of the church has promised that nothing would destroy his church, even those like the Landmarkers who would seek to appropriate that promise to justify their own exclusive rejection of others whether they be of Paul, Apollos, Wesley, Calvin, et al.

Jonathan Edwards wrote that unity is regarded by the Scriptures as "the peculiar beauty of the church of Christ."[68] These attacks by the Landmarkers, spearheaded by Graves, cannot be seen as anything but destructive to the unity and thus the beauty of Christ's church. This sectarian exclusiveness is born when one teaching of Scripture is stressed out of all proportion to the other teachings of Scripture. In the case of Landmarkism their stress on ecclesiology gave rise to the sectarianism which created division and strife within the body of Christ. Criticism of other churches is in order when clear doctrinal principles are being compromised but the highly sectarian views set forth by the Landmarkers could be nothing but destructive. It should be added that sectarianism in any form is destructive and a great evil for it disrupts the unity and catholicity of the Church. It must be said that the Landmarkers' attacks were not confined to other denominations. Other Baptists were not immune. A denomination constantly at war with itself cannot survive and, indeed, the attacks of the Landmarkers threatened their own Baptist Zion.

Attacks on Other Baptists

The attacks of the Landmarkers were not limited to other denominations. Other groups of Baptist and individual Baptists were not immune from the

68. Edwards, "Humble Attempt," 364–65.

same harsh judgment accorded the Presbyterians, Methodists, and others. Graves disputed the contention of many historians that Roger Williams founded the first Baptist church in America.[69] According to Graves, Roger Williams was never a Baptist or a member of a Baptist church much less a Baptist minister. Roger Williams baptized Ezekiel Holliman who then baptized Williams. Graves found this very irregular since it obviously lacked any succession of church or proper administrator. This coupled with the fact that Williams "repudiated what he had done" four months later led Graves to the conclusion: "It can not be shown that any Baptist Church sprang from the Williams' affair."[70] For Graves,

> The oldest Baptist Church in America is the one now existing, with her original articles of faith, in Newport, R. I., and she was planted by Dr. John Clark before Williams was baptized. He received his baptism in Elder Stillwell's Church in London, and that Church received hers from the Dutch Baptists of Holland, sending over a minister to be baptized by them. These Baptists descended from the Waldenses, whose historical line reaches far back and connects with the Donatists, and theirs to the Apostolical Churches.[71]

N. M. Skipworth flatly rejected Graves' version of history. In the *New Orleans Christian Advocate*, after Graves set forth his version of Baptist history in a speech at the Louisiana Baptist State Convention in 1870, Skipworth wrote that Graves' view of history had misled many who were there in his "attempt to establish, through the Clark line, the dogma of apostolic succession." At the end of his letter Skipworth concludes, "I do affirm and am prepared to prove from authentic documentary testimony now in my possession, that Mr. Graves' assertion is false."[72] Graves' answer to Skipworth's letter ran to three

---

69. Roger Williams (1603-1683) is considered by many to be the founder of the first Baptist church in America. Williams was born in London and raised in the Episcopal Church. Later he became a Puritan and came to America and preached in Massachusetts. He was regarded as a zealot for the separation of church and state and complete religious freedom. He created quite a stir, and Cotton Mather wrote of him, "There was a whole country in America like to be set on fire by the rapid motion of a windmill in the head of one particular man." Williams was banished from Massachusetts and founded a settlement on Narragansett Bay which he called Providence. It was at that time that he became a Baptist and was immersed. He later returned to England and received from the Long Parliament recognition of the colony of Rhode Island. The church he established there is said to be the first Baptist church in America. He served as governor of Rhode Island from 1654-1657. See Gaustad, *Liberty of Conscience*.

70. Graves, *Trials and Sufferings*, 121.

71. Ibid., 121-22.

72. Quoted in the *Baptist* (Memphis), 12 November 1870. Skipworth either did not

columns in the paper and in his answer he notes, in response to Skipworth's critique of his historical research methodology, "There is no higher historic authority concerning the important dates and acts of a man's life than the epitaph upon his tomb."[73] (Graves in his presentation stated he made a trip to Newport, Rhode Island, and found on a tombstone an inscription declaring Clark was the founder of the first Baptist Church in America. He should also know full well that epitaphs are most unreliable—witness the praises heaped upon despots and tyrants on their tombstones.) The conclusion of Graves' answer is quite to the point: "No man can prove that the baptism of any person in the world has come by succession from Roger Williams."[74]

About the Freewill Baptists, Graves wrote that they were Baptists in name only because they practiced baptism by immersion. However, they are Arminian in their doctrine, perfectionists, and "open" in their communion. This led Graves to say, "In doctrine they are immersed Methodists, and in church government are modified Presbyterians."[75] The problem with the Freewill Baptists as Graves saw it was that the founder, whom he refers to as Mr. Randall,[76] was ordained by men who were not, at least in Graves' eyes, ministers themselves. After his ordination Randall baptized others and from this sprang the Freewill Baptist Churches caught in the trilemma. Following his usual formula, the pronouncement on the validity of the Freewill Baptist Churches was: "Freewill Baptists can not be churches in any sense, for they are without baptism or a ministry, their first ministers having been baptized by the Baptists [i.e., Freewill Baptist Church], and subsequently all excluded and deprived of their authority."[77]

Even Charles Haddon Spurgeon, the Prince of Preachers, was roundly criticized in the pages of the *Baptist* for his stance on open communion. Spurgeon was accused of being inconsistent in his practice and his preaching and the position of the *Baptist* was that "we have no sympathy with him in this matter."[78] It is worth noting that prior to the Civil War a large number of Spurgeon's books had been burned in Montgomery, Alabama, because he

---

understand Graves' theory of succession, i.e., church succession not apostolic succession, or he is purposely distorting what he knew to be Graves' position to rile him.

73. Ibid.

74. Ibid.

75. Graves, *Trilemma*, 181.

76. The Freewill Baptists were founded by Benjamin Randall (1749–1808) in New Durham, New Hampshire, in 1780. The spellings of Randall's name were inconsistent, with Randall himself using several variations including Randal and Randell. See Bryant, "Awakening of the Freewill Baptists."

77. Graves, *Trilemma*, 188–89.

78. *Baptist* (Memphis), 5 October 1867.

had written "some very foolish things about slaveholders." Quoting from the *Montgomery Mail* of February 28, 1860, Pendleton reports that a large number of books and sermons by Spurgeon were burned. The *Mail* referred to Spurgeon as "the foul-mouthed cockney" and considered the burning of his sermons "all right."[79] It is fair to say that even after the war Spurgeon was a *persona non grata* in the eyes of many in the South and criticism of him was more likely to meet with approval than question, particularly when he was expressing an opinion other than the Landmark-dominated opinion of a large percentage of Southern Baptists in the South at that time.

Just as with the Methodists, other publishing ventures and competitors of Graves' publishing business were open to unusually harsh criticism. John L. Waller was publisher of the *Baptist Banner* in Louisville, Kentucky. He had tried unsuccessfully to partner with R. B. C. Howell and Mason Peck to form a large Baptist paper to serve the West. This venture lasted only three years (1839–1842).[80] Only four years later Graves joined the staff of the *Baptist* as assistant editor and as mentioned previously took over as editor in June 1848. It seemed that Graves never grew tired of editorial polemics with Waller and the two carried on a running debate through the pages of their respective papers. Graves' attacks on Waller began shortly after he became editor of the *Baptist* and centered on the issue of receiving into membership of Baptist churches those baptized by immersion by Pedobaptist preachers, i.e., accepting alien immersions. In August 1848 Waller penned a fourteen-page article aimed squarely at answers given by "Fidus" (Graves) in the *Tennessee Baptist*. Waller accused Graves of "the most gross and palpable misrepresentations, taunts him for his little learning, and that Fidus is intoxicated with the most shallow draughts of ecclesiastical history."[81] Graves answered with a series of articles that stretched on into January of 1849. His determination and resolve to defend what he felt to be the true landmarks of the Baptist Church were admirably summed up in one of the last articles: "I am resolved to stand, *God being my helper*, I will be the last to leave [the old landmarks]. I will stand and battle for these principles, so long as one remains with me, and when he deserts me then I will fight alone."[82] And that is exactly what Graves did. He fought, attacked, castigated, and agitated against all who rejected or watered down his assessment that Baptist churches were the only true churches, could trace their existence back to the first church in Jerusalem, and were the only church that had remained true

79. *Tennessee Baptist* (Nashville), 17 March 1860.
80. Wardin, *Tennessee Baptists*, 160.
81. Quoted in the *Tennessee Baptist* (Nashville), 29 June 1848.
82. *Tennessee Baptist* (Nashville), 24 January 1849 (emphasis in original).

to the Lord's command. It should be noted that despite Graves' attacks on other denominations, other Baptist groups, and all who disagreed with his theological and historical views, and the great following he attracted among Baptists, the *Tennessee Baptist* did nothing to change the relative strength or position of Baptist churches. From the time of Graves' ascendency at the *Tennessee Baptist* (ca. 1850) the next four decades saw no change in the ranking of Baptists at least in Tennessee. The Methodists were first in membership, the Baptist were second, the Presbyterians third, and the Church of Christ fourth. After forty years of dissemination of Landmark views and attacks those rankings were unchanged.[83]

The Trilemma

The attacks by the Landmarkers upon other denominations teach us one thing and explain much of their view of history. The Landmark champion, J. R. Graves, believed he had constructed an argument from which none of the other competing denominations could extricate themselves. If only ministers ordained by true churches and only baptism administered by such ministers were valid, the other denominations were in no sense true churches because they either had come out of the Roman Catholic Church or had been founded by someone whose ordination and/or baptism was deficient in some way rendering them not true ministers. The result of that was that all their acts were invalid and their organizations, to use Graves' words, not true churches but only societies.

It is here that we find the absolute necessity of the Landmark view of history and Baptist church succession. If the Baptist church could not trace its way back across the centuries, if it was formed by some separatist group which pulled away from some "Pedobaptist society," the Baptists would be caught in the same Trilemma in which they saw the competing denominations caught. In order for their claim to be the only true church, the only church that has always been true to the apostolic teaching, to be valid they must maintain a separate and unique heritage from the Protestants and any Pedobaptists. When one entangles his opponent in a dilemma (or in this case, a trilemma) from which he cannot escape, one must be sure that the propositions of the case do not apply to them lest they find themselves hoisted on their own petard.

---

83. Wardin, *Tennessee Baptists*, 291.

Recognition of Other Denominations

At the Southern Baptist Convention which met in Montgomery, Alabama, in 1855 a motion was introduced on the floor of the convention regarding the seating of ministers from other denominations. After amendment the motion that passed stated, "That ministers of our denomination, who are present, be invited seats with us."[84] The following day another motion was introduced which read, "That the clergymen and brethren of other denominations be affectionately invited to seats in this body, that they may witness its deliberations and discussions."[85] This motion was met with vigorous resistance by the Landmark contingent present at the convention. The discussions on this motion took the greater part of one day of the convention and as John A. Broadus wrote it was here for the first time that the term "Landmark" was first used at a meeting of the Southern Baptist Convention.[86] After much discussion, Graves, Pendleton, and the other Landmarkers lost the battle to deny seating of Pedobaptist ministers as corresponding members to the Southern Baptist Convention. The defeat of the Landmarkers at the convention aroused more hostile words between Pedobaptist ministers and Landmarkers and it was all aired in the pages of the *Tennessee Baptist*.

An article written by William Wallace Hill for the *Presbyterian Herald* was reprinted in the pages of the *Tennessee Baptist* on 23 June 1855. The key criticism of the Landmark position taken at the convention was:

> The high church party among the Southern Baptists, with our friend[s] Pendleton, Graves, etc., at its head, met with a most signal defeat in the late Southern Baptist Convention, which held its sessions in Montgomery, Alabama. A motion was made to invite Pedobaptist ministers to sit as corresponding members of the Convention, which called forth a protracted debate, and was finally carried. We hope our friends at Bowling Green and Nashville will not take their signal defeat too seriously to heart.... Let them persevere and they will evidently convince the Baptists that they are bound, in all consistency, either to give up the doctrine that immersion alone is baptism, or take the high ground that there are no churches or ministers but their own.[87]

---

84. *Proceedings of the Southern Baptist Convention, Held in Montgomery, Alabama May 9–10, 1855*, 4.
85. Ibid., 10.
86. Broadus, *Memoir of James Petigru Boyce*, 98.
87. *Tennessee Baptist* (Nashville), 23 June 1855.

Pendleton answered Hill's article. The defeat was convincing: ninety-nine in favor and fifty-three opposed to seating the Pedobaptist ministers; however, Pendleton says of the ninety-nine, "The piety of the ninety-nine who voted seats to Pedobaptist preachers was an *illogical piety*."[88] Pendleton argued that it was illogical to disagree with the baptismal practices of the Pedobaptists and yet recognize them as fellow ministers of the Gospel. He concludes that Hill's argument proves the correctness of the Landmark position.

In a follow-up to the protracted discussion in Montgomery, Pendleton addressed the ones who voted to seat the Pedobaptists: "What say you, ye Baptist opponents of the Landmark? You say immersion alone is baptism and yet you are in favor of recognizing Pedobaptist preachers as gospel ministers . . . you may concede one thing after another to Pedobaptists, but you can never satisfy them until you concede that something other than immersion is baptism."[89]

This issue continued to surface. Thirteen years later an inquiry addressed to the *Baptist* asked about a vote on pulpit affiliation which became a contentious issue at the Alabama Association in that year. The vote on the issue was a tie and had to be decided by the moderator who voted no, and as the *Baptist* termed it, "saved the Baptist character of the association."[90] The remedy that was proposed to the inquirer "and every Landmark brother in that Association" in Alabama was "to circulate The Baptist . . . and give away copies of Pendleton's tract—An Old Landmark Reset—and try it another year and see the result."[91] It was proposed that such a course of action in a few years would result in not a single paper in the South advocating such interdenominational fraternity.

The Southern Baptist Bible Board Controversy

The Southern Baptist Bible Board was established in Nashville, Tennessee, in 1851. In 1854 A. C. Dayton, a member along with Graves and Pendleton of what was called the Landmark Triumvirate, became secretary of the Southern Baptist Bible Board. Dayton along with Graves was a member of First Baptist Church in Nashville, Tennessee. Graves had taken control of the *Baptist* in May 1847 and changed the name of the paper to the *Tennessee Baptist*. In the fall of 1847 Graves formed the Tennessee Baptist Publication Society. During that same period Graves and A. B. Shankland had

---

88. Ibid. (emphasis in original).
89. Ibid.
90. *Baptist* (Memphis), 19 December 1868.
91. Ibid.

formed the publishing firm of Graves and Shankland. In 1854 Shankland was replaced with W. P. Marks, Graves' brother-in-law and the publishing company became known as Graves, Marks, and Company, later as Southwestern Publishing House. With control of one of the more prominent Baptist weekly papers, a publishing house, the Tennessee Baptist Publication Society, and with his friend and fellow Landmarker ensconced as secretary of the Bible Board, Graves was in a position to shape and influence Southern Baptist thought through books, tracts, and teaching materials.

R. B. C. Howell as the president of the Southern Baptist Convention was an ex officio member of the Bible Board. He was also the pastor of the First Baptist Church in Nashville, Tennessee, at the time. Howell introduced a resolution at the Concord Association to address better promotion of Baptist Sunday Schools. The result of this was a meeting held in Nashville on October 23, 1857. When the meeting convened Graves and the Landmarkers were in control and what resulted was the formation of the Southern Baptist Sunday School Union with Dayton as president and Graves as recording secretary.[92] Howell's resolution produced exactly the opposite result from that which he desired, and he was greatly troubled that a Southern Baptist agency under Landmark control would be publishing books and Sunday School materials. (It should be noted that although this was Howell's initiative the result was a competitor for the established Southern Baptist Publication Society in Charleston, South Carolina. Howell was an active supporter of the Publication Society and they had previously published two of his books.)

After this turn of events, Howell was able to persuade the assembly to declare the Sunday School Union was only provisional and would not achieve formal recognition until acted upon by a more representative body of Southern Baptists which was to meet in Americus, Georgia. The meeting was set for the Thursday before the fourth Sabbath in April 1858. Dayton encouraged every state to send representatives to Americus. Late in 1857 Howell wrote a letter to the *Christian Index* in which he declared the board of the Sunday School Union "totally incompetent to the task."[93] One must wonder why he did not send the letter to the editor of the *Tennessee Baptist* who was himself one of the aforementioned board members. Even more telling is the fact that all the board members were members of Howell's church.

Howell may have thought he had a better chance of getting his letter published in the *Christian Index* than in the *Tennessee Baptist*, but, if that

---

92. "Proceedings of the Sunday School Convention," *Christian Index* (Macon, GA), 25 November 1857. See appendix D for constitution.

93. Quoted in the *Tennessee Baptist* (Nashville), 28 February 1858.

was the case, he grossly underestimated Graves' appetite for debate. The question made its way to the pages of the *Tennessee Baptist* in a letter from Dayton to J. M. Pendleton published in the February 13 edition in 1858. Dayton began his letter by laying out the accusation that the Sunday School Union had been formed to compete with the Publication Society.

> It has been intimated that those who were active and earnest in their attempts to secure the organization of the Southern Baptist Sunday School Union, and who desired that it might go into immediate operation with its Board located at Nashville, Tenn., were moved thereto by their desire to *injure the Southern Publication Society and by their wish to secure control of Sunday School literature, in order that they, might make it an instrument of propagation of sentiment upon the "Old Landmark" questions,* which are held only by a portion of the Baptists of the South.[94]

Pendleton begins his answer to Dayton's letter by recounting the calls that were circulated in the *Tennessee Baptist* for a convention to address the subject of appropriate Sunday School materials. "We need," he wrote, "to secure for the children of the South a suitable Sunday School paper, edited and managed by Southern men. If we would have a literature very suitable for Southern Baptist families . . . it must be furnished at the South by Southern minds."[95] Pendleton records also the odd fact that, Howell's comments on the suitability of the Sunday School Union's board notwithstanding, he saw and edited the articles which were circulated in a number of the Baptist papers regarding the need for the convention and when the convention met in Nashville on October 23, 1857, Howell himself was elected moderator. Pendleton reported that there were at least eighty ministers and laymen in attendance.[96]

A committee was appointed to draft a constitution[97] and a nominating committee was elected with Graves serving as chairman. (The nominating committee consisted of one representative from each state. Graves was not originally nominated. Matthew Hillsman of Knoxville, Tennessee, was originally nominated but refused to serve. Graves was suggested as his replacement and chairman since he made the original motion to appoint the committee.) The slate of nominees included A. C. Dayton, president; J. R. Graves, recording secretary; S. C. Rogers, treasurer; and the board of managers included A. B. Shankland. Once the nominations were put forth Howell objected vigorously as did Dr. A. Jones, who according to Pendle-

94. *Tennessee Baptist* (Nashville), 13 February 1858 (emphasis in original).
95. Ibid.
96. Ibid.
97. See appendix D.

ton made the most "incoherent, inflammatory, ranting speech" against the proposed slate of nominees.[98] Howell objected to the make-up of the board and the location of it in Nashville, Tennessee. He said, "The brethren named are known to hold peculiar theological sentiments, that the whole paper has the appearance of partisan prescription for interested purposes."[99]

Then Hillsman, who had refused to serve as chairman of the nominating committee, rose to speak in opposition to the slate of nominees and the whole organization of the Sunday School Union stating that "we had a publication society under the management of devoted Baptists and did not need another."[100] A. M. Poindexter of Virginia rose to speak in opposition to the union and the slate of nominees some of whom he said were "Old Landmark men." Pendleton said that Poindexter was the first to raise the issue of Landmarkism in connection with the formation of the Sunday School Union.[101] After Howell's attacks upon the Landmarkers and upon Dayton, in a number of papers across the South, Graves launched a series of attacks against Howell in the pages of the *Tennessee Baptist*. Graves was his usual critical self and the result was a controversy that extended from the local First Baptist Church in Nashville, Tennessee, to the presidency of the Southern Baptist Convention.

The Graves-Howell Controversy

The assaults by Graves upon Howell continued in the pages of the *Tennessee Baptist*. Finally, in September 1858 the First Baptist Church of Nashville, Tennessee, brought charges against Graves. Howell tried to act as if he was a disinterested, if offended party, and the action was that of the church, but he was involved in the action every step of the way. In a report published by the Concord Baptist Association E. W. Benson (quoting Elder E. P. Walton) said, "[Howell] answered, 'No; we cannot work together. If I go back to Nashville, Graves must be killed off. I have the plan, and it will work.'"[102] The

---

98. *Tennessee Baptist* (Nashville), 13 February 1858.

99. Ibid. Dayton addressed these attacks upon "the new theology with which some persons think this movement was designed to indoctrinate the children and youth of Baptist families" in two letters published in the *Christian Index*. See *Christian Index* (Macon, GA), 9 December 1857 and 16 December 1857.

100. Ibid. Hillsman refers to the Southern Baptist Publication Society of Charleston, South Carolina. In his paper he reported that Howell said, "If he was not mistaken, a quorum of the Board was connected with the office of the *Tennessee Baptist*." *Baptist Watchman* (Knoxville), 5 November 1857.

101. Ibid.

102. Concord Baptist Association (Tennessee), *Both Sides*, 17.

report of the association also concluded, "It was part of the plan adopted by Howell, and which he was so confident he could work, to drive both Elders Dayton and Pendleton from the state, both exercising a powerful Old Landmark influence through the *Tennessee Baptist* . . . Pendleton . . . was to be driven from Union University . . . because he was an Old Landmark Baptist."[103] Pendleton's column in the *Tennessee Baptist* on October 9, 1858 highlighted some of these actions against him.

> News reached me the 22nd of September, that the [First Baptist] Church had passed resolutions in regard to me, requesting me to keep silence in reference to the Graves' trial, and handing me over to the Murfreesboro Church. I suggest to the First Church, Nashville—and I do so as respectfully as the nature of the case will admit—that when I want its advice as to my editorial course, I shall not be backward to make my Desire known.[104]

Regarding Pendleton's post at Union University, he noted:

> That Dr. Howell has been anxious for months past to get me out of the university is unquestionable—and I will if it becomes necessary, publish facts on this subject which will astound the denomination—and, I suppose he now wishes the Church of which I am a member [the Murfreesboro Church] to inflict some disgrace upon me.[105]

Against this background Graves was formally charged with grossly immoral and unchristian conduct, viz., foul, and malicious libels against R. B. C. Howell and having slandered and abused certain distinguished ministers belonging to the Southern Baptist denomination.[106] With this background the trial of Graves was set for October 12, 1858.

Graves appeared before the First Baptist Church on that date and protested the entire proceeding. His assertion was that this was a private matter between two individuals and, based upon Matthew 18:15–18, Howell

---

103. Ibid., 18. It is possible that Howell miscalculated the extent of the opposition to Graves. In 1854 a sharp dispute had arisen between the *Tennessee Baptist* and the *Western Review* published by J. R. Waller in Louisville, Kentucky, over the validity of Campbellite and Pedobaptist immersions. Graves proved to be victorious in that battle of words and the Concord Association noted that "the disaffection of the Kentucky brethren in the Church was made malignant . . . and it silently grew and fed upon a deep-seated opposition to what was then called the too strict and too *high Church* principles and practices advocated by the editor of the *Tennessee Baptist*" (Concord Association, *Both Sides*, 14–15, emphasis added).

104. *Tennessee Baptist* (Nashville), 9 October 1858.

105. Ibid.

106. Concord Baptist Association, *Both Sides*, 8–9.

should have come to him and shown him his fault just between the two of them rather than making this a public matter. Of course, Howell considered this a very public matter as the criticism of him had been spread around the South through the pages of the *Tennessee Baptist*. Howell, however, was not without fault as witnessed by his comments about Graves in a letter to his son: "I ignore him wholly in my congregation, speak to him when I meet him, as I would to a stranger, have no conversation with him, and refuse to receive any correspondence from him. When he has written me notes, I have sent them back unopened."[107] When the church voted to deny Graves' protest and proceed with the trial Graves and a number of other members of First Baptist Church withdrew from the fellowship and declared themselves to be the First Baptist Church but later chose the name Spring Street Baptist Church and elected Graves as pastor.

The First Baptist Church proceeded to try Graves in absentia. The trial lasted until October 18 and Graves was eventually found guilty on all charges. The vote on Tuesday evening October 12 on the question: "Whether Rev. J. R. Graves is guilty of libel as charged" was indicative of the course of the trial. The result was a resounding eighty-four "yes" and zero "no."[108] Although having withdrawn from the church, Graves was nonetheless, at the conclusion of the trial, excluded from the membership.

Graves was not finished, however, and for many months the Graves-Howell controversy dominated the pages of the *Tennessee Baptist*. Everyone who knew Graves knew what to expect. As Basil Manly Jr. wrote to his parents, "What a howl the Tenn. Bap. will raise about this."[109] B. F. Riley also noted in his history of Alabama Baptists that "another cause of distraction [among the Baptists of Alabama] arose from the repeated utterances of Rev. J. R. Graves, through the columns of the *Tennessee Baptist*, of the great injury which had been done him by his exclusion from the First Church, Nashville."[110]

In addition to Graves, A. C. Dayton, deacons A. B. Shankland, H. G. Scovel, and W. P. Marks were excluded from the church. Shankland had been treasurer of the church for ten years. In all forty-seven members were excluded from the First Baptist Church, Nashville for their support of Graves and/or opposition to Howell.[111] In spite of the victory in excluding his opponents from the church, Howell quickly realized he was at a tremendous disadvantage in the battle for the hearts and minds of the members of the

107. R. B. C. Howell to Morton Howell, May 5, 1858.
108. Concord Baptist Association, *Both Sides*, 134.
109. Basil Manly Jr. to Sarah and Basil Manly, 5 March 1859.
110. Riley, *History of the Baptists of Alabama*, 277.
111. Grice and Caudill, "Graves-Howell Controversy," 1:582.

Concord Association, the state, and denomination. That realization brought about the formation of yet another Baptist paper, the *Baptist Standard*, which had as its primary purpose the refutation of Landmarkism, Graves, Pendleton et al.

The aftermath of the trial produced a surprising turn of events. Graves had routinely run a column in his paper under the heading of "Baptist Corollaries." Corollary number three stated: "That a body of immersed believers is the highest ecclesiastical authority in the world, and the only tribunal for the trial of cases of discipline; that the acts of a church are of superior binding force over those of an association, convention, council, or presbytery."[112] Graves had affirmed in *The Great Iron Wheel* that in disciplinary matters the local church is the final authority.[113] All those affirmations to the contrary, the supporters of Graves assembled a council of thirty-eight representatives from nineteen churches in the Concord association. "On the motion of James F. Fletcher of Murfreesboro, visiting members of Concord Association, and members from other Baptist Churches were invited to participate in the deliberations of the Council." Twenty men responded to the invitation.[114]

This council met March 1, 1859, and the meeting lasted until March 3, 1859. The charges that were preferred against Graves were listed one by one and he responded to each charge, speaking for sixteen hours. Some of these proceedings were carried in their entirety in the pages of the *Tennessee Baptist* for all the Baptists of the South to read.[115] The council pronounced Graves innocent of all charges and censured the First Baptist Church and Howell. More damaging, however, was the determination of the council that the church had acted unscripturally and by virtue of their unscriptural actions the majority that had voted to exclude Graves and others was indeed a faction and thus pronounced Graves and the minority, who had removed from First Baptist Church and founded the Spring Street Baptist Church, the true First Baptist Church. Graves printed the transcripts of the testimony before the council in *Both Sides*. The Concord Association at its annual meeting in August 1859 concurred with the decision of the council.

112. *Tennessee Baptist* (Nashville), 11 July 1857.

113. Graves, *Great Iron Wheel*, 311.

114. *Tennessee Baptist* (Nashville), 12 March 1859. Other sources such as *Encyclopedia of Southern Baptists* give the numbers as twenty churches and forty representatives, but the figures quoted here are from the transcribed minutes of the council carried in the *Tennessee Baptist*.

115. The proceedings of Graves' trial had been carried in their entirety in the *Tennessee Baptist*, usually on the front page, beginning with the issue of March 12, 1859, and continuing until the end of June 1859.

Both the Nashville First Baptist Church and the Spring Street Church presented letters purporting to be the Nashville First Baptist Church. Pendleton moved that both letters be referred to a committee and the committee be instructed to report back to the association. After a heated discussion the motion carried. The committee report said that it saw no reason to disagree with the actions taken by the council which had heard the matter in March. The Spring Street Church was recognized as the "orderly and constitutional First Baptist Church, Nashville." The report was approved by a vote of forty-four to one.[116] When the Tennessee General Association met in October 1859, they elected three Landmarkers as officers. All three had been excluded from the First Baptist Church.[117]

All this had to be most embarrassing for Howell who was serving his third term as president of the Southern Baptist Convention. The result of the controversy with Graves at the local and state level had been an embarrassing defeat in which the pastor of the First Baptist Church in Nashville and head of the Southern Baptist Convention was denied a seat in the local and state meetings.

The Landmarkers felt very confident going into the Southern Baptist Convention of June 1859. Graves filled the pages of the *Tennessee Baptist* with attacks upon his opponents in the lead up to the convention, vilifying and demeaning the non-Landmarkers for their persecution of him and all Landmark Baptists. He made clear his intentions in the pages of the *Tennessee Baptist*: "If . . . the Convention exists to support and give honor to certain men, right or wrong, then who will not say, the sooner the convention dies the better?"[118] Graves' intent was to see Howell defeated and humiliated or the Southern Baptist Convention destroyed.

When the convention convened Pendleton offered a resolution to the convention that due to the unscriptural nature of the proceedings against Graves et al. by the First Baptist Church in Nashville that the messengers of First Baptist not be seated. The resolution was tabled by the convention.[119] Graves' primary objective, however, was the defeat of Howell as president of the Southern Baptist Convention. This was the declared end of his propaganda in the run-up to the convention. However, in spite of all his efforts

---

116. Concord Baptist Association, *Proceedings of the Forty-Ninth Annual Session . . . August 6, 8, 1859*, 3–4, 12–15.
117. Grice and Caudill, "Graves-Howell Controversy," 1:582.
118. *Tennessee Baptist* (Nashville), 30 April 1859.
119. *Proceedings of the Southern Baptist Convention at its Seventh Biennial Session*, 6.

Howell was elected on the first ballot but immediately stepped down and Richard Fuller, a non-Landmarker, was elected.[120]

In the end Graves dealt a defeat to Howell but his attempts to take over the convention as he had done with the Concord Association and the Tennessee General Association were defeated. This entire controversy fueled by personal ambition and animosity on both sides brought the Southern Baptist Convention to the brink of dissolution. Graves had overestimated his strength in the broad convention and Howell had underestimated the grip of Landmarkism on the Baptists of the Southwest, i.e., Tennessee, Mississippi, Texas, Arkansas, Kentucky, and parts of Alabama. Howell died less than a decade later still embittered against the Landmarkers but Landmarkism continued to wield considerable influence, particularly among the Baptist churches in the Southwest.

Slavery

A number of the works on Landmarkism and Graves, when treating the subject of the Civil War (1861–1865) and slavery, reflect a general opinion like that expressed by O. L. Hailey (Graves' son-in-law), "Dr. Graves himself had no part in the political and sectional excitement [leading up to the war]."[121] These writers and the sentiments expressed by Hailey would have us to believe that the great polemicist Graves remained silent while denominations split asunder over the issue, and the pulpits and denominational papers of the nation thundered sermons and biblical exegesis to support their side and condemn the other. What one must remember in this is the Graves-Howell controversy just discussed. For the greater part of 1858, 1859, and part of 1860 Graves was preoccupied with his own trial, his counterattacks upon Howell, and his bold move to take over the Southern Baptist Convention. There is ample evidence, however, that prior to and after the Howell affair Graves was anything but silent on the issue of slavery, and that issue eventually sent his friend and confidante Pendleton north while Graves remained true to the Southern states that seceded from the union.

---

120. Ibid., 13–14.

121. Hailey, *J. R. Graves*, 81. Tull, in *History of Southern Baptist Landmarkism and High-Church Baptists in the South*, gives hardly any notice to Graves' prewar editorials and the role of the *Tennessee Baptist* in stirring Baptist emotions before the war. Patterson, in "Theology of J. R. Graves," gives more information than most regarding Graves' activities during the war but again makes little mention of the passionate rhetoric he put forth defending slavery and castigating the Northern politicians, churches, and preachers.

As early as 1853 (eight years after the Southern Baptist Convention was born and the defining issue in that birth was the slavery question) in letter thirteen to Bishop Soule of the Methodist Episcopal Church, South, Graves digressed into a discussion on slavery. It is very telling. He began by asserting that all men are created equal but adds, "Had there been no sin there would have been no slavery—God himself instituted slavery as a *punishment* upon the descendants of Ham. . . . When God removes the curse from Ham, which will not be until every curse is abolished, the slavery of his race will cease, and not until then."[122] His own exegesis of Scripture convinced him that although slavery was not the original condition of man, just as subjection to death was not his original state, it was the present state of the descendants of Ham and was such by God's decree and would remain so. This was very much in line with the rhetoric coming from the pulpits of the South in the lead-up to the war.

Not only the Baptists but the Methodist church and the Presbyterian church eventually divided over the issue of slavery. This was generally along geographical lines as much as along theological lines for some. The Southern economy and way of life had to a large degree been built around the institution of slavery in the decades preceding the war. Graves' Northern heritage and background became fodder for his adversaries and competitors in the religious publishing business particularly among the denominational papers. Samuel Henderson, editor of the *South Western Baptist*, engaged in a running debate with Graves over Landmarkism that often included aspersions to Graves' Northern roots and questioned his loyalty to the South.[123] (It is noteworthy that Graves was able to carry on this debate while embroiled in the Howell controversy.)

To verify Graves' and the Landmarkers' position in general on the issue of slavery one only has to look to the pages of the *Tennessee Baptist* and the *Baptist* both before and even after the war was over and the slaves had been freed. The editor of these papers did as much to promote the justice of the South's cause and the undesired consequences of the North's victory and the emancipation of the slaves as he did for Landmarkism and the Baptist cause.

In 1852, the *Tennessee Baptist* reprinted an article from the *Religious Herald* which advocated the preaching and teaching of the Scripture to one's slaves because "by Christianizing our slave population they will perform their duties more faithfully; for Christ ordered his servant believers to serve and obey their masters."[124] As early as 1856, Graves had urged the secession

---

122. *Tennessee Baptist* (Nashville), 20 August 1853 (emphasis in original).
123. See Terry, "Samuel Henderson."
124. *Tennessee Baptist* (Nashville), 3 January 1852.

of the Southern states unless the constitution was enforced in protecting the rights of all. That "all" would include the rights of slaveholders, who Graves said "would not give up their property without a struggle."[125] The *Tennessee Baptist* carried the following comments in an editorial in September 1858: "From the beginning, abolitionism was based upon a misconception of the physical and moral constitution of the negro. . . . It was everywhere seen, and universally acknowledged that the moral and physical energies of the negro were best developed in the condition of slavery. . . . The subordination of the negro in the relations of society is the result of that inferiority of endowment. . . . It had been already shown that slavery was not absolutely evil, in the sight either of reason or Scripture."[126]

In the aftermath of the Harpers Ferry Raid in 1859,[127] the editorial page of the *Tennessee Baptist* carried an article condemning the Northern fanatics who carried out the insurrection. The lesson to be learned from this blood that was shed, according to the editorial, was this: "The abolition *mad men* of the North have learned a lesson not to be forgotten; *the slaves are faithful to their masters*." The defense of slavery as an institution was again adamantly set forth. The fact that slavery was a Southern institution as opposed to a mere legality as it was in the North was reiterated. "Our institutions are peculiar to us. We believe in them. It is our *right* to do so."[128]

With the presidential election of 1860 looming the *Tennessee Baptist* took a strong editorial stand against the Republican candidate Abraham Lincoln. One article said if he was elected the interests of the South would be sacrificed because his "right hand is against the institutions of the South."[129] However, after Lincoln was elected and passions were running high J. M. Pendleton penned an editorial that was contrary to the views that

125. *Tennessee Baptist* (Nashville), 25 October 1856.

126. *Tennessee Baptist* (Nashville), 11 September 1858.

127. Harpers Ferry was the site of a federal arsenal and John Brown, a radical abolitionist, planned to capture the arsenal, arm local slaves, and lead an insurrection which would start a liberation movement among African American slaves. Brown captured the arsenal on October 16, 1859, but his plans fell apart when the slaves failed to join in the rebellion and authorities in Washington, DC, sent a force of marines led by Colonel Robert E. Lee to quell the rebellion. Brown and his men killed a few of the townspeople of Harpers Ferry, including the mayor, and the local citizenry joined in the attack upon Brown. Ironically, the first casualty in the raid was an African American baggage handler who was shot and killed after confronting the raiders. Brown was tried and convicted of treason and hanged. On the day of his execution church bells rang in many places and some like Emerson and Thoreau joined many in praising Brown. For more details, see Potter, *Impending Crisis 1848–1861*, 378–84, and Hinton, *John Brown and His Men*.

128. *Tennessee Baptist* (Nashville), 5 November 1859 (emphasis in original).

129. *Tennessee Baptist* (Nashville), 21 January 1860.

had been consistently expressed by the paper of which he was an assistant editor. The variance at which this placed Pendleton with Graves, the other Landmarkers, and the readership of the paper was great[130] and warrants a lengthy excerpt from his editorial.

> I regret most profoundly what I learn from various sources is going on in the South. Our citizens are surely acting without reflection. They are condemning the President elect before his inauguration. This is certainly premature. I hoped and thought to the last that Mr. Lincoln would not be elected, but the majority of the people had determined otherwise. I believe all admit he has been elected in accordance with the provision of the Constitution of the United States. Why not then yield gracefully and chivalrously to the expressed will of the people? Why not wait and see whether Mr. Lincoln faithfully performs his duty as President of the United States, all the States? . . . I would have my countrymen of the South consider, what is to be gained by breaking up this United States? . . . For one I am sure the Union will not be dissolved unless the God of heaven intends to chastise this nation. Dissolve the Union on account of slavery? What an absurdity! How preposterous for the men of the South to take this view! . . . I beg I implore my brothers not to lend their influence to weaken the ligament that binds together the States of the Union and makes them in their aggregate capacity the great nation of the world.[131]

In this single expression of and appeal for unity Pendleton put himself at variance with his Landmark brethren and one must believe his appeal to his brothers "not to lend their influence" to the cause of secession had to be directed to the influential editor of the paper in which this very article appeared.

In December 1860 Graves wrote, "To maintain the rights of the South, *out of the Union*, when we can no longer, by fair and honorable measures remain *in it*, we pledge our life, our fortunes, and our sacred honor."[132] That same issue printed a letter by N. M. Crawford of Mercer University in Georgia. The letter addressed the nullification by several Northern states of the fugitive slave law. Crawford condemned the action because, in his words, it trampled "under foot the Constitution [of the United States]." He cited Article IV, section 2, which provided for the rendition of persons held in service. Crawford's letter contained a series of questions, entitled "Can

---

130. A note of thanks to the subscribers of the paper in the issue of January 7, 1860, references "almost fifteen thousand of our patrons."

131. *Tennessee Baptist* (Nashville), 24 November 1860.

132. *Tennessee Baptist* (Nashville), 22 December 1860 (emphasis in original).

the Union Be Saved?" He answers each question and in the response to his question regarding the Constitution he replies that the Union cannot be saved, "Because such a nullifying of the laws of Congress is *de facto* a dissolution of the Union."[133] Crawford's letter expresses the right of a minority of states to be free from the imposition of the will of a majority which violates the laws of the land.

It is no coincidence that on the same page almost column by column is a reply to an inquiry as to the appropriateness of the Concord Association's involvement in the trial of J. R. Graves by the First Baptist Church of Nashville. The answer is very similar to Crawford's answer regarding the oppressive illegality of the action by the Northern states. "Certainly an individual, minority, large or small has not only the right, but is duty bound to protest and withdraw from any participation in any treasonable act against the laws of Christ, and we further believe it is the bounden duty of all loyal subjects of Christ to recognize them as constituting the gospel church."[134] The Landmark faction was equating the Graves-Howell controversy with the North-South controversy and of course the equating of Graves and the Landmarkers with the South was a winning strategy in the eyes of most Southern Baptists.

A Momentous Year (1861)

1861 saw the United States of America plunged into civil war. It was the last year of publication for the *Tennessee Baptist*. Pendleton left Tennessee and moved north, and Graves was soon to see his publishing empire come crashing down. However, before those events unfolded, the Landmarkers were deeply involved in the flood of passions that swept over both sides in the lead up to the great conflict.

The connection between political oppression and ecclesiastical oppression continued to be drawn by the Landmarkers. The year 1861 began with a defense of the idea of secession from the Union. "We do hold and maintain . . . whether in an *ecclesiastical or civil compact,* any one member, or State, may rightfully withdraw, or recede from the compact, and *that it is a sacred and imperative duty to do so, whenever that member* (individual or State) *is oppressed and unrighteously dealt with by a dominant party in that*

---

133. Ibid. It is interesting that Crawford's letter is carried on the front page of the paper. Additionally, Crawford engages in an extended debate in the pages of the *Tennessee Baptist* over the meaning of the Greek word *doulos*, excerpts from that debate to follow in succeeding pages.

134. Ibid.

compact."[135] The connection between Graves' treatment at the hands of the First Baptist Church and the treatment of the Southern states at the hands of the Northern states is unmistakable. This sought to capitalize on an issue that was near and dear to the hearts of the vast majority of Graves' readership and Southern Baptists in general.

Lest this escape the attention of the readers one other article in this edition of the paper and a footnote by the editor raise the question, should the majority always rule regardless of the rights of the minority and regardless of whether the majority is in the right? The argument for the right of a state to secede from the union was turned on its head and applied to church members and cases of church discipline. The question Graves raises in the footnote is: "Will they affirm that any man alienated his natural right of self-preservation when he enters the church, should a majority conspire to work his ruin?"[136] The question, this dilemma posed, concerns the difference between political and ecclesiastical doctrines and practices, particularly when the democratic republicanism of the system of government in the Baptist Church has been so vigorously defended by all good Southern Baptists.

Once the results of the presidential election were confirmed a special South Carolina convention met and declared on December 20, 1860, that the union between it and the other states of the United States of America was dissolved. Within six weeks (February 1, 1861) six other states had followed suit. It was about this time (January 26, 1861) that the *Tennessee Baptist* began to publish, weekly, chapters from the book *Slavery: Its Origin, Nature, and History: Its Relations to Society, to Government, and to True Religion, to Human Happiness and Divine Glory, considered in the Light of Bible Teachings, Moral Justice, and Political Wisdom,* by Thornton Stringfellow. These installments appeared on February 2, 9, and 23, and March 2, 9, and 16. Interestingly these chapters ran side-by-side with the regular column "Baptist Principles, Polity, and Practice." The summation of Stringfellow's argument heads up chapter one of his book:

> It is not many years since our brethren at the North engaged in a crusade against slavery; because (as they said) it was denounced in every page of the Bible as the greatest sin on earth. The Bible has been examined, and it has been found that slavery is fully sanctioned by it. Nevertheless, this crusade has waxed warmer against slavery, as a sin of the deepest dye, because it was a sin (as they have said) against a higher law than the Bible.[137]

135. *Tennessee Baptist* (Nashville), 12 January 1861 (emphasis in original).
136. Ibid.
137. Quoted in the *Tennessee Baptist* (Nashville), 26 January 1861.

The question of whether Tennessee would join the seceding states was discussed in the pages of the *Tennessee Baptist*. The eastern part of Tennessee had strong ties to the union and one editorial feared that "the influences of these strong union men" would prevent Tennessee from joining the other Southern states of the new Confederacy. However, the prediction was made that, no matter the outcome of the impending vote, "Tennessee would be among the first to take up arms" against the outrages of Lincoln and "within twelve months she will be with the majority of the Southern States."[138] This obviously political editorial also contained the observation that these present events meant "we have entered the very twilight of this present dispensation—that its 'last days,' the 'time of the end' are at hand."[139] This was followed with an admonition for the readers to be engaged in prayer and the study of biblical prophecy.

Beginning with the week of March 23 and in succeeding issues of April 6, 13, and 20 a series of letters were printed in the *Tennessee Baptist*. The letters were entitled: "American Slavery and Its English Impugners, In Letters to the Rev. Charles Stovel, of London, Pastor of the First Calvinistic Baptist Church in England." The letters were in response to a "Lecture on American Slavery," delivered by Rev. Stovel, which came into the hands of Graves. The letters defended the institution of slavery, upbraided Stovel and the English in general for their own failures, even among the "laboring masses" who suffered in "degradation and poverty," criticized English philanthropists for aiding the attacks upon the South, and the canonization of John Brown in the English papers. Stovel was reminded that America was not critical of England's handling of her own rebellion in India by that oppressed and enslaved population.[140]

On April 12, 1861, the South fired upon the federal troops stationed at Fort Sumter in Charleston, South Carolina, and the federal troops surrendered the fort to the Southern forces. President Lincoln called for all the states to send troops to recapture the fort and preserve the Union. This led four other states to secede from the Union and the Civil War began.

For the balance of 1861 the rhetoric coming from the pages of the *Tennessee Baptist* only grew in vehemence toward their opponents, unwavering justification of slavery, and support for the Southern war effort. A representative sampling of these attitudes follows.

> This is the real position Mr. Lincoln and his Cabinet, despite their honied [sic] speeches and demure looks have been

---

138. *Tennessee Baptist* (Nashville), 9 February 1861.
139. Ibid.
140. *Tennessee Baptist* (Nashville), 23 March 1861.

occupying towards the Southern States. The serpent of Black Republicanism as long as it could hope to beguile by fraud and falsehood, wore a mild and specious guise, but now that its tail has been trodden on, and it sees the game is up with it, the reptile protrudes its forked tongue, and reeks a deadly slime from every pore. The John Browns and Lloyd Garrisons of the North are jubilant at the prospects which their sanguine expectations conjure up, of carnage, outrage, and negro insurrection in the South. They are now ready to sing their *nunc dimitis*. The year of jubilee is dawning and they are impatient to inaugurate the millennium of abolition and negro equality.[141]

It would be hard to pen more incendiary and offensive rhetoric, but such rhetoric was useful to whip up the Baptists of the South. In a later editorial urging Tennessee to join the Confederacy of Southern states, honor and "sacred rights" are inveighed: "The man who would vote neutrality, would register his own dishonor and *cowardice*. *It is abhorrent* to every sentiment of an honorable heart . . . [to] stand by with folded arms and see their brethren battling for a cause as dear and rights as sacred."[142]

Later, sandwiched between the regular column of "Baptist Polity and Six Important Things" and an article entitled "Are Baptists Protestants?" was a column on "War! Duty!" It tied, as did most of the inflammatory rhetoric of the day, duty to country and duty to God together. Against the Northern states it said, "No consideration—whether of interest or duty—has been strong enough to bind the *Northern conscience* to observe their solemn compact. Even the *Bible* has failed to exert any influence over them."[143]

The vote in the state of Tennessee on the question of whether to secede from the Union was scheduled for June 8, 1861. As that date drew near the pages of the *Tennessee Baptist* were filled with long articles urging the voters of Tennessee to vote in favor of secession. In these articles A. C. Dayton argued that the citizens of Tennessee had the political and religious right to leave the Union and unite with the Confederate states. In fact, the last article in this series which appeared on June 8, the day of the election, Dayton proclaimed it was God's will for Tennessee to secede. He wrote, "Can any doubt what it is his will that we should do? Who does not see that the time has come when in his providence the South and Slavery is to be set free from the exacting and intermeddling of those who feel they do God service by exciting the servant to rebel whom He bade to obey?" The

141. *Tennessee Baptist* (Nashville), 20 April 1861.
142. *Tennessee Baptist* (Nashville), 27 April 1861 (emphasis in original).
143. *Tennessee Baptist* (Nashville), 11 May 1861 (emphasis in original).

summation reveals the deep-seated conviction that marked this struggle. "We are so sure that Providence, by our location, by our interests, by our past associations, and by the character of our people, indicates that we are to go with the slave States, that we shall as a religious duty vote *Separation And Representation* in the Confederate States."[144] Tennessee voted to secede from the Union and became one of the prominent battlegrounds in the war and for the Landmarkers personally.

While this heated rhetoric was proceeding from the Landmarkers by way of the *Tennessee Baptist* (contrary to what many have said was their role in the lead-up to the war), the assistant editor of the paper was not reticent in his criticism of those who supported slavery and urged secession and war. Only weeks after Fort Sumter fell, Pendleton lamented, "Madness is in the hearts of rulers and people. I fear multitudes are thirsting for blood. The time for negotiation and compromise are gone. There is absolutely no hope for this nation but in God . . . Call On God In Prayer."[145] With almost prophetic-like insight Pendleton said that at least five hundred thousand men would fall on the field of battle. That proved to be exactly right. Over five hundred thousand died and another five hundred thousand were wounded and maimed.

Pendleton also engaged in a controversy with N. M. Crawford of Mercer University over the exegesis of the Greek word *doulos*. Pendleton's argument and goal were to refute the political and religious rhetoric which sought to justify slavery with biblical exegesis. Pendleton's contention was that "slave" was used in a dishonorable sense but *doulos*, on the contrary, was used in an honorable sense by the Greeks. He argued that Paul called himself a *doulos* of Christ and Demosthenes called himself a *doulos* of the people but neither meant what was meant by the term slave in the debate that was raging in the country. Pendleton hoped to take away the biblical justification for slavery that was being argued in the pages of the *Tennessee Baptist* and from the Baptist and other pulpits of the South. Pendleton said the argument against his exegesis was driven by "sectional prejudice" and said he was accused of being "the first Southern pen" to be used in defense of servant as the rendering of *doulos*. This controversy was carried in the paper from May 25, 1861, until June 29, 1861.[146] It is no coincidence that Pendleton's co-editorship and writing for the *Tennessee Baptist* ended in June 1861.

---

144. *Tennessee Baptist* (Nashville), 18 May, 1 June, and 8 June 1861 (emphasis in original).

145. *Tennessee Baptist* (Nashville), 11 May 1861 (emphasis in original).

146. *Tennessee Baptist* (Nashville), 25 May, 22 June, and 29 June 1861.

The religious tenor which the war took on and indeed which fanned the flames of bloodlust in the years and months before the war is reflected in several articles in the *Tennessee Baptist* in the latter part of 1861. Against Pendleton who said it was improper for a pastor to leave his flock without a shepherd to go to war, an article appeared in the late summer of 1861 which said, "We are not prepared to condemn those ministers as carnal men who raised companies and led them to war.... No minister should leave his flock desolate, unless he feels that it is his duty to serve his God and his country in the camp.... This is a war *pro aris et focis*, for our firesides, and for the altars of our religion, and every man is called upon to do *his* duty."[147] Later in an article soliciting funds to print New Testaments for soldiers the readers are chided: "Can not and should not Southern Christians afford their soldiers who are defending 'their altars and their fires' a few packages of tracts ... in addition to the Bible?"[148] Of course, Graves' publishing house was the source for the Testaments and tracts. A good summation of the religious nature of this conflict and the religious zeal with which it was approached, not the least by the Landmarkers are seen in the words of A. C. Dayton, "Our cause is just and a just God will answer our requests" for victory and protection for our soldiers.[149]

A fitting end to this momentous and critical year is found in the first edition of the *Tennessee Baptist* in 1862. It is a letter from Jefferson Davis, the president of the Confederate States to J. R. Graves thanking him for the beautiful Bible Graves had sent as a gift. Davis wrote, "The Bible is a beautiful specimen of Southern workmanship, and if I live to be inaugurated the first President of the Confederacy on the 22nd of February next, my lips shall press the sacred volume which your kindness has bestowed upon me."[150]

The Aftermath

The last issue of the *Tennessee Baptist* was published February 15, 1862. Forces of the Union army occupied Nashville on February 24, 1862. J. R. Graves feared he would become a prisoner of war (a strange thought for one who supposedly took no part in the "political and sectional excitement leading up to the war"). Graves made a hasty flight from Nashville after the

---

147. *Tennessee Baptist* (Nashville), 24 August 1861 (emphasis in original).

148. *Tennessee Baptist* (Nashville), 7 September 1861.

149. *Tennessee Baptist* (Nashville), 14 September 1861. A look at this approach and the reality of the "Lost Cause" and its shaping of Baptist life will follow in the next chapter.

150. *Tennessee Baptist* (Nashville), 4 January 1862.

fall of Fort Donelson. "Hasty because [he] had been forewarned that [his] name had been marked for a northern prison."[151] He went to his father-in-law's home in Magnolia, Mississippi. Graves continued to be involved in the Southern war effort from preaching to leading a company of "pikemen" to supervising a salt mine in Louisiana.[152] When Graves returned to Nashville after the war, he found his publishing house ruined and the greatest part of his books, plates, and equipment missing or destroyed.

Pendleton after his separation from the *Tennessee Baptist* remained in Murfreesboro, Tennessee, for a time but the suspension of Union University, the confiscation of his crops by Union forces, and fearing for his life at the hands of his neighbors led him to flee to the North in August 1862. He never returned to the South.

The Whitsitt Controversy

William H. Whitsitt graduated from Union University in 1861 shortly before classes were suspended due to the advancing Union forces. Whitsitt studied theology under J. M. Pendleton and defended his professor against charges that Pendleton was an abolitionist. He served in the Confederate army during the Civil War. After further study at the University of Virginia, Southern Baptist Theological Seminary, and two years in Germany in Berlin and Leipzig, he became professor of church history at Southern Seminary in 1872.

After the death of John A. Broadus in 1895, the trustees chose Whitsitt to be the next president of the seminary.[153] He continued as president and professor of church history until his resignation. In 1895 Whitsitt wrote an article for *Johnson's Universal Cyclopaedia* in which he put forth the belief that a group of English Anabaptists had adopted immersion as the correct form of baptism in 1641 and had thus become Baptists. This denied the theory of Baptist successionism and an unbroken line of Baptist churches, by whatever name, back to John the Baptist. Later, Whitsitt acknowledged that he had written two unsigned articles with the same premise which had been published in the *Independent* in New York some fifteen years earlier.[154] Walter B. Shurden said that these writings "created one of the most bitter and divisive controversies in all of Southern Baptist history."[155] Given the

---

151. Hailey, *J. R. Graves*, 82.

152. For a synopsis of Graves activities during the war, see T. A. Patterson, "Theology of J. R. Graves," 27–36.

153. Wardin, *Tennessee Baptists*, 383–84.

154. Tull, *High-Church Baptists in the South*, 138.

155. Shurden, *Not a Silent People*, 22.

history of the nineteenth century among Southern Baptists that is saying quite a lot.

Whitsitt's thesis which created the furor was a direct contradiction of the Baptist succession theory, which at this point might as well have been called Baptist doctrine, which Graves and the Landmarkers had published, taught, and defended throughout the preceding five decades. As with the controversies of the past this one began in the pages of the Baptist state papers, and the letter writing, and editorial prosecution of the case began in earnest.

The first paper to jump into the fray was the *Western Recorder*. The editor was T. T. Eaton who had been considered for the seminary presidency along with Whitsitt. Eaton was backed by the Landmarkers and they were no doubt disappointed in the selection of Whitsitt. Their disappointment turned to outrage when Whitsitt published, in 1896, *A Question in Baptist History*. However, the faculty at the seminary supported Whitsitt led principally by John R. Sampey and A. T. Robertson. Eaton led the attack on Whitsitt, in the Graves style, through the pages of the *Western Recorder* (Eaton was called the J. R. Graves of Kentucky). To counter Eaton the pro-Whitsitt forces started a paper in Louisville, Kentucky, the *Baptist Argus*. This controversy like others examined earlier also threatened to divide the Southern Baptist Convention. W. O. Carver, a faculty member at Southern Baptist Theological Seminary and one who studied under Whitsitt said, "The election of Whitsitt as president of the seminary was the occasion for the most extensive, the bitterest, and in the issue, the most decisive conflict ever to disturb the Baptists of America."[156] It should be noted that it was not Whitsitt's election as president but the articles and the book he had written which created the conflict.

James E. Tull gives a very good overview of Whitsitt's argument which destroyed the Landmark doctrine of Baptist church successionism and properly baptized administrators of baptism extending back to the Jordan River and John the Baptist. The intent here, as in the other controversies examined, is to probe beyond the established facts of the case and the generally accepted motivations attributed to the main players to examine sources, comments, and influences previously unexamined, ignored, or unknown. The Whitsitt case was quite literally a matter of life and death for Landmark theology because the breaking of the succession of Baptist churches, baptism, and the proper administrators of baptism would destroy the whole Landmark system. As Tull remarked, "Many had regarded Landmarkism as an alien infection in the Baptist body; the Whitsitt Controversy clearly

---

156. Carver, "William Heth Whitsitt," 70.

demonstrated that Landmarkism was a constituent and decisive element in almost every phase of Baptist life."[157]

Whitsitt said of his research, "This is purely a question of modern historical research. It does not affect any items of Baptist principle or practice."[158] Typical of the comments that aroused the ire of the Landmark faction, among others, were: "None of the Anabaptists of Holland or of the adjacent sections of Germany were immersionists . . . in fact, few Anabaptists anywhere were immersionists."[159] In another place, quoting from *Geschichte der Wiedertaenfer* (1836), he wrote, "300 persons were baptized by [Melchior] Hoffman out of a large bucket on this occasion. The act of baptism could not have been immersion, in this case."[160] This type of historical research was branded as heresy by Eaton and the *Western Recorder*. John R. Sampey made this observation near the beginning of the controversy:

> Already the approach to the question of the truth or falsity of Dr. Whitsitt's thesis, that immersion was re-introduced in England in 1641, had become doctrinal rather than historical. The debate was thus open to all lovers of orthodoxy and did not call for any special knowledge of English Baptist history.[161]

The opponents of Whitsitt were forthcoming in their condemnation, as witnessed by the comment of J. H. Spencer of Kentucky, who said, "Dr. Whitsitt's views are heretical."[162] Although as editor of the *Western Recorder* Eaton led the charge against Whitsitt, Sampey gives an interesting bit of history that is ignored in accounts of the conflict. According to Sampey, Eaton was overseas when the Whitsitt controversy first began, but "Mrs. J. E. Peck, widowed older sister of Dr. Eaton, sat in the editorial sanctum and wrote widely for the paper. Her name nowhere appears, but her trenchant pen filled the editorial column, and guided the policy of the paper."[163]

Eaton kept the controversy alive by writing various state conventions and asking that they demand the resignation of Whitsitt. At the 1896 meeting of the Baptist Association in Louisville, Kentucky, an intense debate broke out. Sampey was present and made an impassioned and heated defense of Whitsitt. His rhetoric was so charged that he issued an apology to

---

157. Tull, *High-Church Baptists in the South*, 149.
158. Whitsitt, *Question in Baptist History*, 5.
159. Ibid., 35.
160. Ibid., 42.
161. Sampey, *Memoirs of John R. Sampey*, 82.
162. Ibid., 81.
163. Ibid., 79.

the association the following day.¹⁶⁴ With this type of emotion and feeling sweeping through the Southern Baptist Convention the trustees of the seminary prepared a statement on the matter to be read at the annual meeting of the convention.

The record of the forty-second Southern Baptist Convention of May 7–10, 1897, contains this communication. Key in the communication were the following statements: "We cannot undertake to sit in judgment on questions in Baptist history which do not imperil any of these principles [the articles adopted when the seminary was established], concerning which all Baptists are agreed, but concerning which serious, conscientious and scholarly students are not agreed. We can, however, confidently leave to continued research and discussion, the satisfactory solution of these questions . . . we consider it our duty . . . to foster, rather than repress, the spirit of earnest and reverent investigation."¹⁶⁵

The trustees reported that, after adoption of the communication, a committee was appointed to notify Whitsitt of their action and invite him to meet with them and offer any statement he wished. Whitsitt said that the articles written for the *Independent* were a mistake, but in words that would later be used against him, he added, "What I wrote was from a Pedobaptist standpoint with a view to stimulating historical research."¹⁶⁶ He also stated that he would wish to retract anything from the article in Johnson's encyclopedia that was offensive in any way to any of his brethren. He defended his action in an opinion expressed to a relative that she should join a Pedobaptist church because that was where her husband was a member. On the main question he answered, "That on the historical questions involved in the discussion, I find myself out of agreement with some honored historians; but what I have written is the outcome of patient and honest research, and I can do no otherwise than to re-affirm my convictions and maintain my position. But if in the future it shall ever be made to appear that I have erred in my conclusions, I would promptly and cheerfully say so."¹⁶⁷ After Whitsitt's paper was read the trustees gave him the hand of confidence and fellowship. "The trustees then instructed B. H. Carroll of Texas, and W. E. Hatcher of Virginia to communicate to the Southern Baptist Convention

---

164. Ibid., 85.
165. Southern Baptist Convention, *Proceedings . . . , May 7–10, 1897,* 14–15.
166. Ibid., 15.
167. Ibid., 16. For the full text of the relevant portion of the minutes, see appendix E.

this action, and also give it to the public press."[168] The full report of these actions was carried in the *Baptist and Reflector* of May 13, 1897.[169]

The editorial page of that same issue in commenting on the convention noted, "The main interest of the Convention, however, centered about the Whitsitt matter, which has been a disturbing element in the denomination for the past year or more."[170] The article noted that Whitsitt still held to his position on the reliability of his research, and noted that "we thought he was mistaken about that."[171] Of even more interest was the comment: "We may state that Dr. T. T. Eaton, editor of the *Western Recorder*, who has been the recognized leader of the opposition to Dr. Whitsitt, told us not long ago that if Dr. Whitsitt would do what he has now done, he himself would be satisfied and would cease his opposition to him."[172] This was far from the truth as subsequent events would clearly demonstrate.

Two weeks later the *Baptist and Reflector* carried quotations from eight different Baptist papers concerning the disposition of the Whitsitt affair at the convention. In view of later events these representative samples are particularly telling.

> From the *Arkansas Baptist*: While Dr. Whitsitt's confession and apology are not all that some will demand, it should be accepted as far as it goes and results calmly awaited. The struggle for the *protection of the old landmarks* has not been in vain.
>
> From the *Biblical Recorder*: The Whitsitt controversy is a thing of the past. The banner of peace is again leading the Baptist hosts of the South . . .God be praised!
>
> From the *Evangel*: The Whitsitt matter has been settled, and, we trust, to the satisfaction of everybody. We hope that it is settled "finally," and that our denominational papers will keep all such matter that will tend to reopen the discussion out of their columns in the future.

---

168. Ibid.

169. The *Baptist and Reflector* was the product of a merging and consolidation of the Baptist papers in the state of Tennessee. A period of consolidation in the 1880s saw Graves' *Baptist* acquire the *Baptist Messenger* and the *Baptist Gleaner*. The *American Baptist* of Chattanooga, Tennessee, merged with the Knoxville, Tennessee, *Baptist Beacon*. These two papers merged with the *Baptist Reflector* of Nashville, Tennessee, which was initially called the *American Baptist Reflector* but eventually in 1885 came to be called the *Baptist Reflector*. Finally, in 1889 Graves' *Baptist* merged with the *Baptist Reflector* edited by E. E. Folk and the *Baptist and Reflector* was born. The offices were in Nashville with Folk as editor. Wardin, *Tennessee Baptists*, 243–47.

170. *Baptist and Reflector* (Nashville), 13 May 1897.

171. Ibid.

172. Ibid.

From the *Alabama Baptist*: We are in perfect accord with the action of the Convention.

From the *Florida Baptist Witness*: Dr. W. H. Whitsitt, the beloved President of the Seminary, was thoroughly exonerated by the Board of Trustees . . . the vindication by the Board of Trustees was made known to the Convention . . . a great throng of brethren rushed forward and shook his hand, proving the high esteem and tender affection this sweet-spirited Christian man and great scholar is held by the Southern Baptists. We trust that all the brethren will let the Whitsitt affair be a thing of the past.

From the *Western Recorder*: Let him have full credit [for his apologies and retractions]. His purpose is still to maintain his historical position. . . .We wish he could have seen his way to retract this also, but since he believes it, he cannot be expected to retract it. Perhaps one reason he still believes it is because he has not been reading the evidence we have given in the *Recorder*. It was a great surprise to find that telegrams were sent to the secular papers in various cities that Dr. Whitsitt had been vindicated. . . . There is not the slightest foundation for any such statements. Neither the trustees nor the Convention either justified or condemned him.

From the *Texas Baptist Standard*: After all the criticisms of him—some of them very severe—he bears himself nobly as a Christian gentleman of the highest type. As the *Standard* was the first paper to speak out with emphasis against Dr. Whitsitt's utterances and methods. . . . What has been said about Dr. Whitsitt's teachings and methods has had no malice behind it. . . . While yielding not an atom of our conviction that Dr. Whitsitt's history is not history, and while believing in the end it will be shown by overwhelming evidence to be erroneous, we do feel that it is high time now, in view of his frank apology and retractions, to cease our criticisms of the man and pass out into the broader realm of impersonal historical discussion.[173]

However, the Whitsitt affair was not a "thing of the past" and the sentiments expressed by the Landmarkers in Arkansas, Kentucky, and Texas did not go unnoticed. Barely a month after the convention in Wilmington, North Carolina, a personal letter from T. P. Bell, editor of the *Christian Index* of Georgia, to E. C. Dargan[174] revealed the true sentiments against

173. *Baptist and Reflector* (Nashville), 27 May 1897.

174. Edwin Charles Dargan was professor of homiletics at Southern Baptist Theological Seminary. Tull describes his *Ecclesiology: A Study of the Churches*, as having traces of Landmarkism but his total position as being too large-minded to be squeezed into the Landmark mold. Dargan was later the president of the Southern Baptist

Whitsitt. Bell wrote, the strong "feeling against Dr. W's remaining in the Seminary is deeper and more widespread than it was before Wilmington."[175] What is interesting is the statement that Whitsitt made a terrible mistake writing from a Pedobaptist point of view. This was as offensive to some as the conclusions of his historical research. Bell commented on this, "The feeling is almost universal that he blundered fearfully; and that sentence in his statement, that he wrote those Independent articles from a Pedo-baptist standpoint has stuck in the gizzards of many good men."[176] Bell said the dissatisfaction with Whitsitt was growing throughout the Southern states and the view among the "common people and the plain preachers" was that Whitsitt had betrayed the Baptists.

Bell then discussed a plan to get Furman University to call Whitsitt as president, as that institution was without a president at that moment. That would solve two problems—one for the seminary and one for Furman. Bell saw two other benefits to that plan. Whitsitt could save face, leaving to avoid further contention, and once at Furman "send out a manly defiance to the Landmarkers which would be echoed far and wide.... The Seminary trustees would surely elect a non-succession successor, whom Eaton and Co. could not fight on account of foolish utterances and they could be whipped."[177] One sees in this language a deep divide between the Landmark forces and many Southern Baptists, but Bell closes, wisely, by asking Dargan to keep this in strictest confidence for it would not be advisable to have it known he was saying these things.

Dargan must have been perceived as broad-minded (as Tull suggested) and also viewed as a confidante by many. A. T. Robertson, professor of New Testament at the seminary, wrote Dargan less than two weeks later on June 11, 1897. The rather long letter questioned Eaton's motives for keeping the controversy alive and the effect his victory would have on the seminary in Robertson's opinion. A long quotation from Robertson's letter speaks clearly of his view of Eaton, his motivation, and the result for the seminary.

> If Eaton is to boss the Seminary, I doubt if any of us could do much good. A possibly united constituency wants Eaton in the saddle.... I think I am orthodox, but I cannot have my orthodoxy [spelled?] out to me by Eaton and Mrs. Peck.... If Whitsitt goes,

---

Convention from 1911–1913, editorial secretary of the Sunday School Board of the Southern Baptist convention from 1917–1927, and a member of the International Sunday School Lesson Committee from 1918–1928.

175. T. P. Bell to E. C. Dargan, 30 June 1897.
176. Ibid.
177. Ibid.

what next? There is bound to be a "next." Eaton would instantly claim it as a triumph and vindication by "the denomination" of his orthodoxy and that he represents the denomination in his positions. He would then crack the whip over us with redoubled force. And who would be able to resist? It seems perfect folly not to think this thing through. W. R. L. Smith writes me that he is certain that Whitsitt's going would not be the end, that they come after Sampey's head and mine. . . . If we let Whitsitt go, we accept Eaton's yoke, disgust most of our firmest friends. . . . If we hold our own, we repel Texas and Arkansas, with a good many in Mississippi, Louisiana, Tennessee, Missouri, and Kentucky, and a few other states. But retain the great bulk of the seminary's real constituency, both as to money and students. . . . I would be willing to see [Whitsitt] go for the sake of the Seminary. But if he goes does not the Seminary as we know it and treasure it, go too? If Eaton gets his hand upon it, who can take it off?[178]

Two days later, John Sampey sent a letter to Dargan from Switzerland, where he was vacationing, lamenting the controversy and being especially critical of the role of the Kentucky association, Eaton, Mrs. Peck, and the Landmarkers in resurrecting and keeping alive the whole controversy. Sampey writes, "Well, oughtn't we [Southern Baptists] be ashamed of ourselves in Ky? Just to think that the General Association meeting in Georgetown would stoop as low as to stir up a controversy that all decent men thought buried forever! I had been framing to myself conciliatory speeches that I might make to the leader of the opposition, when lo, in a moment we are notified that it is war to the knife!"[179] Sampey then recounted his impassioned speech at the association meeting and adds this note to the whole affair: "What a pity that as many of our brethren in Ky. should be crammed full of the bitter prejudices of Mrs. Hogshead [a derogatory term for Mrs. Peck], and her bean pole of a brother [Eaton]."[180] Sampey's opinion regarding the possible resignation of Whitsitt and the ensuing consequences are outlined clearly in the letter.

> Shall Uncle Billy resign? That, at first sight, might seem to be the easiest solution; but it would be only the beginning of resignations. It may be that the Baptist cause would be advanced by our leaving the various departments to such men as Eaton, Christian, . . . and Co. Carroll might even be induced to take theology or homiletics under a new management. Of course all

---

178. A. T. Robertson to E. C. Dargan, 11 July 1897.
179. John R. Sampey to E. C. Dargan, 13 July 1897.
180. Ibid.

this is nonsense. Whitsitt's resignation would be a complete surrender on the part of the faculty to the domineering spirits in the Recorder office. For my part I do not intend to serve under such masters.[181]

The implications are clear from this private correspondence. The venting of emotions is more than apparent, and the future of the Southern Baptist Seminary appeared to hang in the balance as the war between the Landmarkers and those who rejected their manufactured view of church history, no matter how civil in public, grew more heated.

The sentiments of the majority of Southern Baptists, however, particularly in the Southwest were with the Landmarkers, and were being strengthened each week by the Landmark press. Charles L. Cocke, superintendent of Hollins Institute in Virginia, commented on this strategy in a letter to Dargan. "The course of the opponents of Dr. Whitsitt can only be compared to that of scheming politicians—they first set to work to create a public sentiment among the masses and then appeal to that sentiment, the '*vox populi*' as the righteous uninspired demand of the whole brotherhood."[182] The *vox populi* was often represented as the impetus behind the call for Whitsitt's resignation. "B. H. Carroll wrote in 1897 that the common people had been aroused, that the followers of J. R. Graves had registered their protest in the Whitsitt affair."[183]

In September the *Baptist and Reflector* carried a letter to the editor from T. J. Eastes to the effect that he would introduce a resolution at the upcoming Tennessee Baptist Convention asking for the resignation of Whitsitt. Eastes wrote that he sincerely believed that the "great majority of Southern Baptists demand Dr. Whitsitt's resignation." Eastes cited Whitsitt's loss of respect in the denomination, the good of the seminary, and a demand that Whitsitt respect the judgment of his brethren as reasons for calling for his resignation. He castigated Whitsitt for "his expressed determination not to resign," saying this had awakened more dissatisfaction than "the blunders he has confessed."[184]

As the time for the Tennessee Convention approached others joined in demanding Whitsitt's resignation. S. C. Hearne was the author of a letter published in the *Baptist and Reflector* in which he outlined Whitsitt's mistakes, which had been previously spelled out, but he adds the damage which these mistakes had done to the Baptist cause.

---

181. Ibid.
182. Charles L. Cocke to E. C. Dargan, 12 September 1897.
183. Mueller, *History of Southern Baptist Theological Seminary*, 121.
184. *Baptist and Reflector* (Nashville), 16 September 1897, 4.

He wrote, "I believe Dr. Whitsitt ought to be removed for the following reasons:"

> Because he does not seem to know what a Baptist is. He says Baptists practiced sprinkling and pouring for baptism.... There is not a Baptist church, Association, or Convention in the South, if in the wide world, that would recognize such a body as a Baptist church.
>
> Because he has published to the world that *all* Baptists practiced sprinkling and pouring as the true mode of baptism until 1641, and that his reading has not furnished him with anything like an authenticated instance of immersion earlier than the year 1644. If these statements are true it follows that there were no Baptist churches (as we now define the term) in the days of the apostles and they have no divine authority for existence today.
>
> Because he says in Johnson's Cyclopedia that the earliest Baptist church belongs to the year 1610 or 1611. If so, then Christ did not build his church, or Baptist churches have no valid claim to be called churches of Christ or any part of the kingdom.[185]

These objections are thoroughly Landmark in their ecclesiology and their view of church history. Hearne's conclusions are based on the lack of an unbroken line of churches that practiced the proper mode of baptism and lacking that connection he concludes that the error he sees in Whitsitt's work is nothing less than the destruction of the validity and authority of the Baptist church.

Not everyone was in favor of a resolution seeking Whitsitt's discharge. In the same issue of the *Baptist and Reflector* another Tennessee writer urged Eastes not to offer his resolution at the State Convention because "Tennessee has had her days of bitter antagonisms and does not wish to return to them.... Our State Convention [must] not be sidetracked for something which ... is not worth the time."[186] Another rather unique perspective was offered in the issue published immediately before the convention. J. M. Phillips cites what many claimed to have been the intentions of the founders of the seminary. "They claim it was the intention of its founders that its teachings should not antagonize the convictions of any considerable portion of its constituents on the subjects of 'Church Succession,' 'Landmarkism,' and 'Alien Immersions'—subjects about which the Baptists of the South are not

---

185. *Baptist and Reflector* (Nashville), 23 September 1897, 4.
186. Ibid.

agreed."[187] Phillips accused Whitsitt of using his position as president of the seminary and his published works to "overthrow the cherished views of a large portion of the denomination in the South . . . [and proposed] that the trustees shall restore [the institution] to these original lines of teaching—*simply that and nothing more*."[188]

These kinds of arguments continued to mark the pages of the religious press and the sentiments were increasingly against Whitsitt remaining as the president of the seminary. During this time, "the State Convention in each of four other states joined the agitation for the retirement of Dr. Whitsitt. They were Mississippi, Louisiana, Arkansas, and Texas. . . . Many district associations in the South especially in Kentucky, kept up the clamor for the elimination of Dr. Whitsitt."[189]

The issue of the *Baptist and Reflector* which was published the day before the Southern Baptist Convention in May 1898 did contain a curious bit of editorial arrangement. Side by side in the columns of the paper were two articles—one seeking donations to either erect a monument or endow a theological chair at Southwestern Baptist University to the "memory of that great and good man, Dr. J. R. Graves." The other article continued the calls for Whitsitt to resign stating, "The controversy has of late changed from 'a question of history' to one of personal veracity . . . [and] it would be in the interest of the Seminary for him to resign."[190]

At the Southern Baptist Convention of May 6 through 10, 1898, in Norfolk, Virginia, the board of trustees of the seminary sustained Whitsitt by an overwhelming majority. They reaffirmed their position of the previous year and affirmed that Whitsitt had done nothing that warranted the calls for his resignation. Many at the convention wanted to bring this issue to the floor of the convention and fight it out until a resolution was reached but just as many opposed the discussion coming before the convention at all.

At this point, B. H. Carroll gave notice of his intention to introduce resolutions to sever the relationship between the Southern Baptist Convention and the Southern Baptist Theological Seminary at the next meeting of the convention in 1899. These resolutions were conveniently already prepared, and it was ordered that they be included in the minutes of the 1898 Convention for all to see. This move placed the Whitsitt supporters in a dilemma for no one wanted the ties between the seminary and the convention

---

187. *Baptist and Reflector* (Nashville), 7 October 1897, 7.
188. Ibid. (emphasis in original).
189. Sampey, *Memoirs of J. R. Sampey*, 87.
190. *Baptist and Reflector* (Nashville), 5 May 1898, 4.

to be severed. Most wanted those ties strengthened.[191] However, Carroll's threat to introduce this resolution at the Southern Baptist Convention the following year meant in essence that the seminary would lose a great deal of its financial support, the Southern Baptist Convention would lose its seminary, or the president of the seminary, who held views of church history that many considered so detrimental to the Baptist cause, would have to be removed from his post.

The editorials in the weeks following the convention in May 1898 still clamored for Whitsitt's removal, but it was the Kentucky General Association that dealt the fatal blow to Whitsitt and his supporters. The Kentucky General Association did not wait for the Carroll resolution to come up the following year. Little more than a month after the 1898 Convention the Kentucky Association by an overwhelming vote of one hundred ninety-eight to twenty-six passed a resolution "to withdraw moral and financial support from the Seminary as long as Dr. Whitsitt retain[ed] his connection with it."[192] This intensified calls for Whitsitt to resign. Many said the matter had gone far enough; "the confidence which has been lost in Whitsitt as a leader can never be restored."[193]

The comment that summarized the new opposition to Whitsitt is quite telling: "If we thought that Dr. Whitsitt [was] standing for a great principle, if his resignation would mean the establishment of an historical test of orthodoxy, or the substitution of tradition for the Bible, or that theological professors [would] not be allowed to think or have freedom of research, then as a Baptist we should say for him to remain."[194] It is clear from the comments of Sampey, Robertson, and others that those conclusions were precisely what the other professors assessed the resignation of Whitsitt to mean.

Whitsitt resigned in a telegram sent to the president of the board of trustees on July 13, 1898. His resignation was to take effect at the close of the 1898–1899 session in May 1899. W. J. McGlothlin, a professor at the seminary, probably spoke for the overwhelming majority of the faculty. "One woe is past; behold a greater cometh I fear. There is before us another most trying year's work. Feverish uncertainty and restless resentments are going to make the best work impossible and good work difficult."[195]

---

191. Southern Baptist Convention, *Annual . . . 1898*, 22–23. See appendix F for complete text of Carroll's resolution.

192. *Baptist and Reflector* (Nashville), 30 June 1898, 2.

193. Ibid.

194. Ibid.

195. W. J. McGlothlin to E. C. Dargan, 15 July 1898.

One would believe that the anti-Whitsitt forces would have been happy over their victory, but such was not the case. The dissatisfaction surfaced almost immediately. Typical of the sentiments was the following: "There is a disposition in some quarters to refuse to consider the resignation of Dr. Whitsitt as a settlement of the Whitsitt matter because it was made to take effect at the end of the next session instead of immediately."[196] The same article claimed to have it on good authority that Whitsitt wanted to resign immediately but acceded to the requests of the other faculty members to remain on until the end of the next session. The article issued a plea that there would "be no further agitation of the matter" in the denominational meetings during the summer and fall.[197]

The fears of the seminary faculty seemed to have been well-founded. W. A. Jarrel, a committed Landmarker, included in the "Texas Notes" feature of the *Baptist and Reflector* in September the following analysis of the situation at the seminary after Whitsitt's resignation:

> As the other professors of the Seminary took part with Dr. Whitsitt, and seemed to agree with his position, it is feared by many Baptists that his resignation does not much relieve the Seminary matter, unless Whitsitt's successor is a *straightout landmarker, seccession* [sic] *Baptist*. By the way, as the Seminary is for all the Baptists of the South, can anyone tell why the trustees should not give the Landmarkers a representation in the Seminary by putting one in as Dr. Whitsitt's successor?[198]

Eaton through the pages of the Western Recorder continued his harangues against Whitsitt until May 11, 1899 when his resignation was a fact at the end of the 1898–1899 session. Sampey records also that, "Dr. Kerfoot [held] that the Seminary president who had resigned . . . had committed grave offenses."[199] This F. H. Kerfoot, along with Eaton, had also been nominated with Whitsitt to succeed Broadus as president of the seminary. Whitsitt became president and one must question if the attacks by Eaton and Kerfoot did not take on a personal nature, masked by their asserted desire for historical accuracy. One thing that is not up for speculation, however, is that Eaton and to a lesser degree Kerfoot, were the voices of a great number who had idolized J. R. Graves and had accepted as Baptist doctrine

---

196. *Baptist and Reflector* (Nashville), 28 July 1898, 9.

197. Ibid.

198. *Baptist and Reflector* (Nashville), 1 September 1898, 4 (emphasis added). Jarrel would write in 1894, *Baptist Church Perpetuity*. The book was a defense of the Landmark doctrine of church succession and was dedicated to J. R. Graves, among others.

199. Sampey, Memoirs of J. R. Sampey, 73.

his view of church succession. Whitsitt's work destroyed the entire premise that Baptists had existed in an unbroken chain since the days of the first church in Jerusalem. Whitsitt's work destroyed the Landmark ecclesiology and sectarian, high church claims to be the only true church.

Whitsitt got in one final word. It would not be the last word as the Landmark theology continued to play a part in Southern Baptist life, but it was a parting salvo from Whitsitt. From his final address at the commencement exercises on June 1, 1899, we find these words: "I solicit them [all who ever studied with me in the seminary] to maintain and industriously proclaim the fundamental Baptist doctrine of the universal spiritual church ... the only church that has received and enjoyed the promise of unbroken succession."[200]

Missions Controversy

Different scholars give varying accounts of controversies within the Southern Baptist Convention over mission work. Walter Shurden says that the seeds of mission work for which the Southern Baptist became known were sown in the anti-missions controversy of the early part of the nineteenth century, even before there was a Southern Baptist Convention. According to Shurden as the western expansion of the country grew in momentum the Baptists were the greatest beneficiaries of the independent people who tamed the wilderness. The bi-vocational Baptist preacher was able to move quickly with the population, but this uneducated, passionate group of preachers proved to be the breeding ground for the Anti-Missions Controversy that rocked the frontier from 1820 to 1840. Initially the Baptists responded positively to the idea of missions but that soon changed and anti-missionism spread rapidly.[201]

Although this preceded the Landmark movement, Shurden's analysis of the factors involved, in many cases, point directly to later controversies in which the Landmark theology was the key factor. Shurden's list was comprised of first, the ministerial jealousy of the largely uneducated pastors of the West toward their more educated counterparts from the settled and refined East. Second, there was a growing suspicion of missionary organizations. The frontier preachers saw this as a movement toward a centralized church government that threatened the independence of the local church. The third factor was money. It was very difficult to ask churches to contribute to the support of a missionary when they did not even pay

200. Ibid., 100.
201. Shurden, *Not a Silent People*, 37–38.

their own preachers. Fourth, Shurden cited the hyper-Calvinism of many of the frontier Baptists as the theological reason behind the anti-mission movement.[202] It is worth noting that one of the key figures in the Baptist ranks who was virulently opposed to mission work was Graves' old nemesis Alexander Campbell, who separated from the Baptists over this issue taking thousands of Baptists with him into the Disciples of Christ. James Tull also noted, "The anti-mission sentiment assumed its most intense form in the churches of Tennessee."[203]

The Landmarkers, however, were not anti-missional. As Pendleton stated in a sermon carried in the *Tennessee Baptist*, "Every church should, according to its ability, supply the needy at home and abroad with the bread of life. I do not see how any church in this age of the world, can be in a healthful state that does nothing for Home or Foreign Missions."[204] The bigger problem for the Landmarkers was the whole concept of mission boards managing the contributions of local churches and setting standards by which missionaries were either accepted or rejected. Of course, the problem with this was the usurpation of the authority of the local church. As John E. Steely wrote later, "[The] schism in the Baptist fellowship [near the end of the nineteenth century] . . . ostensibly over the methods of missionary work [was] actually due to a radical disagreement in the field of ecclesiology."[205] The missions' controversy centered precisely on the question of whether or not conventions, associations, and boards had ecclesiastical authority to call missionaries and collect and administer funds from the various Baptist churches. Graves himself had questioned the authority of the Foreign Mission Board as early as 1859.

The Gospel Mission Movement was a continuation of the Landmark controversies that surfaced in earlier decades. The strict advocates of Gospel Missionism insisted that those who received support should be supported by individual churches. The Foreign Mission Board was to be simply the agent for passing these funds to the missionaries without deducting any administrative costs or overhead.[206] In 1894 E. E. Folk, editor of the *Baptist and Reflector*, engaged in an exchange worthy of the old Graves' editorial battles. Folk's opponent was J. H. Grime, a committed Landmarker and editor of the *Baptist Freeman*.[207] Grime was highly critical of the operating

202. Ibid., 40–45.
203. Tull, *History of Southern Baptist Landmarkism*, 89.
204. *Tennessee Baptist* (Nashville), 9 September 1854.
205. Steely, "Landmark Movement," 134.
206. Tull, *High-Church Baptists in the South*, 136–37.
207. Grime (1851–1941) authored *History of Middle Tennessee Baptists* and a

expenses and salaries paid to the mission boards pointing out that the salary of the executive director was four times that of the average missionary and far above the salary of the average pastor.[208]

The following year A. J. Holt, corresponding secretary of the Tennessee Baptist Convention, wrote a series of nine articles for the *Baptist and Reflector* entitled "The Missionary Controversy." These articles were in fact an unabashed critique of a pamphlet, "Are Mission Boards Scriptural?" The pamphlet was written by J. A. Scarboro of Georgia.[209] Again, in good Landmark fashion, Scarboro followed up with an answer to Holt point for point. Holt's arguments highlighted what he considered the impractical nature of moving away from a board system. Holt argued, "In swinging from centralization these brethren appear to be tending to segregation, where no church will cooperate with any other church."[210] In a rather questionable appeal to Scripture Holt affirms, "There appears no Scripture warrant for such separate work as they advocate. We have not found a single instance in the Scriptures where a missionary was appointed, sent out, and sustained by any one church."[211] Holt adds that there is no mutual sharing of responsibility. The missionary is responsible to no one and no one is responsible to the missionary. Holt also enumerated eight advantages of the board system, number one being its accord with scriptural precedent and the eighth he considered the pragmatic proof of the other seven, "All the real advancement in missionary work at home or abroad has been accomplished under the Board plan." This was bolstered by such statistics as sermons preached, converts, baptisms, pages of tracts distributed, and religious family visits.[212]

Scarboro answered Holt's objections and refuted the advantages he listed as a product of the board system, but Scarboro's reply was far more revealing when he answered Holt's objection that the missionary is responsible to no one under the Gospel Mission plan. Scarboro recounts Holt's visit to Jerusalem in the company of an independent missionary "appointed

---

number of pamphlets, among them "Close Communion and Baptists" and "History of Alien Immersion," in which he defined alien immersions as "immersions performed outside Baptist churches."

208. Wardin, *Tennessee Baptists*, 380–81.

209. Scarboro (1857–1932) is best known as author of *The Bible, the Baptists and the Board System* (1904). He served as a home missionary serving in Georgia, Alabama, Mississippi, Arkansas, Kentucky, Tennessee, North Carolina, and South Carolina. In his missionary report to the convention in 1907 he estimated he had written six hundred letters and two hundred columns for various newspapers.

210. *Baptist and Reflector* (Nashville), 21 April 1898, 6.

211. Ibid.

212. Ibid., 7.

by no church, just as the Board missionaries are appointed by no church." The problem with the visit was the fact that Holt engaged in open communion in this company and baptized a Methodist without church authority. Scarboro's full comments are important for their tone and emphasis:

> Bro. Holt was glad to be with him—for a wonder: and preached for him too! How strange! . . . What a pity! And Bro. Holt actually helped him to administer the Lord's Supper to baptized people. Let me see! Did I read it right? Yes, he administered free communion in Jerusalem; that is Bro. Holt and Bro. Joseph did . . . Shades of the Jerusalem Mission Board. Here is a good orthodox Board man, Bro. Holt, from whose keen organized and orthodox eyes no heretical missionary can escape, right in Jerusalem, in the place where he says the first Board was organized to look after the orthodoxy of missionaries and he himself—the *Ego*, corresponding secretary actually falling in and administering free communion. But more, he dipped a Methodist in the Jordan, and then with his Methodist, dipped without church action or authority, he sits down to the Lord's table and holds a free communion service.[213]

The key elements of Scarboro's attack against Holt really centered around the key Landmark principles of pulpit affiliation, close communion, alien immersion, and local church authority. It is also impossible to miss the sarcasm that laces the invectives Scarboro levels at Holt. Graves himself probably could not have been sharper in criticizing Holt.

As James E. Tull records, two schisms within the Southern Baptist Convention occurred at this same time, one in Texas and one in Arkansas. The Baptist Missionary Association of Texas and the Baptist General Association of Arkansas both grew out of Landmark ideology clashing with the board system and particularly with the right of individual churches to commission and send forth missionaries.[214] (It is interesting that the opponents of the schismatic Landmarkers in the Texas battle included B. H. Carroll and J. M. Carroll.) The withdrawal of these Landmark associations from the Southern Baptist Convention quieted at least the overt opposition to the board system within the Southern Baptist Convention.

---

213. *Baptist and Reflector* (Nashville), 14 June 1898, 7.
214. Tull, *High-Church Baptists in the South*, 150–51.

The Fundamentalist—Moderate Controversy

The Fundamentalist-Moderate controversy which recently plagued the Southern Baptist Convention and which had its roots in the Fundamentalist-Modernist debates of the early twentieth century was not a result of Landmark distinctives. However, the contesting of the issue in the pages of the Baptist press, the firing of respected and beloved seminary presidents and professors, and the battle for control of the various boards of the convention all bear remarkable similarity to the Landmark inspired controversies described above. While it may be true that Landmarkism played no definitive part in shaping the Fundamentalist-Modernist controversies of the early twentieth century, the fundamentalism that has shaped the Southern Baptist Convention in recent years has an unmistakable Landmark flavor.

In *Hardball Religion: Feeling the Fury of Fundamentalism*[215] Wade Burleson explained how he "aroused the wrath of denominational power-brokers carrying out a well-orchestrated effort to further restrict missionary qualifications (according to strict Landmark Baptist doctrine)."[216] For his part, Burleson repeatedly points out the Landmark positions of leading Southern Baptist power brokers like Paige Patterson, Paul Pressler, John Floyd, Keith Eitel, and Bill Sutton.[217] These men all held key trustee and board positions within the Southern Baptist Convention.

In view of the direction in which fundamentalism in the Southern Baptist Convention has gone it would be reasonable to conclude that although the original issues in the fundamentalist-modernist controversy were decidedly not Landmark issues, the direction which that controversy has assumed in the fundamentalist-moderate debates of recent years has been marked by decidedly Landmark tendencies and beliefs. A full discussion of this topic follows in the next chapter as current attitudes within the Southern Baptist Convention regarding Landmarkism are examined.

Conclusion

Controversy, debate, and editorial attacks are an inherent part of the fiber of the Landmark legacy. From the great polemicist, J. R. Graves, to the schisms of the early twentieth-century Landmarkers have not only been marked by controversy but have worn those controversies as a badge of

---

215. Burleson, *Hardball Religion: Feeling the Fury of Fundamentalism*, 195–200, 221–31.

216. Ibid., 32–33, 37.

217. Ibid., 48.

honor. Furthermore, these controversies were not disputed in isolation but were unabashedly played out in the pages of the religious press. No one was above attack if their beliefs conflicted with Landmark ecclesiology, the Landmark view of history, or Landmark missiology. While many look upon these controversies as a sad and better-to-be-forgotten part of Southern Baptist history, the truth is that during these controversies Landmarkism was exercising its considerable influence in the Southern Baptist Convention and becoming a major force in the shaping of the life and future direction of the denomination. The next chapter will examine the various ways Landmarkism has projected itself into the Southern Baptist Convention in more recent days.

5

Gone in Name but Present in Doctrine

Incredible Staying Power of Landmark Doctrines

IN THE PREVIOUS CHAPTER the controversies in Texas and Arkansas at the beginning of the twentieth century were highlighted. The dispute in Texas followed the Graves' pattern of personal attacks and competition between opposing religious newspapers. The result in both Texas and Arkansas was the formation of new conventions composed entirely of churches with Landmark beliefs. It is noteworthy that these two separate conventions met November 24–26, 1905, in the church pastored by O. L. Hailey.[1] This group was known as the Baptist General Association. In 1924 the Baptist General Association changed its name to the American Baptist Association. To the casual observer it would appear that the Landmark elements in the Southern Baptist Convention, particularly in the Southwest where they were the strongest, had been removed and the tenets of Landmarkism would soon be just a footnote in Baptist history. That assumption was to be far from the truth, as the history of the twentieth century would prove.

Leon McBeth, noted Baptist historian, wrote, "I will affirm that there is a Baptist tradition of the Southwest and that it centers in Texas . . . that Southwestern Baptist Theological Seminary is its major institutional expression . . . that the *Texas Baptist Standard* has been and continues to be a major force both in creating and sustaining that tradition. I will nominate B. H. Carroll as the primary architect of the new tradition."[2] As mentioned

---

1. Moore, "Landmark Baptists and Their Attack," 67.
2. McBeth, "Texas Tradition," 38.

in the previous chapter Carroll used Pendleton's texts at the seminary and was instrumental in the Whitsitt controversy. McBeth quotes Carroll in saying, "In Texas the spirit of J. R. Graves goes marching on."[3] McBeth added, "This was written in 1911, but I can testify that these practices continue.... This Landmark residue provides the basis of much of the conservatism that marks Baptist life in the Southwest today."[4]

James Tull wrote in the conclusion of his thesis, "By 1905 Landmarkism had entered the blood-stream of Southern Baptists and had become a chronic virus, even though it had been held in check by more healthy elements in the denomination's life."[5] He added, in explaining that the period from 1905 to the present had been compressed into a single short chapter, "The aim of this chapter is to show that Landmarkism, though in decline as a specific set of issues, has insinuated itself into virtually every challenge Southern Baptists have faced."[6]

These assessments of Landmark influence are several decades old and one would logically ask: Has the Landmark influence waned even more in recent times? According to Timothy George, such is not the case. George says, "Landmarkism is very much alive and well within the Southern Baptist Convention."[7] George said that this manifested itself in several ways:

> In the exclusivity of Baptist churches, probably not to the extent that Graves, et al., carried it but there is a certain exclusivism in the eyes of many Southern Baptists; probably not to the extent of denying the validity of other churches but a certain sectarian, exclusive view of the Southern Baptist Convention and particularly their church.
>
> You see this today in closed communion practices by many churches, the re-baptizing of new members, even people who may have been baptized by immersion upon profession of faith in another Baptist church. To a lesser extent you see this in the expression of the continuity of the Baptist Church and the affirmation of the Baptist Church as the only true church.[8]

Bearing out what George said, a recent search of the internet turned up a Landmark discussion group for Southern Baptists. Their self-described

---

3. Ibid., 49.

4. Ibid., 49–50. (This continuation of which he speaks is in 1991.)

5. Tull, *History of Southern Baptist Landmarkism*, vii.

6. Ibid.

7. Timothy George, dean of Beeson Divinity School, interview by author, Birmingham, AL, 9 February 2010.

8. Ibid.

description states, "The Landmark Southern Baptist is an e-mail discussion group and resource center for those interested in studying *historic Baptist ecclesiology, also known as Old Landmarkism*."[9]

The Legacy of J. R. Graves

One would think the legacy of controversy, a new denomination, schisms, and internal wrangling within the Southern Baptist Convention would have relegated Graves and Landmarkism to the dusty memory of times better forgotten. This did not prove to be the case, even after the death of Graves and the defection of the staunch Landmark Baptists from the convention.

There were some among the Southern Baptists who, like J. B. Jeter, editor of the *Religious Herald* of Virginia, consistently opposed Graves. In a letter to Graves in 1879 Jeter asks Graves to make fair quotations of his opposing views (something for which Graves was not noted). He adds, "I think their [Landmarkers'] views are a serious hindrance to the progress of Baptist principles."[10] Jeter engaged in a series of editorial debates with J. B. Gambrell, editor of the *Baptist Record* of Mississippi. Gambrell was one who was deeply influenced by Landmarkism as Tull said but "did not stand in awe of Graves."[11] This is clear in a letter from Gambrell to E. C. Dargan. Gambrell wrote, "Dr. Graves wrote much on the subject [alien immersion], but in the course of his editorial work. There is more or less of it in nearly all his books but his writings, as you know, were usually crude and his facts over-colored."[12]

Later proponents of Landmarkism tended to follow Gambrell's method, i.e., slight to moderate criticism of Graves' methods while yet defending and promoting some facet(s) of Landmark doctrine. This is not to say that Graves did not have his staunch supporters and defenders among Southern Baptists. These tended to fade away over time, as we will see, and his name as well as the term Landmarkism became a largely forgotten expression among Southern Baptists except among historians. However, this did not happen immediately as the following examples will show.

Frank L. Wilkins, noted Southern Baptist pastor, in a sermon reprinted in the *Baptist and Reflector* in 1897, noted the march of the Baptist church through the centuries and those who were ready "to resist these corrupting

9. See https://groups.yahoo.com/neo/groups/LandmarkSouthernBaptist/info (emphasis added).
10. J. B. Jeter to J. R. Graves, 17 September 1879.
11. Tull, *High-Church Baptists in the South*, 133.
12. J. B. Gambrell to E. C. Dargan, 4 November 1895.

influences" [of the Roman Catholic Church]. Among the spiritually-minded men and women who resisted, even at the cost of martyrdom, he listed the Montanists, Novatians, Donatists, Paulicians, Albigenses, and Pickards.[13] These groups are the same set forth by Orchard and widely published by Graves. Wilkins adds that these groups were Baptists because, "They fearlessly repudiated all baptisms administered by the apostate church as no baptisms, and led anew to the waters of baptism ever convert they made from Rome.... The popish authorities ... retorted by calling the baptism administered by the dissenters 'ana' or 're'-baptism, hence the title 'Anabaptists' ... dropping of the prefix gives us 'Baptists' the term commonly used today."[14] We see no mention of Graves or Landmarkism, but church succession is set forth and this by a pastor who later was not in the Southwest but pastor of the First Baptist Church of Glouster, Massachusetts, a church of around six hundred members.

However, the name of J. R. Graves and his influence did not just disappear. A survey of relevant articles in the decade following his death (June 26, 1893) shows not only a fondness for his memory but an embracing of the basic tenets of Landmarkism.

H. C. Vedder, professor of church history at Crozer Theological Seminary from 1894–1927, wrote an article for the *Watchman* which was later carried in the *Baptist and Reflector* on "The Folly of Open Communion." Vedder did not specifically identify the names of the sects who passed down the Baptist distinctive of believer's baptism but his argument for close communion suggests that it would dishonor the sacrifice of so many martyrs down through the ages. He adds, "To abandon strict communion, therefore, is to admit that we have no valid reason of denominational existence."[15] Another article followed one week later in which he says, "We have a definite 'Thus saith the Lord' for strict communion and we have it in the Great Commission."[16] Vedder makes this associative jump from the word "baptizing" in Matthew 28:19 to the proper mode of baptism, to the implied administrators of that mode, to communion being restricted to those of the true church, i.e., those who have been baptized in the proper way.

One week later J. M. Phillips, pastor of the Baptist Church at Mossy Creek, Tennessee, and son-in-law of A. C. Dayton, wrote an article on the

13. *Baptist and Reflector* 8.40 (Nashville), 27 May 1897.
14. Ibid.
15. *Baptist and Reflector* 9.21 (Nashville), 13 January 1898. Vedder's description of what the Baptists of antiquity suffered is compared to that of the role of the faithful in Hebrews 11, i.e., "sawn asunder, slain with the sword, went about in sheepskins and goatskins..."
16. *Baptist and Reflector* 9.22 (Nashville), 20 January 1898.

scriptural grounds for close communion. Again, without listing the sects in the line of Baptist church succession, he added as an aside that the Catholics, "with the exception of the Baptists, are the oldest denomination." In reference to communion with Pedobaptists he said, "To practice open communion would be to admit this claim and endorse their baptism as Scriptural."[17]

Though neither Graves nor Landmarkism were mentioned specifically in the above examples it was not long before Graves' name was in the pages of the *Baptist and Reflector*. The occasion was a solicitation of funds for an endowment of a professorship at Southwestern Baptist University, Jackson, Tennessee, to be known as the J. R. Graves Professorship.[18] Among the reasons given to justify such a tribute to Graves were: to "perpetuate his memory . . . this Institution . . . was nearer in accord with his doctrinal teachings than any other institution."[19] This article was followed a week later by an appeal for funds, first for the endowment and second for a marble monument to mark the burial site of Graves, "as a more personal tribute to the great hero who did so much for our Baptist cause in all this Southwestern part of the country."[20]

There were also some who ever stood ready to come to the defense of Graves' views when called into question by others. One key figure in this effort was O. L. Hailey, Graves' son-in-law and biographer, whose defense of Graves was noted in chapter 2. Hailey was one of the leaders of the campaign to endow the professorship in memory of Graves. He was a professor at Southwestern Baptist University.[21] Illustrative of Hailey's defense of Graves was a request for a retraction/correction regarding an article about Graves:

> It has been published in the Western Recorder . . . that Dr. J. B. Hawthorne, at the Alabama Convention said Dr. Graves believed in Spiritism. I have been unwilling to believe that the magnanimous and chivalrous Dr. Hawthorne could do such a thing. I hope he will enter his public denial. But if he or anyone else ever got the idea that Dr. Graves believed in Spiritism let me say that he believed in nothing less.[22]

---

17. *Baptist and Reflector* 9.23 (Nashville), 27 January 1898. A previous article about Phillips' preaching at Carson-Newman College described him as "one of the strongest men in the state" (*Baptist and Reflector* [Nashville, TN] 30 December 1897.)

18. It was Graves' wish that this chair be named the Chair of Logic and Moral Philosophy. *Baptist and Reflector* 9.33 (Nashville), 7 April 1898.

19. *Baptist and Reflector* 9.31 (Nashville), 24 March 1898.

20. *Baptist and Reflector* 9.32 (Nashville), 31 March 1898.

21. Wardin, *Tennessee Baptists*, 323.

22. *Baptist and Reflector* 9.33 (Nashville), 7 April 1898.

It must be said that Graves did not hold to Spiritism but many of his views of the intermediate state of the soul as outlined in chapter 2 could easily lie behind Hawthorne's critique. Hailey and other prominent Baptists through the early part of the twentieth century repeatedly came to defend Graves against any suggestion that his doctrine was anything less than orthodox.

Even when the names of the Landmarkers or Landmarkism itself are not mentioned the doctrines they espoused are clearly seen in articles and correspondence. In a letter to the editor another Tennessee Baptist argued against receiving "Hardshell Baptists"[23] into membership on the basis of their baptism, even if by immersion. The writer said of them, "I am unwilling to ask any Baptist church to receive [members] on their baptism. . . . We are the only true church. Christ didn't say, 'I will build my churches,' but 'my church.' The Hardshells or the Baptist denomination one is wrong: both can't be the true church of Christ."[24]

As was pointed out in chapter 2, even the criticism of Graves was couched in terms like "peculiar." *Ford's Christian Repository* carried an article on Graves and said of his Christology: "Graves held somewhat peculiar views of the twofold nature of the Lord Jesus—views with which I cannot agree. He supposed that the soul, or spirit of the man Christ Jesus, was not a human soul, but the Deity incarnate, and as a consequence that 'the travail of His soul' involved suffering in the Deity."[25] The church historically has not called this view "peculiar' but rather a form of Apollinarianism.

It must be noted that during this period some periodicals, most notably the *Religious Herald* of Richmond, Virginia, carried articles by several various authors that repudiated the doctrines of an authorized administrator and church succession. They also noted that many of these controversies like pulpit affiliation and seating of ministers of other denominations which had marked many of the earlier conventions were now, thankfully, a thing of the past.[26]

Landmark Doctrine Propagated

As the twentieth century moved on the name of Landmarkism and Graves et al. were seen and referenced less and less but the Landmark doctrines

---

23. The Hardshell Baptists grew up in opposition to mission boards, tract societies, and cooperation with other churches in such efforts.

24. *Baptist and Reflector* 9.51 (Nashville), 11 August 1898.

25. *Ford's Christian Repository and Home* Circle 64.6, 350.

26. For examples, see the *Religious Herald* of June 5, 1902, August 21, 1902, and August 28, 1902.

were promoted and fostered by many Southern Baptists in positions of influence. A look behind the scenes, by way of personal correspondence, in the preparation of *A History of the Baptists, Together with Some Account of Their Principles and Practices*, by John T. Christian, will give some insight into one of the ways in which this was affected. A survey of other writings and religious periodicals will also shed light on the spread of Landmark principles throughout the Southern Baptist Convention.

Christian's History of the Baptists and Church Succession

In September 1916 I. J. Van Ness wrote to Christian regarding the fact that "the [Southern Baptist] Convention ordered" the preparation of a Southern Baptist history.[27] Van Ness says that the author of this history has been somewhat determined by events which have taken place although nothing is finalized at this time. He asks Christian in the letter for any resources he might have to aid in the project.[28]

The other author that had been somewhat determined was B. F. Riley. Riley had been president of Howard College in Birmingham, Alabama, from 1888–1898, a professor at the University of Georgia from 1898–1900 and pastor of First Baptist Church in Houston, Texas, from 1900–1906. Riley had written on Baptist history, having previously produced histories of Baptists in Alabama and Texas.[29] In ways that are not exactly clear, however, Christian was the one selected to compile the Baptist history.

Some indications of the factors which motivated that decision are found in Van Ness' correspondence. He writes to Christian of the difficulties in getting all the committee members together to review "the Riley history." He adds, "I think we are all agreed about certain matters; as for example . . . the material dealing with the earlier centuries."[30] Later he wrote, "I am hoping to get a memorandum from you about the Riley History. Dr. Dargan and I have been going over it carefully. There is one section of it from 1814–1848

---

27. Van Ness worked at the Sunday School Board as editorial secretary from 1900–1917 at which time he became executive secretary and treasurer of the Sunday School Board. He also served as president of the Sunday School Editor's Association of the United States and Canada, chairman of the editorial section of the Sunday School Council of Evangelical Denominations, a member of the International Sunday School lesson committee, president of the Sunday School Council of Evangelical Denominations, and a member of World's Sunday School Executive Committee. He retired from the Sunday School Board in 1935 (see "I. J. Van Ness Papers").

28. I. J. Van Ness to J. T. Christian 22 September 1916.

29. See Riley, *History of the Baptists of Alabama* and *History of the Baptists of Texas*.

30. I. J. Van Ness to J. T. Christian 17 September 1919.

which, with the exception of the discussion of Landmarkism, is very finely written."[31]

Although that is not definitive, in and of itself, a later letter clarified the difficulty. Van Ness acknowledges receipt of a letter from Christian which included letters form I. N. Penick, professor at Union University, and H. E. Watters, president of Union University. Van Ness writes, "I am sure you have understood and appreciated, as they do not seem to do, the difficulties in which we found ourselves through our venture in Baptist history."[32] Penick had written to Christian, "Some of us have had fears that the Riley move did not come from the right source."[33] Apparently, the selection of Christian over Riley was a matter of some concern. Van Ness continued, "Until we went past the Southern Baptist Convention we were not fairly into the open. I think the passing of that point left us clear on this subject. It is of course impossible for either you or for me to explain to some of your friends the delicate situation."[34]

The delicate situation becomes clear later in that same correspondence.

> I confess I do not exactly understand the tone of Dr. Penick's letter. Surely he has not been very well informed as to the Riley matter and its course. I can hardly imagine what he could mean—can you? Perhaps it is a pity that he has not had to wrestle with some of the problems, and especially the ones which Dr. Hailey and myself have been worrying over in the treatment of the Graves matter. So far as you are concerned you never got so far as the Whitsett [sic] question, but you would have had some sensations if you had done so.[35]

If Hailey was wrestling with the problem one can be sure that it was one which held views contrary to Graves or views critical of him.

A brief review of Christian's *History* shows how Graves' ideas and the continuation of the position against Whitsitt's views were propagated. Christian devotes seventeen chapters to the tracing of the heritage of the Anabaptists and a defense of the antiquity and perpetuation of baptism of believers by immersion. Five of those chapters are devoted to ancient and medieval Baptist churches. He defends the Montanists because "they insisted that those who had 'lapsed' from the true faith be rebaptized . . . on

---

31. I. J. Van Ness to J. T. Christian, 11 October 1919.
32. I. J. Van Ness to J. T. Christian, 3 July 1920.
33. I. N. Penick to J. T. Christian, 29 June 1920.
34. Van Ness to Christian, 3 July 1920.
35. Ibid.

this account they were termed 'Anabaptists,' and some of their principles reappeared in Anabaptism."³⁶

He speaks approvingly of the Novatians and quotes Robinson (*Ecclesiastical Researches*) as tracing "a continuation of them up to the reformation and the rise of the Anabaptist movement . . . all over the Empire Puritan churches were constituted and flourished through two hundred succeeding years."³⁷ He treats the Cathari similarly, "They rebaptized those who came to them from other communions [thus] they were called Anabaptists."³⁸

The Albigenses he called, quoting approvingly from Robinson, "Trinitarian Baptists," and noted, "They held to the independence of the churches."³⁹ In discussing the Donatists, he noted the caution with which David Benedict had treated them in his history, but noted, "In his last days he went into the original sources and produced a remarkable book called a 'History of the Donatists' (Pawtucket, 1875). In that book he recedes from his noncommittal position and classes them as Baptists. He quite freely shows . . . that the Donatists rejected infant baptism and were congregational in their form of government."⁴⁰ That is, as Christian would admit, a very loose and far-reaching definition of a Baptist. He also quotes approvingly from Osiander, "Our modern Anabaptists are the same as the Donatists of old."⁴¹

As Christian continues to trace Baptist origins, he says of the Paulicians, "The Paulician churches were of apostolic origin."⁴² He acknowledges that the Paulicians were considered by many to be Manichæans but he comes to their defense and says, "They held to the orthodox view of the Trinity; and to the human nature and substantial sufferings of the Son of God." He added quite boldly, "Baptist views prevailed among the Paulicians . . . they baptized and rebaptized by immersion."⁴³ Once again there is a very minimalist view of what constitutes one a Baptist. He does say, "It is possible that the Paulicians were Adoptionists." However, he justifies that later by adding, "It is certain that the Adoptionist views of the Paulicians accentuated their opposition to infant baptism."⁴⁴ One fails to see the connection or justification for such a position.

36. Christian, *History of the Baptists*, 43.
37. Ibid., 44. He quotes Robinson, *Ecclesiastical Researches*, 1792.
38. Ibid., 45.
39. Ibid.
40. Ibid. He quotes from Benedict, *History of the Donatists*, 1875.
41. Ibid., 46.
42. Ibid., 49.
43. Ibid., 55.
44. Ibid., 56–57.

Regarding the Reformation and the Anabaptists, Christian portrays the Anabaptists as the one branch of the Reformation who revived the authority and sufficiency of Scripture. He writes, "The Reformers aimed to reform the Roman Catholic Church by the Bible; the Baptists went directly to the apostolic age and accepted the Bible alone as their rule of faith and practice.... They were orthodox in the articles of the Christian faith."[45] In contrast with the *solas* of the Reformation (*sola fide, sola gratia, sola Scriptura*), Christian held "the nature of a church was the fundamental contention of the Baptist movement of the Reformation."[46] The nature of the church is the *sine qua non* of the Landmark movement and in Christian's judgment what it means to be a Baptist.

Christian was not ignorant of the views of many of these so-called Baptists. In the preface to his *History* he explains the theological inconsistencies of these various groups:

> Many examples might be introduced to show that some of these parties might not be recognized by some Baptists now-a-days. The Montanists, the Novatians, and the Donatists held diverse opinions, not only from each other but from the teachings of the New Testament; but they stressed tremendously the purity of the church. It is possible that the Paulicians were Adoptionists. There have always been different views in regard to the birth of Jesus. Some of the Anabaptists held that Jesus was a man, and that he did not derive his manhood from Mary, but passed through her as a channel. The Adoptionists held that Jesus was endowed with divinity at his baptism. Most modern Baptists hold that Jesus became incarnate at his birth.... No effort is here attempted to minimize, or dismiss as trivial, these variations.
>
> Through all these variations, however, there has been an insistence upon some great fundamental truths. There has ever been the vital necessity of a regenerated life; a church pure and separate from the ungodly; believers' baptism; a simple form of church government; the right of free speech and soul liberty; and the permanent and paramount authority of the New Testament. Whatever may have been the variations in any or all of these parties, on the above or kindred subjects the voice of the Baptists has rung clear and distinct.[47]

The questions which hang over this explanation are: how can one hold to the "paramount authority" of the New Testament and hold

---

45. Ibid., 103.
46. Ibid.
47. Ibid., 5.

different views about the person of Christ; how can those like the Donatists hold views different from the New Testament and be considered Baptists; how can issues like free speech, soul liberty, and a simple form of church government be equated with fundamental truths like regeneration and the authority of Scripture?

The position of influential Baptists toward Christian's *History* is epitomized by the comments of E. Y. Mullins.[48]

> I am very much pleased with the manner you approach the subject of Baptist history, and especially Baptist succession. I think the position which you take in the Preface, and which you observe in the treatment of the subject, is the true and wise one for the Baptist historian. You frankly recognize the fact that many of the parties of the middle ages and others which have frequently been claimed as in all particulars conforming to modern Baptist churches, and therefore in the line of succession, have varied to greater or less extent from present day Baptist doctrines. This has been my objection to some of the histories which have been printed heretofore. They have proved too much. The facts of the case showed that there were divergencies and variations, but show clearly that Baptists have always allowed a certain degree of latitude in belief without necessarily ceasing to be classified in a general way among Baptists.
>
> I believe there have always been genuine spiritual witnesses to the Gospel and people who have been, in the fundamental and spiritual phases of our Baptist belief, true to the convictions of the Baptists of today.[49]

It is highly probable that following immediately after Whitsitt's resignation, prompted by this very issue, that Mullins was careful in his criticism of the medieval groups claimed to be Baptist in the line of church succession. However, the questions remain, what are the fundamental Baptist beliefs, and how much "latitude" does one have when it comes to the Person and work of Christ and the authority of Scripture? The unmistakable inference from what has been written in the early decades after the death of the original Landmarkers is that church government, the mode and subjects of baptism, and freedoms associated with the American political experience often trump biblical doctrine in the determination of the true, i.e., Baptist churches. For all the academic hair-splitting, to the casual reader Christian's

---

48. Mullins succeeded Whitsitt as president of Southern Baptist Theological Seminary and served there from 1899–1928. He was president of the Southern Baptist Convention from 1921–1924.

49. E. Y. Mullins to J. T. Christian, 12 July 1918.

History did little to dispel any notions of church succession as promoted by the Landmarkers.

C. C. Carroll's "Sonnets of John the Baptist"

C. C. Carroll, son of B. H. Carroll, was a Southern Baptist pastor and professor. He pastored the Third Baptist Church, Owensboro, Kentucky. After a very public conflict there he went on to the First Baptist Church, Winchester, Kentucky, and later to New Orleans Baptist Bible Institute (later New Orleans Baptist Theological Seminary).[50] Carroll authored a chapter in Victor Masters' compilation *Re-thinking Baptist Doctrines*. Carroll's chapter bore the title "Baptists Not Protestants." It followed the Landmark assertion that the Baptist churches did not come out of the Reformation but could be traced to the formation of the first church when Jesus called some from the disciples of John the Baptist.

Carroll also wrote eighteen sonnets devoted, as he said, "to bringing out in concrete form at least some of the salient features and fundamental principles in the life and teachings of John the Baptist."[51] There is no record of the publication of Carroll's poetry but a look at the correspondence with Van Ness of the Sunday School Board is revealing. In his original correspondence he noted, "You will note I have written from a Baptist standpoint which it seems to me is fairly appropriate since it is a Baptist under discussion. . . . This effort of mine has at least the merit of Baptist integrity."[52] Later Carroll wrote to Van Ness and his correspondence includes a rather curious phrase. He wrote, "There are some particular phases of Baptist doctrine and Baptist Democracy brought out in these sonnets that I am hopeful would be of help in our great indoctrination campaign."[53] One has to ask: who is being indoctrinated and for what purpose? But this follows close on the resignation of Whitsitt, the efforts to publish Christian's *History* are underway, and Carroll's uncle J. M. Carroll is giving his lectures on *The Trail of Blood* which in time will prove to have the widest circulation of all these works.

---

50. Moody, *Heaven for a Dime*, 4. There seems to be some confusion surrounding the date Carroll went to New Orleans. His own letter to Van Ness, however, gives the date as October 1919 (C. C. Carroll to I. J. Van Ness, 11 August 1919.)

51. C. C. Carroll to I. J. Van Ness, 23 July 1919.

52. Ibid.

53. C. C. Carroll to I. J. Van Ness, 10 January 1920.

Baptist Periodicals

The Baptist newspapers and other periodicals were key in originally shaping and propagating Landmark doctrines. In the papers of Rufus W. Weaver[54] an undated rough manuscript (the date is ca. 1928 as he refers to the Whitsitt affair as being "thirty years ago") makes the point that "the important factor in the moulding [sic] of public opinion among Baptists have been and are the Baptist papers."[55] He discusses the impact of the various newspapers in the Whitsitt controversy (see chapter 4) but he adds interestingly, "The episode to the study of which I invite your attention is one that probably will never have a place in any standard Baptist history."[56] What would exclude the Whitsitt controversy from any Baptist history? Weaver is not clear, but the treatment Whitsitt received at the hands of the Landmarkers and the influence of the Baptist papers in molding public opinion may have led him to conclude the details of Whitsitt's case would remain buried.

Control of those papers in Kentucky, Tennessee, Arkansas, Texas, and parts of Alabama remained for the most part firmly in the hands of Landmarkers or those with Landmark leanings. A prime example was E. E. Folk who was the owner and editor of the *Baptist and Reflector* from 1888–1917. Folk purchased the *Baptist Reflector* of Chattanooga, Tennessee, in 1888. In 1889 he merged that paper with Graves' *Baptist* published in Memphis, Tennessee, and the new paper took the name the *Baptist and Reflector*. That same year Graves' son-in-law O. L. Hailey bought the interests of Graves and J. B. Moody, whose paper had merged with the *Baptist*, and Folk and Hailey were the proprietors and editors of the *Baptist and Reflector*.[57] Graves maintained his own column in the paper until his death. Folk agreed with Landmark principles although he worked to unify Baptists and did not attack those with differing opinions as Graves had done.

Folk leaned more toward Christian's view that a strict succession of Baptist churches could not be maintained but nonetheless Baptists had existed in every time since the founding of the church in Jerusalem. Folk wrote, "You cannot put your finger upon any year this side of the Apostles

---

54. Rufus W. Weaver was an influential Baptist who held a variety of positions within the Southern Baptist Convention and pastored several different Baptist churches. In 1919 he was the president of the Education Committee of the Southern Baptist Convention. He served from 1917–1920 as president of the Education Board of the Tennessee Baptist Convention and from 1918–1927 as president of Mercer University. From 1927–1928 he was corresponding secretary of the Education Board of the Southern Baptist Convention (see "Introduction to Rufus W. Weaver Papers").

55. Weaver, "Episode in Baptist History."

56. Ibid. Weaver was the last student to receive a degree at the hands of Whitsitt.

57. Wardin, *Tennessee Baptists*, 246–47.

and say that the Baptists originated then. The only place to look for their origin is in the New Testament."[58]

Despite admitted meager historical evidence Folk writes that down through the ages there have been people holding to essential Baptist principles. Among those people he lists the "Novatianists [sic], Donatists, Cathari, Paulicians, Vaudois, Petrobrusians, Henricians, Albigenses, Waldenses, Anabaptists, and Mennonites." He adds, "It is not claimed that all of these sects held all Baptist principles, but that all of them held some Baptist principle—some essential Baptist principle—so as to differentiate them from other denominations besides Baptists and classify them more or less distinctly as Baptists."[59] The implications of this line of thinking are all too obvious. A group may be heretical in many aspects but practice baptism by immersion and be essentially Baptist. Folk ends his remarks thus, "While we may not be able to trace a succession of Baptist churches all down the line of history, we can, as we have seen, trace a succession of essential Baptist principles. The existence of the principles would indicate the existence of the churches."[60] Such were the views of the editor of the Baptist paper published in the city where the offices of the Southern Baptist Convention made its home. Such were the views of the paper which Weaver said was instrumental in molding the views of Baptists.

Dissenting Voices

Of course, not every article or paper was sympathetic to the Landmark view. Just as it had been in the glory days of Graves and the *Tennessee Baptist* not all Baptists held to or were even receptive to the furtherance of Landmark doctrines. A. T. Robertson, one of the great Southern Baptist scholars, was quite critical of the Landmarkers and their attacks on Whitsitt (see chapter 4). The *Baptist World* carried a long article by Robertson in 1916 entitled "Heresy among Southern Baptists." This was emblazoned on the front page of the paper. The chief subject of the article was J. R. Graves. In it Robertson takes Graves to task over his views of mission boards, ecclesiology, pulpit affiliation, alien immersion, and cooperation with other denominations. Several long quotations will serve to illustrate Robertson's position.

> The career of Dr. J. R. Graves has also left a deep mark upon the life of Southern Baptists. Dr. B. H. Carroll once spoke of the

58. E. E. Folk, unpublished notes of speech.
59. Ibid.
60. Ibid.

region "where the soul of J. R. Graves goes marching on" . . . it was chiefly in doctrine that his influence was felt. . . . He taught a more rigid Baptist ecclesiasticism that regarded Pedobaptists as outside of the Kingdom of God, which is composed entirely of Baptist churches . . . he insisted that Baptists have existed through all the centuries since Christ as the sole Kingdom of God. He restricted the term "church" to a local body, but used the word Kingdom as practically Baptist church in the general sense. . . . Baptists who accepted the teaching of Graves assumed a more hostile and less fraternal attitude toward other evangelical denominations like the Methodists and Presbyterians, who did not relish being told that they were outside the pale of the Kingdom of God.

Pulpit affiliation was the first test of this view. It was demanded of orthodox Baptists that they refuse to affiliate with Pedobaptist ministers in any way at all. [In addition], the Graves view added a new argument to the dispute already on hand about alien immersion. Southern Baptists had long been divided over the wisdom of accepting immersion at the hands of those not Baptists, but they were willing to disagree in theory and practice and work together as brethren. The Graves view made the rejection of alien immersion a test of fellowship. This position has probably caused more trouble among Southern Baptists than any other doctrinal issue. [This is still the case as will be shown later.]

Another corollary of the Graves theory of Baptist doctrine is to make Baptist church succession a test of fellowship. If the Kingdom of God is composed only of Baptist churches, then Baptist churches must have existed always, else the Kingdom of God has been snapped in two. It is due to the imperative demand of this view that various sects in the early centuries with all sorts of heretical teachings have been called Baptists by some modern Baptist theologians. . . . It is now openly demanded by advocates of the Graves' view as an article of sound Baptist faith that, in spite of any evidence we must believe that Baptist churches have always existed.[61]

Robertson added that the attempts to make the Graves views a test of orthodoxy had failed and said, "We do not call the followers of Graves heretics, but we deny the right of his adherents to call the other Baptists heretics."[62]

---

61 Robertson, "Heresy among Southern Baptists," 5–6.
62. Ibid.

Of course, with Baptist papers being the shapers of Baptist thought, such charges could not go unanswered and it was not long before Robertson was answered by Graves' chief protagonist, O. L. Hailey. Hailey's response published in the *Baptist Advance* was reprinted in the *Baptist World*. Hailey accused Robertson of "either carelessness or lack of discrimination" in his treatment of Graves views.[63] Hailey repeats throughout the article that Robertson "finds that Dr. Graves was a divisive force and a leader into heresy."[64] If Robertson stopped short of calling the adherents of Graves" views heretics, as he did, Hailey is overstating the case.

Hailey's arguments in defense of Graves are equally telling. He writes, "Dr. Robertson finds that Graves was a divisive force and a leader into heresy because of his views concerning the 'Kingdom and the church.'" But he adds, as has been the case in the defense of Graves' positions by many, "Dr. Graves was not always clear as to his views about these questions . . . but [he believed] that Baptist churches were and are the 'executives of the Kingdom.'"[65] On the question of pulpit affiliation, Hailey merely summarizes Graves' doctrine that no one "except a church of Jesus Christ could make a man a Gospel minister . . . [and to give] official recognition to a Pedobaptist minister as if he were a Scripturally qualified minister . . . was leading the church to an endorsement of what the church did not believe."[66] He challenges Robertson to call that heresy, if he dare, "and he will find the views of Dr. Graves as to this point are still held by Southern Baptists."[67] Hailey is asserting that Robertson's views of Graves' theology are outside the mainstream of Southern Baptist thought. On the question of alien immersion, Hailey notes that Robertson admits there are two different opinions among Baptists and asks if Robertson is willing to call Graves a heretic because he differs with him on the question. Hailey's summation is quite telling. He said, "The views held by Dr. J. R. Graves were not and never were intended to be divisive. And one would be inclined to believe that there is a concerted and long-sustained effort to discount Dr. Graves before the denomination."[68]

Hailey understood the power of the religious press and was quick to come to the defense of Graves, as were others. Hailey's influence was even seen in some subtle ways. Graves' opposition to the historical view that

---

63. Hailey, "Dr. Robertson's Reflections," 25.
64. Ibid.
65. Ibid.
66. Ibid.
67. Ibid.
68. Ibid.

Roger Williams established the first Baptist church in America has been discussed earlier. When a movement was begun in the Southern Baptist Convention to build a Roger Williams Memorial Church, Hailey responded in a letter to Van Ness: "The other thing that I would say is that I do not approve the undertaking to build that Roger Williams Memorial Church, at all. I do not tax you to give my reasons now, as I can do."[69] The reason is clear. Such an undertaking would run counter to the views of Graves and serious damage is done to Baptist church succession by accepting the view that Williams was pastor of the first Baptist church in America.[70]

Regarding Hailey's view of history and his constant defense and promotion of Graves it should be noted that the Tennessee Baptist Convention authorized the publication of a Baptist state history. "O. L. Hailey was contracted to write a history, but in 1930 his manuscript, 'History of the Baptists of Tennessee,' was rejected and placed in the archives."[71] Hailey's manuscript represents Graves as the paragon of Tennessee Baptists in publishing, education, preaching, and as the champion of the Baptist cause. He mentions that Graves was largely self-educated but never explains how he became "Dr. Graves." He mentions that the controversy with Howell and the First Baptist Church of Nashville "could have a lasting influence upon the Baptists of Middle Tennessee . . . and we are not beyond its influence."[72] He notes, "If five of the most gifted geniuses of the 19th century should be named, Dr. J. R. Graves would be one of the five."[73] By comparison Hailey gives scant mention to Pendleton in the thirty-eight pages he devotes to the history of Union University and gives no biographical sketch of Pendleton although he lists many obscure and little-know Tennessee Baptists. He does not mention Pendleton's association with Graves and merely says, "Because of his pronounced political views he decided to move to the North."[74] Examples of this type must be considered when we see Hailey constantly coming to the defense of Graves. This biased view of history led to the rejection of Hailey's manuscript.

One of the stranger voices of dissent was E. P. Alldredge who did not find fault with Graves, Pendleton, et al., but in fact blamed the Landmark Baptists who split from the Southern Baptist Convention for advancing the

69. O. L. Hailey to I. J. Van Ness, 29 April 1919.
70. See Graves, *First Baptist Church in America*.
71. Wardin, *Tennessee Baptists*, 483.
72. Hailey, "History of the Baptists of Tennessee," photocopy of typewritten manuscript, 212
73. Ibid., 422.
74. Ibid., 217.

idea that the Landmarkers held different doctrinal positions from mainline Southern Baptists. Alldredge was the first secretary of the Department of Survey, Statistics, and Information of the Sunday School Board of the Southern Baptist Convention and he served in that position for twenty-five years from 1920–1945. Tull says of Alldredge, he was "a Landmark extremist."[75]

This is clearly demonstrated in a letter written by Alldredge to A. A. Riner, Holly Grove, Arkansas. The occasion of the letter was Riner's request for counsel regarding a pending lawsuit by the Landmark Baptists. Alldredge's advice centers on his contention that the Landmarkers have no basis for a lawsuit as they hold to the same doctrinal positions as the Southern Baptists. For example, he writes, "Now coming to the supposed doctrinal differences between Convention Baptists and Landmark Baptists, let me say there is no difference."[76]

To substantiate that there were no differences Alldredge offered up the following proofs: "Both Convention Baptists and Landmark Baptists agree with the doctrinal positions held by J. M. Pendleton, J. R. Graves, J. N. Hall, and so on. For example, the standard statement of the doctrinal position of this school of Baptist writers and leaders is summed up in a little book by J. R. Graves entitled 'Old Landmarkism.'"[77] Alldredge goes on to list the seven marks of a gospel church as outlined by Graves. He then adds, "There is not a Baptist church in Arkansas which does not hold these seven marks of the gospel church."[78] He follows the reference to Graves' description of the church in chapter three of *Old Landmarkism* with the assertion that it is that doctrine to which "every Convention Baptist of Arkansas heartily subscribes."[79] Alldredge quotes approvingly from Graves throughout the four-page letter and equates Graves' doctrine with the position of all Southern Baptists. It was Alldredge's true belief that Graves, Pendleton, and the other Landmark voices were not Landmark voices at all but rather the true voice of the Southern Baptist Convention. He wrote to J. T. Sheppard, "I have had considerable experience in combating Landmarkism."[80] Yet he combats Landmarkism with a book entitled *Old Landmarkism* which sets forth the essence of Landmark doctrine.

The Landmark doctrine found its way, if even very subtly, into the educational materials of the Southern Baptist Convention. *The Doctrines of*

---

75. Tull, *High-Church Baptists in the South*, 170.
76. E. P. Alldredge to A. A. Riner, 25 September 1920.
77. Ibid.
78. Ibid.
79. Ibid.
80. E. P. Alldredge to J. T. Sheppard, 3 July 1920.

Our Faith, by E. C. Dargan, was part of the "Convention Normal Course" for which credit was awarded to church members as part of the education ministry of Southern Baptist Churches. Dargan was described by Tull as too large-minded to be squeezed into the Landmark mold. However, Dargan showed the influence and pervasiveness of Landmark doctrine, along with the good sense to refrain from openly disagreeing with the Landmark positions.

For example, regarding the relation of Baptist churches to the church of the New Testament, Dargan asked the question, have the Baptist churches of today any real historic connection to the New Testament church? To this he replied,

> As to the historic connection, we can only say in brief that many of the sects all through Christian history endeavored to conform their churches in idea and organization to the model of the New Testament. Through these there may be some historic, though not always demonstrable, connection, down to the Anabaptists in Europe and the Baptists in England and America.[81]

While Dargan's view could not be called dissent in the same way as Robertson's, he clearly does not subscribe wholeheartedly to the Landmark view. However, being at Southern Baptist Theological Seminary during the Whitsitt controversy may have tempered his explanation of the succession of Baptist churches.

In the same way, he describes the "church universal" as "the whole number of the Lord's true people in all times and places," but he quickly adds, "We should always remember that there is no mention or even suggestion of a great organized body in any passage of Scripture which speaks of the church."[82] He says that we use this phrase only for convenience and not as an expression of the nature, construction, or constitution of the church.

During the first quarter of the twentieth-century Landmark doctrine found its way into much of the Southern Baptist educational material both at the seminary level and at the local church. Due to the Landmark Baptist schism and the pulling away of a number of churches the terms Landmark and Landmarkism disappeared from Southern Baptist writings and teachings but the Landmark doctrines remained quite well established and were fostered by many in key positions within the Southern Baptist Convention which controlled publication and propagation of teaching materials.

---

81. Dargan, *Doctrines of Our Faith*, 166–67.
82. Ibid., 145.

Landmark Doctrine Mainstreamed

As the Southern Baptist Convention moved into the second quarter of the twentieth century the terms Landmark and Landmarkism were seen and heard even less than in the preceding quarter century. However, Landmark doctrine was very visible. These doctrines were not identified as Landmark doctrines, but they were set forth in journals, periodicals, speeches, and instructional materials as Baptist doctrine, i.e., Southern Baptist doctrine. Some like E. P. Alldredge clearly identified Landmarkism as the true Baptist doctrine. In 1922 Alldredge wrote regarding the "difference between Landmark Baptists and Convention Baptists," i.e., Southern Baptist Convention Baptists, "that there were no such things as Landmark Baptists anywhere on the earth until 1902 when Ben Bogard and Dr. W. A. Clark originated this trouble."[83] Apparently, he ignored the title of Graves et al. as Landmarkers and Landmark Baptists. Alldredge, however, in true Graves' form, says of Bogard, "[He] is the most unscrupulous man whom I know in religious work anywhere in the United States."[84] Alldredge says of the Landmark Baptists that they are not Landmarkers at all but use precisely the same arguments "used by the first four Hardshell Baptists: John Taylor, Alexander Campbell, Gilbert Parker, and Elder Bebee."[85] The schismatics who claimed to be Landmark Baptists were labeled by Alldredge as "not real Landmark Baptists [but] modernized Hardshell Baptists."[86] We see here efforts to remove any stigma from the title Landmark and claim Landmark Baptist principles as the true doctrines of the Southern Baptists.

While others were not as obvious as Alldredge there was a very clear affirmation of many key Landmark doctrines during the second quarter of the twentieth century. One article of the period contrasted liberalism with "the strict interpretations of the Baptist faith, known as Landmarkism. The germinal difference between the two phases of doctrine were, open and close communion, alien and anti-alien Baptism, and official sectarian affiliation."[87] In order to make this even more clear these examples are grouped in the sections that follow under the headings of prominent Landmark principles as articulated by Graves and the Landmarkers.

---

83. E. P. Alldredge to J. C. Cochcroft, 22 December 1922.
84. Ibid.
85. E. P. Alldredge to S. B. Rogers, 18 July 1925.
86. Ibid.
87. Anderson, "Trend of Baptist Faith and Practice," 25 March 1920.

Alien Immersion

Despite the various controversies spawned by this doctrine in earlier days and the difficulties which entered in as one tried to establish that the one baptizing had himself been properly baptized, this doctrine is set forth as a test of fellowship and orthodoxy. The *Southwestern Journal of Theology*, the quarterly publication of the Southwestern Baptist Theological Seminary, carried in editorial form a strong condemnation of baptism administered by an unauthorized administrator. The article said that "the fountains of truth and life of our churches can be poisoned by doing violence to the ordinances of Jesus Christ, in depreciating their value and emasculating their testimony."[88] This violence is done "when a Baptist church receives baptism administered at the hands of some other organization than a Baptist church."[89] The Landmark influence is clearly seen in the reference to the church administering the baptism as an "organization" as opposed to the Baptist "church." In what amounts to a very serious warning to Baptist preachers the article said,

> If a Baptist preacher admits into the fellowship of his church Christians who have received baptism at the hands of pedo-baptists, without requiring them to be baptized by a Baptist church, he violates the truth of God and is guilty of heresy in ecclesiology which will eventually ruin the testimony of the ordinances and vitiate the witness of Christ's churches.[90]

The article does not specify whether the baptism in question was by immersion but the example that follows in the article makes the point even more demonstrable. The example concerned a woman who came to "one of the leading churches of Texas" seeking membership on transfer of letter from another Baptist church. However, upon being questioned more closely it was found that she was admitted to the previous church based on her baptism in a Campbellite church and had not been required to be re-baptized. Upon learning of this the pastor "promptly refused to admit this woman into the fellowship of his church."[91]

The influence of the seminaries was felt in the pastorate and echoed in the religious press. J. W. Porter was a noted Southern Baptist pastor who succeeded T. T. Eaton as editor of the *Western Recorder*. Porter, writing on

---

88. Scarborough, "Ways to Poison These Fountains," 91. Scarborough was the second president of Southwestern Seminary, following B. H. Carroll in that post.

89. Ibid., 92.

90. Ibid.

91. Ibid.

alien immersion, defined it as "a baptism that is not administered by Baptist churches, but is alien to, different from, and not belonging to Baptist churches . . . the very name itself offers strong presumptive proof against its acceptance by our churches."[92] As with the Landmarkers, Porter ties alien immersion closely with the recognition of other bodies as scriptural churches and the authority of the administrator. He says, "To admit other churches differing from us in faith and polity are scriptural churches, as many alien immersionists do, leads to 'confusion worse confounded.'" He adds, "A majority of the cases of alien immersion that are received by our churches are administered by ministers who have never been baptized. How can a man communicate that which he never possessed?"[93] He means the minister in question has never been immersed or baptized himself by an authorized administrator.

L. R. Scarborough, editor-in-chief of the *Southwestern Journal of Theology*, quoted J. B. Gambrell, four-time president of the Southern Baptist Convention, as saying, "One of the great perils to the life of the churches of Jesus Christ in recent years and at this time was the heresy in ecclesiology along the lines of inter-denominationalism, unionism, and along the lines of alien immersion."[94] The danger for the Baptist Church lies in the fact, according to Porter, that Pedo-Baptist or other churches are baptizing people and those baptisms are being accepted by Baptist churches. This necessarily means "Baptist churches are not essential to the carrying out of the commission of Christ. If Baptist churches are not essential to the carrying out of the commission of Christ, then [they] have no scriptural authority for . . . existence."[95] Apparently, Porter believes that the Great Commission has only been carried out through the efforts of Baptist churches.

Over a decade later the definition of the church in an article which appeared in the *Baptist and Reflector* leaned heavily on opposition to alien immersion without actually using the term. The article said, "A church (*ekklesia*) of Christ is an organized assembly of those who have repented of sin and trusted in Jesus Christ for salvation; who have been baptized (immersed) by a Scriptural authority."[96] That scriptural authority is defined as "a regular Baptist church through a regularly ordained Baptist preacher of the Word."[97] In that same year O. W. Taylor, editor of the *Baptist and Reflector*,

---

92. Porter, "Alien Immersion," 1.
93. Ibid., 4.
94. Scarborough, "Ways to Poison These Fountains," 93.
95. Ibid.
96. Bronson, "New Testament Church and Its Ordinances Defined," 4.
97. Ibid.

answered charges made by Ben Bogard that the Tennessee Baptist Convention had endorsed alien immersion by receiving into their membership churches of the Stone Association in 1919. The issue revolved around the fact that the churches of the Stone Association were Freewill Baptists. That, as Taylor explained it, was "a superficial matter and was not descriptive of the *real faith* of the body as a whole."[98] Taylor concluded the article with the following examples:

> There may be a *few individual* cases of men in the state who favor alien immersion and open communion, but the Tennessee Baptist Convention as a whole *does not* favor these things. Only last Sunday (Nov. 19), the editor's pastor, R. Kelly White, of Belmont Heights Baptist Church, Nashville, a Southern Baptist Convention man and the immediate past president of the Tennessee Baptist Convention and the chairman of the Executive Board of the Convention, declined to receive a lady on her Freewill baptism, and the lady agreed to be baptized. Our state secretary, Chas. W. Pope, is opposed to alien immersion and open communion. So is the editor.[99]

Taylor clearly marshals the testimony of prominent Southern Baptist and Tennessee Baptist figures to make his case. Also, very clear is the relationship between alien immersion and close communion.

Close Communion

The link between alien immersion and close communion as stated by Taylor is very clearly defined. Close communion was another Landmark tenet that was repeatedly defended as biblical, i.e., Southern Baptist doctrine, as the twentieth century progressed. A short tracing of its defense and propagation follows.

J. W. Porter saw very clearly the connection between alien immersion and close communion. He wrote, "Another fatal objection to receiving alien immersion is that to do so forces us to surrender the doctrine of restricted [close] communion."[100] To receive the baptism of Pedobaptists, Campbellites, Free Will Baptists, or others in effect would recognize their authority as scriptural churches. Thus, Porter affirmed, "Neither scripturally nor logically can we acknowledge their baptism and then deny

---

98. Taylor, "Tennessee Baptist Convention," 2 (emphasis in original).
99. Ibid. (emphasis in original).
100. Porter, "Alien Imersion," 4.

them the Supper. . . . No logically constructed mind can subscribe to the doctrine of restricted communion and alien immersion at the same time; to accept one is to reject the other."[101]

Charles Bronson, cited above, said of the Lord's Supper, it "is a memorial ordinance engaged in by the members of a New Testament church (a regular Baptist church)."[102] His parenthetical expression leaves little doubt as to the identity of the New Testament Church. He makes that even more clear later when he says, "Open communion cannot be here. It is twin brother to Alien Immersion for baptism. They both go down or up together. For my part, they always go down. They both lack a New Testament church in some way."[103] With added emphasis he concludes, "To Have A True Church, A True Baptism, Or A True Lord's Supper, We Just Must Have All Three! They *all three* go together! If one of these is lacking, *all three are necessarily* lacking!"[104]

Editorials in Alabama, Tennessee, and North Carolina in 1932 noted the breakdown of close communion among some Baptist churches. Editor J. S. Farmer of the *Biblical Recorder* of North Carolina noted, "If the practice of open communion was the first step that led to mixed churches and decay of Baptist principles in Northern states and in England, we may be sure that its acceptance in the South will lead to the same things."[105] The root of the falling away by some churches was summarized at the end of the article and is quite telling.

> The Baptists made the mistake of their lives when they did not hold the supper to the local churches and refuse communion even among other Baptist churches. This was the contention of Dr. J. R. Graves—that the right of communion in any church did not extend any further than the influence and discipline of that church. Since with Baptists the local church is the autonomous religious unit, his contention was thoroughly logical, and had the Baptists come to his position they would have been relieved of all the criticism of other denominations on what they call "close" communion of the Baptists. Of course, we will get nowhere by making the suggestion, but it is a matter of such importance that we believe, even at this date, the churches ought to come to Dr. Graves' position.[106]

101. Ibid.
102. Bronson, "New Testament Church," 4.
103. Ibid.
104. Ibid., 5 (emphasis in original).
105. "Concerning the Lord's Supper," 3.
106. Ibid.

Turning from the strict Landmark doctrine, according to these editors, had resulted in the current problems, and Graves is held up as the model of orthodox ecclesiology.

Hugh Tully, pastor of the Wylam Baptist Church, Wylam (Birmingham), Alabama, was at the time of his death the longest serving pastor in the Birmingham Baptist Association. He was a graduate of Southern Baptist Theological Seminary, Louisville, Kentucky, and professor of Greek at Southeastern Bible College for thirteen years. Tully wrote, "According to the Scriptures, scholarship and history, Baptists alone have the authority to administer the ordinances of baptism and the supper." He carries this to the extreme as he writes, "The supper is not a Christian but a church ordinance. It is not for all Christians. The apostles were alone members of His church during His earthly ministry, and they alone ate with Him."[107] The claim of course is that different denominations may not partake of the Lord's Supper together. Tully follows that up with the following explanation:

> It is commonly believed that one denomination has as much scriptural authority for its existence as another. This is untrue. Only one has authority. The question is which one? Christ founded His Church while upon earth and said that churches like it would continue until His return. . . . All denominations that have come into existence since the days of Christ do not have Scriptural authority to baptize. . . . New Testament Churches were Baptist Churches. . . . Baptists alone have continued from days of Christ, and consequently alone have authority to baptize.[108]

His conclusion is simply that the Supper can be eaten only by those who hold to the teachings of the New Testament and the only ones who do that are the Baptists.

Ten years later at the halfway mark of the twentieth century these same principles were standard fare in the religious press. It is quite telling that in an article of February 26, 1948, which also quite tellingly was entitled "Landmarks of Our Faith," the doctrines of close communion and alien immersion were put side-by-side with the doctrines of the infallibility and inerrancy of Scripture, the virgin birth, the deity of Christ, the fall, and original sin.[109] Later that same year, we read, "The Baptist is the only church that has the same doctrines that are obtained in the New Testament Church. . . . The reason why we do not observe the Lord's Supper with other

---

107. Tully, *Brief History of the Baptists*, 38.
108. Ibid., 36.
109. Thurman, "Landmarks of Our Faith," 4–6.

denominations is that they do not follow the teachings of Jesus."[110] Alien immersion and close communion were regarded by many Baptists as essential New Testament doctrine. In the words of L. R. Scarborough, "The Baptist church which practices these things [open communion and alien immersion] will sooner or later cease to be a Baptist church and lose its witness to the truth set forth by Jesus Christ in His Holy Word."[111]

Baptist Church Succession

Several decades after the Whitsitt controversy many within the seminaries were less adamant about the succession of Baptist churches from the time of John the Baptist to the present. However, one finds shadows of that doctrine even when the question of Baptist history is not the primary subject. In discussing the Baptist position on the authority of Scripture and the individual's right to interpret the Word of God for himself, H. E. Dana wrote, "Far back in the shadows of the dark ages we catch occasional glimpses of our doctrinal progenitors, coming into the light of history purely by reason of their aggressive and intrepid advocacy of this theory."[112] He adds, "All down through history Baptist blood has been copiously spilled in defense of this great principle."[113] It should be noted that this is the time when J. M. Carroll was beginning his lectures later published as *The Trail of Blood*.

If the seminaries were somewhat reserved in their avowals of Baptist succession, it certainly was not the case in the religious press and convention addresses. W. L. Compere, addressing the Arkansas Baptist Convention in 1922 in defense of the convention system, asserted, "Our Convention system . . . is strictly in line with New Testament principles."[114] In defending the work of Baptists through different missionary organizations (a long-standing contentious issue) Compere went to Baptist history for his example. "When old-time Baptists like Paul and Barnabas could not agree

---

110. "History of the Baptist Church," 7.

111. Scarborough, "Ways to Poison These Fountains," 93.

112. Dana, "Influence of Baptists," 21. Dana was professor of Greek at Southwestern Seminary.

113. Ibid.

114. Compere, "What Is the Proper Attitude of Convention Baptists toward Other Baptists?," address delivered before Ministers and Laymen's Conference Arkansas Baptist Convention, December 1922, 8, typewritten. Compere served for a time as president of Clarke College in Mississippi.

as to how the work should be done, they simply exercised their Baptist privilege to quit working together."[115]

Others left no doubt as to their belief in the origin of the Baptist Church. C. M. Pickler wrote, "Some claim there is a Catholic Church; others say there is a universal, invisible church; and still others assert that all denominations are branches of the church. But all these theories and claims can not invalidate historical and Biblical facts."[116] Those "facts" go to the same scriptural interpretation essentially articulated by Graves:

> Jesus said in Matthew 16:18, "I Will Build My Church; and the gates of hell shall not prevail against it." Then he said in Matthew 18:17, "And if he shall neglect to hear them, Tell It To The Church." When He made the former statement this world was without a Christian Church but when He spoke the latter word the first church teaching the doctrinal truth that Baptists of today teach had already been organized at Jerusalem.[117]

Some would probably fault Pickler for not taking the founding of the Baptist church back to John the Baptist. He ended the article "Since others do not claim the church that Jesus founded in Jerusalem from the time He organized it until the day of Pentecost, what harm could there be in granting the Baptists' claim that it was a Baptist church?"[118] There was an editorial note appended to the article (editor John D. Freeman) which read, "And why will Baptist scholars spend their time trying to prove the contentions of Pedo-Baptists and Catholics?"[119]

Hugh Tully's *Brief History of the Baptists* was essentially a conflation of Orchard, Graves, Carroll, and other Landmark exponents of Baptist successionism, which went a little further in some of its claims. For instance, he writes, "The first New Testament preacher was a Baptist."[120] "Every denomination whose origin dates this side of Christ's earthly ministry cannot Scripturally and historically claim Christ as its founder."[121]

Tully follows in the footsteps of Graves and Hailey's defense of Graves in asserting, "Roger Williams was never a Baptist. Baptists in America do not owe their existence to him; nor is Baptist succession broken by the

---

115. Ibid., 9.

116. Pickler, "First Baptist Church," 4. Pickler was pastor of the Boulevard Church, Memphis, TN.

117. Ibid.

118. Ibid.

119. Ibid.

120. Tully, *Brief History of the Baptists*, 5.

121. Ibid., 17.

Williams' affair."[122] Here in plain words is the significance of denying Roger Williams to be the founder of the Baptist church in America: it would break the line of Baptist succession. Tully's history is unclear and contradictory in regard to Menno Simons, whom he calls "Simon Menno, a great Baptist preacher."[123] Later he says Simon Menno was a "great Baptist preacher among [the] Waldensian Baptists of Germany."[124] His entire thesis may be summed up thusly: *"Baptists may be considered the only Christian community which has stood since the days of the Apostles. . . . Baptists have a succession back to Christ!"*[125]

As the first half of the twentieth century ends the idea of Baptist succession, not to mention Baptist exclusivism, is still clearly visible in the religious press. In yet another article outlining the history of the Baptist Church the argument is made that God made Adam and Eve in order to begin the human race. Similarly, "in order to begin the Baptist Church, God prepared John the Baptist." In words reminiscent of Graves' exposition of "the gates of hell," the article goes on, "The Baptist Church was established by Christ during his own personal ministry. The Baptists believe in the perpetuity of their church because Christ said that the gates of hell would not tear the church apart."[126] Furthermore, the Great Commission was given to none but Baptists. As evidence of this the article says, "All the members at the time Christ gave this commission were Baptists because they had been baptized by John or the twelve disciples who had been baptized by John the Baptist."[127] This raises the Roger Williams' type of question, i.e., were any baptized by Judas?

As strange as some of these assertions may sound the reading of Baptist history into the pages of the New Testament was a common practice. One article urged Baptists to know their history and heritage and the way to know both was simply to "Know your history. Know your Bible."[128] The same article affirmed that "Baptists are not and never have been Protestants."[129] This affirmation now stretches back across almost one hundred years of articles, books, tracts, sermons, debates, and speeches.

---

122. Ibid., 26.
123. Ibid., 37.
124. Ibid., 41.
125. Ibid., 40 (emphasis in original).
126. "History of the Baptist Church," 7.
127. Ibid.
128. "Origin of Sprinkling and Pouring," *Baptist and Reflector*, 4 (reprint from *Arkansas Baptist*).
129. Ibid.

This highly sectarian view and disavowal of any kinship with other denominations was just as strong in some quarters as it was in Graves' day. For many the uniqueness of the Baptists' claim of being the New Testament church and existing ever since that time necessarily excluded other denominations from the true church. "Since Jesus instituted His church during His earthly ministry . . . and since His church has continued on earth until the present time, He then did not need Luther, Calvin, Henry VIII, Wesley, Campbell . . . to organize or start a new denomination."[130] These other denominations, as Graves said, cannot trace their origins back but a few hundred years. They have no connection to Christ's church. "Every denomination that has come into existence since the days of Christ's earthly ministry is man-founded and cannot be composed of the Churches of Christ."[131] If such doctrines are maintained, one can easily see the *onus probandi* that rests on the Baptist church to preserve the idea of Baptist church succession irrespective of the facts of history. The exegesis of Matthew 16:18 by the Landmarkers and their successors, i.e., that Christ's church as a local, independent body would never cease to exist on earth until his return, placed them in a position whereby they had to disavow all other denominations and cling to some form of succession or admit their exegesis of the Scripture was faulty.

Landmarkism Subsumed and Eclipsed

As the second half of the twentieth century opened, Southern Baptists were embroiled in and overtaken, as was most of the country, in the civil rights struggle, the Vietnam war, and the cultural revolution known now simply as the sixties. These controversies pushed many other issues into the background for many Southern Baptists. Landmarkism was one of those issues. It was subsumed in Baptist doctrine in many places and was eclipsed in the religious press by the more pressing issues of that time.

Moving Out of the Old Southwest

As the first half of the twentieth century was winding down, Southern Baptists were making an expansive thrust into the West and Northwest. Stephen Stookey made the case that Landmarkism had a great influence

---

130. Tully, *Brief History of the Baptists*, 3.
131. Ibid.

on the westward expansion of the Southern Baptist Convention.[132] One of the key figures in that westward expansion, particularly in the Pacific Northwest, was R. E. Milam. It is interesting that W. A. Criswell, a paragon among Southern Baptist pastors and pastor of First Baptist Church, Dallas, Texas, wrote to Milam after reading a draft of Milam's book *Westward, Ho*, "Your book is revealing—we all need to know what you have to say. Keep on saying it! Send it to everybody."[133]

What Milam was "saying" was the basic Landmark doctrine articulated by Graves, Pendleton, and other Landmarkers. The doctrinal emphasis of Milam was primarily in the three areas of alien immersion, close communion, and the authority of the local church. Milam was not a strict successionist but held that "some churches in ages past that were not called Baptist were in reality Baptist churches."[134] He held that churches could slip from their New Testament moorings but could be restored. "Historical connection is not enough. There must be a constant realignment of the church with its foundation as found in the New Testament."[135]

A very clear example of the criticism that could often accompany any deviation from a strict view of alien immersion, close communion, and recognition of other churches as true churches of Christ was seen early in the ministry of Billy Graham. Graham was raised to national prominence in a tent meeting in Los Angeles, California, in 1949. The Billy Graham Evangelistic Association was formed in 1950. Graham's success, in part, was founded on a policy of not going to a city for a crusade unless supported by local church councils, i.e., the Methodists, Baptists, Lutherans, Episcopalians, and even the Roman Catholics had to agree to promote and support the event. This would naturally cause some concern for those with Landmark leanings. In witness of this David M. Gardner wrote to Milam shortly after a Graham crusade in Portland, Oregon, in 1950. Gardner's concerns involved alien immersion and whether Graham was a true Baptist.[136] In reply Milam said he believed Graham had been misquoted by the press. However, "he missed an opportunity to make a clear-cut statement of his conviction on immersion. His wife is a Presbyterian and he stated that she

---

132. See Stookey, "Impact of Landmarkism."
133. W. A. Criswell to R. E. Milam, 20 December 1949.
134. R. E. Milam to Will Vernon, 7 June 1950.
135. Milam, *Fortress of Truth*, photocopy of manuscript, chs. 5, 6.
136. David M. Gardner to R. E. Milam, 6 September 1950. Gardner was the editor of the *Baptist Standard, Inc.*, the state denominational paper of Texas.

had not been immersed and left an opening so that the press quoted him as though he thought it was not important how one was baptized."[137]

Milam was more concerned about Graham's association with others who advocated an interdenominational cooperation in evangelism. He wrote, "I am uneasy when I see that Graham is being drawn more and more toward men like Fuller and the interdenominational 'set-up.' I am wondering if a group of you Texas Baptists ought not to have a conference with him and ask him some very direct questions. Right now his career might hang in the balance."[138] What is obvious in these words is the old Landmark doctrine that recognition of these other denominations, as cooperation would entail, recognizes their legitimacy as churches of Christ. All staunch Landmarkers, many who have been quoted, would say that recognition of these other "societies," as they would term them, would mean a virtual rejection of the authority of Baptist churches.

An Uncooperative Spirit Based on Ecclesiology

The vitriol against any kind of interdenominational cooperation was evident in some personal correspondence between John Partain and Milam. As Partain wrote, "For my part, I have no hesitancy in saying that the F. C. [Federal Council of Churches] is led by the most unscrupulous liars and treacherous scoundrels God ever let live . . . they are at least communists, atheists (in the true Christian sense), and anti-Christs."[139] Partain continued to blast these non-Baptists and criticize the Baptists who expressed "Christian charity" toward them. He summed up his attack saying, "In spite of all their asinine conceit, they are pathetically ignorant of the Bible, history, speculative systems, historical theology, and logic."[140]

Partain then turned his remarks to the real reason for the letter, i.e., his review of Milam's manuscript for *Westward Ho*. His critique of Milam's work centered on two key points, namely, his ecclesiology and the view of the kingdom and the church. He indicated that he would like to discuss Milam's treatment of the church because, in his mind, "Carrolistic [sic] Ecclesiology departed from the historic position."[141] "In the matters of 'kingdom' and 'church,' I can't follow Carroll."[142] Having said that, however, he immediately

137. R. E. Milam to David M. Gardner, 14 September 1950.
138. Ibid.
139. John Partain to R. E. Milam, 11 June 1950.
140. Ibid.
141. Ibid.
142. Ibid.

issued a disclaimer, that no church had any authority "to administer these [ordinances] other than an autonomous New Testament Church, and that, to me, means Baptist."[143] He added, "I'm 'agin' [against] 'alien Baptism' and 'open communion' as much as any Carrollite." Although Partain may have shied away from a strict Landmark ecclesiology, the Landmark strain had thoroughly influenced his regard, or lack thereof, for other churches and the place of the Baptist Church as the only authorized administrator of baptism and the Lord's Supper.

C. M. Pickler in a sermon before the Tennessee Baptist Convention in 1954, fittingly entitled "Keep the Old Landmarks," had three main points. In those points he laid the Landmark ecclesiology alongside the Bible, as God's revealed truth, and salvation by grace. The text of his sermon shows no Scripture references under the heads "The Bible Is God's Revealed Truth" or "Salvation Is by Grace." He gave eleven Scripture references in the section on the church which was somewhat longer than the other two points. Notable among the things he said in reference to the church were the continued unbroken existence of the church Jesus instituted based on Matthew 16:18, the denial of any invisible or catholic church, and the exclusive Baptist claim to be the church Jesus himself instituted. In excluding other churches Pickler said, "A church beginning on the day of Pentecost or any time later could not qualify as the one Jesus built."[144] Although not stated, this necessarily means that Baptist churches have always existed and precludes any date later than the ministry of Jesus for the founding of the Baptist church (such as sixteenth-century England as Whitsitt asserted). He added, "No people today claim this church that existed before Pentecost except Baptists . . . since Baptists claim this kinship we are not Protestants . . . since no other people claim such kinship, then why not allow this Baptist claim, especially as our doctrine today is still the same as that taught by this first church?"[145] One has to question whether or not Pickler is aware that the early church had no fully articulated doctrine of some great biblical and theological truths, e.g., the two natures of Christ and the Holy Spirit. This retreat into the purity of the doctrine of the "first church" proves more than desired.

Although the opinions of Graves and even the mention of his name had decreased dramatically in the religious press there were still those like O. W. Taylor willing to come to his defense.[146] An article by Taylor defends

143. Ibid.

144. Pickler, "Keep the Old Landmarks," 5.

145. Ibid.

146. O. W. Taylor was a pastor, editor, and author and served as editor of the *Baptist and Reflector* for seventeen years. He was the author of *Early Tennessee Baptists 1769–1832*.

Graves' assertion that "the begetter must exist before the begotten—the Father before the Son. And it is no less contradictious to say that Father and Son eternally self-existed in these same relationships."[147] For those who attributed heretical leanings to Graves for such remarks Taylor answers, "This conclusion is not true unless one reads into the statements made by Dr. Graves meaning that he never intended."[148] We have to judge Graves by what he wrote (with the benefit of reflection and editing) not what he "intended to say" as Taylor presumes to know.[149] This was not the only time that Graves made such assertions (see chapter 2).

Religious Periodicals' Continuing Influence

Lest some would doubt the impact of these weekly papers in a time wherein radio and television were quickly becoming the dominant media it should be noted that the editors of the various papers were still quite sure of their impact and reach. W. Barry Garrett, editor of the *Baptist Beacon*, reported in 1954 that the Baptist state papers had a circulation of well over one million one hundred thousand subscribers. He said that an additional two million people were influenced by shared copies and repeated information. This brought the reach of the weekly papers to well over three million.[150] Garrett's opinion of the influence of the Baptist papers was clear: "Aside from the preachers' personal appearance in the pulpit the most powerful and effective implement for informing and influencing our people is the Baptist state paper."[151]

The thrust of his article was to encourage churches to grow this influence. He suggested that every family in every church subscribe and the subscription be paid out of the church budget. In addition, he says, every organization within the church should use the articles in the papers and every member of every household should read the papers every week. He

---

147. Taylor quotes from Graves, *Work of Christ*, 61–62.

148. Taylor, "In the Interest of Fairness," 3.

149. Taylor seems to ignore other comments from even that same page of Graves' book. For example, Graves wrote, "Before the birth of creation there could have been no relationship existing as that of Father and Son . . . these terms . . . demand time" (Graves, *Work of Christ*, 61.) He also said, "The phrases 'Eternal Father,' and 'Eternal Son,' are inadmissible, since they involve a manifest contradiction" (ibid.). Taylor does not even begin to defend some statements of Graves, such as, "The Person of the Son of God, being the Second Person of the Trinity is Divine, and only relatively human" (ibid., 87).

150. Garrett, "Free Voices for Free People," 3.

151. Ibid.

emphasized repeatedly that "the Baptist state paper is the pastor's best assistant and the denomination's most powerful instrument."[152]

All the news, however, was not good news for the staunch Landmarkers within the convention. They suffered a defeat at the Southern Baptist Convention in Detroit, Michigan, in 1966. The issue was an old one—the seating of messengers at the convention (see chapter 4). This matter came up in 1855, 1914, and again in 1954. The convention began with a motion to deny seats to messengers of an Arkansas Baptist church. "The motion charged that the Russellville [First Baptist] Church 'has departed from the traditional practice of regular Baptist churches by officially adopting a doctrinal statement which advocates the practice of open communion and the acceptance of alien immersion.'"[153] The motion was ruled out of order because, "The constitutional requirements for membership in the Southern Baptist Convention . . . [do] not make these two positions tests of fellowship for membership in this convention."[154] In addition the recently adopted "Baptist Faith and Message" did not "make alien immersion and open communion grounds for excluding membership."[155]

The following year Wayne E. Ward, professor of theology at Southern Seminary, wrote that one of the hottest debates at the time (and we might add one of the hottest debates for over one hundred years) "centers on the question of receiving into our membership people who have been immersed by someone other than Baptists."[156] While Ward attacks such attitudes in his article, he begins with a revisionist explanation of Graves' beliefs in this regard. He says, "Not even Graves argued that the Baptist name was required because he knew better than to add a requirement that goes beyond the words of the New Testament."[157] There is ample evidence, as already shown, that Graves considered the New Testament churches Baptist churches and he had little reticence in adding what he thought was the true interpretation regardless of what Scripture had to say. Ward does come around to that explanation after somewhat defending Graves. He adds, "His narrow restriction of the term 'New Testament church' to Baptist churches (and not all of them) did result in a practical limitation of valid scriptural baptism to the Baptist churches as he defined them."[158]

152. Ibid.
153. "SBC Seats Russellville Messengers," 8.
154. Ibid.
155. Ibid. The Baptist Faith and Message was adopted in 1963.
156. Ward, "Should Baptists Receive Non-Baptist Immersion?," 9.
157. Ibid.
158. Ibid.

Ward continued, "Anyone who stands up today and says that valid scriptural baptism can be performed only in the Baptist name or authority is flying in the face of Holy Scripture. . . . If we go around re-baptizing, just to put the Baptist label on it, we are mocking baptism and calling unholy what is sacred before God!"[159] But as in the case of Graves, he adds a disclaimer saying that the receiving of alien immersions (he singles out Campbellites but does not go so far as to identify the others of whom he speaks) is an even worse practice. A worse practice than calling unholy what God has called holy? One has to wonder. The pendulum swings within this article represent the difficulty within the Southern Baptist Convention, even one hundred years later, of flatly speaking out against the Landmark doctrine.

Others, however, not only speak out but reinforce Landmark doctrine and practice. T. A. Patterson whose treatment of Graves' theological "peculiarities" was noted in chapter 2 cited an article from the *Baptist Record* of Mississippi. Patterson said, "The last paragraph of [that] editorial is so clear and forceful that I should like to give it verbatim."[160] What the editorial spelled out as the way to destroy Baptists was this:

> Cause them to turn away from their belief in the authority of the Word of God, the distinctive divinity of Jesus Christ, redemption through the blood, the bodily resurrection of Christ and His glorious personal return. Get them to quit preaching salvation by grace and the eternal security of the believer. *Lead them to practice alien immersion and open communion.*[161]

What is striking is the place given to alien immersion and open communion. These errors are ranked alongside the denial of the deity of Christ, denial of the authority of Scripture, the resurrection, and redemption by Christ's substitutionary atonement as errors that would bring down the church. This makes clear the reason that Ward and others must tread lightly or attach some sort of disclaimer to their remarks on these subjects. The pervasive influence and impact of Landmarkism one hundred years after the Civil War and the high-water mark of Landmark influence is clearly seen in these examples.

---

159. Ibid.

160. Patterson, "How to Stamp Out Baptists," 8. Patterson was executive secretary, Baptist General Convention of Texas.

161. Ibid.

Relegated to the Shadows

While Landmark doctrines, principles, and beliefs still circulated throughout the Southern Baptist Convention, the turbulent events of the 1960s proved to be in a different way as distracting as the Civil War had been in the 1860s. Riots, cities ablaze, and marches to protest segregation, the Vietnam War, and the draft enveloped the land. Baptist churches and the Southern Baptist Convention were not immune to these forces and like the Civil War in the last century this civil war swept many up into it and took many of the former debates from the pages of the religious press. The threat of spreading communism, the sexual revolution, and the battle over civil rights consumed churches and the convention. Although the convention tried to take a mediating position on the most divisive issue, the question of equal rights for Negroes, the autonomy of the local church rendered such pronouncements essentially null and void.

This mediating position was described as "mediating, paralyzed 'silence' on the race question. 'Silence' in this usage refers not to a complete failure to address the South's 'great matter.' Rather, it describes a situation in which public pronouncements, so encumbered with the need to mediate, were perceived merely as vague and vacuous platitudes."[162]

Illustrative of that was the note, oddly enough at the end of an article about Billy Graham's political views in the 1960 presidential race, which said, "One of the surprises of the convention was the endorsement without opposition of the Christian Life Commission report urging Southern Baptists to make use of every opportunity to help Negro citizens to secure equal rights."[163] It should be noted that the same issue of the *Baptist and Reflector* carried a report of the Tennessee Baptist Convention's action which "declined three pleas to act on the controversial race issue. In annual session, it turned aside three efforts to instruct Convention agencies to accept all persons regardless of race, color, or creed."[164] The policy which existed by way of silence was one of non-acceptance. As the article reports, "The Tennessee Baptist Convention has never adopted a policy on segregation. Currently no Negroes are enroled [sic] in its schools. Hospitals, though not admitting Negro patients give them emergency treatment. The Negro cases are later move [sic] to other hospitals."[165] The Convention rationalized its action by saying that the determination of such policies was made by the individual

---

162. Manis, *Southern Civil Religions in Conflict*, 102.
163. "Graham Voices Political Opinion," 3.
164. Ibid., 8.
165. Ibid.

directors of the three hospitals and four schools. Apparently, they would have people believe all seven made the same decision independent of one another or the convention boards overseeing their activities.

New Problems from the Shadows

Irrespective of the explanations and surprise offered up by the Baptist press, conditions in the churches were far more disturbing. The convictions expressed in the press concerning the inferiority of the Negro, as noted in chapter 4, were the beliefs held by many Southern Baptists. These assertions of the inequality of the races, the superiority of the white race, and the dangers of recognizing these inferiors as equals were spread throughout the Southern Baptist Convention by respected papers, educators, pastors, and figures of note. This extreme racism was nowhere more evident than among the Landmarkers. The autonomy of the local church combined with the belief that Baptist churches and Baptist churches alone were the true church of Christ made it difficult if not impossible for the Southern Baptist churches to accept that they could be wrong in their declarations regarding racial inequality and inferiority.

Landmarkism and Racism

Several examples will serve to document that the version of events reported at the convention level in the religious press was fanciful if not an outright distortion of the facts. In 1966 the Tatnall Square Baptist Church in Macon, Georgia, forced the pastor and two assistants to resign because they insisted that the church should accept as members people of all races. The Tatnall Square Baptist Church was on the campus of Mercer University. Mercer had been the subject of news stories and editorials in the *Christian Index* as the debate over the integration of the school raged throughout 1962 and 1963. The Southern Baptist Convention appointed a committee to study the issue and counsel with the university's trustees. This committee in the end "expressed the opinion that Baptists in Georgia were not yet ready for such a change in policy."[166]

Ready or not the decision had to be made in 1963. Sam Oni, a Ghanaian Negro, applied for admission to Mercer. Oni had been converted through the efforts of Southern Baptist missionaries and one of Mercer's missionary alumni recommended Mercer to Oni. "In April 1963, the Mercer

---

166. Holmes, *Ashes for Breakfast*, 22.

trustees voted to admit [Oni as] the first black student to the University."[167] Through a series of events, Oni presented himself for membership in the Tatnall Square Church. The result, after a long and protracted struggle, was the dismissal of the pastor, Thomas J. Holmes, the assistant pastor, Douglas Johnson, and music director, Jack W. Jones. Although there were notable exceptions who criticized the Tatnall Square Baptist Church for sending money to support missionaries to win converts to Christ who would subsequently be denied membership in their church, most of the Southern Baptist Convention was silent on the issue. It was a local church matter.

Holmes voiced a poignant observation regarding the autonomy of the local church and the power of a congregation made up solely of baptized believers as the Landmarkers would have characterized it. He said, "Baptist churches have operated for centuries under the belief that the congregation rules. In fact, Baptists have practically substituted the doctrine of congregational infallibility for the doctrine of papal infallibility."[168] Against the Landmark doctrine of republicanism, democratic government, and local autonomy Holmes added, "A Baptist church . . . can become the most ruthless political machine imaginable. Matters of morals and faith are then decided by the counting of noses. No single dynamic in Baptist life is in greater need of change."[169]

The First Baptist Church in Birmingham, Alabama, suffered through a similar situation. Birmingham had been the scene of some of the most widely publicized and deadly struggles of the Civil Rights movement. Things exploded (figuratively) at First Baptist Church on June 27, 1970, when a Negro woman and her daughter presented themselves for membership. The daughter came on profession of faith and wanted to be baptized into the membership of the church. This began a long and bitter struggle which resulted in the division of the church and the effective ouster of the pastor, Herbert Gilmore. Because of Birmingham's history the struggle received much national news coverage, making the pages of *Newsweek*, *Time*, the *Christian Century*, the *New York Times*, and the *Washington Post*.[170]

Perhaps one of the most insightful comments on the whole situation at First Baptist Church, Birmingham, was offered by federal judge H. H. Grooms Sr. in addressing a church conference there in September 1970. In relating his comments to Matthew 23:15 he said, "It has been suggested that in lieu of taking black people in, we increase our gifts to foreign missions. . . . The last

---

167. Ibid., 22–23.
168. Ibid., 63.
169. Ibid., 46.
170. See Gilmore, *They Chose to Live*, for the history of these events.

version that I have read on this [woe] reads this way: 'You lock the doors of the Kingdom of Heaven in men's faces, yet you sail the seas and cross whole countries to win one convert.'"[171] Judge Grooms' address had no noticeable impact on the situation at the First Baptist Church. The church split, the pastor was removed, and the First Baptist Church continued to have no Negro members. It is more than a little dichotomous that the fallback position of the Southern Baptist Convention continued to be its commitment to foreign missions and taking the gospel to all people—all people except the people in their own community if they are of a different color.

The odd thing about the Birmingham situation is the fact that it came almost two years after the adoption of a very clear statement by the Southern Baptist Convention regarding the shortfalls of the convention in the area of race relations. This followed a summer of riots and civil unrest. The document was entitled, "A Statement Concerning the Crisis in Our Nation." It said in part, "We have come far short of our privilege in Christian brotherhood. . . . [We commit to] personally accept every Christian as a brother . . . and welcome to the fellowship of faith and worship every person irrespective of race or class."[172] What the executives of the convention failed to recognize was the powerful influence of the sectarian Baptist stance which was only further entrenched by the great loss of life, pride, and material well-being brought on by the Civil War and its aftermath as outlined in chapter 4. The decades of racism, high-church Baptist attitudes, and a disdain for other Christians was not going to be erased by a pronouncement from the annual convention. Luther Copeland makes the case that most of the instances in which the Southern Baptists have wandered from the truth of Scripture throughout their history can be traced back to the original sin of defending slavery, the thing that precipitated their formation as a separate denomination although certain revisions of history today seek to deny that as the formative cause.[173]

Copeland relates the highly sectarian attitudes of Southern Baptists, which he calls "denominational conceit or arrogance," directly to the Landmark traditions which were still part of the Southern Baptist claim of distinctiveness. He says, "Landmarkism continued to have a powerful influence upon Southern Baptists and was not only strongly sectarian but also fiercely polemical, engaging in continuous warfare with other denominations. . . . It occasioned acrimonious controversy within the ranks of Southern Baptists

---

171. Ibid., 190.
172. *Annual . . . Nineteen Hundred and Sixty-Eight*, 67–69.
173. See Copeland, *Southern Baptist Convention*.

as well."[174] At the root of this acrimony was the claim that only Southern Baptist churches are New Testament churches. This coupled with the constant tirade of criticism against and distrust of other denominations produced an attitude of superiority and contempt for other denominations as clear as what had been set forth in the writings of Graves et al. As Copeland wrote, "We Southern Baptists, under Landmark influence, did not hesitate to assert that we had sole possession of the truth or at least had more truth than any other denominational body."[175]

Copeland makes the case that the Southern Baptist air of supremacy was closely tied to the alleged superiority and purity of many white Southerners. As proof he quotes Ben Bridges, executive secretary of the Arkansas Baptist Convention, who said, "We believe our theology, our doctrines . . . are complete within themselves . . . our utter reliance upon the pure word of God has preserved us from error and reserved to us a purer faith than that of any other people under heaven."[176] Copeland followed that with numerous quotes from various Southern Baptist sources regarding the supremacy and superiority of the Anglo-Saxon race. His conclusion was, "Landmarkism . . . allied itself with Southern sectionalism and racism to produce exaggerated notions of Southern Baptist superiority."[177] Further to this point Samuel S. Hill contended that Southerners have usually regarded theirs as "the most moral type of arrangement for human living . . . and that the southern churches are the purest in Christendom."[178]

Andrew Manis called "such a perspective the quintessential religious legitimation, and its use by Southern clergy continued into the Second Reconstruction"[179] Manis made the same point made in chapter 4, i.e., that in the lead-up to the Civil War both sides claimed God's divine sanction of their position and both sides vigorously defended their position from Scripture. He said in the religious wars of the civil rights movement "both groups . . . found divine sanction for their views and actions."[180]

Manis cited the example of Carey Daniel, pastor of First Baptist Church, West Dallas, Texas.[181] Daniel preached a sermon that harkened back to the

---

174. Copeland, *Southern Baptist Convention*, 86.

175. Ibid., 87.

176. Ibid., 88.

177. Ibid., 89.

178. Hill et al., *Religion and the Solid South*, 36.

179. Manis, *Southern Civil Religions*, 91. Second Reconstruction is a name for the civil rights battles of the mid-twentieth century.

180. Ibid.

181. Daniel was the brother of Texas Democratic Senator Price Daniel who was also a candidate for governor.

editorial affirmations of the nineteenth-century Landmark press which tied the biblical basis of segregation to the division of Noah's sons after the flood and the curse of Ham. Daniel's sermon was heralded by many in the press who supported segregation and is still one of the quintessential examples of Southern Baptist sectarian superiority and the use of Scripture to defend such positions.[182] It may be an overstatement to classify Daniel as a Landmarker but he was a prominent pastor in the Landmark belt, was educated at Southwestern Seminary, and had not deviated from the post-Civil War Landmark position on the place of the Negro in American society. Manis asserted that the Civil War never really ended but was now being waged on the "civil religious front as well."[183] The leaders of the Southern whites in this war were the Southern Baptist Convention according to Manis. The Convention, he said, "manifested their indecision through mediating, paralyzed 'silence' on the race question . . . [their] public pronouncements, so encumbered with the need to mediate, were perceived merely as vague and vacuous platitudes."[184] On that same subject, Ellen Rosenberg noted, "By the late 1960s, the topic that was convulsing the entire region was the subject of so much compromise at the national [Convention] that the resolutions sounded nearly incoherent and incomprehensible."[185]

If the expressions at the national level were vague, the local expressions against integration and recognition of blacks were anything but incoherent. A letter from Selsus E. Tull to the editor of the *Arkansas Baptist* who had expressed a favorable opinion regarding integration is a prime example. Tull accused the editor of using his position to try to defeat the convictions of the Baptists of Arkansas who were against integration (a number Tull claimed to be 95 percent of Arkansas Baptists.) Tull suggested to the editor that there were two honorable choices open to him: "one is to apologize to the Baptists of Arkansas for using their paper in your attempt to put over your views in favor of integration; and the other is to resign and take your fight for mongrelization to other fields."[186] Tull was a long-time Southern Baptist pastor and leader and solidly Landmark in his ecclesiology. He said, "I assert the first Baptist church was organized by Jesus Christ." While perhaps

---

182. Daniel circulated a petition of pastors who opposed integration in the pages of the *Dallas Morning News*, Sunday, 18 May 1958. In addition to Manis, others from *Time* November 5, 1956, to Jane Dailey, *Journal of American History* (2004) 91.1 have referred to Daniel's comments.

183. Ibid., 99.

184. Ibid., 102.

185. Rosenberg, "Southern Baptist Response to the Newest South," in Ammerman, *Southern Baptists Observed*, 149.

186. Selsus E. Tull to Erwin L. McDonald, 21 February 1959. .

not a strict successionist he believed Baptist doctrine had been preserved through all ages. "Throughout the Christian ages, the pure Baptist teaching has survived." Then he added, "[Any] church which cannot bear this historical test . . . can never claim to be 'The Bride of Christ.'"[187] Tull would have been in step both ecclesiologically and racially with the Landmarkers of one hundred years earlier.

As had been the case in the days of the Landmark ascendency the seminaries were targeted for lack of compliance to the Southern Baptist mandate. Martin Luther King Jr. had been invited to speak at the Southern Baptist Theological Seminary (King gave the Julius B. Gay Lecture at the seminary on April 19, 1961). Taylor Branch said that King's name was so sensitive "the white Southern Baptist Convention forced its seminary to apologize for allowing King to discuss religion on the Louisville campus. Within the church, this simple invitation was a racial and theological heresy, such that churches across the South rescinded their regular donations to the seminary."[188] Although the president did not lose his job over the incident the similarities to the Whitsitt controversy are obvious.

The vacuous pronouncements coming from the convention regarding civil rights masked the true sentiments of a very large number of Southern Baptists. As shown above the attacks against Herbert Gilmore at First Baptist Church in Birmingham and Thomas Holmes at Tatnall Square Baptist Church in Macon were at their heart retribution wreaked upon pastors who tried to open the doors of the church to all people—the very thing many of the resolutions of the Southern Baptist Convention proclaimed. However, those attacks were subsumed in other arguments about liberalism and modernism, historical-critical approaches to the Old Testament and over-literal renderings of the biblical text, and the ever-present Baptist church supremacy in regard to other churches. These all have roots in Landmarkism and the exclusivist, sectarian, high-church attitudes associated with being the only true church in the minds of many Southern Baptists.

Landmarkism and the Fundamentalist/Moderate Controversy

Most historians will argue that the fundamentalist/moderate controversy and the resultant "fundamentalist takeover"[189] in the Southern Baptist Conven-

---

187. Tull, "Denominationalism Put to the Test," 16–17.

188. Taylor Branch, *Parting the Waters*, 488. Taylor Branch is an American author known for his groundbreaking history of the civil rights movement. This work, *Parting the Waters*, won the Pulitzer Prize in 1989.

189. The term fundamentalist takeover is used by the moderates who lost control

tion had nothing to do with the Landmark controversies of a century earlier. However, to the extent that the racial strife and antagonism flowed out of Landmark doctrines, the "lost cause" mentality of the South, and the racial prejudice fostered by the Baptist religious press as noted above, it can be argued that the fundamentalist/moderate controversy within the convention stemmed from those same causes. Walker Knight and Ellen Rosenberg contend that there is a close connection between the fundamentalist position and the segregationists. The conservative movement within the Southern Baptist Convention "has been identified with a segregationist position."[190]

Knight referred to a speech given in 1956 by W. A. Criswell, in which "the 'godfather' of SBC fundamentalists, called integrationists 'a bunch of infidels, dying from the neck up,' and he charged that they were 'good-for-nothing fellows who are trying to upset all things we love as good Southern Baptists.'"[191] Criswell later changed his stance as did many of the leading conservatives within the Southern Baptist Convention. However, Ammerman's research showed in 1993 only "fifty-three percent of self-identified fundamentalists agreed with the statement [the civil rights movement helped to move this country in the right direction] as opposed to ninety percent of the self-identified moderates."[192]

How is this related to Landmarkism? There may seem to be no direct connection if one looks strictly at ecclesiology, authorized administrators of baptism, and ordination and recognition of ministers, however, the focal point of the integration struggles came in the "Southwest," i.e., Tennessee, Arkansas, Texas, Alabama, and Mississippi, as the Landmarkers liked to call their area of dominant influence. Beyond mere geographic considerations, one must consider the key ecclesiological principles of local church autonomy, democratic church government, and the often unspoken but clear confidence that comes with being the only "true church of Christ." As the invectives of the post-Civil War editorials rested on a certain Baptist supremacy, in the same way, the harsh rhetoric of the racial battles a century later was rooted in the same feelings of supremacy and autonomy. Many of

---

of the convention with the election of Adrian Rogers as president in 1979. The implication in that term is that the "takeover" did not truly represent the wishes of the many churches of the convention but was instead a highly orchestrated political move by the fundamentalists. Many books have dealt with this controversy. See, e.g., Morgan, *New Crusades*; Merritt, *Betrayal of Southern Baptist Missionaries*; Ammerman, *Baptist Battles*; Leonard, *God's Last and Only Hope*.

190. Knight, "Race Relations: Changing Patterns and Practices," in Ammerman, *Southern Baptists Observed*, 176.

191. Ibid., 177.

192. Ibid., 178.

the leaders in these racial battles became leaders in the fundamentalist takeover. One must say that the connection in this regard is much clearer than the connections of the successionists through the centuries that have been defended with tragic consequences for some as previously documented.

However, the positions of some of the significant figures in the fundamentalist camp are not ascertained merely by connection. Southern Baptist Convention International Mission Board member Bill Sutton, one of the prominent fundamentalists, said, "I'm a Landmarker and proud of it."[193] Wade Burleson wrote, "Many of our SBC's [Southern Baptist Convention's] influential trustees and administration leaders over the past few years have had strong Landmark tendencies."[194] These key leadership positions since the "fundamentalist takeover" would be in the fundamentalist camp. There is a certain thread running through the segregationists to the fundamentalists and that thread has certain Landmark tendencies.

Unseen Transmission

William Barnes wrote in 1934, "In every direction this emphasis upon the central idea of Landmarkism—the local church—has affected Baptist thinking."[195] On the other hand, Wiley Richards wrote in 1991, "The doctrine of the church in Southern Baptist theology shows evidence of widespread rejection of its Landmark heritage and acceptance of an existentialist understanding of the meaning of the church."[196] Richards added, "Southern Baptists are well on their way to a complete break with their . . . Landmark heritage. . . . The widespread practice of open communion and the beginning stage of accepting other modes of baptism than immersion, reinforce that conclusion."[197] Additionally he said, "The old Landmark dogmas about the ordinances are practically dead. The enforcement of closed communion rarely occurs among Southern Baptists. In spite of the fact that most Southern Baptists still believe that immersion is the only proper mode of baptism, the doctrine has little practical significance beyond restriction placed on church membership."[198] Restriction of church membership would seem to be very significant, particularly if one believes that church to be the only true church.

193. Burleson, *Hardball Religion*, 37.
194. Ibid., 48.
195. Barnes, *Southern Baptist Convention*, 50.
196. Richards, *Winds of Doctrine*, 199.
197. Ibid., 208.
198. Ibid., 215.

The works of Barnes and Richards were separated by almost six decades and one could surmise that Richards' comments represent the movement away from the Landmark theology during that period. Twenty years beyond Richards' assessment it may be said that most evangelicals have never heard of Landmarkism and despite the fact that Landmarkism had a very significant influence in the early years of the Southern Baptist Convention most Southern Baptists have never heard of Landmarkism.[199] Barnes and Richards do not represent even a sampling of the views on this question but illustrate the widely divergent views on the present impact of Landmarkism in the Southern Baptist Convention.

Methods and Evidences of Transmission

Earlier in this chapter reference was made to Hugh Tully and his Landmark views. Tully was one who carried Landmark theology to the extreme, but the transmission of those ideas through the church and into the succeeding generations is illustrated by the following story. As a young girl ten years of age Jane Miller was told by her Sunday School teacher, "When the Bible called the church the 'Bride of Christ' it meant the Wylam Baptist Church. Other churches would be there like bridesmaids, but the Bride would be the Wylam Baptist Church."[200] The transmission of Landmark theology (very extreme interpretations of that theology) is evidenced in this example from pastor to Sunday School teacher (whether or not the teacher understood correctly what was being taught) on to the next generation.[201]

This was by no means an isolated case. James McGoldrick (cited earlier in chapter 2), while professor of church history at Cedarville University, Cedarville, Ohio (1973–2001), said he encountered students from various Baptist churches who were distressed because church history classes did not teach a successionist view of Baptist history. Some students withdrew from the university because they were so distressed over the non-successionist teaching. The successionist view was not ascribed to or taught by the professors at the university but quite a few students came to the university with this view inculcated in them by their local pastors.[202] McGoldrick added

199. Data gathered from surveys taken will bear this out. Surveys are discussed at the end of this section.

200. Interview and handwritten notes of Jane Miller. Interview by author.

201. The Wylam Baptist Church is no longer in existence, but the influence of such teaching persisted throughout its lifetime. Ms. Miller eventually left the church and joined the Wylam Presbyterian Church.

202. James McGoldrick, professor of church history Greenville Presbyterian Theological Seminary. Interview by author Greenville, SC, 2 August 2010. Cedarville College

that as far as he knew there were no members of the faculty that accepted the successionist view. There were some who denied the idea of the universal church but no strict successionists. Some would have said that rather than a succession of Baptist churches what you have is an unbroken line of Baptist doctrine.[203] This is striking for two reasons: First, the widespread reach of Landmarkism outside what is usually thought of as the "Landmark belt," and second, the number of students and their commitment to Landmark doctrine and the way this doctrine is transmitted through the local church in the examples cited above.

Robert Baker, professor of church history at Southwestern Baptist Theological Seminary for twenty-nine years and chairman of the Southern Baptist Historical Commission, said, "There are many Southern Baptists who have adopted some of Graves' emphases and thus in varying degrees have been influenced by Landmarkism."[204] Harold S. Smith wrote that "over eighty years later [1975] the impact of the Landmark movement which he [Graves] helped to inaugurate is still very much alive."[205] It would seem that Richards' assertions were overly optimistic if not just completely off the mark; however, as will be seen in the next section that largely depends on the definition of what constitutes one a Landmarker. How many tenets of the Landmark theology does one have to ascribe to in order to be fairly described as one who is a Landmarker?

Landmark or Not?

Defining or identifying a pastor, agency head, or seminary professor as holding Landmark beliefs became rather imprecise, and one could easily be accused of falsely identifying someone as a Landmarker. The person in question very often could simply say they did not hold to Landmark doctrine. Strict successionists became almost non-existent within faculties of the various seminaries. Other Landmark questions regarding the authority of the local church, close communion, alien immersion, and authorized administrators were often put forth but most often in very temperate language and in a much more general way than the sectarian pronouncements of the preceding one hundred and fifty years.

---

was founded as a Presbyterian college but after problems left it unviable Cedarville became affiliated with the Baptist Bible Institute of Cleveland, Ohio, in 1953. In 2000 the trustees changed the designation of the institution to university.

203. Ibid.
204. Baker, "Factors Encouraging the Rise of Landmarkism," 103.
205. Smith, "Life and Work of J. R. Graves (1820–1893)," 19.

Of course, this was not always the case. Some who unabashedly held to Landmark doctrines were proud of the fact and said so, often quite clearly. R. L. Hymers Jr. was a longtime Southern Baptist and his stance was clearly articulated. In 2004 he proclaimed in a sermon, "We do not believe in a universal church."[206] He went on in the sermon to hold up the primacy of the local church insisting that the New Testament "does not teach that the church is universal, invisible [and] made up of all that are saved."[207] Hymers asserted that he had long held these beliefs but added that holding such beliefs led some to label him as a Landmark Baptist. "So be it," he replied, "put me down as Landmark when it comes to these doctrines concerning the local church and its primacy . . . because that's what the Bible teaches!"[208]

Interestingly, that is the same position taken by those who shun the label Landmark Baptist. The theological positions are the same as those held by Graves et al. in many cases, but the insistence is simply that these are not Landmark doctrines; they are biblical doctrines. Many times, the doctrines were compared with and/or contrasted with the doctrines of other denominations. Often these were "straw-man arguments" whose aim was to justify the doctrine in question. One pastor wrote,

> There is no such thing as an open communion. All people of all denominations have some restrictions which may or may not be stated publicly at the time of the observance, but there are still restrictions. The conclusion is that some churches have more restrictions or they are closer in their observance of the Lord's Supper than others.[209]

Other instances of familiar controversies bore no outward trace or affirmation of Landmarkism other than a methodology and practice that hearkened back to the glory days of Landmarkism. "The dismissal on 25 October 1962, of Midwestern Baptist Theological Seminary professor Ralph Elliott over his book *The Message of Genesis* sent shock waves through six Southern Baptist Seminaries."[210] This was written by the president of the Southern Baptist Theological Seminary and he "read the situation as potentially disastrous."[211] The similarities with the Whitsitt controversy, irrespective of one's view of the content, were unmistakable.[212] During what

206. Hymers, "Last Hope of Man on Earth."
207. Ibid.
208. Ibid.
209. Dangeau, "Unity at the Lord's Table," 7.
210. McCall, "History of the Baptist Cooperative Program," 241.
211. Ibid.
212. For more on the Elliott controversy, see Shurden, *Not a Silent People*, 103–19.

many Baptists styled "the Fundamentalist Takeover" of the Southern Baptist Convention, Randall Lolley, president of Southeastern Seminary, resigned in 1987 in protest over fundamentalist-imposed guidelines for hiring professors and Russell Dilday, president of Southwestern Seminary, was summarily fired in 1994 by what many have called a hostile fundamentalist board who found him out of step with their views.

Just as in the Whitsitt controversy Dilday was supported by the faculty. They affirmed that Dilday was conservative theologically and held "traditional, conservative Southern Baptist views of the Scriptures."[213] It is interesting that the faculty of Southern Baptist Theological Seminary did the same thing in the Whitsitt controversy.[214]

The avowed purpose of these actions outlined above was to protect the denomination from the alleged danger posed by professors and seminary leaders who did not believe in the inerrancy of the Bible. Although many would dispute any connection to Landmark beliefs, James Garrett, professor of theology at Southwestern Baptist Theological Seminary, said that the contentions raised by the fundamentalists were found only in the twentieth century and such applications are "found exclusively in Landmark and Fundamentalist confessions."[215]

During this period of controversy and infighting both sides returned to one of Graves' primary weapons for the propagation of doctrine and marshaling support for issues whether they were appointments and dismissals from boards and seminaries or voters at the convention. This was the Baptist newspaper. It is worth noting that during this period that many believe eclipsed the Landmark movement in bitterness and vitriol no less than eight newspapers were launched. The fundamentalists had the advantage in sheer numbers of publications. Those newspapers include: (1) the *Southern Baptist Advocate*, 1980, the editor was Russell Kaemmerling, brother-in-law of Paige Patterson; (2) the *Southern Baptist Watchman*, 1991; (3) the *Southern Baptist Communicator*, 1991; (4) the *Baptist Observer*, 1992; (5) the *Baptist Banner*, 1994; (6) *SBC Today* (later

---

213. "Open Letter to Southern Baptists," 21. This appeared as a full-page advertisement in the *Baptist Standard*, the Texas Baptist state newspaper.

214. Mueller, *History of Southern Baptist Theological Seminary*, 162–64.

215. Garrett, "Concept of Biblical Authority," 47. Garrett was a Baptist theological educator for more than fifty years and taught at Southwestern Baptist Theological Seminary for twenty-eight years (1949–1959 and 1979–1997). See Richardson, "Baptist Theology with James Leo Garrett, Jr.: An Interview and Review," 10. The review was of Garrett's book *Baptist Theology: A Four Century Study*.

Baptists Today), 1983.[216] Fully half of these papers were published in what the Landmarkers liked to call the great Southwest.

As much as these papers sought to stir up the average Baptist and encourage attendance for at least the crucial presidential vote during the years which marked the controversy the Landmark tradition worked against the Fundamentalists. As Nancy Ammerman wrote, "For a few of the pastors of the smallest and most conservative churches, supporting SBC fundamentalists meant getting involved in a denomination that had always been held at arm's length. Landmark traditions were still strong enough to keep some Baptists away from full Convention participation."[217] What is noteworthy here is the clear alignment of Landmark traditions with the fundamentalist movement as Garrett proposed.

Different Time Same Issues

As was noted in an earlier section R. E. Milam was instrumental in moving Landmark doctrine into the Pacific Northwest as the Southern Baptist churches expanded far beyond their original "southern" roots. In *The Fortress of the Truth (The New Testament Church)* some of the issues with which Milam dealt were the definition and nature of the church and the problem of alien immersion. He attributed, as did Graves, the disciples as the authorized and first church of Christ. He seems to miss the fact that Judas was not a regenerate "member" of that church. He says, "It is plain that the twelve and later the eleven all through His ministry, and even at His resurrection, were recognized as His authorized church. . . . Before His ascension Jesus directed that the twelve locate the church in Jerusalem."[218] He quotes Luke 24:49 in support but it is obvious that Judas is dead by that time. This may be relegated to a mistake which later editing would correct but he repeats, "This proves that the twelve were not a hierarchy for a worldwide church, but the charter membership of the authoritative model church which Jesus built and stationed in Jerusalem."[219] For one who insists on the principle of regenerate church membership this "authoritative model" proves less than what is desired.

As was the case with Graves, Milam insisted that the New Testament church was an independent, democratic church. He adds, "The departure from the New Testament form of independent, democratic churches was

216. James et al., *Fundamentalist Takeover*, 86–87.
217. Ammerman, *Baptist Battles*, 191.
218. Milam, *Fortress of the Truth*, 3:5.
219. Ibid.

the first step which led to the repudiation of the gospel of salvation by grace."[220] The thrust of this is simply that democratic church government is the guardian of the truth.

When one considers the case of alien immersion the basis rests on the autonomy and judgment of the local church. The validity of one's baptism depends on the local church's view of the church and the administrator who initially administered the baptism. As Milam said, "Baptism must do more than satisfy the individual conscience; it must also satisfy the conscience of the church."[221] He adds, "A New Testament church cannot be consistent, and recognize the baptism performed by a church which it considers alien to New Testament truth."[222] This would, based on his beliefs, include a church whose polity was other than congregational even if all the other elements of the baptism were correct.

Another key word in much of what Milam affirms is the word "considers." It is the sole judgment of the church in question, i.e., the autonomy of the local church which is the determining factor, even though that determination may be made by a vote that includes unregenerate members as would have been the case in the original church in Jerusalem under his mistaken scenario above. The conclusion this leads to is not left to speculation. Milam says, "The whole genius of their [Baptist's] work is based on the sovereignty and democracy of the local congregation."[223]

The controversies examined herein have had connection either directly or indirectly to Landmark doctrines of pulpit affiliation, alien immersion, close communion, and an anti-convention, anti-board sentiment which appeared primarily in areas of mission work. Howard Stewart says, "At the heart of each controversy, express in one form or another, was the ever-present emphasis on 'local autonomy.'"[224] Paul Harrison states what should be obvious when one views comments such as Milam's. The doctrine of local autonomy stands firmly against the sovereignty of God and the freedom of the Holy Spirit.[225] Although Harrison's study concerned the American Baptist Convention the doctrine involved was the same one. Harrison holds that the origin and spread of this doctrine is due to Landmark influence.

The issue of local autonomy was directly related to alien immersion as seen in a paper by Frank Barnes. Barnes related a story of an evangelist who

220. Ibid., 5:5.
221. Ibid., 3:6.
222. Ibid.
223. Ibid., 9:2.
224. Stewart, *Baptists and Local Autonomy*, 43.
225. Harrison, *Authority and Power*, 19–21.

baptized converts after a revival meeting. He said, "If these converts are received into the membership of a Baptist church on the basis of that immersion, it will be a case of alien immersion, because the man who immersed them did not have the scriptural authority to do so."[226] One has to ask the question based on this line of thought, was the baptism of the Ethiopian eunuch by Philip an alien immersion? Barnes says, "The local church alone has been commissioned to authorize and administer baptism."[227] He also traces the problem of alien immersion to the third century when certain churches regarded other groups as so heretical that they would not accept their baptisms. He cites no names, but the description fits Carroll's and Graves' description of the actions of the Novations.

Barnes cited approvingly R. E. Milam's words that "no Baptist group has long continued to grow and have unity when they have lost their stand against alien immersion."[228] He then cites the "prophecy" of B. H. Carroll when Carroll was asked if he knew that Charles Spurgeon disagreed with him on alien immersion. Carroll said, "When Spurgeon's Tabernacle is in ruins, the First Baptist Church of Waco, Texas will be going stronger than ever."[229] Barnes validated the fulfillment of Carroll's prophecy by relating the size of the offering and membership at the Metropolitan Tabernacle with the four thousand plus members of the Waco church and the size of the offering and the value of the church property.[230] Herein lies one of the validations of these doctrines. It is a pragmatic analysis. If the doctrines were not correct the Southern Baptist Convention would not be the size it is, have such growth as it has experienced, nor have the resources to fund such tremendous missionary efforts as it does. This is not often said as plainly as Barnes and Carroll set it forth.

However, all is not as it seems. The *Southern Baptist Texan* devoted a large part of one issue in 2006 to the issue of unregenerate church members. This sounds like an oxymoron in a Baptist church, particularly considering the doctrines espoused by Baptists quoted herein, but the truth is that less than 38 percent of Southern Baptists attend church on any given Sunday. This means that more than ten million of the supposed sixteen million plus

---

226. Barnes, "Problem of Alien Immersion." Barnes was a Southern Baptist pastor and leader. He spent thirty-five years in the Pacific Northwest as pastor of two churches and director of missions for Washington state. He was a trustee of Golden Gate Seminary for ten years and president of the Northwest Baptist Convention for two years.

227. Ibid., 2.

228. Ibid., 6.

229. Ibid., 8.

230. Ibid.

members are not actively involved in their respective churches.[231] The ramifications of this statistic alone for local autonomy and democratic rule of the church are staggering. As was the case at Tatnall Square Baptist Church and First Baptist Church Birmingham many of these "members" are marshaled in get-out-the-vote campaigns for certain issues but show no evidence of being a regenerate member of said church. Mark Dever, senior pastor of Capitol Hill Baptist Church in Washington, DC, said, "Some of those [missing members] will not have been our brothers and sisters in Christ and so slip into a Christless eternity."[232] What does that say about the claims of competency and autonomy and the decisions which were democratically voted on by these unregenerate members of a church whose membership is solely and exclusively supposed to be regenerate and who stand in judgment (some of these same members in all likelihood) of the validity of another's baptism, the authority of another minister of the gospel, or the place of another Christian at the Lord's table? As was the case with Graves, some of these deficiencies in theology and practice are overlooked rather than admit that the champions and proofs of Southern Baptist exclusiveness are somehow tarnished or without merit.

The Impact in the Local Church

While the controversies among the convention elites, authors, and scholars may make for interesting reading, one has to ask, how does this translate to the local church, to the people in the pew, and to the students who will be, in some cases, the leaders of the next generation? In order to assess this, a number of surveys have been examined and one of more recent date has been conducted by the author. Two reviews of Tull's *High-Church Baptists in the South* take somewhat different tacks on the influence of Landmarkism on the current generation of students. William Brackney says, "Perhaps most valuable of all is Tull's demonstration of the flexibility of Landmarkist ideas to reach across generations."[233] James Garrett, in reviewing Tull's work, said, "[It] seems to stretch unduly the connections, which are not documented, between Landmarkism and present SBC leadership, partly because he . . . seems to be out of touch with the present-day student mind-set. Most students entering Southwestern Seminary today, for example, have no

---

231. "Born-Again Baptists?" 8.
232. Ibid.
233. Brackney, review of *God So Loved the World*, Humphreys et al., *High Church Baptists in the South*, Tull, *Priesthood of Some Believers*, 168.

background in or knowledge of Landmarkism."²³⁴ As we will see, Garrett's assessment of the student's knowledge of Landmarkism is correct but not the influence upon their theological views wrought by pastors, teachers, and other church leaders who have been influenced by Landmark theology through the years.

The lack of background was not because there were no study materials available for Southern Baptists. A videotape program, *Southern Baptist Heritage*, by Walter Shurden, was produced in 1982 and made clear the place of Landmarkism in the development of the Southern Baptist Convention and exposed some of its fallacies particularly regarding successionism. The study guide by Earl Stroup which accompanied the series said in the introduction that there were three theories of Baptist beginnings. The first theory listed was the "Successionist Theory." The author noted, "Many Baptists today [1982] still hold to this view."²³⁵ Stroup noted also the "Anabaptist Kinship Theory" and the "English Separatist Dissent Theory" and added that the latter "is the most historically valid."²³⁶ In the pretest for the course, question number 1 (to which a true or false answer is required) states, "Southern Baptists may be traced as a denomination back to John the Baptist, through the early apostolic church of the first century, and down to the present Southern Baptist Convention."²³⁷ The answer is unambiguous: "False, Although this opinion is still held by many Baptists. It is not historically correct."²³⁸ No statistics are available as to how many people viewed the course or how many churches did not use the material because they found the teaching out of accord with their particular view. (The course also made the point that immersion was not the mode of baptism practiced by the first Baptist church.) This study course shows that Landmarkism was being taught in some places as the history of Baptist development and needed to be refuted.

One measure of the impact of Landmarkism in the life of the local church, and how it reached across generation lines, is to look at the surveys done by the agencies of the Southern Baptist Convention which addressed Landmark beliefs. Not every survey, of course, addressed every issue, as that was not their purpose, but certain issues were raised with enough frequency to obtain a picture of what the average Baptist church member and/or pastor believed regarding these doctrines. The surveys will be examined in

234. Garrett, review of *High-Church Baptists in the South*, 104.
235. Stroup, "Learning Guide to Southern Baptist Heritage," 11.
236. Ibid.
237. Ibid., 14.
238. Ibid., 71.

chronological order to assess the growth or diminution of Landmark theology among Southern Baptists.

A 1966 survey among Southern Baptist pastors in Arkansas revealed that slightly over 18 percent state when presiding at the Lord's Supper "that only members of the particular Baptist church in which the ordinance is being observed are eligible to partake."[239] Pastors in 60 percent of the churches, however, described their own practice as "closed communion." The disparity is seen in the pastors' own definition of closed communion. Asked to define closed communion, 44 percent said it meant only the members of the particular church where the ordinance was being observed could participate. Thirty-eight percent said it meant only Baptists can partake, 7 percent only immersed Christians can partake, and 4 percent said it meant only Christians could participate.[240] Even though there is a wide disparity of definition among those surveyed, it is clear that nearly 20 percent of Arkansas Southern Baptist churches in 1966 practiced close communion as the Landmarkers would have defined it.

In a survey of Southern Baptist students conducted in 1967 the question of the call to the preaching ministry was examined. It is interesting that among the students surveyed over 16 percent said they believed the call to the ministry came "mainly through the influence of friends, education, desire to help others, and background experiences."[241] One would have trouble holding any view opposed to pulpit affiliation if this is indeed the basis for the "call" to the gospel ministry.

A survey of Southern Baptist members who came into Southern Baptist churches from other denominations was conducted in 1968. Of the 1,296 members surveyed three-fourths indicated that they had been rebaptized when they joined a Southern Baptist church. This survey was broken down into geographic zones and interestingly the highest percentage of people who were rebaptized was in the Southwest where slightly over 85 percent said they were rebaptized when coming for membership.[242] This is

---

239. "Survey of Pastors," *Arkansas Baptist* 65.3 (20 January 1966): 7.

240. Ibid.

241. Sullivant et al., "Southern Baptist Students Speak Out." It is worth noting that this survey revealed in the decade before the fundamental resurgence in the Southern Baptist Convention that slightly more than 56 percent of students said they did not fully agree with the statement: "[The Bible] has God for its author, salvation for its end, and truth, without any mixture of error, for its matter."

242. Lowry et al., "Southern Baptist Membership Survey," 36–37. This same survey revealed that 73 percent of Southern Baptist pastors surveyed agreed with the statement "Jesus Christ was little interested in seeing his mission develop into widespread groups of believers on an organized basis." It seems to say that Jesus was interested in the one true church and not a number of different groups of believers.

clearly reflective of the Landmark theology of an authorized administrator in a true church which holds to the doctrine of the New Testament church.

A survey of small churches in 1970 showed a very slight decrease in the number of churches among that group who practiced true closed communion with 17.5 percent stating that only members of the particular church where the ordinance is being observed are eligible to partake.[243] This may not represent an actual decrease because the 1966 figures were from Arkansas in the heart of the "Landmark belt" and the later figures represent a sampling of small churches across the denomination, which would include areas where Landmark theology never gained a strong following.

A 2008 survey of 778 Southern Baptist pastors on the subject of alien immersion was quite revealing. One of the statistics that revealed quite a lot in regard to beliefs regarding alien immersion was the 92 percent response of Southern Baptist pastors who said they would not require baptism of new members who were immersed after conversion in a church that has the same beliefs as a Southern Baptist church.[244] One has to ask if there are in fact other churches that have exactly the same beliefs as Southern Baptist churches. The old adage that you have three opinions when you have two Baptists together, the local autonomy of each church, the soul competency of each believer,[245] and the democratic government of the individual church raises the question that has been asked by many, what is Southern Baptist belief, and could 92 percent of these pastors agree completely on the content of those beliefs in every point? One must also ask the source of the other church's belief. Does it come from the member seeking admission to the Southern Baptist church, is research conducted, is it derived from some denominational handbook, or is it merely the opinion held by the pastor or officers of the Baptist church receiving the person into membership? What does one do about independent non-denominational churches? This statement has the appearance of a cooperative spirit without any practical foundation.

Even more revealing in regard to Landmark doctrine and practice was the statistic that 16 percent of pastors would require a candidate for membership to be rebaptized if they had been baptized by immersion after conversion in another Southern Baptist church. In line with the 2000 Baptist Faith and Message, 74 percent of pastors said they would require rebaptism of candidates who had been immersed after conversion in another church

---

243. Faulkner et al., "A Look at the Small Church."

244. "Opinions of Southern Baptist Pastors."

245. Soul competency is a term popularized by E. Y. Mullins in *The Axioms of Religion* (1908). This doctrine holds that every believer is accountable to God and competent without outside assistance of interpreting the Scripture.

that does not believe in the eternal security of the believer. Apparently, this is true regardless of the beliefs of the candidate on this issue.[246] The issue at the heart of these rebaptisms seems to be the idea of cooperating with other evangelical churches which many Baptists, due in part to the Landmark influence, find not only inadvisable but striking at the heart of what it means to be a Southern Baptist.

In order to assess what this means for the next generation of Southern Baptists and what influence Landmarkism has had in shaping their beliefs the author undertook to survey students at three predominantly Baptist colleges in Tennessee and Alabama. The large percentage of students holding Landmark beliefs coming to Baptist colleges and universities, as related by James McGoldrick above, was the impetus for considering such a survey. The results were quite revealing. One hundred twenty-nine students at Union University (where Pendleton was the first chair of theology) in Jackson, Tennessee, Carson-Newman College in Jefferson City, Tennessee, and Samford University in Birmingham, Alabama, were surveyed in the fall of 2010 and the spring of 2011. (The methodology and statistical information is found in appendix G.) Of the 129 students surveyed 84 identified themselves as Southern Baptists. Of this group over 39 percent said that Baptists could be traced as a denomination from John the Baptist to the present-day Baptist churches. Sixty-two percent said that although Baptists could not be traced as a succession of churches back to the first century, Baptist churches can be traced through groups of various names back to the first church in Jerusalem. That probably explains the fact that 74 percent of those surveyed said the first Baptist church used immersion as the mode of baptism. The statistics on closed communion and alien immersion were much lower. Only 6 percent said their church invited only members of their particular church to partake of the Lord's Supper. The same percentage said that candidates for membership in their churches had to be rebaptized regardless of the mode or administrator of their former baptism. The make up of the respondents in the 6 percent were not the same in both questions.

Quite surprisingly, given the statement of the 2000 "Baptist Faith and Message" that "a New Testament church of the Lord Jesus Christ is an autonomous local congregation of baptized believers,"[247] over 76 percent

---

246. Ibid.

247. The 2000 Baptist Faith and Message does acknowledge that "the New Testament speaks also of the church as the Body of Christ which includes all the redeemed of all the ages, believers from every tribe, and tongue, and people, and nation." The words universal and invisible are studiously omitted. This language is also different from other statements within the Faith and Message. The other articles read: "Baptism *is* . . . ," "justification *is* . . . ," "the Lord's Supper *is* . . . ," "is" is strangely missing here and instead we

of those surveyed said the true church was invisible, universal, and made up of all believers of all ages. One of the choices available to the survey participants was the one given above from the "Baptist Faith and Message" but only 12 percent chose that response. This underlines the fact that pronouncements made at the convention level do not always translate into the pews as has been graphically demonstrated in other examples which have been considered.

Perhaps the most revealing statistic given the large percentage of students holding to some Landmark principles was the result which showed over 98 percent of those surveyed could not identify Landmarkism from a list of multiple choice answers. Eighty-four percent chose the answer which said, "Landmarkism is a term with which I am not familiar." This indicates the extent to which Landmark doctrine has been absorbed into the fabric of Southern Baptist life. As the above examples have shown Landmarkism was propagated and spread through denominational leaders, pastors, Sunday School teachers, and has been in some respects, as this next generation of Southern Baptists demonstrate, accepted as Baptist history, doctrine, and to a more limited extent Baptist exclusivism.

Landmarkism, although a term with which most Southern Baptists are unfamiliar, did not die out with the original progenitors. It did not cease to trouble the Southern Baptist Convention with the formation of the American Baptist Association. Landmarkism has influenced, to some greater or lesser extent, every significant controversy within the Southern Baptist Convention in the twentieth century. The name Landmarkism and the knowledge of Landmark precepts have faded from view. James Garret was correct in his assessment that students today "have no background in or knowledge of Landmarkism." But this nameless, faceless system of doctrine still influences much of Southern Baptist life and practice. Tull equated it to a virus but it is more akin to a strand of genetic code. It is no longer a foreign invader which has infected the blood stream of the Southern Baptist Convention as he metaphorically described it. A virus is something that runs its course or may be treated with various remedies but Landmarkism is much more akin to a strand of DNA which has influenced and is continuing

---

are told that the New Testament "speaks of." The definition of the church also plays into the definition of the Lord's Supper, which leaves room for closed communion. When the Faith and Message says, "The Lord's Supper is a symbolic act of obedience whereby members of the church . . . ," it leaves ample room for those who want to practice closed communion to be in step with the statement of faith since the church is defined as "an autonomous local congregation." See Southern Baptist Convention, "Baptist Faith and Message: A Statement Adopted by the Southern Baptist Convention June 14, 2000," articles 6–7.

to influence and shape the Southern Baptist Convention over one hundred fifty years after its introduction and most visible presence.

6

Conclusion

Concluding Observations

WALTER SHURDEN WROTE, "BYGONES are not *just* bygones. Our bygones are not has beens. They are still with us, helping and short-changing us, damning, and redeeming us, perverting, and saving us. Bygones are present. They are present whether you know it or not, whether you care or not."[1] The "us" Shurden refers to are Southern Baptists and while he speaks of Baptist controversies in general what he says can be applied to Landmarkism. It is not a forgotten piece of Southern Baptist history. On the contrary, as has been shown, Landmarkism is alive and well within the Southern Baptist Convention and is, in fact, one of the shapers of thought and practice for many Southern Baptists. It was a desire to understand the power of what seems to be an obscure movement in Baptist history to shape and form opinions of many Southern Baptists that motivated this study.

Although some has been written on the subject virtually all the works of any depth terminated in the early twentieth century and gave little insight into the impact of Landmarkism in the Southern Baptist Convention over the last century. In addition, there were some voids in what had been studied primarily regarding the Civil War, slavery, and how the passions and heartbreak surrounding these events would later play out in the civil rights struggles of the twentieth century. Some even suggested the Landmarkers played no part in this great moral struggle. In addition, many took the position that the formation of the American Baptist Association, which was founded by churches with strong Landmark beliefs which separated from the Southern Baptist Convention at the beginning of the twentieth century, spelled the end

1. Shurden, *Not a Silent People*, 21 (emphasis in original).

of Landmark influence among Southern Baptists. It was the goal of this work to fill in those voids and determine if and how Landmark influence was carried forward and the impact on present day Southern Baptists.

To add to the existing knowledge on this subject and uncover the answers sought much of the research focused on influential Baptist periodicals from the founding of Landmarkism to the present day. In addition, various unpublished letters, sermons, journals, speeches, and papers were examined to gain insight into the depth and influence of Landmark doctrines, their impact, and effect among Southern Baptists. This study was restricted to the Southern Baptist Convention the denomination in which Landmarkism was born, and one in which Landmarkism is alive and well even though largely unrecognized. The study did not examine the American Baptist Association and certain strains of Black Landmarkism which are openly and unabashedly Landmark in their beliefs. The focus was on the question: How have Landmark beliefs, particularly in the areas of ecclesiology, church history, and church polity, been propagated and become part of the accepted doctrine of many Southern Baptists when these beliefs in large part lie outside normative theological and historical boundaries?

Summary of Findings

J. R. Graves was the father of Landmarkism and for the better part of five decades its chief promoter and champion. He did more than any other single individual to inculcate Landmark views into Southern Baptist life. It was well said of Graves that you either loved him or hated him. He was a fiery and persistent adversary to all who opposed his views of Baptist church succession, baptism, the Lord's Supper, missiology, local church autonomy, authorized administrators of the ordinances, rejection of the legitimacy of other denominations, and slavery. Graves saw himself as the champion of Christ's truth over against every system of what he considered to be error. His great polemical skills and the publishing enterprises he controlled were key elements he used in that struggle and in the spread of Landmark theology throughout what was then called the Southwest (Kentucky, Tennessee, Alabama, Mississippi, Arkansas, and Texas). This was the center of critical mass, in those early days, of the Southern Baptist Convention.

Graves' theology, however, was very troubling in many respects, and one who examines it with an unbiased eye will see many disturbing aspects that many of his contemporaries merely termed "peculiar." Because many of Graves' works were published in the latter part of the nineteenth century most writers have seen his theological views as being developed later in his life.

However, Graves' early mentor, R. B. C. Howell (later turned upon by Graves), claimed the Baptist church was the true church and this influence early in Graves' career (1846) shaped his thinking. Howell brought Graves onto the editorial staff of the *Baptist* and thereby gave Graves a platform from which to project his theological views into the churches of the Southern Baptist Convention and the homes of its members. The formation of the Tennessee Publication Society by Graves in 1847 would prove to be the foundation of a publishing empire that served to foster and promote Landmark doctrines throughout the Southern Baptist Convention. Through consolidations and acquisitions the remnants of Graves' various publishing houses are even today producing denominational magazines for Southern Baptists. As early as 1848 Graves began to express positions in those publications on close communion, authorized administrators of baptism, and Baptist church succession. He repeated these beliefs and grew more adamant in his rejection of those who did not share his views all through the 1850s. His later works were merely recapitulations of positions he had held for decades.

Some of Graves' theological views were quite troubling and have been treated dismissively by most writers if they were treated at all. Many used terms like "peculiar" or "unsatisfactory" to describe Graves' views. The views he articulated, editorialized, and published on certain elements of ecclesiology, the atonement, the Trinity, and Christology were particularly notable for their divergence from historic Christianity.

In the area of ecclesiology he denied that the kingdom of Christ is composed of persons saying it was composed of churches. He declared that the locale of the kingdom of God is on earth and no where else. He equated the kingdom of God with the total of all Baptist churches. With that view of the "true church" as the standard he affirmed that ministers of other denominations were not true ministers of the gospel and demanded that all true Baptists cease from any pulpit affiliation with ministers of other denominations and refuse to accept their acts, particularly baptism, as legitimate.

His views on the Trinity were a product of his over-literal interpretation of Scripture. He denied that the terms Father and Son regarding the Trinity are eternal because, in his extreme literal view, the Son cannot be as old as the Father. He reduced the mysteries of the Trinity to strictly human experience and univocal predication.

Even the defenders of Graves called his Christology "one the most unsatisfactory aspects of his theology."[2] It is far from satisfactory to say as Graves did that the Son of God is divine and only relatively human. This view smacks of Apollinarianism and his views of the Son of God in his

---

2. Patterson, "Theology of J. R. Graves," 194–95.

Trinitarian formulations come perilously close to the Arian view and although Graves went to great lengths to avoid that his words are what they are. Graves denied that Christ is reigning in heaven and in fact says he will never reign there. Graves also held a kenotic theory of Christ and such a self-emptying of the Son of his divine attributes as Graves espoused is in essence a destruction of the Trinity. It is not merely an unsatisfactory Christology that Graves professed but rather a theology with far-reaching implications because such views cannot stand in isolation from one's doctrine of God.

These views also impacted the doctrine of the atonement which Graves affirmed. He asserted that Christ could not fulfill all righteousness in his human nature. He denied that saints go to heaven at their death because their redemption was not fully accomplished at the cross and actually awaits its fulfillment at Christ's return. He also refers to purgatory as the place where souls are purified of sin by the fires of punishment.

The extent of these views has been lightly treated or passed over by previous writers. The motivation behind such is unknown and, in some cases, may be due to their particular research objectives but could have been motivated in some cases by a desire to avoid arousing the wrath of Landmarkers. One of the objectives set forth here was an examination of the views of key Landmarkers and the extent to which such views were disregarded.

J. M. Pendleton's tract *An Old Landmark Re-set* was the source of the term Landmarkism, Landmark, etc., and he and Graves collaborated in promoting Landmarkism throughout the Southwest primarily through the pages of the *Tennessee Baptist* for ten years. Pendleton was much more the theologian than Graves and avoided some of the questionable formulations of Graves. Pendleton in his *Christian Doctrines* condemned those who said Christ had no human soul. He stated specifically that the work of the atonement was completed on the cross, contra Graves. Pendleton also explicitly rejected any assertion that the redeemed will not enter heaven until after the judgment and he dismissed ideas that represented Paradise as a place other than heaven. These expressions were in direct contradiction to Graves. Where he agreed with Graves, however, was on the issues of church government, baptism, authorized administrators of the ordinances, and Baptist church succession. Pendleton vacillated on the doctrine of the universal church. In the years before the Civil War and his parting with Graves his writing reflected much of Graves' influence. Later works showed a noticeable shift in this doctrine. After Pendleton moved north at the beginning of the Civil War there is a noticeable softening and even a shift in his sermons and much of his writing away from a hard-line Landmark position.

The Carroll brothers represent two different types of influence which spread Landmarkism through the Southern Baptist Convention. B. H.

Carroll was a theologian, pastor, and educator. He was the founder and first president of Southwestern Baptist Theological Seminary. Through that seminary Carroll was instrumental in promoting the Landmark view of Baptist church succession. He cited much of Graves' scriptural exegesis in his own works and used Pendleton's *Church Manual* as a textbook at the seminary. This played a part in shaping the theology and view of Baptist church history of many pastors who attended that seminary and went on to pastor churches throughout the Southern Baptist Convention. Examples of that influence have been cited herein and the generational preservation of Landmark ideas can be directly tied to such influence.

J. M. Carroll on the other hand although involved in theological education made a most significant contribution to the promotion and normalization of the Landmark view of Baptist church succession through his little book *The Trail of Blood*. The influence, longevity, and reach of this little book are nothing short of amazing if not perplexing. The perplexity arises because definitive historical scholarship has ably refuted the claims made by Carroll that the groups represented in his "trail" were indeed the true church and that these churches were in fact a continuous, unbroken line of Baptist churches even though known by other names. Despite definitive scholarship refuting Carroll's entire thesis this book continues to sell over eight thousand copies per year almost a century after it was first published.

The various groups claimed as Baptists by Graves and the Landmarkers and popularized and engraved upon the hearts and minds of many Southern Baptists by Carroll's *Trail of Blood* shared to a greater or lesser degree an exclusivist mentality about their church, even to the point of saying that there was no salvation outside their particular church. This led to a re-baptizing of all who joined their churches on the grounds that they had not been baptized in a true church by an authorized administrator. They shared a rejection of ecclesiastical authority and many of them were persecuted by the Church at Rome. This in the view of the Landmarkers made them true churches and hence Baptist churches.

The key to the Landmark claim to be the one and only true church rested squarely on the succession of Baptist churches. An unbroken line of properly baptized administrators of the ordinances traced back to the first church in Jerusalem was necessary to support the Landmark claims. Even the Landmarkers knew this was impossible to prove but they held (based on their interpretation of Matthew 16:18) that as Christ had said the forces of hell would not destroy his church that church had to exist in the pure form in every age. This succession of true churches could not be identified in particular individuals but rather in churches which held to the true doctrine of the original church founded by Christ (and John the Baptist as many insisted). The root and sustenance of the Baptist high churchism is in this historical continuity.

This highly sectarian, exclusivist view was bound to produce conflict and it did. These conflicts, frequently instigated by the Landmarkers, embroiled Baptists in controversies with other denominations. However, the Landmarkers were quick to bring the full force of their attacks to bear on many, even ones within their own Southern Baptist Convention, who dared to challenge, question, or offer an opposing view to the Landmark view of Baptist history, baptism, the Lord's Supper, local church autonomy, or mission work. During most of Graves' lifetime he was the chief protagonist in these efforts. Nothing describes his single-mindedness in many of these attacks better than his own words addressed toward others. He wrote, "I have known some professors to err greatly in this matter. They have been very strict over one point, and they have blamed every body who did not come up to their strictness."[3] Those who did not come up to the Landmark strictness in regard to the old Landmarks were certainly blamed, castigated, and defamed in many cases.

This Baptist pedigree was at the root of many of the controversies with other denominations as well as those that tore at the fabric of the Southern Baptist Convention through the last half of the nineteenth century and on into the twentieth century. Landmark attacks and attempts to diminish and destroy the authority and practice of other denominations were grounded in this Landmark view of church history. Any church or denomination which could not trace its lineage back to the first church in Jerusalem was not a true church in the Landmark view. The officers of those churches having been baptized in "societies," as the Landmarkers disparagingly called them, were, therefore, not true ministers of the gospel and hence were not entitled to recognition, nor were their acts. Southern Baptists who tried to interject any reputable scholarship into the Landmark view of Baptist church history were viciously and relentlessly attacked. In many cases like the Whitsitt controversy they were hounded out of office. The private correspondence examined herein reflects the chilling effect this had on other scholars, pastors, and officials of the Southern Baptist Convention.

The Landmarkers regarded Baptist church succession as their most powerful defense against encroachment by other denominations and even other interests with whom they disagreed within the Southern Baptist Convention. It should be said that apostolic doctrine produces apostolic living not sectarian, high church exclusiveness. Apostolic doctrine in the Landmark sense produced little more than an interest in the historical succession of baptismal subjects, mode, and administrators which became the *sine qua non* of their

---

3. Graves, *Relation of Baptism to Salvation*, 61.

ecclesiology. J. C. Ryle said, "No visible Church has any right to say, 'We are the only true Church. We are the men, and wisdom shall die with us.' No visible Church should ever dare to say, 'We shall stand for ever. The gates of hell shall not prevail against me.'"[4] No church may have that right but the Landmarkers certainly claimed that right for the Baptist Church. This methodology did not die with Graves, but rather, was one of the hallmarks of disputes arising over conflict with Landmark doctrines on into the twentieth century. This appetite for conflict has been a recurrent source of problems within the Southern Baptist Convention and its roots go deep into Landmarkism.

Landmarkism was born in the crucible of passions leading up to the American Civil War. The Southern Baptist Convention was formed out of a split among the Baptists over the question of slavery. This debate raged from the pulpits and in the pages of the religious press for decades before war began. The Baptists of the South found in the Landmark doctrines a ready answer to their critics in the North and other anti-slavery forces. They were the only true church. Therefore, any criticism was clearly the work of the devil and his forces marshaled against the one true church of Christ. The abusive nature of the attacks in the Landmark controlled religious press is a thing most Southern Baptists today would rather forget. The disparagement of the Negro included everything from physiology, mental capacity, primeval inclinations, and social development to biblical justification for their enslavement. Convinced by their own biblical exegesis, which in its own way was as flawed as their view of history, the Landmarkers hardened the already entrenched positions of many Southern Baptists on the issue of slavery and endeared themselves to many in the process.

Although Landmarkism and the staunch Landmarkers seemed to fade from prominence and even withdraw from the Southern Baptist Convention, the number of Landmarkers who ascended to positions of influence within the convention was remarkable. In the majority of the organizations of the convention Landmarkers found themselves publishing and editing denominational curricula for Sunday School and editing denominational publications, as Graves had done. Some of the denominational periodicals were outgrowths of Graves' old publishing concerns. Because of this influence doctrines like alien immersion, Baptist church exclusivity, and close communion were still loudly proclaimed and defended well past the midpoint of the twentieth century. The hottest debate among Southern Baptists in the decade of the 1960s, other than integration, was alien immersion. As in the nineteenth century, the debate was joined by the editors of the religious press, influential pastors, and seminary professors. The view most

---

4. Ryle, *Holiness*, 186.

widely held was one that rejected baptism, even by immersion, if performed by other than a Baptist church. In some cases, baptism by other Baptist churches was rejected because one could not be sure of the pedigree of that particular administrator.

The other debate, as mentioned above, regarded the acceptance of Negro members in Southern Baptist churches. This debate bore all the hallmarks, or one could say the landmarks, of the debates and fiery rhetoric of a century before in the lead up to the Civil War. Many Baptist churches were ripped apart over the question of whether to admit black candidates for membership. The defense of slavery, the segregation of the first half of the twentieth century, and the divisive and damaging struggle over civil rights and what it meant for the church were tied substantively if not directly to Landmark traditions and positions from the mid-nineteenth century. This Landmark, and one could say Southern Baptist, exclusivity and supremacy was fostered and closely tied to the alleged superiority and purity of white Southern Baptists.

Many of the recent controversies within the Southern Baptist Convention can be tied either directly or indirectly to a persistent Landmark theology that is part of much Baptist belief. As presented herein, although the words Landmark or Landmarkism fell out of favor and common usage, Landmark doctrines continued to be spread by many influential Southern Baptists. These doctrines came to be known, in many cases, as historic Baptist doctrine rather than Landmark doctrine. Many leaders recoiled at having the Landmark epithet hung on them, but others welcomed it and wore it proudly. The old antagonisms seem to surface in both the expected and quite unexpected places. For example, James Patterson's recent work, *James Robinson Graves: Staking the Boundaries of Southern Baptist Identity*, was met with almost instant criticism in the blogosphere by Landmark sympathizers. Most of the attacks accused Patterson of bias toward Graves and a failure to deal with the scriptural nature of the Landmark claims. The Landmark belief runs deep and those who hold such beliefs are not easily swayed by recent scholarship or history even as taught in Southern Baptist seminaries. Another recent example occurred in Virginia during a seminar on conflict resolution for Southern Baptist leaders. When the subject of church discipline was introduced the first comment from the audience was, "That smacks of Landmarkism."[5] Of course, Virginia was home to some of the most strident opposition to Graves and the Landmarkers. The passions aroused in the nineteenth century are still cherished by some and, as seen in this example, are still resented by others as the twenty-first century begins.

---

5. Glenn Waddell, president, Birmingham Theological Seminary, Birmingham, AL, interview by author.

CONCLUSION

There are substantive reasons in the eyes of a large percentage of Southern Baptists to consider other traditions as outside the normative expression of true and sound Christian tradition. These reasons are largely rooted in the Landmark doctrine of exclusivity, continuity, and purity of the Baptist Church. The number of Southern Baptists who hold such views has diminished since the time of Graves and the high tide of Landmarkism but still is manifest in many Southern Baptists who take a certain pride in what they consider to be their exclusive heritage, a heritage which they believe stretches back to the first church in Jerusalem. This view has been soundly refuted by many Baptist historians, but the pervasiveness of this view continues to be something that defies explanation.

As has been pointed out, Graves' success in promoting and furthering Landmark doctrine and beliefs was due in large part to his vast publishing empire which provided much of the material for Sunday School instruction, Bible study helps, and the weekly denominational periodicals. This influence of the denominational periodicals has been attested with many examples and many of the key editorial figures surveyed have been unabashedly Landmark in their views. This not so subtle and constant reinforcement of these views has proved to have a lasting impact. For nearly one hundred and fifty years these materials were the primary source of information, teaching, and instruction for the average Southern Baptist. When that is coupled with the preaching of many pastors, some examples which have been noted herein, you have a powerful influence on the minds of church members. This continues to some extent through denominational periodicals but the accessibility of the blogosphere, the ease of setting forth such views on the internet, familial traditions, and the instructional influence of the local church may prove to be the defining influence for succeeding generations. The propagation of this view through over a century of Landmark champions from preachers to convention officials has proven to have remarkable staying power. Midway through the twentieth century an eighteen-year-old student wrote an essay published in the *Baptist and Reflector* in which she said, "The Baptist Church was established by Christ during his own personal ministry."[6] She went on to affirm that "the Baptist is the only church that has the same doctrines that are obtained in the New Testament Church. . . . The reason we do not observe the Lord's Supper with other denominations is that they do not follow the teachings of Jesus. . . . The [Great] Commission was given to none except Baptists."[7] The fact that this essay was published (chosen from multiple submissions) in the leading

---

6. Mackay, "History of the Baptist Church," 7.
7. Ibid., 7–8.

denominational periodical of the time gives a clear indication of the sentiments of those who controlled that periodical. This essay written nearly a half century after Landmarkism faded from the minds of most Southern Baptists demonstrates what the various interviews, surveys, and personal correspondence referenced herein show, i.e., the remarkable staying power of Landmark doctrine, and the hold it has on many laypersons in the Southern Baptist Convention.

This power of Landmark doctrine remains unbroken in some respects. There is no doubt, based on what is presented herein, that there is a long-standing belief among many Southern Baptists that an unbroken succession of true churches must have always existed stretching back to the first church in Jerusalem. That these true churches were always Baptist churches is a foregone conclusion among this same group. While there is no historical basis for such belief and the vast majority of, if not all, Baptist historians, college, and seminary professors refute such beliefs; these beliefs have become part of what many regard as Baptist history and their unique ecclesiology. Surveys done by the author reveal that 62 percent of the Southern Baptist students surveyed still believe that although Baptist churches cannot be traced in an unbroken line back to the first century, Baptist doctrine can be traced through a succession of churches of various names back to the first century. The persistence of such beliefs testifies to the deep-seated hold which certain Landmark beliefs and doctrines have within the Southern Baptist Convention even today.

Contribution, Confirmation, and Contradiction

The contributions of this work on Landmarkism are in four primary areas. First, there has been much written on J. R. Graves. Relatively little of it has been of any length. Only James Tull and James Patterson have probed very deeply into his actions and analyses of the so-called peculiarities of his theology have been treated somewhat superficially by all writers and ignored by many. This research specifically set out to identify those peculiarities and assess them. Much of what has been discovered and recorded is disturbing and raises significant questions about his theology. However, every effort has been made to let Graves' own words define his questionable positions without any attempt to read into his words or attribute to him by inference questionable positions. The fact that these disturbing views were and have been ignored merely testifies to the appeal of his Landmark doctrines of Baptist church exclusivity and perpetuity.

The second area in which a noticeable void existed was the research and reporting of the part the Landmarkers played in the run up to the Civil War and the attitudes which formed toward the Negroes in its aftermath. Reading what has been written in the past one would be led to believe as O. L. Hailey said of Graves that he had no part in the bitter disputes leading up to the war. This research has discovered and reported that such was not the case. Not only Graves but the overwhelming majority of the Landmarkers, with the notable exception of Pendleton, participated in this controversy and its aftermath with what at times was venomous rhetoric. The connection with the civil rights struggles of a century later has been lightly treated. These struggles which tore many churches apart were reminiscent of the high-water mark of Landmarkism and are a part of recent Southern Baptist history most would rather forget.

Third, the impact and spread of Landmarkism in the twentieth century has been largely ignored in existing works. The term faded from popular use and most felt that the schism which saw the hard-line Landmarkers withdraw from the Southern Baptist Convention spelled the end of Landmarkism among Southern Baptists. This research has demonstrated that not to be the case and has shown Landmarkers, or at least persons sympathetic to some Landmark beliefs, continuing to occupy positions of influence within the convention and in the pulpits of many churches.

Finally, the continuing reach and impact of Landmarkism although it is a term unknown to those surveyed is somewhat remarkable. Large percentages of current students in predominantly Baptist colleges and universities hold to some key Landmark doctrines yet have no familiarity even with the term itself. All this shows the extent to which the views of Graves and his successors have succeeded in making their unique beliefs and doctrines part of what are now the beliefs of many Southern Baptists.

There were certain areas where this research led to different conclusions than what others have asserted. One such area was regarding the doctrinal positions held by J. M. Pendleton. It seems that many other writers were more influenced by Graves' assertion that he was unaware of any theological issues on which he and Pendleton disagreed. The conclusions reached from this research do not bear that out. Particularly after Pendleton moved north at the beginning of the Civil War, his positions, even on some of the key Landmark doctrines, seemed to soften considerably. Much of this was gleaned from over one thousand pages of handwritten sermon notes which were examined and perhaps neglected in other research.

Another area, as mentioned above, was the rhetoric that poured forth from the Landmark press regarding the Negro, slavery, states rights, and other issues leading up to and in the decades following the Civil War. These same words resurfaced in the civil rights struggles in the mid-twentieth century and it seems most researchers want to leave these things unsaid. Historical research, however, must not leave unsaid that which is now embarrassing, regrettable, and rather to be forgotten instead of reported.

Going Forward

There are many areas in which this research built on the work of those who have gone before. The effort has been made to build upon that work and advance the base of knowledge regarding Landmarkism and its considerable influence within the Southern Baptist Convention. The legacy of Landmarkism is in many respects one of controversy with those who rejected their unique view of the church, its history, government, and ordinances. There are more controversies emerging among Southern Baptists even at the present day and some bear a resemblance to those of the nineteenth century and early twentieth century. From mission boards, administration of baptism, alien immersion, seminary subscription to certain doctrines, a resurgent Landmarkism, and the new effort to root out Calvinists from positions of power in the convention, many issues loom for the Southern Baptist Convention. This may well prove to be fertile ground for further study regarding the effect and extent to which Landmarkism plays a part in the outworking and resolution of these issues.

This kind of study will be even more challenging as time passes. In spite of the high percentages of Southern Baptist who hold some Landmark views, as revealed by the various studies referenced in this work, Landmarkism is a term that is practically unknown among many Southern Baptists, most notably in the millennial generation. Irrespective of the views of Baptist historians and the clear majority of professors who teach at predominantly Baptist colleges and seminaries, the Landmark views of ecclesiology and church history have become accepted Baptist doctrine among many and at the same time these views have lost any distinctive designation that would indicate these views are outside the mainstream of Southern Baptist belief. Landmarkism is no longer a movement, a sectional oddity, or a curious piece of Baptist history. It has become for far too many the essential Baptist position.

Appendix A

Tennessee Publication Society
Preamble and Constitution of an Auxiliary Publication Society

WHEREAS, WE BELIEVE IT to be our duty, as Christians and good citizens enjoying as we do so many, and rich privileges, secured to us by our holy religion, to aid by all means in our power in its widespread dissemination in all sections and communities of our land and especially in our own State & the South West. It is a fact to be deplored that thousands of families in our own State, and tens of thousands in the great West and Southwest are without a copy of the Bible to direct them and their children in the way of life. While Papists are pouring in upon us like a flood, and by their Priests, and schools, and books, and Sisters of Charity, are seeking to infect the rising population with the poison of their creed, have we nothing to do to stay the tide? Believing as we do that in no way can we accomplish more good (save by the living preacher) than by encouraging the wide spread circulation of our Religious Periodicals and the gratuitous distribution of Bibles, testaments, religious books and tracts, through our ministers, missionaries, colporteurs, and *whole body of the church.*

And whereas, to procure these books for gratuitous circulation will require a large permanent fund for the purpose of purchasing and publishing books and tracts, the interest of which to be applied annually in books for this purpose:

Resolved, That we do heartily commend and approve of the organization of the Tennessee Publication Society which has in view this great and glorious purpose, and to aid in its operations and to secure to ourselves its advantages, we hereby form ourselves into a society with the following constitution:

Constitution

Art. I. This society shall be called the _____ Baptist Publication Society auxiliary to the Tennessee Publication Society.

Art. II. The objects of this society shall be to raise funds for supplying the destitute in our own neighborhood with the word of God, and religious books and tracts, and to aid the parent society in its effort to publish and purchase such books as are needed by the Baptist denomination, and to circulate the Bible and religious books throughout the destitute places in our State and country.

Art. IV [*sic*] [actually III]. All the funds raised by this society shall be sent to the parent society one half of which to be applied to the permanent fund, and one half received by the society in books for the formation of a church library for the benefit of this church and neighborhood. The interest on the money contributed to the permanent fund to be received each year in books to be placed in the library, or gratuitously distributed.

Art. IV. Each contributor of $2 or more annually, shall be a member of this society and enjoy a life interest in the library—being entitled to the use of four books each month or more, according to the sum contributed. Each member contributing fifty cents for each reader in the family shall be entitled to draw one book for each.

Art. V. The officers of this society shall consist of a President, Vice President, a Secretary and Treasurer, who shall perform the duties of like officers in similar societies and chosen by ballot.

Art. VI. This society shall make a report through its Corresponding Secretary, annually, upon the first _____ of Sept., to the State Society, of all its proceedings; giving a list of the names of the contributors—the amounts given; the No. of copies of religious (Baptist) papers taken in the church and neighborhood; the number of volumes of books in the library; the number of pages of religious books and tracts circulated, or sold by the society, and the results of their efforts.

Art. VII. This society shall appoint at each annual meeting, two special solicitors, one a Fund Solicitor, and one a Publication Solicitor. It shall be the duty of the Fund Solicitor to solicit members and contributors to this Society. It shall be the duty of the Publication Solicitor to ascertain the extent of the destitution of the word of God, or religious papers and books, and to introduce the bible and one weekly religious periodical into every family within the reach of the society, each Solicitor making a report of advancement to the Corresponding Secretary at the regular meetings of this society. This society shall furnish one Bible and one religious paper to each destitute family within its bounds, unable or unwilling to provide one for itself.

Art. VIII. This society shall have one annual meeting, on the _____ Saturday in September, at the place selected by the Society, at which time the Preamble and Constitution shall be read, and an anniversary address delivered by some one previously and specially invited; after which a public contribution shall be taken, to promote the general objects of the Society, to enlarge the library and circulate the word of God—also names of new subscribers to this constitution.

Art. IX. This society shall have the power to make by-laws, from time to time, as expediency may seem to demand, not annulling any article of this constitution.

Art. X. This society shall not be dissolved so long as two members are willing to adhere to this constitution, and they shall continue to control the interests and library of this society.

Art. IX [sic] [actually XI]. This Constitution can be amended, but *not repealed*, by a vote of two thirds of the contributing members of this society, at a regular meeting.

Note: There are numerous inconsistencies in the capitalization of certain words and expressions in this document. All are reproduced as in the original as carried in the *Tennessee Baptist*, May 18, 1848.

It is worth noting that the logo for the Tennessee Publication Society featured a printing press with rays of light emanating from it and forming an arch over the press. The "stones" of the arch were books and bore the names of authors like Gill, Carson, and Howell. However, the keystone of the arch was not the Bible as one might expect, but rather the *Tennessee Baptist*. The constitution makes it clear that at least next to the Word of God each family should receive a religious periodical and the constitution makes it equally clear by parenthetical definition that religious equals Baptist.

(Source: *Tennessee Baptist*, May 18, 1848)

Appendix B

Mass Meeting at Cotton Grove

June 24, 1851

ON THE MOTION OF Rev. J. R. Graves, Rev. E. Collins was called to the chair. The meeting was then called to order by the President, by reading a chapter of Scriptures, and prayer by Rev. G. Wright.

On motion and second, J. R. Woolfolk, Esq., was appointed Secretary, and Rev. J. V. E. Covey, assistant.

Brother Graves then proceeded briefly to explain the reasons that suggested the call of the present meeting and its objects; and when, on motion, seconded by Rev. Peter S. Gayle, he proceeded to offer the following resolutions:

Resolved. That it is our duty, as the professed followers of Jesus Christ, to use our utmost efforts and exertions to aid in every possible way the fulfillment of the Savior's prayer, as recorded in John 17:20, 21. "Neither pray I for these alone , but for them also which shall believe on me through their word: That they may all be one, as thou Father art in me, and I in thee, that they also may be one in us: that the world may believe that thou hast sent me."

In sustaining the resolution he said:

1st. It is blasphemous to pray for the accomplishment of an object which we are unwilling and refuse to aid in accomplishment—the measure of our doing, is the exact measure of the sincerity of our prayers.

2d. He explained the oneness sought to be effected.

3d. How can it be effected? Can we recognize those sects as churches or branches of the Church of Christ, which have not the organization, doctrines, membership, or ordinances of the primitive churches? Will we not aid in deceiving those Christians in them? Will they not say, I am a branch of Christ's Church, it is all enough? Is not one branch as good as another? It is a serious question.

Brother Gayle followed at some length, glancing at the history, principles and position Baptists had always occupied, and the persecutions they have been called upon to endure.

The resolution was passed unanimously.

Rev. J. R. Graves then proceeded to offer the following queries, which he wished to be considered at this meeting and referred to some adjourned meeting.

1st. Can Baptists consistently with their principles or the Scriptures recognize those societies, not organized according to the pattern of the Jerusalem Church, but possessing a *government*, different *officers*, a different *class of membership*, different *ordinances, doctrines* and *practices*, as the Church of Christ?

2d. Ought they to be called Gospel Churches or Churches in a religious sense?

3d. Can we consistently recognize the ministers of such irregular and unscriptural bodies, as gospel ministers in their official capacity?

4th. Is it not virtually recognizing them as official ministers to invite them into our pulpits, or by any other act that would or could be construed into such a recognition?

5th. Can we consistently address as brethren those *professing* Christianity, who not only have not the doctrines of Christ, and walk not according to his commandments, but are arrayed in direct and bitter opposition to them?

After considerable discussion, which showed an unanimous feeling and sentiment,

On motion and second, the above queries were referred to a subsequent meeting.

(Source: *Tennessee Baptist* [Nashville], September 20, 1851.)

Appendix C

The Trail of Blood

From J. M. Carroll, *The Trail of Blood*, 1931, reprinted by permission, Ashland Avenue Baptist Church. This work is in the public domain. Ashland Baptist Church was original publisher and still publishes the book today. Note: The "red circles" mentioned in Carroll's explanation show up as the dark black circles in the reproduction.

THE TRAIL OF BLOOD

By DR. J. M. CARROLL

	100	200	300	400	500	600	700	800	900	1000	1100	1200
IRREGULAR CHURCHES		CHURCH GOVERNMENT CHANGED			LEO II POPERY OFFICIALLY ESTABLISHED							
JESUS ORGANIZES HIS CHURCH MARK 3:16-18		BAPTISMAL REGENERATION	CONSTANTINE 313	CHURCH AND STATE UNITED (HIERARCHY)					INFANT COMMUNION			CELIBACY 1123
			INFANT BAPTISM	PERSECUTION ACT 303	MARIOLATRY							TRANSUBSTANTIATION PETROBRUSIANS & ARNOLDISTS 1139
			NON FELLOWSHIP DECLARED 251	TOLERATION ACT 311	INFANT BAPTISM ESTABLISHED BY LAW	INDULGENCES	PURGATORY	SAINT AND IMAGE WORSHIP 787	DIVISION 869			
					(CATHOLIC)				GREEK			CATHO
									ROMAN			
CHRISTIANS		MONTANISTS NOVATIONS PUTERINS	PATERINS CATHARI								ARNOLDISTS HENRICIANS	
					(ANA) (BAPTIST)				DARK AGES	(ANA) BAPTIST		
ITALY WALES ENGLAND	ITALY WALES		AFRICA		SPAIN FRANCE	WALES ARMENIA	ITALY ARMENIA ENGLAND	ITALY ARMENIA BULGARIA	ITALY FRANCE		ENGLAND WALES	

EXPLANATION OF THE CHART

By DR. J. M. CARROLL

ILLUSTRATING the History of the Baptist Churches from the time of their founder, the Lord Jesus Christ, until the 20th Century.

1. The purpose of this book and chart is to show according to History that Baptists have an unbroken line of churches since Christ and have fulfilled His prophecy, "I WILL BUILD MY CHURCH AND THE GATES OF HELL SHALL NOT PREVAIL AGAINST IT." In the irregular churches is clearly seen the growth of Catholicism and Protestantism. Baptists are not Protestants since they did not come out of the Catholic Church.

2. The numbers at the top and bottom represent 20 centuries. The first vertical line is A.D. 1, and the second, A.D. 100, and so on.

3. The horizontal lines at the bottom have between them the nicknames given to Baptists during the passing years and ages — Novations, Montanists, Paulicans and Waldenses.

4. THE RED CIRCLES REPRESENT BAPTIST CHURCHES beginning with the first Church at Jerusalem, founded by Christ during His earthly ministry, and out of which came the churches of Judea, Antioch and others. The red indicates they were persecuted. In spite of the bitterest opposition and persecution Baptist Churches are found in every age. The first nickname given them was Christians, the next Ana-Baptists, and so on. You will notice that the dark ages are represented by a dark space. Even during this time you will notice a continual bitterly persecuted even unto death by the Catholic Baptists, and they were simply called Baptists.

5. THE BLACK CIRCLES REPRESENT IRREGULAR, THEREFORE CALLED — IRREGULAR Pastors assumed authority over them and other smaller churches. Thus in the 3rd Constantine issued a call in 313 inviting a churches — that is Baptist Churches — ref

TRAIL OF BLOOD

By DR. J. M. CARROLL

	00	1000	1100	1200	1300	1400	1500	1600	1700	1800	1900	2000

INFANT COMMUNION

GREEK CATHOLIC

ROMAN CATHOLIC

TRANSUB-STANTIATION

1123 CELIBACY

1139 PETROBR-USIANS & ARNOLDISTS

1215 AURICULAR CONFESSION

1215 DEPOSED FREDERICK

1229 BIBLE FORBIDDEN

1231 INQUISITION

WYCLIFF 1330-1384

HUSS 1373-1415

SAVONAROLA 1452-1498

1483-1546 LUTHER

ZWINGLI 1484-1531

1530 LUTHERAN

1535

1509-1564 CALVIN

1541

1555 AUGS-WESTPHALIA

BURG

1602 PRESBYTERIAN

1648

BUNYAN 1628-1688

CHURCH OF ENGLAND

1785 METHODIST

1810 CUMBERLAND

1812 DISCIPLES

DARK AGES

ARNOLDISTS-ALBIGENSES

HENRICIANS WALDENSES

(ANA-BAPTISTS)   BAPTISTS

ARMENIA BULGARIA   FRANCE ITALY   ENGLAND WALES   ITALY GERMANY   POLAND ALPS GERMANY   FRANCE   AMERICA   RUSSIA CUBA

TRENT

CONGREGATIONALIST

at vertical line is A.D. 1, and the during this time you will notice a continual line of churches called Ana-Baptists. They were continually and bitterly persecuted even unto death by the Catholics. Near the first of the 16th Century the Ana was dropped and they were simply called Baptists.

THE BLACK CIRCLES REPRESENT CHURCHES INTO WHICH ERROR CAME AND ARE THEREFORE CALLED IRREGULAR CHURCHES. The first error was in church Government. Pastors assumed authority not given them by Christ. Pastors of larger churches claimed authority over other and smaller churches. Thus in the 3rd Century the Roman Hierarchy was established. The Emperor Constantine issued a call in 313 inviting all churches to send representatives to form a council. The red churches — that is Baptist Churches — refused the invitation but the irregular churches responded. The Emperor was made the head and thus the group of churches known as irregular churches became the State Church. The Emperor continued to head the churches until Leo II claimed authority as the successor of Peter. Thus is seen the error in church Government developed into Popery in the 16th Century the Protestant Churches began to come out of the Roman Catholic Church. They are called Protestants because they protested against the errors of Catholicism.

6. It was in the year 251 that Baptist Churches declared nonfellowship with the irregular churches. They refused to accept Baptism administered in infancy or for Salvation and thus came the oldest nickname — Ana-Baptists which means rebaptizers.

Copyrighted 1931 by Ashland Avenue Baptist Church, Lexington, Ky.

Appendix D

Constitution of the Southern Baptist Sunday School Union

Constitution

Art. 1 This body shall be called the Southern Baptist Sunday School Union.

Art. 2 The objects of this Union shall be to call the attention of the Baptists of the South to the importance of Sunday Schools; to provide and recommend to them suitable books and other publications; and by whatever means we can, to advance the interests of Sunday Schools among our brethren.

Art. 3 Any person may become an annual member of this Union by the paying to our Treasurer of the sum of one dollar. Any person paying thirty dollars at one time, or in three annual installments of ten dollars each, shall receive a certificate of Life Membership. The payment of one hundred dollars at one time, or in five annual installments of twenty dollars each, shall constitute one a Life Director and Honorary Member of the Board of Managers. Any Church, Association, Sunday School, Missionary Society, or other organization of the sort, that shall contribute to the funds of the Union, shall be entitled to one member for every five dollars contributed within the previous year to any regular meeting; and any such body contributing, as above specified, thirty dollars, be entitled to a perpetual representation by any one to whom they may select from year to year. See also Article 7.

Art. 4 The officers of this Union shall consist of a President, fourteen Vice Presidents, Corresponding and Recording Secretary, Treasurer, and seven Managers, who shall be members in good standing of some Baptist Church of Christ. They shall be elected every two years at the Regular

Biennial meeting, held at the same time and place with the Southern Baptist Convention, and shall hold their respective places until others are chosen.

Art. 5 It shall be the duty of the President, Vice Presidents, Corresponding and Recording Secretary to perform such services as usually devolve upon such officers. The Corresponding Secretary shall conduct the correspondence, visit Churches, Associations, etc. to present the claims of the Union, and by all means within his power, advance the influence and interests of the organization, and report his work as often as required by them to the Executive Board, attested by the President and Recording Secretary, and shall report the state of his accounts as required by the Board. The Managers with the other officers shall constitute the Executive Board of the Union, and in the intervals of its meetings shall have the power to manage all the business that properly belongs to it. It shall be authorized to fill all its own vacancies in the intervals of the meeting of the Union; to establish a depository of Sabbath School books in the city of Nashville, with branches wherever it may be thought necessary, make contracts with authors, publishers, agents, and do what ever else may be necessary to the efficient accomplishment of the objects of this organization as specified in Article 2.

Art. 6 The Union shall hold its regular meeting at the time and place of the Southern Baptist Convention every two years, but it shall also hold a meeting in the intermediate year, at such time and place as may be determined by vote.

Art. 7 Any Baptist Sunday School, Church or Association, which shall purchase our books or publications, shall be entitled to a representation in the next annual meeting of the Union thereafter, of one member for every twenty dollars invested.

Art. 8 This Constitution may be altered or amended by a vote of two-thirds at any regular meeting, provided, notice of the proposed alteration be given and recorded at the previous annual or biennial meeting.

(Source: *Christian Index* [Macon, GA], November 25, 1857.)

Appendix E

Whitsitt's Statement before the Board of Directors at the Southern Baptist Convention 1897

Wilmington, N.C., May 7, 1897
To the Board of Trustees of the Southern Baptist Theological Seminary

DEAR BRETHREN: —I BEG leave to return sincerest and heartiest thanks for the noble and generous treatment that you have bestowed upon me. I have only words of affection for every member of the Board. After consulting with the committee I have the following to say:

1. That in regard to the articles written as editorials for the *Independent*, I have long felt that it was a mistake, and the generous action of the Board of Trustees renders it easy for me to make this statement. What I wrote was from a Pedobaptist standpoint with a view to stimulating historical research, with no thought that it would injure the Baptists, and with no intention to disparage Baptist doctrines or practices.

2. That the article in *Johnson's Encyclopedia* has probably passed beyond my control; but it will be very pleasing to me if I can honorably procure the elimination from it of whatever is offensive to any of my brethren.

3. Regarding the charge that I expressed a conviction that a kinswoman of mine ought to follow her husband into a Pedobaptist church, that it was never my intention to indicate a belief that the family outranked the Church of God. I believe that obedience to God's commands is above every other human duty, and that people in every relation of life ought to obey God rather than man.

4. That on the historical questions involved in the discussion, I find myself out of agreement with some honored historians; but what I have written is the outcome of patient and honest research, and I can do no otherwise than to re-affirm my convictions and maintain my position. But if in the future it shall ever be made to appear that I have erred in my conclusions, I would promptly and cheerfully say so. I am a searcher after truth, and will gladly hail every helper in my work.

5. That I cannot more strongly assure the brethren that I am a Baptist than by what I have recently declared with regard to the abstract of principles set forth in the Fundamental Laws of the seminary. I am heartily in accord with my Baptist brethren in every distinctive principle that they hold. My heart and life are bound up with the Baptists, and I have no higher thought on earth than to spend my days in their fellowship and service, in the name of the Lord Jesus Christ.

Respectfully submitted.
Wm. H. Whitsitt

(Source: *Proceedings of the Southern Baptist Convention held at Wilmington, NC, May 7–10, 1897* [Atlanta: Franklin Printing and Publishing, 1897], 15–16.)

Appendix F

Resolution Presented By B. H. Carroll at the Southern Baptist Convention, 1898

WHEREAS, AS APPEARS FROM report adopted at Chattanooga Convention and from the charter and fundamental laws of the Seminary, the connection between this Convention and the Southern Baptist Theological Seminary is but slight and remote; and

Whereas, This connection cannot well be made stronger or more equitable to the several States in representation on the Board of Trustees because of legal difficulties and of hazard to investments, which might result from necessary charter changes; and

Whereas, There have developed serious differences among our people relative to certain Seminary matters, which threaten harmony and jeopardizing that unity in mission work; which was the great object of the institution of the Convention; and

Whereas, The dissolution of the slight and remote bond between the body and the Seminary would in no wise affect the legal status of the Seminary; and

Whereas, Unity in mission work is more important than unity in Seminary work; now therefore,

Resolved, That this Convention without expressing any opinion whatever on the merits of the controversy concerning Seminary matters, about which good brethren among us honestly differ, but in the interest of harmony, particularly with a view to preserve and confirm unity in mission work, does now exercise its evident right to divest itself of responsibility in the Seminary management, by dissolving the slight and remote bond between this body and the Seminary; that is, that this body declines to nominate trustees for the seminary or entertain motions or receive reports relative thereto, leaving that institution to stand on its own merits and be managed by its own trustees.

(Source: *Annual of the Southern Baptist Convention 1898, Containing the Proceedings of its Forty-Third Session, Fifty-Third Year, Held at Norfolk, VA., May 6–10, 1898* [Atlanta: Franklin Printing and Publishing, 1898], 22–23.)

Appendix G

SURVEYS WERE CONDUCTED WITH the assistance of professors in church history and Baptist history classes at Samford University, Carson-Newman College, and Union University in the fall semester of 2010 and the spring semester of 2011. Additional surveys were done by the author in campus coffee shops, common areas, and various restaurants and coffee shops adjacent to campus.

The purpose of the surveys was to measure current beliefs and attitudes of students at predominantly Baptist colleges and universities in regard to Landmark doctrines.

The students from the classes were asked to identify themselves as Southern Baptists, other Baptist denominations, or other denominations other than Baptist. Only the responses of self-identified Southern Baptist students were measured. The surveys were composed of twelve true/false or multiple choice questions. The students were not identified in any way other than their self-identified denominational affiliation. Participation in the surveys was voluntary and the subjects were not compensated. The type of procedure was psychosocial-non-manipulative and there was no relationship between the researcher and the participants.

The following pages contain a sample of the survey and the statistical analysis.

APPENDIX G

Student Survey

Please Note: Participation in this survey is entirely voluntary and is not part of the requirements for this course. Participation in this survey, or lack thereof, will not affect your grade in this course.

1. Denominational affiliation:

    ___ Southern Baptist   ___ Independent Baptist
    ___ Missionary Baptist ___ American Baptist
    ___ Other

2. ___ T ___ F Baptists may be traced as a denomination from John the Baptist, through the early apostolic church, and through the ages to the present day Baptist churches.

3. ___ T ___ F Baptists are the only denomination (other than the Roman Catholic Church) that did not emerge from the Protestant Reformation.

4. ___ T ___ F Although Baptists may not be traced through a succession of churches back to the first century, Baptist doctrine can be traced through groups of various names back to the first church in Jerusalem.

5. ___ T ___ F Baptists as a denomination had their beginning in 17th century England.

6. ___ T ___ F The first Baptist congregation used immersion as their mode of baptism.

7. ___ T ___ F John Smyth is considered to be the founder of the Baptists.

8. When your church observes the Lord's Supper does your pastor
    a. make no reference as to who may partake
    b. invite all Christians present to partake
    c. state that only members of your particular church may partake
    d. state that only Baptists who are present may partake

9. In order for a person who has been baptized after profession of faith in another church to be received into membership in your church
    a. they must be re-baptized if it was not a Baptist church
    b. they will be received by statement if it was a Baptist church
    c. they must be re-baptized by our pastor regardless of the

church since we cannot know what another church taught
- d. they will be received as long as their baptism was by immersion
- e. don't know

10. What does the term "close" (or closed) communion mean to you?
    - a. only Christians may partake
    - b. only immersed Christians may partake
    - c. only Baptists may partake
    - d. only members of the particular Baptist church observing communion may partake

11. The true church is
    - a. the Baptist Church, the true representative of Christ on earth
    - b. invisible, universal, and consists of the whole body of believers that have been or will be gathered into one under Christ
    - c. a visible, local body of baptized believers, voluntarily united
    - d. made up of all who profess the true religion and their children
    - e. I would define differently than the above choices.

12. The kingdom of God is
    - a. the sovereign rule or reign of God, either in grace or in judgment
    - b. the aggregate of all Baptist churches
    - c. the aggregate of all churches that preach the Gospel
    - d. the rule of God on earth through proper administrators in properly organized churches
    - e. I would define differently than the above choices.

13. Landmarkism:
    - a. is a term with which I am not familiar
    - b. was what could be called a "high church" movement among Southern Baptists in the mid-nineteenth century
    - c. was one of the early church growth movements of the early twentieth century
    - d. was a movement among Southern Baptists in the late nineteenth century characterized by a distinctive view of Scripture
    - e. is a term used by the Disciples of Christ and often wrongly attributed to Baptists

John the Baptist #2		Succession of Doctrine #4		Baptism Immersion #6	
Population	10600	Population	10600	Population	10600
Sample Size	84	Sample Size	84	Sample Size	84
Answer	33	Answer	52	Answer	62
Percentage	39.29%	Percentage	61.90%	Percentage	73.81%
95% CI	+/-10.44%	95% CI	+/-10.39%	95% CI	+/-9.40%

Closed Communion #8		Alien Immersion #9		Church Inv., Univ. #11	
Population	10600	Population	10600	Population	10600
Sample Size	84	Sample Size	84	Sample Size	84
Answer	5	Answer	5	Answer	64
Percentage	5.95%	Percentage	5.95%	Percentage	76.19%
95% CI	+/-5.06%	95% CI	+/-5.06%	95% CI	+/-9.11%

Landmarkism #13	
Population	10600
Sample Size	84
Answer	83
Percentage	98.81%
95% CI	+/-2.32%

"CI" = Confidence Interval

Bibliography

Primary Sources

Unpublished Sources

Alldredge, Eugene Perry. "E. P. Alldredge Collection." Southern Baptist Historical Library and Archives, Nashville, TN.

Barnes, Frank. "The Problem of Alien Immersion." Typewritten manuscript. Original in the Southern Baptist Historical Library and Archives, Nashville, TN.

Bell, Marty G. "James Robinson Graves and the Rhetoric of Demagogy: Primitivism and Democracy in Old Landmarkism." PhD diss., Vanderbilt University, 1990.

Compere, Ebenezer Lee. "E. L. Compere Collection." Southern Baptist Historical Library and Archives, Nashville, TN.

Folk, Edgar Estes. "E. E. Folk Collection." Southern Baptist Historical Library and Archives, Nashville, TN.

George, Timothy. Interview by author. Birmingham, AL, February 9, 2010.

Graves, James Robinson. "J. R. Graves Collection." Southern Baptist Historical Library and Archives, Nashville, TN.

Howell, Robert Boyte Crawford. "A Memorial of the First Baptist Church, Nashville, Tennessee from 1820 to 1863, by a Member of the Church." Typescript copy. 2 vols. Dugan-Carver Library, Nashville, TN.

Hymers, R. L., Jr. "The Last Hope of Man on Earth—the Local Church." Sermon. Baptist Tabernacle, Los Angeles, CA, July 11, 2004.

"Manly Family Correspondence." Southern Baptist Historical Library and Archives, Nashville, TN.

McDonald, Erwin L. "Erwin L. McDonald Papers." University of Central Arkansas Archives and Special Collections, Fayetteville, AR.

McGoldrick, James. Interview by author. Greenville, SC, August 2, 2010.

Milam, Robert Edward. "R. E. Milam Collection." Southern Baptist Historical Library and Archives, Nashville, TN.

Moore, David O. "The Landmark Baptists and Their Attack upon the Southern Baptist Convention Historically Analyzed." ThD diss., Southern Baptist Theological Seminary, 1949.

Mullins, Edgar Young. "E. Y. Mullins Collection." Southern Baptist Historical Library and Archives, Nashville, TN.

Patterson, Thomas Armour. "The Theology of J. R. Graves and Its Influence on Southern Baptist Life." ThD diss., Southwest Baptist Theological Seminary, May 1944.

Pendleton, James Madison. "Proctor-Pendleton Papers." Department of Library Special Collection, Kentucky Library and Museum, Western Kentucky University, Bowling Green, KY.

Smith, Harold Stewart. "A Critical Analysis of the Theology of J. R. Graves." ThD diss., Southern Baptist Theological Seminary, 1966.

Stookey, Stephen M. "The Impact of Landmarkism upon Southern Baptist Western Geographical Expansion." PhD diss., Southwestern Baptist Theological Seminary, 1994.

Terry, William Martin. "Samuel Henderson and His Response to J. R. Graves and Landmarkism through the South Western Baptist 1857–1859." MA thesis, Samford University, May 1977.

Van Ness, Isaac Jacobus. "I. J. Van Ness Collection." Southern Baptist Historical Library and Archives, Nashville, TN.

Weaver, Rufus W. "An Episode in Baptist History." Unpublished manuscript, ca. 1928. Original in Southern Baptist Historical Library and Archives, Nashville, TN.

———. "Rufus W. Weaver Collection." Southern Baptist Historical Library and Archives, Nashville, TN.

Journals, Magazines, Newspapers

Ashland Avenue Baptist (Lexington, KY), April 13, 1924–July 20, 1956.

Baptist and Reflector (Nashville, TN), May 13, 1897–September 13, 1973.

Baptist Watchman (Knoxville, TN), November 5, 1857.

"Born-Again Baptists?" *Southern Baptist Texan*, December 18, 2006.

Bronson, Charles. "The New Testament Church and Its Ordinances Defined." *Baptist and Reflector*, July 6, 1944.

Carver, William Owen. "William Heth Whitsitt: The Seminary's Martyr." *Review and Expositor* 51 (1954) 449–69.

Christian Index (Macon, GA), November 25–December 16, 1857.

"Concerning the Lord's Supper." Reprint, *Alabama Baptist* (August 18, 1932); *Baptist and Reflector*, August 25, 1932.

"Concerning the Satisfaction of Christ." Introduced and translated by J. C. Wenger. *Mennonite Quarterly Review* 20 (1946) 249–51.

Dana, H. E. "The Influence of Baptists upon the Modern Conception of the Church." *Southwestern Journal of Theology* 6 (1922) 21–24.

Dangeau, Orvind M. "Unity at the Lord's Table." *Baptist and Reflector*, September 13, 1973.

Ford's Christian Repository and Home Circle (St. Louis) 64.6 (1900) 350.

Garrett, James Leo, Jr. "The Concept of Biblical Authority in Historic Baptist Confessions of Faith." *Review and Expositor* 76.4 (1979) 43–54.

———. Review of *High-Church Baptists in the South*, edited by James E. Tull and Morris Ashcraft. *Southwestern Journal of Theology* 45.2 (2003) 103–5.
Garrett, W. Barry. "Free Voices for Free People." *Baptist and Reflector*, July 1, 1954.
"Graham Voices Political Opinion." *Baptist and Reflector*, June 2, 1960.
Graves, J. R. "Church History." *Southern Baptist Review and Eclectic*, April-May 1855.
Hailey, Orren L. "Dr. Robertson's Reflections upon Dr. J. R. Graves." *Baptist World*, September 7, 1916.
Hall, Chad W. "When Orphans Became Heirs: J. R. Graves and the Landmark Baptists." *Baptist History and Heritage* 37 (2002) 112–27.
Hillerbrand, Hans Joachim. "Anabaptism and the Reformation: Another Look." *Church History* 29.4 (1960) 404–23.
"History of the Baptist Church." *Baptist and Reflector*, June 24, 1948.
"Old Landmarkism: A Historiographical Appraisal." *Baptist History and Heritage* 25 (1990) 31–40.
"Origin of Sprinkling and Pouring." Reprint, *Arkansas Baptist*. *Baptist and Reflector*, August 19, 1948.
Patterson, James A. "The J. R. Graves Synthesis: American Individualism and Landmark Ecclesiology." *Tennessee Baptist History* (Fall 2005) 11–15.
Porter, J. W. "Alien Immersion." *Baptist and Reflector*, April 7, 1932.
Religious Herald (Richmond, VA), September 18, 1879–August 28, 1902.
Robertson, A. T. "Heresy among Southern Baptists." *Baptist World*, July 13, 1916.
Scarborough, L. R. "Ways to Poison These Fountains." *Southwestern Journal of Theology* 6.1 (1922) 91.
"Survey of Pastors." *Arkansas Baptist*, January 20, 1966.
The Baptist (Nashville, TN), August 31, 1845–November 14, 1846.
The Baptist (Memphis, TN), August 1867–December 1889.
The Baptist Messenger (Oklahoma City, OK), January 15, 1931.
The Christian Baptist (Buffalo Creek, VA), July 4, 1823.
The Tennessee Baptist (Nashville, TN), January 6, 1847–February 1, 1862.
Ward, Wayne E. "Should Baptists Receive Non-Baptist Immersion?" *Arkansas Baptist*, May 4, 1967.

Minutes of Associations, Conventions, Meetings

Concord Baptist Association (Tennessee). *Both Sides: A Full Investigation of the Charges Preferred against Elder J. R. Graves by R. B. C. Howell and others, September 8, and October 12, 1858, by a Council Composed of Delegates from Twenty Churches of Concord Association, Held in Odd Fellows' Hall, March 1–3, 1859. Together with the Report of the Council and the Action of the Church.* Nashville: published by order of the Spring Street Baptist Church, 1859.
———. *Proceedings of the Forty-Ninth Annual Session of the Missionary Baptist, Concord Association Held with the Church of Spencer's Lick, Wilson Co., Tenn. . . . August 6, 8, 1859.* Nashville: Southwestern, Graves, Marks, 1859.
Southern Baptist Convention. *Annual of the Southern Baptist Convention 1898 containing the Proceedings of the Forty-Third Session, Fifty-Third Year held at Norfolk, VA, May 6–10, 1898.* Atlanta: Franklin, 1898.

———. *Annual of the Southern Baptist Convention Nineteen Hundred and Sixty-Eight, One Hundred Eleventh Session, One Hundred Twenty-Third Year, Houston, Texas, June 4–7, 1968*. Nashville: Executive Committee Southern Baptist Convention, 1968.

———. *Proceedings of the Southern Baptist Convention at its Seventh Biennial Session Held in the First Baptist Church, Richmond, VA, May 6th, 7th, 8th, 9th, 10th, 1859*. Richmond, VA: Ellyson, 1859.

———. *Proceedings of the Southern Baptist Convention held at Montgomery, Alabama May 11–15, 1855*. Richmond, VA: Ellyson, 1855.

———. *Proceedings of the Southern Baptist Convention held at Wilmington, N. C. May 7–10, 1897*. Atlanta: Franklin, 1897.

Published Books

Carroll, B. H. *An Interpretation of the English Bible*. 17 vols. Edited by J. B. Cranfill. Nashville: Broadman, 1947.

———. *Baptists and Their Doctrines: Sermons on Distinctive Baptist Principles*. Compiled by J. B. Cranfill. New York: Revell, 1913.

Carroll, J. M. *A History of Texas Baptists: Comprising a Detailed Account of Their Activities, Their Progress, and Their Achievements*. Houston: Historical Publishing Society, 1977.

———. *The Trail of Blood: Following the Christians Down through the Centuries from the Days of Christ to the Present Time; or, The History of Baptist Churches from the Time of Christ, Their Founder, to the Present Day*. 2nd ed. Lexington: Ashland Avenue Baptist Church, 1931.

Dayton, A. C. *Baptist Facts against Methodist Fictions*. Nashville: Southwest, 1859.

———. *Pedobaptists and Campbellite Immersions: Being a Review of the Arguments of Doctors Waller, Fuller, Johnson, Wayland, Broadus, and others, with an introductory essay by J. R. Graves*. Nashville: Southwest; Graves and Marks, 1858.

———. *Theodosia Ernest; or, The Heroine of Faith*. 2 vols. Nashville: Graves, Marks & Rutland, 1856–57.

Gilmore, J. Herbert, Jr. *They Chose to Live: The Racial Agony of an American Church*. Grand Rapids: Eerdmans, 1972.

Graves, J. R. *The Act of Christian Baptism*. Texarkana, AR-TX: Baptist Sunday School Committee, 1928.

———. *The Biblical Doctrine of the Middle Life as Opposed to Swedenborgianism and Spiritism*. Memphis: Baptist Book House, 1873.

———. *Campbell and Cambellism Exposed: A Series of Replies to A. Campbell's Articles in the Millennial Harbinger*. Nashville: Graves and Marks, 1854.

———. *Christian Baptism: The Profession of Faith of the Gospel*. Memphis: Baptist Book House, 1881.

———. "Church History." *Southern Baptist Review and Eclectic*, April-May 1855.

———. "Communion: or The Distinction between Christian, and Church Fellowship." *The Southern Baptist Almanac, and Annual Register, for the Year of Our Lord, 1851*. Nashville: Graves and Shankland, 1851.

———. *Denominational Sermons*. Memphis: Baptist Book House, 1881–1882.

———. *The Dispensational Expositions of the Parables and Prophecies of Christ.* Memphis: Graves and Mahaffy, 1887.

———. *The First Baptist Church in America: Not Founded or Pastored by Roger Williams.* Texarkana, AR-TX: Baptist Sunday School Committee, 1939.

———. *The Graves-Ditzler, or, Great Carrollton Debate on the Mode of Baptism.* Memphis: Southern Baptist Publication Society, 1876.

———. *The Great Iron Wheel; or, Republicanism Backwards and Christianity Reversed.* Nashville: Southwest; Sheldon, 1853; Nashville: Graves, and Marks, 1855.

———. *Intercommunion: Inconsistent, Unscriptural and Productive of Evil.* Memphis: Baptist Book House, 1881.

———. *John's Baptism: Was It from Moses or Christ? Jewish or Christian? Objections to Its Christian Character Answered.* Texarkana, AR-TX: Baptist Sunday School Committee, 1939.

———. *The Lord's Supper: A Church Ordinance, and so Observed by the Apostolic Churches.* Texarkana, AR-TX: Baptist Sunday School Committee, 1928.

———. *The New Great Iron Wheel: An Examination of the New M.E. Church, South, in a Series of Letters Addressed to Bishop McTyeire, D. D.* Memphis: Baptist Book House, 1884.

———. *Old Landmarkism: What Is It?* Memphis: Baptist Book House; Graves, Mahaffey, 1880.

———. *The Relation of Baptism to Salvation.* Texarkana, AR-TX: Baptist Sunday School Committee, ca. 1928.

———. *Satan Dethroned and Other Sermons.* New York: Revell, 1929.

———. *Tracts for the People.* Special Collection, Samford University. Nashville: Graves and Shankland for the Tennessee Publication Society, 1849. Microfilm.

———, ed. *Trials and Sufferings for Religious Liberty in New England: The Oldest Baptist Church in America Is Not the Providence Church.* Nashville: Southwest, 1857.

———. *The Trilemma; or, Death by Three Horns. Protestants Can Not Answer This Question: "Are the Baptisms of the Romish Church Valid?" Catholics, Free-Will Baptists, Campbellites, and Anti-Missionary Baptists Can Not Answer This: "Are the Baptisms of Baptist Churches Valid?"* Nashville: Southwest, 1860.

———. *The Watchman's Reply.* Nashville: Graves and Shankland for the Tennessee Publication Society, 1853.

———. *What Is Conscience? Have You a Good Conscience?* Texarkana, AR-TX: Baptist Sunday School Committee, 1928.

———. *What Is It to Eat and Drink Unworthily?* Texarkana, AR-TX: Baptist Sunday School Committee, 1928.

———. *The Work of Christ in the Covenant of Redemption, Developed in Seven Dispensations.* Memphis: Baptist Book House, 1883; Texarkana, AR-TX: Bogard, 1971.

Hailey, Orren L. *J. R. Graves, Life, Times, and Teachings.* Nashville: published by the author, June 21, 1929. Historical Commission, Southern Baptist Convention, 1964. Microfilm.

Holmes, Thomas J. *Ashes for Breakfast.* Valley Forge, PA: Judson, 1969.

Howell, Robert Boyce Crawford. *The Evils of Infant Baptism.* Charleston, SC: Southern Baptist, 1851.

———. *Terms of Sacramental Communion.* Philadelphia: American Baptist, 1847.

Orchard, G. H. *A Concise History of Foreign Baptists: Taken from the New Testament, the First Fathers, Early Writers, and Historians of All Ages: Chronologically Arranged: Exhibiting Their Distinct Communities, with Their Orders in Various Kingdoms, Under Several Discriminative Appellations from the Establishment of Christianity to the Present Age: with Correlative Information, Supporting the Early and Only Practice of Believers' Immersion: Also Observations and Notes on the Abuse of the Ordinance, and the Rise of Minor and Infant Baptism.* Introductory essay by J. R. Graves. Nashville: Graves, Marks, and Rutland, agents of Tennessee Publication Society; Sheldon Lamport, 1855.

Pendleton, J. M. *The Atonement of Christ.* Philadelphia: American Baptist, 1885.

———. *Christian Doctrines: A Compendium of Theology.* Valley Forge, PA: Judson, 1976.

———. *Church Manual, Designed for the Use of Baptist Churches.* Reprint. Philadelphia: American Baptist Publication Society, 1912.

———. *The Condition of the Baptist Cause in Kentucky in 1837.* S.1.: S.N., 18--?

———. *Distinctive Principles of Baptists.* Philadelphia: American Baptist, 1882.

———. *Landmarkism, Liberalism and the Invisible Church.* St. Louis: National Baptist, 1899.

———. *Notes of Sermons.* Philadelphia: American Baptist, 1886.

———. *An Old Landmark Re-Set.* 2nd ed. Nashville: Southwest, 1857.

———. *Questions to the Impenitent.* Memphis: South-Western, 1857.

———. *Reminiscences of a Long Life.* Louisville: Press Baptist Book Concern, 1891.

———. *Three Reasons Why I Am a Baptist with a Fourth Added on Communion.* Louisville: Baptist Book Concern, 1905.

Tull, Selsus E. "Denominationalism Put to the Test." Address by S. E. Tull to Murray Bible Conference Murray, KY. Published by author, 1912.

Tully, Hugh L. *A Brief History of the Baptists with Chapters on Baptism, Lord's Supper, etc.* Ensley, AL: Jefferson, 1938.

Whitsitt, William Heth. *A Question in Baptist History: Whether the Anabaptists in England Practiced Immersion before the Year 1641? With an Appendix on the Baptism of Roger Williams at Providence, Rhode Island in 1639.* Louisville: Dearing, 1896.

Surveys and Articles by Associations and Other Religious Bodies

Faulkner, Brooks R., et al. "A Look at the Small Church: A Survey of Small Churches in the Southern Baptist Convention." Nashville: Sunday School Board of the Southern Baptist Convention, 1970.

Lowry, James A., et al. "Southern Baptist Membership Survey." Nashville: Sunday School Board of the Southern Baptist Convention, June 1968.

"Opinions of Southern Baptist Pastors on Various Topics of Interest." Nashville: Lifeway Christian Resources, 2008.

Sullivant, Charles, and Tom Morris. "Southern Baptist Students Speak Out." Nashville: Research and Statistics Department Sunday School Board of the Southern Baptist Convention, 1967.

Secondary Sources

Journals, Magazines, Newspapers

Anderson, S. G. "Trend of Baptist Faith and Practice." *Baptist Advance* (Little Rock, AR), March 25, 1920.

Baker, Robert A. "Factors Encouraging the Rise of Landmarkism." *Baptist History and Heritage* 10 (1975) 1-2, 18.

Brackney, William Henry. Review of *God So Loved the World*, by Fisher Humphreys and Paul E. Robertson, *High-Church Baptists in the South*, by James E. Tull, and *The Priesthood of Some Believers*, by Colin Bulley. *Perspectives in Religious Studies* 28.2 (2001) 164-70.

Compton, Bob. "J. M. Pendleton: A Nineteenth-Century Baptist Statesman (1811-1891)." *Baptist History and Heritage* 10 (1975) 30-36.

Krahn, Cornelius. "Prolegomena to Anabaptist Theology." *Mennonite Quarterly Review* 24, no.1 (January 1950) 5-11.

Ledbetter, Gary. "Straight Talk." *Southern Baptist Texan*, February 6, 2006.

Mackay, Roberta LaVerne. "History of the Baptist Church." *Baptist and Reflector*, June 24, 1948.

McBeth, H. Leon. "The Texas Tradition: A Study in Baptist Regionalism." *Baptist History and Heritage* 26.1 (1991) 37-57.

"An Open Letter to Southern Baptists." *Baptist Standard*, April 20, 1994.

Patterson, T. A. "How to Stamp Out Baptists." *Baptist Standard*, September 8, 1965.

Patterson, W. Morgan. "The Influence of Landmarkism among Baptists." *Baptist History and Heritage* 10 (1975) 44-54.

Pickler, C. M. "The First Baptist Church." *Baptist and Reflector*, February 25, 1932.

———. "Keep the Old Landmarks." *Baptist and Reflector*, November 11, 1954.

Richards, Jim. "IMB Disagreement Not All Bad News for SBC." *Southern Baptist Texan*, February 6, 2006.

"SBC Seats Russellville Messengers." *Arkansas Baptist*, June 2, 1966.

Smith, Harold Stewart. "The Life and Work of J. R. Graces (1820-1893)." *Baptist History and Heritage* 10 (1975) 18-22.

Taylor, O. W. "In the Interest of Fairness." *Baptist and Reflector*, December 16, 1954.

———. "The Tennessee Baptist Convention Did Not Indorse Alien Immersion and Open Communion When It Received Stone Association." *Baptist and Reflector*, November 30, 1944.

Wamble, Hugh. "Landmarkism: Doctrinaire Ecclesiology among Baptists." *Church History* 33 (1964) 429-47.

Published Books

Allis, Oswald T. *Prophecy, and the Church: An Examination of the Claim of Dispensationalists That the Christian Church Is a Mystery Parenthesis which Interrupts the Fulfillment to Israel of the Kingdom Prophecies of the Old Testament.* Phillipsburg, NJ: Presbyterian and Reformed, 1947.

Ammerman, Nancy Tatom, ed. *Southern Baptists Observed: Multiple Perspectives on a Changing Denomination.* Knoxville: University of Tennessee Press, 1993.

Barnes, William Wright. *The Southern Baptist Convention: A Study in the Development of Ecclesiology*. Seminary Hill, TX: published by author, 1934.

Bascom, Henry B. *The Little Iron Wheel: A Declaration of Christian Rights and Articles, Showing the Despotism of Episcopal Methodism*. With J. R. Graves. Nashville: Southwest, 1856; Graves, Marks, 1857.

Benedict, David. *A General History of the Baptist Denomination in America and Other Parts of the World*. New York: Lewis Colby, 1848; reprint Lafayette, TN: Church History Research and Archives, 1977.

———. *History of the Donatists*. Pawtucket, RI: Nickerson, 1875.

Branch, Taylor. *Parting the Waters: America in the King Years 1954–1963*. New York: Simon and Schuster, 1988.

Broadus, John A. *Memoir of James Petigru Boyce*. New York: Armstrong, 1893.

Brownlow, William G. *The Great Iron Wheel Examined; or, Its False Spokes Extracted and an Exhibition of Elder Graves, Its Builder in a Series of Chapters*. Nashville: for the author, 1856.

Brownson, Orestes A. *The Works of Orestes A. Brownson*. 3 vols. Collected and arranged by Henry F. Brownson. Detroit: Thorndike Nourse, 1883.

Burleson, Wade. *Hardball Religion: Feeling the Fury of Fundamentalism*. Macon, GA: Smyth and Helwys, 2009.

Burnett, James John. *Sketches of Tennessee's Pioneer Baptist Preachers*. Nashville: Marshall and Bruce, 1919.

Calvin, John. *Institutes of the Christian Religion*. Translated by Henry Beveridge. Grand Rapids: Eerdmans, 1997.

Campbell, Alexander. *A Debate between Rev. A. Campbell and Rev. N. L. Rice, on the Actions, Subject, Design and Administrator of Christian Baptism*. Jacksonville, IL: Roberts, 1857.

Christian, John Tyler. *Baptist History Vindicated*. Louisville: Baptist Book Concern, 1899.

———. *A History of the Baptists, Together with Some Account of their Principles and Practices*. Nashville: Sunday School Board of the Southern Baptist Convention, 1922.

Copeland, E. Luther. *The Southern Baptist Convention and the Judgement of History: The Taint of an Original Sin*. Lanham, MD: University Press of America, 1995.

Cramp, John Mockett. *Baptist History from the Foundation of the Christian Church to the Close of the Eighteenth Century*. Philadelphia: American Baptist, n.d.

Cranfill, J. B. *Sermons and Life Sketch of B. H. Carroll*. Philadelphia: American Baptist, 1893.

Crosby, Thomas. *A History of the English Baptists from the Reformation to the Beginning of the Reign of King George I*. 4 vols. Reprint of 1738 edition. Lafayette, TN: Church History Research and Archives, 1978.

Crowder, W., ed. *Dr. B. H. Carroll, the Colossus of Baptist History*. Fort Worth: n.p., 1946.

Dargan, Edwin Charles. *The Doctrines of Our Faith*. Nashville: Sunday School Board of the Southern Baptist Convention, 1920.

Davis, Georgene Webber. *The Inquisition at Albi 1299–1300: Text of Register and Analysis*. New York: Octagon, 1974.

Davis, Jonathan. *History of the Welsh Baptists, from the Year Sixty-Three to the Year One Thousand Seven Hundred and Seventy*. Pittsburgh: Hogan, Lloyd, 1835.

Eaton, Thomas Treadwell. *The First Annual Meeting of the Kentucky Baptist Historical Society . . . June 14th, 1904. So much of the Exercises of the Evening as pertain to the Life of Rev. James Madison Pendleton are here preserved . . . by Mr. and Mrs. B. F. Proctor*. Louisville: Baptist Book Concern, 1904.

Estep, William R. *Anabaptist Beginnings (1523–1533)*. Nieuwkoop: B. De Graaf, 1976.

———. *The Anabaptist Story: An Introduction to Sixteenth-Century Anabaptism*. 3rd ed. Grand Rapids: Eerdmans, 1996.

Friedmann, Robert. *Theology of Anabaptism*. Scottsdale, PA: Herald, 1966.

Furcha, E. J. *Selected Writings of Hans Denck, 1500–1527: Texts and Studies in Religion*. Lewiston, NY: Mellen, 1990.

Gardner, W. W. *Church Communion as Practiced by the Baptists Examined and Defended*. Cincinnati: Blanchard, 1869.

George, Timothy. *Theology of the Reformers*. Nashville: Broadman and Holman, 1988.

Gross, Alexander, et al. *A History of the Methodist Church, South, the United Presbyterian Church, the Cumberland Presbyterian Church, and the Presbyterian Church, South in the United States*. New York: Christian Literature, 1894.

Hill, Samuel S., et al. *Religion and the Solid South*. Nashville: Abingdon, 1972.

James, Rob, and Gary Leazer. *The Fundamentalist Takeover in the Southern Baptist Convention: A Brief History*. Timisoara, Romania: Impact, 1999.

Jarrel, Willis Anselm. *Baptist Perpetuity; or, The Continuous Existence of Baptist Churches*. Dallas: published by the author, 1894; Fulton, KY: National Baptist, 1904.

Lambert, Malcolm. *Medieval Heresy: Popular Movements from Bogomil to Hus*. New York: Holmes and Meier, 1977.

Lefever, Alan J. *Fighting the Good Fight: The Life and Work of Benajah Harvey Carroll*. Austin: Eakin, 1994.

Lofton, George Augustus. *English Baptist Reformation (from 1609 to 1642 A.D.)*. Louisville: Dearing, 1899.

———. *A Review of the Question: Being a Review of Dr. William H. Whitsitt's "Question in Baptist History."* Nashville: University Press, 1897.

Manis, Andrew M. *Southern Civil Religions in Conflict: Civil Rights and the Culture Wars*. Macon, GA: Mercer University Press, 2002.

Masters, Victor I. *Re-thinking Baptist Doctrines: Adapted for Use by the General Reader and for Church Study Classes*. Louisville: Western Recorder, 1937.

McBeth, H. Leon. *A Sourcebook for Baptist Heritage*. Nashville: Broadman, 1990.

McCall, Duke K. "The History of the Baptist Cooperative Program." In *The Struggle for the Soul of the SBC: Moderate Responses to the Fundamentalist Movement*, edited by Walter B. Shurden, 241–51. Macon, GA: Mercer University Press, 1994.

McGoldrick, James Edward. *Baptist Successionism: A Crucial Question in Baptist History*. Metuchen, NJ: American Theological Library Association, 1994.

Milam, R. E. *The Fortress of Truth (The New Testament Church)*. Photocopy of manuscript. Portland, OR, July 1949.

Moody, Dwight A. *Heaven for a Dime: Memoirs of a Small Town Preacher*. Lincoln, NE: Writer's Showcase, 2002.

Mosheim, John Lawrence. *An Ecclesiastical History, from the Birth of Christ to the beginning of the Eighteenth Century in which the Rise, Progress and Variation of Church Power Are Considered in Their Connection with the State of Learning and*

Philosophy and the Political History of Europe During the Period. Trans. Archibald MacLaine. London: Tyler, 1842.

Mueller, William. *A History of Southern Baptist Theological Seminary*. Nashville: Broadman, 1959.

Neff, Christian, and Walter Fallmann. "Denck, Hans (ca. 1500–1527)." *The Mennonite Encyclopedia: A Comprehensive Work on the Anabaptist-Mennonite Movement*. Vol. 2. Hillsboro, KS: Mennonite Brothers, 1955.

Newman, Albert Henry. *A History of Anti-pedobaptism: From the Rise of Pedobaptism to A.D. 1609*. Philadelphia: American Baptist, copyright 1896, published 1902.

———. *A Manual of Church History*. 2 vols. Valley Forge, PA: Judson, 1931–1933.

Patterson, W. Morgan. *Baptist Successionism: A Critical View*. Valley Forge, PA: Judson, 1969.

Peters, Edward, ed. *Heresy and Authority in Medieval Europe: Documents in Translation*. Philadelphia: University of Pennsylvania Press, 1980.

Renfroe, John Jefferson Deyampert. *Vindication of the Communion of Baptist Churches: A Review of the Present Views of J. R. Graves, L.L.D., as Found in His Book Entitled "Intercommunion Inconsistent, Unscriptural and Productive of Evil."* Selma, AL: West, 1882.

Richards, W. Wiley. *Winds of Doctrine: The Origin and Development of Southern Baptist Theology*. Lanham, MD: University Press of America, 1991.

Riley, B. F. *History of the Baptists of Alabama from the Time of Their First Occupation of Alabama in 1808, until 1894: Being a Detailed Record of Denominational Events in the State during the Stirring Period of Eighty-six years, and Furnishing Biographical Sketches of Those Who Have Been Conspicuous in the Annals of the Denomination, besides Much Other Incidental Matters Relative to the Secular History of Alabama*. Birmingham: Roberts, 1895.

———. *History of the Baptists of Texas: A Concise Narrative of the Baptist Denomination in Texas; from the Earliest Occupation of the Territory to the Close of the Year 1906: with a Copious Topical Index*. Dallas: published for the author, 1907.

Robinson, Robert. *The History of Baptism*. Reprinted from the original London edition of 1790. Introduction and notes by J. R. Graves. Memphis: South-Western Baptist Publishing House, 1860.

Ross, Bob L. *Campbellism: Its History and Heresies*. Pasadena, TX: Pilgrim, 1981.

———. *Old Landmarkism and the Baptists: An Examination of the Theories of "Church Authority" and "Church Succession."* Pasadena, TX: Pilgrim, 1979.

Runciman, Steven. *The Medieval Manichee: A Study of the Christian Dualist Heresy*. Cambridge: Cambridge University Press, 1969.

Sampey, John R. *Southern Baptist Theological Seminary: The First Thirty Years, 1859–1889*. Baltimore: Wharton, Barron, 1890.

Schaff, Philip, ed. *Creeds of Christendom*. Rev. ed. 3 vols. Grand Rapids: Baker, 2007.

———. *History of the Christian Church*. 6 vols. Grand Rapids: Eerdmans, 1979.

Shackleford, J. A. *Compendium of Baptist History, Showing the Origin and History of the Baptists, from the Days of the Apostles to the Present Time, with an Original Chart, Giving a Comparative View of Some of the Denominations of Christians with which They Have Come in Contact*. Louisville: Press Baptist Book Concern, 1892.

Shurden, Walter B. *Not a Silent People: Controversies That Have Shaped Southern Baptists*. Nashville: Broadman, 1972.

Smith, Morton H. *Studies in Southern Presbyterian Theology*. Phillipsburg, NJ: Presbyterian and Reformed, 1962.
Steely, John E. "The Landmark Movement in the Southern Baptist Convention." In *What Is the Church? A Symposium of Baptist Thought*, edited by Duke K. McCall, 134–37. Nashville: Broadman, 1958.
Stewart, Howard R. *Baptists and Local Autonomy: The Development, Distortion, Decline and New Directions of Local Autonomy in Baptist Churches*. Hicksville, NY: Exposition, 1974.
Summers, T. O., ed. *The Confederate States Almanac for the Year of Our Lord 1862*. Nashville: Southern Methodist, 1862.
Thomas, Jesse Burgess. *Both Sides: Review of Dr. Whitsitt's Question in Baptist History, along with Four Editorials in the New York Independent by W. H. Whitsitt*. Louisville: Baptist Book Concern, 1897.
Tull, James E. *High-Church Baptists in the South: The Origin, Nature, and Influence of Landmarkism*. Edited by Morris Ashcraft. Macon, GA: Mercer University Press, 2000.
———. *A History of Southern Baptist Landmarkism in the Light of Historical Baptist Ecclesiology*. New York: Arno, 1980.
———. *Shapers of Baptist Thought*. Macon, GA: Mercer University Press, 1984.
Wakefield, Walter L., and Austin P. Evans. *Heresies of the High Middle Ages: Selected Sources Translated and Annotated*. New York: Columbia University Press, 1991.
Wardin, Albert W., Jr. *Tennessee Baptists*. Brentwood, TN: Executive Board of the Tennessee Baptist Convention, 1999.
Wenger, John Christian, ed. *The Complete Writings of Menno Simmons*. Translated by Leonard Verduin. Scottsdale, PA: Mennonite, 1956.
White, Thomas, ed. *Selected Writings of James Madison Pendleton*. Paris, AR: Baptist Standard Bearer, 2006.

Tertiary Sources

Published Books, Theses, Dissertations, and Journals

Ammerman, Nancy Tatom. *Baptist Battles, Social Change and Religious Conflict in the Southern Baptist Convention*. New Brunswick, NJ: Rutgers University Press, 1990.
Ayers, Joseph Cullen, Jr. *A Source Book for Ancient Church History*. New York: Scribner, 1952.
Bainton, Roland H. "The Left Wing of the Reformation." *Journal of Religion* 21 (1941) 125–34.
———. *The Reformation of the Sixteenth Century*. Boston: Beacon, 1952.
Baldwin, Marshall W., ed. *Christianity through the Thirteenth Century*. New York: Walker, 1970.
Barnes, William Wright. *The Southern Baptist Convention 1845–1953*. Nashville: Broadman, 1954.
Bašić, Denis. "The Roots of Religious, Ethnic, and National Identity of the Bosnian-Herzegovinan Muslims." PhD diss., University of Washington, 2009.

Bender, Harold S., and C. Henry Smith, eds. *The Mennonite Encyclopedia: A Comprehensive Reference Work on the Anabaptist-Mennonite Movement*. Hillsboro, KS: Mennonite Brethren, 1955.

Brackney William Henry. *Baptist Life and Thought, 1600-1980: A Source Book*. Valley Forge, PA: Judson, 1983.

Bryant, Scott E. "The Awakening of the Freewill Baptists: Benjamin Randall and the Founding of an American Baptist Tradition." PhD diss., Baylor University, 2007.

Burrage, Champlin. *The Early English Dissenters*. Vols. 1-2. Cambridge: Cambridge University Press, 1912.

Campbell, Will D. *The Stem of Jesse: The Costs of Community at a 1960s Southern School*. Macon, GA: Mercer University Press, 1995.

Cathcart, William. *The Baptist Encyclopedia: A Dictionary of the Doctrines, Ordinances, Usages, Confessions of Faith, Sufferings, Labors, and Successes, and of the General History of the Baptist Denomination in all Lands. . . .* Philadelphia: Everts, 1881.

Christian, John Tyler. *Did They Dip? or, An Examination into the Act of Baptism as Practiced by the English and American Baptists before the Year 1641*. 2nd ed. Louisville: Baptist Book Concern, 1899.

———. *A History of the Baptists*. 2 vols. Nashville: Broadman, 1922.

Dargan, Edwin Charles. *Ecclesiology: A Study of the Churches*. Louisville: Dearing, 1905.

Dyck, Cornelius J. *The Writings of Dirk Phillips*. Translated and edited by William E. Keeny and Alvin S. Beachy. Scottsdale, PA: Herald, 1992.

Early, Joseph, Jr. *Readings in Baptist History: Four Centuries of Selected Documents*. Nashville: B & H, 2008.

Edwards, Jonathan. "Humble Attempt." In *Apocalyptic Writings: The Works of Jonathan Edwards*, edited by Stephen J. Stein, 5:307-436. New Haven: Yale University Press, 1977.

Eusebius. *The History of the Church from Christ to Constantine*. Translated by G. A. Williamson. New York: Penguin, 1965.

Everts, W. W. "The Old Landmark Discovered." *Christian Repository and Literary Review* 37 (January 1855) 20-34.

Ford, S. H. "Review of Dr. Whitsitt's Editorial in the Independent." *Christian Repository and Home Circle* 60.8 (August 1896) 475-78.

Fuller, Richard. *Baptism and the Terms of Communion: An Argument*. Charleston, SC: Hoff, 1850.

———. *Domestic Slavery Considered as a Scriptural Institution*. Macon, GA: Mercer University Press, 2008.

Furniss, Norman F. *The Fundamentalist Controversy 1918-1931, Yale Historical Publications, Miscellany 59*. New Haven: Yale University Press, 1953.

Gaustad, Edwin S., ed. *Baptist Ecclesiology*. New York: Arno, 1980.

———. *Baptists, the Bible, Church Order and the Churches: Essays from "Foundations"; American Baptist Journal of History and Theology*. New York: Arno, 1980.

———. *Liberty of Conscience: Roger Williams in America*. Valley Forge, PA: Judson, 1999.

George, Timothy. "The Reformation Roots of the Baptist Tradition." *Review and Expositor* 86 (1989) 9-22.

Gould, Stephen J. *The Panda's Thumb*. New York: Norton, 1980.

Graham, Balus Joseph Winzer, ed. *Baptist Biography*. Atlanta: Index, 1917.

Grice, Homer L., and R. Paul Caudill. "The Graves-Howell Controversy." In *Encyclopedia of Southern Baptists*, 1:580–85. Nashville: Broadman, 1982.

Grime, John Harvey. *History of Middle Tennessee Baptists*. Nashville: Baptist and Reflector, 1902.

Harper, Keith. "Old Landmarkism: A Historiographical Appraisal." *Baptist History and Heritage* 25 (1990) 31–40.

Harrison, Paul M. *Authority and Power in the Free Church Tradition: A Special Case Study of the American Baptist Convention*. Princeton: Princeton University Press, 1959.

Hill, Samuel S., ed. *Varieties of Southern Religious Experience*. Baton Rouge: Louisiana State University Press, 1988.

Hinton, Richard J. *John Brown and His Men*. New York: Arno, 1968.

Hodge, Charles. *Systematic Theology*. 3 vols. Philadelphia: Judson, 1979.

Hudson, Winthrop S., ed. *Baptist Concepts of the Church*. Philadelphia: Judson, 1959.

———. *Baptists in Transition: Individualism and Christian Responsibility*. Valley Forge, PA: Judson, 1980.

———. "Baptists Were Not Anabaptists." *Chronicle* 16 (1953) 171–79.

Ivimey, Joseph. *A History of the English: Including an Investigation of the History of Baptism in England from the Earliest Period . . . to the Close of the Seventeenth Century . . . Extracted from Dr. Gill's Piece Entitled the Divine Right of Infant Baptism Examined and Disproved*. 4 vols. London: printed for the author, 1811–1830.

James, Frank. *History of Christianity I*. Class lectures (audio cassette). Charlotte: Reformed Theological Seminary, 2003.

Jeter, Jeremiah B. *Baptist Principles Reset, Consisting of a Series of Articles on Distinctive Baptist Principles, by the Late Jeremiah B. Jeter, D. D., Editor of the "Religious Herald."* Richmond, VA: Religious Herald, 1901.

Johnson's Universal Cyclopedia: A New Edition . . . under the Direction of Charles Kendall Adams. 8 vols. New York: Appleton, Johnson, 1897.

Jürgen-Goertz, Hans. *The Anabaptists*. Translated by Trevor Johnson. New York: Routledge, 1996.

Keegan, M. M. "Introduction to E. P. Alldredge Papers." Southern Baptist Historical Library and Archives. Nashville: n.p., 1975.

———. "Introduction to Rufus W. Weaver Papers." Southern Baptist Historical Library and Archives. Nashville: n.p., August 3, 1962.

Klassen, William, and Walter Klassen, ed., trans. *The Writings of Pilgram Marpeck*. Scottsdale, PA: Herald, 1978.

Leedy, Paul D. *Practical Research Planning and Design*. 6th ed. Upper Saddle River, NJ: Prentice Hall, 1997.

Leonard, Bill J. *God's Last and Only Hope: The Fragmentation of the Southern Baptist Convention*. Grand Rapids: Eerdmans, 1990.

Loos, Milan. *Dualist Heresy in the Middle Ages*. Translated by Iris Lewitová. Prague: Akademia, 1974.

Loveland, Anne. *Southern Evangelicals and the Social Order, 1800–1860*. Baton Rouge: Louisiana State University Press, 1980.

McBeth, H. Leon. "Baptist Fundamentalism: A Cultural Interpretation." *Baptist History and Heritage* 13.3 (1978) 12–19, 32.

———. *The Baptist Heritage: Four Centuries of Baptist Witness*. Nashville: Broadman, 1987.

———. "Baptist or Evangelical: One Southern Baptist's Perspective." In *Southern Baptists and American Evangelicals: The Conversation Continues*, edited by David S. Dockery, 68–76. Nashville: Broadman and Holman, 1993.

———. "God's Last and Only Hope: The Fragmentation of the Southern Baptist Convention." *Review and Expositor* 88, no. 4 (Fall 1991) 449–450.

———. "Southern Baptists and Race Since 1947." *Baptist History and* Heritage 7.3 (1972) 155–69.

McGoldrick, James Edward. "Baptists and the Reformation." *Reformation Today* 68 (1982) 14–20.

———. "The Trail of Blood." *Reformation Today* 100 (1987) 11–14.

McGregor, J. F. "The Baptists: Fount of All Heresy." In McGregor and Reay, *Radical Religion in the English Revolution*, 30–37.

McGregor, J. F., and B. Reay, eds. *Radical Religion in the English Revolution*. Oxford: Oxford University Press, 1984.

McMillan, James H., and Sally Schumacher. *Research in Education: A Conceptual Introduction*. Glenview, IL: Foresman, 1989.

Merritt, John W. *The Betrayal of Southern Baptist Missionaries by Southern Baptist Leaders, 1979-2004*. S.l.: s.n., 2004.

Milam, R. E. *Keep on the Scriptural Track: A Southern Baptist Must*. Portland: Milam, 1982.

———. *Win America Now, God's Call to Southern Baptists and Two Other Manuscripts, The Fortress of Truth, the New Testament Church, and Believer's Baptism, Practical Key to New Testament Doctrines*. Lincoln, NE: Bison, 1954.

Miller, Samuel C. *After Whitsitt, What? An Open Letter to the Trustees of the Southern Baptist Theological Seminary*. Pamphlet. Louisville: Dearing, 1899.

Morgan, David T. *The New Crusades, the New Holy Land: Conflict in the Southern Baptist Convention 1969-1991*. Tuscaloosa: University of Alabama Press, 1996.

Morland, Samuel. *The History of the Evangelical Churches of the Valleys of Piedmont: Containing a Most Exact Geographical Description of the Place, and a Faithful Account of the Doctrine, Life, and Persecutions of the Ancient Inhabitants. . . .* Collected and compiled by Samuel Morland. H. Hills for A. Byfield, 1658. Reprint. Fort Smith, AR: Franklin, 1955.

Mullins, Edgar Young. *Baptism and the Remission of Sins: Paper Read at the National Congress of Disciples April 25, 1906*. Philadelphia: American Baptist, 1906.

Newman, Albert Henry. *A History of the Baptist Churches in the U.S.* Rev. ed. Philadelphia: American Baptist, 1898.

———. "Recent Researches Concerning Medieval Sects." *Papers of American Society of Church History* 4 (1892).

Patterson, James A. *James Robinson Graves: Staking the Boundaries of Southern Baptist Identity*. Nashville: B & H, 2012.

Patterson, T. A. "The Theology of J. R. Graves." ThD diss., Southwest Baptist Theological Seminary, 1944.

Potter, David M. *The Impending Crisis 1848–1861*. New York: Harper and Row, 1976.

Ray, David Burcham. *Baptist Succession: A Handbook of Baptist History*. St. Louis: St. Louis Baptist, 1869. Reprint, Rosemead, CA: Kings, 1949.

Ray, Jefferson Davis. *B. H. Carroll*. Nashville: Sunday School Board of the Southern Baptist Convention, 1927.

Robertson, A. T. "The Baptist Preacher in the Modern World." *Review and Expositor* 16.2 (1919).

———. *A Grammar of the Greek New Testament in the Light of Historical Research.* Nashville: Broadman, 1934.

Robinson, Robert. *Ecclesiastical Researches.* Cambridge, UK: Hudson, 1792.

Rodgerson, Philip E. "A Historical Study of Alien Baptism among Baptists since 1640." ThD diss., Southern Baptist Seminary, 1952.

Ryle, J. C. *Holiness.* Cedar Lake, MI: Readaclassic, 2010.

Sampey, John R. *Memoirs of John R. Sampey.* Nashville: Broadman, 1947.

Scarboro, Joseph Addison. *The Bible, the Baptists and the Board System: An Examination, Investigation and Trial of the System Scriptural, Legal, Moral, Economical and Practical . . . An Appeal for Biblical Missions.* N.p.: Published by the author, 1904.

Shurden, Walter B. "The Southern Baptist Synthesis: Is It Cracking?" *Baptist History and Heritage* 16.2 (1981) 2–11.

Stringfellow, Thornton. *Slavery: Its Origin, Nature, and History; Its Relation to Society, to Government, and to True Religion, to Human Happiness and Divine Glory, considered in the Light of Bible Teaching, Moral Justice, and Political Wisdom.* New York: Trow, 1861.

Strong, Augustus Hopkins. *Systematic Theology.* Philadelphia: Judson, 1907.

Stroup, Earl. "Learning Guide to *Southern Baptist Heritage*." Jefferson City, TN: Video Equipping Ministries, 1982.

Taylor, O. W. *Early Tennessee Baptists 1769–1832.* Nashville: Executive Board of the Tennessee Baptist Convention, 1957.

Thurman, J. H. "Landmarks of Our Faith." *Baptist and Reflector*, February 26, 1948.

Tull, James E. "The Landmark Movement: An Historical and Theological Appraisal." *Baptist History and Heritage* 10 (1975) 3–18.

Vedder, Henry C. "Origin and Early Teachings of the Waldenses." *American Journal of Theology* 4.4 (1900) 465–89.

———. *A Short History of the Baptists.* Valley Forge, PA: Judson, 1907.

Villari, Luigi. *The Republic of Ragusa: An Episode of the Turkish Conquest.* London: Dent, 1904.

Waller, John L. "The Administrator of Baptism". *Western Baptist Review* 3.12 (1848).

———. "Reformation." *Christian Repository* 1.1 (1852); 1.9 (1852); 1.10 (1852).

———. "The Validity of Baptism by Pedobaptist Ministers". *Western Baptist Review* 3.7 (1848).

Walther, Daniel. "A Survey of Recent Research on the Albigensian Cathari." *Church History* 34.2 (1965) 146–77.

Weaver, Ralph W. "Life and Times of William Heth Whitsitt." *Review and Expositor* 37.2 (1940).

Wenger, John Christian. *Glimpses of Mennonite History and Doctrine.* Scottsdale, PA: Herald, 1947.

Williams, George Huntston. *The Radical Reformation.* 3rd ed. Kirksville: MO: Sixteenth Century Journal, 1992.

Williams, Lawrence H. "Black Landmarkism: Sectarian Theology among the National Baptists." *Baptist History and Heritage* 28.4 (1993) 45–54.

Wilson, Charles. *Baptized in Blood: The Religion of the Lost Cause, 1865–1920.* Athens: University of Georgia Press, 1980.

Wright, David F. "The Donatists in North Africa." In *The Eerdmans Handbook to the History of Christianity*, edited by Tim Dowley, 202–3. Berkhamsted, UK: Lion, 1977.

Zöckler, O. "New Manichaens." In *New Encyclopedia of Religious Knowledge*, edited by Albert Hauck, 8:143–44. New York: Scribner, 1899.

Index of Names

Abraham, 36
Adam, 56, 176
Agassiz, Louis, 55–56, 55n191
Alldredge, Eugene Perry, 63, 64n225, 76n43, 165–66, 166n76, 166n80, 168, 168n83, 168n85
Allis, Oswald T., 36, 36n94
Ammerman, Nancy Tatom, 191, 191n189, 197, 197n217
Anderson, S. G., 168n87
Andrew, James, 25n28
Anselm, 31
Apollinaris, 30n64
Arius, 30n65
Arnold, 84
Ashcraft, Morris, 15

Baker, Robert A., 194, 194n204
Ballamie, 92n6
Barnabas, 174–75
Barnes, Frank, 198–99, 199n226
Barnes, William, 192, 192n195, 193
Bebee, Elder, 168
Beecher, Henry Ward, 48n156
Bell, T. P., 135–36, 136n175
Benedict, David, 68, 70, 70n17, 157, 157n40
Benson, E. W., 115
St. Bernard of Clairvaux, 84
Beza, Theodore, 105
Boardman, G. D., 52
Bogard, Ben, 168, 171
Boyce, James P., 43
Brackney, William Henry, 200, 200n233

Branch, Taylor, 190, 190n188
Breckinridge, R. L., 53, 53n178
Bridges, Ben, 188
Broadus, John A., 111, 111n86, 130
Bronson, Charles, 170n96, 172, 172n102
Brown, John, 122n127, 126
Brownlow, William G., 8
Bryant, Scott E., 108n76
Bullinger, Heinrich, 85
Burleson, R. B., 20
Burleson, Wade, 147, 147n215, 192, 192n193
Burnett, James John, 17n6, 40n109

Calvin, John, 34, 104, 105, 177
Campbell, Alexander, 20n13, 94, 95–96, 144, 168, 177
Carroll, Benajah Harvey, 11, 12–13, 16, 57, 58–61, 63, 65, 73–74, 76, 77, 78, 79, 133, 138, 140–41, 141n191, 146, 149, 150, 162–63, 169n88, 199, 210–11, 231–32
Carroll, C. C., 160, 160n50, 160n51, 160n53
Carroll, James Milton, 7, 11, 12–13, 16, 57, 61–64, 65, 66, 67, 68–69, 68n7, 70, 75–86, 76n43, 87, 88, 146, 160, 174, 175, 211, 224
Carroll brothers, 17, 57–64, 210–11
Carver, William Owen, 131, 131n156
Cathcart, William, 84n76, 85n78, 90n2
Caudill, Paul, 117n111, 119n117
Chafer, Lewis Sperry, 36n93

Christ, 26, 28, 29, 30, 30n64, 31, 34, 36n93, 37, 38, 49, 63, 67, 72, 76, 88, 121, 154, 159, 175, 176, 208, 210, 211. See also Jesus Christ
Christian, John Tyler, 9, 9n9, 74n39, 155–60, 155n28, 155n30, 156n31, 156n32, 156n33, 156n34, 157n36, 159n49
Clark, John, 107, 108
Clark, W. A., 168
Cochcroft, J. C., 168n83
Cocke, Charles L., 138, 138n182
Collins, E., 222
Compere, W. L., 174, 174n114
Compton, Bob, 42, 42n116
Copeland, E. Luther, 187–88, 187n173, 188n174
Cornelius, 82n60
Covey, J. V. E., 222
Cramp, John Mockett, 70, 70n18
Cranfill, J. B., 58n199
Crawford, N. M., 123–24, 124n133, 128
Criswell, W. A., 178, 178n133, 191
Crosby, Thomas, 67, 67n6, 68
Crowder, J. W., 58n199

Dailey, Jane, 189n182
Dana, H. E., 174, 174n112
Dangeau, Orvind M., 195n209
Daniel, Carey, 188–89, 188n181, 189n182
Daniel, Price, 188n181
Darby, John Nelson, 36, 36n93, 54
Dargan, Edwin Charles, 135–36, 135n174–36n174, 136n175, 137, 137n178, 137n179, 138, 138n182, 141n195, 151, 151n12, 155, 167, 167n81
David, 30, 32, 35
Davis, Jefferson, 129
Davis, Jonathan, 69, 69n14
Dayton, A. C., 91, 112, 113, 114, 115n99, 116, 117, 127–28, 129, 152
Demosthenes, 128
Dever, Mark, 200
Dilday, Russell, 196

Ditzler, Jacob, 93, 102n52

Eastes, T. J., 138
Eaton, Thomas Treadwell, 131, 132, 134, 136, 137, 142, 169
Edwards, Jonathan, 106, 106n68
Eitel, Keith, 147
Elliott, Ralph, 195
Emerson, 122n127
Eve, 176

Farmer, J. S., 172
Faulkner, Brooks R., 203n243
Fletcher, James F., 118
Floyd, John, 147
Fly, Mr., 99
Folk, Edgar Estes, 74, 74n36, 134n169, 144, 161–62, 162n58
Freeman, John D., 175
Friedmann, Robert, 86n84
Fuller, Charles E., 179
Fuller, Richard, 53, 120

Gambrell, J. B., 151, 151n12, 170
Gardner, David M., 178, 178n136, 179n137
Garrett, James Leo, Jr., 196, 196n215, 200–201, 201n234
Garrett, W. Barry, 181–82, 181n150
Gaustad, Edwin S., 107n69
Gayle, Peter S., 222, 223
George, Timothy, 150, 150n7
Gilmore, J. Herbert, Jr., 186, 186n170, 190
Gomer, 69
Goodwin, John, 91–92
Gould, Stephen J., 55n191
Graham, Balus Joseph Winzer, 62n218
Graham, Billy, 178–79, 184
Graves, James Robinson, 2, 6–9, 10, 11, 12, 13, 16, 16n2, 17–39, 40, 41, 41n114, 42, 43, 43n122, 44, 46, 47–48, 49, 51, 54, 55, 56, 57, 58, 59, 60, 65, 66, 66n3, 67, 67n4, 69, 70, 71, 72–75, 79, 80, 81, 82, 83, 83n68, 85–86, 85n80, 86n83, 87, 88, 90, 90n2, 91,

INDEX OF NAMES

92–94, 93n8, 93n10, 95–125, 96n24, 100n41, 102n52, 103n58, 103n59, 103n60, 104n63, 107n70, 108n72, 108n77, 116n103, 118n113, 120n121, 129–30, 131, 138, 140, 142, 144, 147, 149, 150, 151–55, 151n10, 152, 153, 153n18, 154, 156, 161, 162–66, 165n70, 168, 172, 173, 175, 176, 178, 180–81, 181n147, 181n149, 182, 183, 194, 196, 197, 200, 208–10, 212, 212n3, 213, 214, 215, 216, 217, 222, 223
Grice, Homer L., 117n111, 119n117
Grime, John Harvey, 144–45, 144n207–45n207
Grooms, H. H., Sr., 186–87
Gross, Alexander, 25n30, 97n25

Hailey, Orren L., 11, 11n13, 12, 12n15, 19, 29n56, 39n108, 40, 97, 97n27, 120, 120n121, 130n151, 149, 153, 156, 161, 164, 164n63, 165n69, 165n72, 175, 217
Hall, J. N., 42
Ham, 53, 121, 189
Harrison, Paul M., 198, 198n225
Hatcher, W. E., 133
Hawthorne, J. B., 153–54
Hearne, S. C., 138–39
Henderson, Samuel, 121
Henry of Lausanne, 84
Henry VIII, 177
Hill, Dr., 50–51
Hill, John L., 64
Hill, Samuel S., 188, 188n178
Hill, William Wallace, 111–12
Hillsman, Matthew, 114, 115, 115n100
Hinton, Richard J., 122n127
Hodge, Charles, 28, 28n52
Hoffman, Melchior, 132
Holliman, Ezekiel, 107
Holmes, Thomas J., 185n166, 186, 190
Holt, A. J., 145–46
Howell, Morton, 117n107

Howell, Robert Boyte Crawford, 10, 10n12, 11, 17, 18, 19, 20, 90, 98, 109, 113–14, 115, 116–20, 116n103, 117n107, 209
Hudson, Winthrop S., 67
Humphreys, Fisher, 200n233
Hymers, R. L., Jr., 195, 195n206

James, Rob, 197n216
Japheth, 69
Jarrel, Willis Anselm, 9, 9n10, 68, 68n9, 75, 75n41, 142, 142n198
Jesus Christ, 29, 47, 48, 58, 59, 60, 71, 72, 76, 94, 154, 158, 164, 174, 175, 177, 180, 183, 189, 197, 202n242, 204, 222. See also Christ
Jeter, Dr, 43
Jeter, Jeremiah B., 151, 151n10
John, 38, 59
John the Baptist, 7, 26, 34, 36, 37, 43, 58, 67, 72, 88, 131, 160, 175, 176, 201, 211, 234, 236
Johnson, Douglas, 186
Jones, A., 114–15
Jones, Jack W., 186
Joseph, Bro., 146
Judas Iscariot, 44, 176, 197

Kaemmerling, Russell, 196
Keegan, M. M., 64n224
Kerfoot, F. H., 142
King, Martin Luther, Jr., 190
Knight, Walker, 191, 191n190
Knox, John, 34, 104, 105

Lee, Robert E., 122n127
Lefever, Alan J., 58n199
Leonard, Bill J., 191n189
Lincoln, Abraham, 122, 123, 126
Lofton, George Augustus, 9
Lolley, Randall, 196
Lowry, James A., 202n242
Luther, 34, 104, 105, 177

Mackay, Roberta LaVerne, 215n6
MacLaine, Archibald, 70

INDEX OF NAMES

Manis, Andrew M., 184n162, 188–89, 188n179, 189n182
Manly, Basil, Jr., 90, 90n1, 91, 91n3, 117, 117n109
Manly, Basil, Sr., 90n1, 91n3, 117n109
Manly, Sarah, 90n1, 91n3, 117n109
Marks, W. P., 113, 117
Mary (mother of Jesus), 158
Masters, Victor, 160
Mather, Cotton, 107n69
McBeth, H. Leon, 58, 58n200, 59, 61, 149, 149n2, 150
McCall, Duke K., 195n210
McDonald, Erwin L., 189n186
McFerrin, Dr., 97
McGlothlin, W. J., 141, 141n195
McGoldrick, James Edward, 67–68, 76, 76n42, 81, 81n57, 82n62, 193–94, 193n202, 204
McGregor, J. F., 92n6
Menno, Simon. See Simons, Menno
Merritt, John W., 191n189
Milam, R. E., 178–80, 178n133, 178n134, 178n135, 178n136, 179n137, 179n139, 197–98, 197n218, 199
Miller, Jane, 193, 193n200, 193n201
Montanus, 81
Moody, J. B., 160n50, 161
Moore, David O., 149n1
Morgan, David T., 191n189
Moses, 60
Mosheim, John Lawrence, 70, 71, 77
Mueller, William, 138n183, 196n214
Mullins, Edgar Young, 74, 74n39, 159, 159n48, 159n49, 203n245
Murdock, J., 70

Newman, Albert Henry, 9, 67, 83n70, 88, 88n86
Nicodemus, 26
Noah, 69, 189

Oni, Sam, 185–86
Orchard, George Herbert, 9, 21, 66, 66n2, 68, 70, 70n16, 71, 72, 73, 82, 82n61, 84, 84n77, 87, 88, 152, 175

Osiander, 157

Parker, Gilbert, 168
Partain, John, 179–80, 179n139
Patterson, James A., 35–36, 35n91, 214, 216
Patterson, Paige, 147, 196
Patterson, Thomas Armour, 28–29, 29n53, 130n152, 183, 183n160, 209n2
Patterson, W. Morgan, 9, 9n8, 66, 66n1, 67
Paul, 52, 106, 128, 174–75
Peck, Mason, 109
Peck, Mrs. J. E., 132, 136, 137
Pendleton, James Madison, 2, 6, 8, 11, 12, 16, 17, 39–57, 59, 60, 65, 82, 87, 101, 101n49, 102, 109, 111, 112, 114, 115, 116, 119, 120, 122–23, 124, 128, 129, 130, 144, 150, 178, 204, 210, 211, 217
Pendleton, John, 56
Penick, I. N., 156, 156n33
Peter, 32, 60
Peters, Edward, 84n73
Philip, 199
Phillips, J. M., 139–40, 152–53, 153n17
Pickler, C. M., 175, 175n116, 180, 180n144
Poindexter, A. M., 115
Pope, Chas. W., 171
Porter, J. W., 64, 79, 169–70, 170n92, 171–72, 171n100
Potter, David M., 122n127
Pressler, Paul, 147

Randall, Benjamin, 108, 108n76
Randolph, Mr., 101
Ray, David Burcham, 71, 71n19
Reay, B., 92n6
Renfroe, John Jefferson Deyampert, 8, 8n6
Richards, W. Wiley, 192, 192n196, 193
Richardson, Wyman, 196n215
Riley, B. F., 117, 117n110, 155, 155n29
Riner, A. A., 166, 166n76

INDEX OF NAMES

Robertson, A. T., 12, 12n14, 59n202, 131, 136–37, 137n178, 141, 162, 163, 163n61, 164
Robinson, Robert, 69, 69n10, 72, 157, 157n37
Rogers, Adrian, 191n189
Rogers, S. B., 168n85
Rogers, S. C., 114
Rosenberg, Ellen, 189, 189n185, 191
Runciman, Steven, 81n58
Ryle, J. C., 213, 213n4

Sampey, John R., 131, 132–33, 132n161, 137, 137n179, 140n189, 141, 142, 142n199
Scarboro, Joseph Addison, 145–46, 145n209
Scarborough, L. R., 169n88, 170, 170n94, 174, 174n111
Schaff, Philip, 77
Scobee, J. S., 100–101
Scofield, C. I., 36n93
Scovel, H. G., 91, 117
Shackleford, J. A., 71–72, 71n24, 78, 78n47, 78n48
Shankland, A. B., 19, 91, 112–13, 114, 117
Sheppard, J. T., 166n80
Shurden, Walter B., 42, 42n118, 130, 130n155, 143–44, 143n201, 195n212, 201, 207, 207n1
Simons, Menno, 176
Skipworth, N. M., 107–8, 107n72–8n72
Smith, Harold Stewart, 29n54, 194, 194n205
Smith, Morton H., 104n62
Smith, W. R. L., 137
Solomon, 61
Soule, Joshua, 24–25, 97, 100, 121
Spencer, J. H., 132
Spurgeon, Charles Haddon, 108–9, 199
Steely, John E., 91, 91n5, 144, 144n205
Stewart, Howard, 198, 198n224
Stookey, Stephen M., 177–78, 178n132
Stovel, Charles, 126

Stringfellow, Thornton, 125
Strong, Augustus Hopkins, 28, 28n51
Stroup, Earl, 201, 201n235
Sullivant, Charles, 202n241
Summers, Dr., 97
Summers, T. O., 97n25
Sutton, Bill, 147, 192

Taylor, George B., 68
Taylor, John, 168
Taylor, O. W., 170–71, 171n98, 180–81, 180n146, 181n147, 181n148, 181n149
Terry, William Martin, 121n123
Thoreau, 122n127
Thurman, J. H., 173n109
Tull, James E., 2n1, 8n5, 10, 15n1, 18, 18n9, 40, 40n111, 42, 42n117, 43, 43n124, 44, 44n132, 73, 73n35, 85n80, 88, 88n85, 91n4, 94n14, 95, 95n18, 120n121, 130n154, 131–32, 132n157, 135n174–36n174, 136, 144, 144n203, 144n206, 146, 146n214, 150, 150n5, 151, 151n11, 166n75, 167, 200, 200n233, 205, 216
Tull, Selsus E., 189–90, 189n186, 190n187
Tully, Hugh L., 9, 9n11, 173, 173n107, 175–76, 175n120, 177n130, 193

Valdès (Waldo), 85
Van Ness, Isaac Jacobus, 64, 155, 155n27, 155n28, 155n30, 156n31, 156n32, 156n34, 160, 160n50, 160n51, 160n53, 165n69
Vedder, Henry C., 71, 71n22, 152, 152n15
Vernon, Will, 178n134

Waddell, Glenn, 214n5
Walker, Clarence, 79–80, 80n53
Waller, J. L., 73, 85, 85n80
Waller, J. R., 116n103
Waller, John L., 109
Walton, E. P., 90, 115
Ward, Wayne E., 182–83, 182n156

Wardin, Albert W., Jr, 10, 90n2, 98n30, 109n80, 110n83, 130n153, 134n169, 145n208, 153n21, 161n57, 165n71
Watters, H. E., 156
Weaver, Dr., 43, 44
Weaver, Rufus W., 161, 161n54, 161n55
Wesley, John, 102, 105, 177
White, R. Kelly, 171
Whitsitt, William Heth, 7, 7n3, 9, 11, 63, 67, 74, 75, 76, 78, 130–43, 132n158, 159n48, 180, 229–30
Wilkins, Frank L., 151–52
William (monk), 84
Williams, Roger, 107, 107n69, 108, 165, 175–76
Woolfolk, J. R., 222
Wright, David F., 83n69
Wright, G., 222

Zwingli, 104

Index of Subjects

abolitionism, 122
administrator. *See* authorized administrators of baptism; unauthorized administrator
Adoptionist views, of the Paulicians, 157
Adoptionists, beliefs of, 158
Agassiz, Louis, 55–56, 55n191
Alabama Baptist, on the Whitsitt controversy, 135
Albigenses
    aberrant Christology of, 87
    Benedict on, 70
    Christian on, 157
    Folk on, 162
    J. M. Carroll on, 68, 84–85
    as just nicknames for Baptists, 85
    as Waldenses by different names, 71
    Wilkins on, 152
alien immersion, 169–71
    acceptance of, 109, 182
    debated among Southern Baptists in the 1960s, 213–14
    defined, 145n207
    as essential New Testament doctrine, 174
    Graves view of, 18, 163
    issue of, 43, 198
    Landmark case against, 34
    local autonomy directly related to, 198
    Pendleton on, 40
    practicing, 183
    relationship with close communion, 171
    student survey statistics, 204
    survey of Southern Baptist pastors in 2008, 203
    as twin to open communion, 172
Alldredge, E. P., 165–66, 168
American Baptist Association, 207–8. *See also* Baptist General Association
American Civil War (1861-1865), 10–11
    aftermath of, 129–30
    beginning of, 124–29
    Landmarkers role in, 207
    as a religious war, 3, 129
    victory in as arbiter of theological differences, 53
amillennialist, Pendleton as, 54–55
"Anabaptist Kinship Theory," 201
Anabaptists
    Christian on, 158
    Crosby on, 68n6
    few were immersionists, 132
    focused on the *ekklesia*, 86
    Folk on, 162
    as God's servants, 73
    Graves on, 72
    groups bearing the name of, 63
    J. M. Carroll on, 68
    Montanists use of the term, 157
    origin of, 68
    rejecters of infant baptism, 87
    separate from and preceding the Reformation, 85–86
Anglo-Saxon race, supremacy and superiority of, 188

INDEX OF SUBJECTS

Anselmian views, of Christ's active obedience, 31
anthropology
   Graves views, 35–36
   Pendleton's views, 51–53
anti-missions controversy, 143
Apollinarianism, 30, 154, 209
Apollinaris, 30n64
apostasy, long periods of, 88
apostolic doctrine, producing apostolic living, 212
apostolic succession, through the Clark line, 107–8
"Are Mission Boards Scriptural?" pamphlet, 145
Arian view, Trinitarian formulations of Graves close to, 210
Arius, on a time when the Son was not, 30n65
Arkansas Baptist, on the Whitsitt controversy, 134
Arkansas Baptist church, motion to deny seats to messengers of, 182
Arnold, died as a martyr of the "true church," 84
Arnoldists
   Benedict on, 70
   J. M. Carroll on, 68
   opposition to the Roman Catholic Church, 84
   rejection of infant baptism, 87
   rejection of unworthy ministers, 87
Ashland Avenue Baptist Church, 79, 224
Ashland Avenue Baptist weekly newspaper, 79–80
atonement
   Graves on, 31–33, 210
   necessity of, 49
   Pendleton on, 48–49
authorized administrators of baptism, 33
   articles repudiating, 154
   holding to the doctrine of the New Testament church, 203
   immersion of, 95
   issue of, 73
   John the Baptist as, 34
   question of, 21
   validity of baptisms by, 21, 198

Baker, Robert, 194
baptism
   accepting other modes of, 192
   encouraging valid, 44
   essential to the existence of a visible church, 50
   Graves on, 33–35
   held together the Landmark theology, 51
   by immersion as true baptism, 16
   ordinance of, 10
   Pendleton on, 49–51
   as the root of the Landmark movement, 50
   by an unauthorized administrator, 169
   by an unbaptized administrator, 102
   valid, 33, 34
   validity of, 21, 103n59, 198
baptismal succession
   chain broken, 105
   theory of, 95
Baptist(s)
   accepted the Bible alone, 158
   attacks on other, 106–10
   beginnings, theories of, 201
   caught in the same Trilemma, 110
   disowned Alexander Campbell, 20n13
   divided over the issue of slavery, 121
   form of church government, 45
   historical documents of, 77
   J. M. Carroll on, 68, 77
   martyred in large numbers, 70
   as never Protestants, 176, 180
   not springing from the Reformation, 69
   as the only Christian community since the days of the Apostles, 176
   as the only denomination established by Christ, 72

INDEX OF SUBJECTS

position of influential toward
  Christian's *History*, 159
regarding baptism as a mere symbol, 96–97
as the true church through the centuries, 22
Baptist (newspaper), 17, 18, 18n8, 98n30
Baptist and Reflector (newspaper), 134, 134n169, 138, 161
Baptist Argus paper, 131
Baptist Banner (1994), 196
Baptist Church(es)
  as always existing, 180
  commission of Christ and, 170
  effects of admitting blacks for membership, 214
  established by Christ, 176
  exclusivity of, 73, 150
  as the "executives of the Kingdom," 164
  existence of depending on Landmark tenets, 50–51
  first called "Christian" and then "Ana-Baptists," 80
  Landmark positions on the history of, 7
  making up the kingdom of God, 26
  not coming out of the Reformation, 160
  as the only true church, 15, 72, 93, 150
  organized by Jesus in Jerusalem, 175
  preserving the idea of Baptist Church succession, 177
  as ruthless political machines, 186
Baptist Church Perpetuity (Jarrel), 142n198
Baptist Church succession, 174–77
  absolute necessity of, 110
  acceptance of, 6–7
  articles repudiating, 154
  back to apostolic times, 9
  back to John the Baptist, 7
  brief history of, 69–75
  in-depth refutations of, 67
  doctrine of, 16

evaluating the claims of, 66–69
evaluation of, 66–89
from the first century to the present, 2
Folk on, 162
influencing a disproportionate number of Southern Baptists, 63
as key to the Landmark claim to be the one only true church, 211
Landmark view of, 3, 15
as the Landmarkers most powerful defense, 212
Pendleton on, 43–44
refuted by competent scholarship, 9
set forth by Wilkins, 152
summary of works claiming, 69–72
as a test of fellowship, 163
Whitsitt's direct contradiction of, 131
Baptist colleges, surveying students at, 204
Baptist confessions of faith, 402
"Baptist Corollaries" column, run by Graves, 118
Baptist doctrine, 194, 216
"Baptist Don't Go Back to Christ," Catholic article, 80
Baptist Faith and Message (2000), 204n247
Baptist family, tracing through the centuries, 21–22
Baptist General Association. *See* American Baptist Association
Baptist General Association of Arkansas, 146
Baptist Missionary Association of Texas, 146
Baptist newspapers, as weapons, 196
Baptist Observer (1992), launching of, 196
Baptist periodicals, shaping and propagating Landmark doctrines, 161–62
Baptist press, promoted Carroll's book, 80
Baptist principles, holding essential, 74
Baptist Standard newspaper, 118

Baptist Successionism: A Critical View (Patterson), 67, 68
Baptists Today, 197
baptistic principles, found in Robinson's groups, 69
"Baptists Were Not Anabaptists" (Hudson), 67
baptizing, done by Jesus, 60
Barnabas, as an old-time Baptist, 174
Barnes, Frank, 198–99, 199n226
Beecher, Henry Ward, 48n156
Beecherism, 48, 48n156
believers
  persecution of by the established church, 66
  rebaptized for not being regenerate, 51
Bell, T. P., 135–36
Benedict, David, 70, 157
Beza, Theodore, 105
Bible, as the sole rule of faith and practice, 39
Biblical Recorder, on the Whitsitt controversy, 134
Big Hatchie Association, resolutions adopted by, 24
biographical method, 5
Black Landmarkism, not examined, 208
board system, advantages per Holt, 145
Bogomils, claimed by Robinson as Baptists, 69
Bride of Christ, meaning of, 37–38
Brief History of the Baptists (Tully), 175
Broadus, John A., 111, 130
Bronson, Charles, 172
brotherhood, union with Christ creating, 49
Brown, John, 122n127, 126
Brownlow, William G., 8
Bullinger, Heinrich, 85–86

Calvary, as not the atonement, 31
Calvin, John, 104, 105
Campbell, Alexander
  doctrine of, 95–96
  opposed to mission work, 144
  teachings of, 20n13
  written debate with Graves, 94
Campbell and Campbellism Exposed: A Series of Replies to A. Campbell's Articles in the Millennial Harbinger (Graves), 96
Campbellite church, baptism in, 169
Campbellites (Disciples of Christ)
  attacks on, 94–97
  claim to be the true church, 93
  founding of, 20n13
  receiving the baptism of, 171
Carroll, Benajah Harvey, 58–61, 73–74
  architect of the new tradition, 149–50
  biographical information, 11
  encouraging his brother to begin his lecture series, 79
  on Graves, 162–63
  on honor due to Christ's church, 60–61
  influence in the beliefs of rank and file Southern Baptists, 74
  instrumental in the removal of W. H. Whitsitt, 76
  opposed schismatic Landmarkers in Texas, 146
  promoted Landmark view of Baptist church succession, 211
  "prophecy" of, 199
  quotes Graves' questionable interpretation of Matthew 11:11, 59
  read several works of J. R. Graves, 58
  on the relationship between the Southern Baptist Convention and the Southern Baptist Theological Seminary, 140–41
  resolution presented at the Southern Baptist Convention, 1898, 231–32
  softening his approach versus that of Graves, 60
  used Pendleton's *Church Manual, Designed for the Use of Baptist Churches*, 59

INDEX OF SUBJECTS 263

on the Whitsitt affair, 138
Carroll, C. C., "Sonnets of John the
    Baptist," 160
Carroll, James Milton, 61–64
    achievements of, 62
    on Ana-Baptists by the end of the
        sixteenth century, 86
    biographical information, 11
    chart identifying groups of "true
        Baptists," 67
    dating the time when non-fellow-
        ship was first declared between
        the true churches and the irregu-
        lar churches, 82n60
    enduring contribution to Baptist
        Church succession, 75
    lectures vastly popular with South-
        ern Baptists, 76–77
    library donated to Southwestern
        Baptist Seminary, 77
    opposed schismatic Landmarkers
        in the Texas, 146
    promotion and normalization of
        the Landmark view of Baptist
        church succession, 211
    The Trail of Blood, 211, 224–26
Carroll brothers
    aspects of theology of, 57–64, 65
    spread Landmarkism through the
        Southern Baptist Convention,
        210–11
Carson-Newman College, 204
Cathari
    Benedict on, 70
    Christian on, 157
    Folk on, 162
    J. M. Carroll on, 68, 82–83
    Orchard on, 84
    rejection of the organized church,
        87
    as Waldenses by different names, 71
Cathars, 87
Catholics. *See* Roman Catholic
    Church
Chafer, Lewis Sperry, 36n93
Christ. *See* Jesus Christ
Christian, John Tyler, 9, 155, 156, 158
Christian Baptist newspaper, 20n13

Christian bodies, as not true
    churches, 99
Christian Church, Graves' views on,
    96
*Christian Doctrines, A Compendium
    of Theology* (Pendleton), 46
Christian Doctrines (Pendleton), 8,
    41–42, 210
Christian Life Commission report,
    184
Christians
    accepting everyone, 187
    classes or states of, 37–38
    equating with Baptists, 76
    essential beliefs, 94
    not going to heaven when they
        die, 32
    outside of Baptist churches, 101
Christology
    of Graves, 29–31, 209–10
    of Pendleton, 46–48
church
    defined by Pendleton, 41
    as distinct from Israel, 36
    as local, visible, independent, and
        democratic, 16
    as pure democracy, 60
    as strictly a New Testament institu-
        tion, 59
    as visible, 25
church (*ekklesia*) of Christ, definition
    of, 170
church at Jerusalem, 41, 68, 93
church government
    B. H. Carroll on, 60
    Graves on, 22
    Pendleton on, 45–46
church history, Landmark view of, 2
*Church Manual, Designed for the Use
    of Baptist Churches* (Pendleton),
    8, 42, 43, 59, 211
Church of Christ
    essential features of, 23–24
    left in obscurity according to
        Graves, 70
    not needing Luther, Calvin, Henry
        VIII, Wesley, Campbell, 177

church of the Old Testament, not existing according to Graves, 37
church succession. *See* Baptist Church succession
"church triumphant in heaven," 43
church universal, 43, 167
churches of Christ
    analogy to the American Republic, 23
    as independent bodies, 45
    theory of the co-existence on earth of two, 60
civil rights movement, religious wars of, 188
civil rights struggles, 217, 218
Clark, John, 107, 108
close (closed) communion
    B. H. Carroll on, 61
    breakdown of among some Baptist churches in 1932, 172
    defense and propagation, 171–74
    enforcement rarely occurring among Southern Baptists, 192
    as essential New Testament doctrine, 174
    evolved into "closed" communion, 21n17
    Graves' views on, 8
    known as "closed communion" today, 8n6
    leaving room for, 205n247
    link with alien immersion, 171
    number of churches practicing, 203
    Pendleton on, 45
    practice of, 15, 202
    practices, 150
    student survey statistics, 204
Compendium of Baptist History (Shackleford), 71, 78
Compere, W. L., 174, 174n114
"Concept of Biblical Authority" (Garrett), 196n215
Concise History of Foreign Baptists (Orchard), 9, 21, 70
Concord Association, 118, 124
Confederacy of Southern states, urging Tennessee to join, 127

confessions, historic at Nicea, Constantinople, and Chalcedon, 4n2
congregational authority, attitude of, 2
congregational church government, 46
congregational infallibility, for Baptists, 186
contending, for the faith, 90
controversies
    connection to Landmark doctrines, 198
    generated by Landmarkers, 90–148
    involving Landmarkers, 11
    as the legacy of Landmarkism, 218
"Convention Normal Course," 167
Copeland, Luther, 187–88
Cotton Grove, mass meeting at in 1851, 222–23
Cotton Grove Resolutions, 24
Covenant of Redemption, not eternal, 27
Cramp, John, 70–71
Crawford, N. M., 123–24
Criswell, W. A., 178, 191
Crosby, Thomas, 67n6
Cur Deus Homo (Anselm), 31

Dana, H. E., 174
Daniel, Carey, 188–89, 189n182
Darby, John Nelson, 36, 36n93
Dargan, Edwin Charles, 135n174–36n174, 167
Davis, Jefferson, letter to J. R. Graves, 129
Davis, Jonathan, 69–70
Dayton, A. C., 112
    excluded from the First Baptist Church, 117
    on the justness of the Southern cause, 129
    on right of Tennessee to leave the Union, 127–28
    on the Sunday School Union formation, 114
    death, 35, 54
democratic church government, 22, 198

democratic republicanism, in the Baptist Church, 125
Demosthenes, 128
denominational newspapers, importance of, 18, 80
denominational periodicals, influence of, 215
denominations
    attacks on other, 92–110
    controversies with other, 212
    disavowal of any kinship with other, 177
    fragmentation into new denominations, 17
    only one having authority, 173
    other having no connection to Christ's church, 177
    recognition of, 179
    recognition of other, 111–12
Dilday, Russell, 196
disciples
    became the church, 26–27
    not a hierarchy for a worldwide church, 197
Disciples of Christ, 20n13, 94–97
dispensational views, of Graves, 32
dispensationalism, essential factors in, 36
dissident groups, compared to modern day Baptists, 71
The Doctrines of Our Faith (Dargan), 166–67
Donatists
    Christian on, 157, 158
    Folk on, 162
    J. M. Carroll on, 68, 83
    rejection of infant baptism, 87
    rejection of unworthy ministers, 87
    repudiation of the link between church and state, 83
    Robinson on, 69
    views different from the New Testament, 159
    Wilkins on, 152
doulos, exegesis of the Greek word, 128
Dual Being, Christ as, 29
Dutch Baptists of Holland, 107

early church, having no fully articulated doctrine, 180
Eastes, T. J., 138
Eaton, T. T., 131, 132, 142
ecclesia, cannot be applied to all denominations, 60
ecclesiastical authority, of conventions, associations, and boards, 144
Ecclesiastical History (Mosheim), 70, 77
ecclesiology
    of B. H. Carroll, 58–61
    of Graves, 209
    of J. M. Carroll, 62–64
    of J. R. Graves, 20–27
    Landmarkism stress on, 106
    of Montanists, 81
    of Pendleton, 41–46
    uncooperative spirit based on, 179–81
Edwards, Jonathan, 106
1861, as a momentous year, 124–29
eisegesis, defending one's doctrine, 59
ekklesia, meaning of, 26, 41
Elliott, Ralph, dismissal of, 195
Emerson, 122n127
"English Separatist Dissent Theory," 201
Episcopalians, not the Church of Christ, 99
eschatology
    of Graves, 36–38
    of Pendleton, 54–55
Eternal Father and Son, involving a contradiction, 27–28
Evangel, on the Whitsitt controversy, 134
evangelical churches, cooperating with other, 204
exclusive Baptist claim, to be the church Jesus himself instituted, 180
exclusivism, of many Southern Baptists, 150

Father, Son, and Holy Spirit, as official and relative terms, 27
Father and Son, eternally self-existed, 181
Fatherhood in God, brotherhood in Christ establishing, 49
Fatherhood of God, as a doctrine of spiritual paternity, 48
Fidus
  Graves' pseudonym, 72–73
  letters from, 19
First Baptist Church in Birmingham, Alabama, 186
first church in Jerusalem, 41, 68, 93
Florida Baptist Witness, on the Whitsitt controversy, 135
Folk, E. E., 74, 144, 161–62
"The Folly of Open Communion" (Vedder), 152
Foreign Mission Board, 144
Fort Sumter, 126
The Fortress of the Truth (The New Testament Church) (Milam), 197
Freewill Baptists, 108, 108n76, 171
frontier Baptists, 144
Fuller, Richard, 53
fundamentalism, 147
fundamentalist controversy/takeover, roots in the Landmark movement, 15
fundamentalist position, connection with segregationists, 191
"the Fundamentalist Takeover," of the Southern Baptist Convention, 190n189–91n189, 196
Fundamentalist-Moderate controversy, 147
fundamentalists, contentions raised by, 196
Furman University, 136

Gambrell, J. B., 151, 170
Gardner, David M., 178, 178n136
Garrett, James Leo, Jr., 196, 196n215
Garrett, W. Barry, 181–82
George, Timothy, 150, 150n7
God, 52
Gomer, 69
Goodwin, John, 91–92
gospel church, seven marks of, 166
Gospel Mission Movement, 144
grace, 35, 49
Graham, Billy, 178–79, 184
Graves, James Robinson
  appealing to republicanism and individual rights, 36
  attacks of, 92, 100, 106, 109, 115
  attitude toward other Protestant churches, 93
  Baptist and Reflector seeking donations for, 140
  as chairman of the nominating committee for the Sunday School Union, 114
  as the champion of Baptists, 97
  as the champion of Christ's truth, 208–10
  charged with libels against R. B. C. Howell, 116
  debate with Mr. Fly of the Methodist Church in 1851, 99
  as the defender of the true faith, 93
  differences with J. M. Pendleton, B. H. Carroll, and J. M. Carroll, 65
  differences with Pendleton, 57
  on the Donatists, 83
  editor of the *Tennessee Baptist*, 19
  effect on wide acceptance of Baptist succession, 66
  "eternal" not to be used with the names Father and Son, 47
  excluded from membership in the First Baptist Church of Nashville, 117
  father of Landmarkism, 2
  as Fidus, 19, 72–73
  flight from Nashville in 1862, 129–30
  on identifying the true church, 67
  intent to see Howell defeated and humiliated or the Southern Baptist Convention destroyed, 119
  judging by what he wrote, 181
  key principles of, 39
  legacy of, 151–54

literal interpretation of Scripture, 28
on maintaining the rights of the South, 123
marks upon the life of Southern Baptists, 162–63
as the model of orthodox ecclesiology, 172–73
narrow restriction of the term "New Testament church" to Baptist churches, 182
not aware of differences with Pendleton, 47
on other denominations, 16, 92–93
popularized Orchard's *Concise History of Foreign Baptists*, 9
preaching at Pendleton's church, 40
proclaiming Baptist policy, 39
promoting the justice of the South's cause, 121
on a properly organized church, 81
questionable positions of, 216
rejection of the universal church, 36–37
on the relationship of the Father and Son, 181n149
reminding the Campbellites that they were no church of Christ, 96
resolution and queries at Cotton Grove, 222–23
revisionist explanation of beliefs of, 182
on the right of communion, 172
Robertson taking to task, 162–63
shaping and influencing Southern Baptist thought, 113
single-mindedness in attacks, 212
on slavery, 11, 120–22
spirit of marching on, 150
Spiritism and, 153, 154
support of Baptist Succession, 72–73
taking on all comers from the Methodist camp, 99
taste for controversy, 90–92
theology of, 8, 17–39
trial of in 1858, 116–17
unable to take over the Southern Baptist Convention, 120
upbraided Stovel and the English in general, 126
urged the secession of the Southern states, 121–22
using "person" as synonymous with soul, 30
validating the Baptist Church as the one true church, 65
on the Waldenses, 85
works of, 7–8
Graves, Marks, and Company, 113
Graves-Ditzler debate, 8, 102, 102n52, 103
Graves-Howell controversy, 11, 115–20
Great Commission, 170, 176
"The Great Iron Wheel," 100
The Great Iron Wheel, or Republicanism Backwards and Christianity Reversed (Graves), 22
great tribulation, 38
Grime, J. H., 144–45, 144n207
Grooms, H. H., Sr., 186–87
groups
claimed as Baptists by the Landmarkers, 80–81
J. M. Carroll on, 68

hades, as the abode of spirits, 32–33
Hailey, Orren L.
on alien immersion, 164
arguments in defense of Graves, 164
biased view of history, 165
campaign to endow a professorship in memory of Graves, 153
defense of Graves, 12, 153
giving scant mention to Pendleton, 165
on Graves' landmark view, 97
on Graves' part in the Civil War, 120
Graves' son-in-law, 19
part owner of the *Baptist and Reflector*, 161

Hailey, Orren L. *(cont.)*
  on the problem of the Riley history, 156
  relationship to Graves, 11
  on Robertson's treatment of Graves views, 164
Ham, curse of, 121, 189
Hardball Religion: Feeling the Fury of Fundamentalism (Burleson), 147
Hardshell Baptists, 154, 154n23, 168
Harpers Ferry, 122n127
Hearne, S. C., 138–39
heaven, Paradise as, 54
Henderson, Samuel, 121
Henricians
  Benedict on, 70
  Folk on, 162
  J. M. Carroll on, 68, 84
  rejection of infant baptism, 87
  rejection of original sin, 88
  as Waldenses by different names, 71
Henry of Lausanne, 84
"Heresy among Southern Baptists" (Robertson), 162
"high churchism," of the Landmarkers, 16
high-church accusations, leveled against Southern Baptists, 50
"high-church" attitude, of Landmarkism, 2
High-Church Baptists in the South (Tull), 200
high-church exclusiveness, tendency toward, 91
high-church mentality, reflective of their traditions, 93
high-church movements, in the mid-nineteenth century, 93
historic Baptist doctrine, Landmark doctrines known as, 214
historic connection, to the New Testament church, 167
historical Baptist position, Landmark doctrine known as, 12
historical continuity, as root and sustenance of Baptist high churchism, 212
historical data, analysis of, 5

historical scholarship
  in Orchard's work, 88
  refuted the claims made by J. M. Carroll, 211
historiographical method, described, 5
history, revised by Graves, 106
A History of Anti-Pedobaptism: From the Rise of Pedobaptism to A. D. 1609 (Newman), 67
The History of Baptism (Robinson), 69, 72
The History of English Baptists (Crosby), 67n6–68n6
History of Foreign Baptists (Orchard), 66
History of Middle Tennessee Baptists (Grime), 144n207
"History of the Baptists of Tennessee" (Hailey), 165
History of the Baptists (Orchard), 72
A History of the Baptists, Together with Some Account of Their Principles and Practices (Christian), 155
History of the Welsh Baptists (Davis), 69
ho mikroteros, translation of, 59n202
Holliman, Ezekiel, baptized by Roger Williams, 107
Holmes, Thomas J., 186
Holt, A. J., 145
Howell, R. B. C., 17, 113
  attacks on the Landmarkers and on Dayton, 115
  attempting to drive both Dayton and Pendleton from the state, 116
  debate with Methodists, 98
  elected on the first ballot but stepped down, 120
  influence of Graves, 209
  miscalculated the extent of the opposition to Graves, 116n103
  objected to the make-up of the board of the Sunday School Union, 115
  strong opposition against Pedobaptists and Campbellites, 20

human system, supporting as a veritable Church of Christ, 102
Hymers, R. L., Jr., 195

immersion. *See also* alien immersion; Pedobaptist immersions
   baptism by, 16, 33
   as essential to baptism, 51
   as the mode of baptism, 201, 204
individualism, of Graves, 17, 35
infant baptism, 83, 84, 87
infants
   admitting into membership, 102
   as recipients of God's grace, 35
interdenominational cooperation, vitriol against, 179
An Interpretation of the English Bible (B. H. Carroll), 58
invisible, universal church, 25, 42, 180
The Iron Wheel, burning as "anti-Landmark," 102
"irregular churches," non-fellowship with, 68

J. R. Graves Professorship, at Southwestern Baptist University, 153
James Robinson Graves: Staking the Boundaries of Southern Baptist Identity (Patterson), 214
Japheth, 69
Jarrel, Willis Anselm, 9, 75, 142
Jesus Christ. *See also* Son of God
   appointed Apostles and the first seventy elders, 59
   atonement of, 48
   denial of full humanity of, 88
   established a visible kingdom on earth, 27, 67, 72
   failure to recognize the eternal and essential deity of, 88
   on the forces of hell not destroying his church, 211
   Graves' kenotic theory of, 210
   Graves on the offices of, 30
   Graves on the two natures of, 29, 154
   having no throne in heaven, 30
   instituted His church, 177
   made disciples before he baptized, 59
   named as the founder of the Baptist church, 76
   not having a human soul, 30, 30n64
   as truly and properly man according to Pendleton, 47
   union of a human body and a human soul, 47
Jeter, J. B., 151
John the Baptist
   as "an authorized administrator," 34
   as a demon, 88
   duly called and qualified Christian minister, 34
   as "the first Baptist preacher," 43
   inaugurated the church, 37
   prepared by God to begin the Baptist Church, 176
   sonnets about, 160
   succession back to, 211
Johnson, Douglas, 186
Jones, Jack W., 186
judgment of God, falling upon ungodly nations, 54

"Keep the Old Landmarks" sermon (Pickler), 180
kenosis, theory of, 30–31, 30n68–31n68
Kentucky General Association, 141
Kerfoot, F. H., 142
King, Martin Luther, Jr., 190
kingdom of Christ, composed of churches, 26, 209
Knox, John, 104, 105

Landmark assessment, of Reconstruction, 3
Landmark Baptist principles, as true doctrines of the Southern Baptists, 168
Landmark beliefs, identifying, 194–97
Landmark claim, of baptisms resting on an unbroken succession of churches, 105–6
Landmark discussion group, for Southern Baptists, 150

270 INDEX OF SUBJECTS

Landmark DNA, as an unseen part of Baptist life, 65
Landmark doctrine(s)
absorbed into the fabric of Southern Baptist life, 205
as biblical doctrines, 195
described, 198
in the educational materials of the Southern Baptists Convention, 166
mainstreamed, 168–77
propagation of, 154–67
reinforcing, 183
remarkable staying power of, 216
spread by many influential Southern Baptists, 214
spread through Baptist periodicals, 10
staying power of, 149–51
Landmark ecclesiology
centering around autonomy of the local church and its actions, 2
fostered an exclusive sectarian view of the local Baptist church and the Southern Baptist Convention, 15
of J. R. Graves, 172–73
Landmark faith, church succession theory as a compact summary of, 73
Landmark forces, many Southern Baptists dividing with, 136
Landmark movement
adding to the historiography of, 4
compared to Puritans and Separatists, 92
distinctive beliefs of, 6
on the Graves-Howell controversy, 124
influence in the Southern Baptist Convention, 91
influenced Partain, 180
on local autonomy, 198
official beginning of, 24
Landmark positions
as a departure from Baptist doctrine and practice, 16

on doctrine of the church, baptism, and the Lord's Supper, 7
leading Southern Baptist power brokers within the Southern Baptist Convention, 147
in objections to Whitsitt by Hearne, 139
seen as Southern Baptist principles, 2
toward other denominations, 92
tracing during the last century, 4
Landmark press, rhetoric regarding the Negro, slavery, states rights, and other issues, 217
Landmark tendencies, of SBC's (Southern Baptist Convention's) influential trustees and administration leaders, 192
Landmark traditions, 197
Landmark Triumvirate, 112
Landmark views
answering with scholarly research, 9
of ecclesiology and church history accepted as Baptist doctrine, 218
voices dissenting from, 162–67
Landmarkers
appeal of groups to, 81–86
attacks destructive to the unity and the beauty of Christ's church, 106
attacks on other Baptists, 106–10
on Baptist church succession, 73–75
biographies of major, 11
claiming that Baptists had no heritage from the Protestant churches, 85
confident going into the Southern Baptist Convention of June 1859, 119
conflicts instigated by, 212
on the connection between political oppression and ecclesiastical oppression, 124–25
control of newspapers by, 161
controversies involving, 11, 90–148
defeat at the Southern Baptist Convention in 1966, 182

INDEX OF SUBJECTS 271

defeated in denying seating of Pedobaptist ministers, 111–12
definition of, 194
doctrines as historic and long-held, 16
extreme racism among, 185
holding the same doctrinal positions as the Southern Baptists according to Alldredge, 166
on the issue of slavery, 213
no one above attack by, 147–48
not anti-missional, 144
occupying positions of influence in the Southern Baptist Convention, 217
positions of influence within the Southern Baptist Convention, 213
role in the run up to the Civil War and attitudes formed toward the Negroes, 217
works in the area of baptism and the Lord's Supper, 10

Landmarkism
advancing the base of knowledge regarding, 218
akin to a strand of DNA, 205–6
allied with Southern sectionalism and racism, 188
born in the passions leading up to the American Civil War, 213
chief promoter and champion, 208
connections with present SBC leadership, 200
continuing to have a powerful influence upon Southern Baptists, 187
criticizing Graves' methods while defending Landmark doctrine, 151
destroying claims of other denominations, 93
effects of, 1
embrace and defense of traditional Baptist principles, 93
entered the blood-stream of Southern Baptists, 150

as the essential Baptist position, 218
fondness for after the death of Graves, 152
fundamentalist/moderate controversy and, 190–92
impact and spread of ignored in existing works, 217
impact in the local church, 200–206
influence in many controversies, 3
influence on the westward expansion of the Southern Baptist Convention, 177–78
influence upon theological views, 201
influenced controversies within the Southern Baptist Convention in the twentieth century, 205
insinuated itself into virtually every challenge Southern Baptists have faced, 150
methods and evidences of transmission, 193–94
not a forgotten piece of Southern Baptist history, 207
not identifiable to current students, 205
not just a footnote in Baptist history, 149
overlooking theological inconsistencies, 4
pervasive influence and impact of, 183
present impact of in the Southern Baptist Convention, 193
racism and, 185–90
reached across generation lines, 201–2
relegated to the shadows, 184–92
staying power of, 3, 215
stress on ecclesiology giving rise to sectarianism, 106
subsumed and eclipsed, 177–83
tenets of as basic Baptist doctrine, 1
as a term practically unknown among many Southern Baptists, 218
theology of early, 15–65

Landmarkism *(cont.)*
  within the Southern Baptist Convention, 207
  works on, 12
  writings of, 7–8
Landmarkism, Liberalism, and the Invisible Church (Pendleton), 42, 43
landmarks
  Graves' determination and resolve to defend, 109–10
  struggle for the protection of the old, 134
"Landmarks of Our Faith" article, in 1948, 173
"last days," as at hand, 126
Lee, Robert E., 122n127
liberalism, contrasted with Landmarkism, 168
limited atonement, doctrine of, 49
literal interpretation, of the Scriptures, 36
local church
  alone commissioned to authorize and administer baptism, 199
  autonomy of, 45, 172, 198
  emphasis upon, 192
  as the final authority in disciplinary matters, 118
  losing visibility, 43
  Pendleton's stance on, 44
  place and importance of, 20
  primacy of, 195
local self-government, of churches, 22
Lofton, George Augustus, 9
Lolley, Randall, 196
London Confessions, First and Second, 4n2
Lord's Supper
  definition of, 205n247
  not for all Christians, 173
  ordinance of, 10
Luther, baptisms of, 104

man, as depraved and inclined to sin, 52
Manicheans, Robinson on, 69
Manis, Andrew, 188–89

man's constitution, Pendleton's trichotomous view of, 52
"markers," of Landmark influence, ix–x
marks, of the true church, 79, 81, 86
Marks, W. P., 117
Masonry, Pendleton on, 56
Mather, Cotton, on Roger Williams, 107n69
McGoldrick, James, 81, 193–94, 193n202–94n202
Menno, Simon. *See* Simons, Menno
Mennonites, Folk on, 162
Mercer University, 185–86
The Message of Genesis (Elliott), 195
Methodism, without Scriptural baptism, 34
Methodist Church
  divided over the issue of slavery, 121
  Graves criticism of, 25
  sects of, 98
  as unscriptural according to Graves, 100
Methodist Episcopal Church, South
  competing with Southern Baptist Churches for members, 97
  formed over the issue of slavery, 24n28–25n28
  Graves' constant battle with, 25n30
Methodists
  attacks on, 97–103
  not "inside the church" according to B. H. Carroll, 61
"Middle Life," as that which "Christ called Paradise," 32
mikros, Graves on the use of, 59
Milam, R. E., 178, 179, 197–98
ministers, rejection of non-Baptist, 16
minority, rights of, 125
mission boards, 11, 144
mission work, controversies over, 143–46
missionary organizations, suspicion of, 143
missionary societies, Campbell's opposition to, 94
Montanism, beliefs of, 81

Montanists
  Benedict on, 70
  Christian on, 156–57, 158
  ecclesiology of, 81
  J. M. Carroll on, 68, 81
  rejection of the organized church, 87
  Wilkins on, 152
Montanus, 81
Mormons, 93, 99
Mullins, E. Y., 74, 159, 159n48

Nashville Christian Advocate, of the Methodist Episcopal Church, South, 98–99
Nashville Indian Mission Association, 19
Negroes
  acceptance in Southern Baptist churches, 214
  asserting the inferiority of, 53
  disparagement of, 213
  equal rights for, 184
  Pendleton's defense of, 53
New School Presbyterians, 104n62
New Testament
  authority over that of the Old, 94
  form of church government recognized in, 46
  as the law of Christianity, 59
  reading of Baptist history into the pages of, 176
New Testament church
  as an autonomous local congregation of baptized believers, 204
  historic connection to, 167
  as an independent, democratic church, 197–98
  uniqueness of the Baptists' claim of being, 177
New Testament churches, as Baptist churches, 173, 182
New Testaments, printing for soldiers, 129
Newman, Albert Henry, 9, 88
Nicodemus, Christ's answer to, 26
1960s, turbulent events of, 184
Noah, 69

nominees, for the board of the Sunday School Union, 114–15
non-acceptance, existed by way of silence, 184
non-Baptist baptisms, rejection of all by Graves, 21
Novatianists, Folk on, 162
Novatians
  actions of, 199
  on baptism in the Catholic Church, 82
  Benedict on, 70
  Christian on, 157, 158
  clash with Cornelius the bishop of Rome, 82n60
  J. M. Carroll on, 68, 82
  opposed Rome and were persecuted for doing so, 82
  Ray on, 71
  rejection of unworthy ministers, 87
  Vedder on, 71
  Wilkins on, 152

An Old Landmark Re-Set (Pendleton), 8, 40, 112, 210
Old Landmarkism, e-mail discussion group, 151
"Old Landmarkism" (Graves), 166
Old Landmarkism: What Is It? (Graves), 21
"Old Landmarks," establishing, 67
Old School Presbyterians, 104n62
Old Southwest, Southern Baptists moving out of, 177–79
Old Testament, church in, 36
one Lord, one faith, one Immersion, 39
Oni, Sam, 185–86
open communion
  advocating the practice of, 182
  B. H. Carroll against, 61
  criticized by Graves, 20–21
  as "humbug" according to Pendleton, 45
  no such thing as, 195
  practicing, 183
  Taylor on, 171
  widespread practice of, 192

open communion, Charles Haddon Spurgeon on, 108
Orchard, George Herbert, 21, 70, 82, 84
ordination, 44, 51
organization
  continuity of, 67
  opposed to the Baptist "church," 169
organizational succession, not resulting in doctrinal succession, 106
organized church, rejection of, 87
original sources, evaluating, 5
"outer darkness," meaning of, 38

parable, of the sower, 52–53
Paradise, Pendleton on, 54, 210
"paramount authority," of the New Testament, 158–59
Partain, John, 179–80
pastors
  continuity of, 67
  requiring a candidate for membership to be rebaptized, 203–4
  trying to open the doors of the church to all people, 190
Paterines (Paterins)
  aberrant Christology of, 87
  Benedict on, 70
  docetism of, 87
  Graves on, 82
  J. M. Carroll on, 68, 82
  as Waldenses by different names, 71
Patterson, T. A., 183, 183n160
Paul
  called himself a *doulos* of Christ, 128
  condemning sectarian exclusivity, 106
  as an old-time Baptist, 174
Paulicians
  aberrant Christology of, 87
  adoptionist Christology of, 88
  Benedict on, 70
  Christian on, 157, 158
  claimed by Robinson as Baptists, 69
  Folk on, 162
  J. M. Carroll on, 68, 82, 83–84
  rejection of the organized church, 87
  Wilkins on, 152
Peck, Mrs. J. E., 132, 137
"peculiar" aspects, of Graves' theology, 154, 208–10, 216
Pedobaptist churches, not true churches, 22
Pedobaptist immersions, validity of, 95
Pedobaptist point of view, Whitsitt's mistake in writing from, 136
Pedobaptist preachers
  conceding one thing after another to, 112
  as not gospel ministers, 50
  those baptized by immersion by, 109
"Pedobaptist societies," 50, 98
Pedobaptists
  accepted by Baptist churches, 170
  attacks on, 91
  Baptists communing with, 45
  communion with, 153
  maintaining a separate and unique heritage from, 110
  receiving the baptism of, 171
  substituted sprinkling and pouring, 50
Pelagian view, of salvation, 88
Pendleton, James Madison
  agreed with Graves on the Baptist doctrine of baptism, 57
  author of *An Old Landmark Re-Set*, 2, 8
  avoided some of the questionable formulations of Graves, 210
  biographical information, 11
  on Christ not having a human soul, 46–47
  on church government, 45–46
  on church succession, 43–44
  controversy with N. M. Crawford over the exegesis of the Greek word *doulos*, 128
  defined the church, 41
  doctrinal positions held by, 217
  dogmatic assertions on baptism, 50

INDEX OF SUBJECTS

editorial after Lincoln was elected, 122–23
first meeting with Graves, 40
fled to the North in 1862 and never returned, 53, 124, 130
on God existing from eternity, 48
on Graves' critique of Methodism, 102
on the idea of the universal church, 42
on intercommunion, 44–45
on at least five hundred thousand men falling on the field of battle, 128
on Masonry, 56
on Methodist church government, 101
on mission work, 144
on the need for a suitable Sunday School paper, 114
not consistent in doctrine, 43
on Paradise, 54
post at Union University, 116
as a puzzle, 42
rejected the rhetoric on inferiority of the Negro, 55
reluctance to join Graves in every facet of his virulent attacks, 101
on seating to Pedobaptist preachers, 112
on slavery, 53, 128
swayed by Graves to become the theological base, advocate, and codifier of Landmarkism, 57
as theologian, 56
theology of, 39–57
on the universal visible church, 42–43
Pendleton, John, 56
periodicals, promoted Carroll's book, 80
Person of Christ, Pendleton on, 48
Peter, on David not ascending to heaven, 32
Petrobrusians, Folk on, 162
Petrobrussians, as Waldenses by different names, 71
Philadelphia Confession, 4n2

Phillips, J. M., 139–40, 152–53
physical death, as the penalty for sin, 35
Pickards, Wilkins on, 152
Pickler, C. M., 175, 180
pneuma, Pendleton on, 52
Poindexter, A. M., 115
political conflict, in the 1850s, 92
Poor Lombards. See Waldenses
Popery, conflict between true Christianity and, 93–94
Porter, J. W.
  on alien immersion, 169–70
  asked J. M. Carroll for permission to publish his lectures, 64, 79
  on the connection between alien immersion and close communion, 171–72
pragmatic analysis, validating doctrines, 199
preaching ministry, call to, 202
premillennial dispensationalist, 36, 36n93
Presbyterian Church
  divided over the issue of slavery, 121
  ministers as unbaptized, 104
  schism in 1837, 104n62
Presbyterians
  attacks on, 103–6
  baptisms by, 34
  Graves' challenges to, 104–5
  not "inside the church" according to B. H. Carroll, 61
  not the Church of Christ, 99
primary sources
  described, 6
  for J. M. Carroll's book, 80–81
Primitive Church, government of, 22
proper administrators, Graves assertions regarding, 34
proper officers of the church, Graves on, 22
Protestant Reformation, churches out of, 73
Protestants, maintaining a separate and unique heritage from, 110

psyche or soul, denoting pneuma or spirit, 52
publication houses
  under Graves control, 18–19
  remnants of Graves' producing denominational magazines for Southern Baptists today, 209
publishing competitors of Graves, open to unusually harsh criticism, 109
publishing empire, of Graves, 18, 215
pulpit affiliation
  as the first test of the Graves view, 163
  Hailey on, 164
"pure individuality," of every man in eternity, 54
purgatory
  doctrine of, 33
  Graves referring to, 210
purification, of souls "by the fires of punishment," 33

"The Querist" column, in the *Tennessee Baptist*, 19
A Question in Baptist History (Whitsitt), 67, 131

race question, mediating, paralyzed "silence" on, 184
races, inequality of, 185
racial battles, harsh rhetoric of, 191
Randall, Benjamin, 108, 108n76
Ransom Theory, which Anselm refutes, 31
Ray, D. B., 71
rebaptizing
  of all who joined Southern Baptist churches, 211
  of new members, 15, 150
redemption
  application of, 32
  doctrine of, 56
Reformation
  Christian on, 158
  churches of not true churches, 21
  Shackleford on, 72
Reformers, baptisms of, 104
regenerate church membership, principle of, 197
regenerate person, for baptism, 33
regeneration, agents in, 39
religious periodicals, continuing influence of, 181–83
religious societies, having legislative powers and clerical or aristocratical governments as illegal, 99–100
religious war, American Civil War as, 10
Renfroe, J. J. D., 8
republican, executive body of the true church as, 23
republicanism
  argument of Graves, 99
  issue of, 3
resurrection, of the just and the unjust, 54–55
Re-thinking Baptist Doctrines (Masters), 160
Revelation (book of), figurative language of, 55
Richards, Wiley, 192
Riley, B. F., 155
Robertson, A. T.
  accusing Landmarkers of heresy, 12
  critical of the Landmarkers and their attacks on Whitsitt, 162–63
  supported Whitsitt, 131
  wrote Dargan questioning Eaton's motives, 136–37
Robinson, Robert, 69
Roger Williams Memorial Church, 165
Roman and Orthodox churches, Paulicians refused to recognize the clergy of, 84
Roman Catholic Church
  Arnoldists opposition to, 84
  asserted as no true church by the reformed churches, 104
  "Baptist Don't Go Back to Christ" article, 80
  claimed to be the only true church, 93
  as the mother of Harlots, 93

INDEX OF SUBJECTS

not the Church of Christ, 99
Novatians on baptism in, 82
Reformers aimed to reform, 158
as a true Church of Christ, 103
Ryle, J. C., 213

sacraments, Landmark view of, 15
sacred writers, infallibly preserved from error, 55
saints, perseverance of, 39
salvation
  election to proved by regeneration, 55
  by grace through faith alone, 39
Samford University, in Birmingham, Alabama, 204
Sampey, John R.
  impassioned and heated defense of Whitsitt, 132–33
  sent a letter to Dargan, 137–38
  supported Whitsitt, 131, 132
SBC Today (1983), launching of, 196
Scarboro, J. A., 145, 146
Scarborough, L. R., 170, 174
Schaff-Herzog Encyclopedia, cited by Carroll, 77
scholarship, refuting J. M. Carroll's entire thesis, 211
Scobee, J. S., attacked Graves, 100–101
Scofield, C. I., 36n93
Scofield Reference Bible, 36n93
Scovel, H. G., 117
scriptural authority, baptized by, 170
Scripture, literal interpretation of, 28
secession from the Union, defense of, 124–25
Second Great Awakening, produced great revivals, 17
Second Person, of the Trinity came to be called the Son, 31
Second Reconstruction, 188n179
sectarian exclusivity, condemned by Paul, 106
sectarian view, 177
segregation, biblical basis of, 189
segregationist position, conservative movement within the Southern Baptist Convention identified with, 191
seminaries
  influence of felt in the pastorate, 169
  targeted for lack of compliance to the Southern Baptist mandate, 190
seminary faculty, fears of as well-founded, 142
"Sermon on the Law" (Campbell), 94
Shackleford, J. A., 71–72
Shankland, A. B., 19, 117
Simons, Menno, 176
sinner, suffering a self-procured damnation, 54
"Six Fundamental Doctrines of Baptist Churches," 99
Skipworth, N. M., 107–8
slave population, Christianizing, 121
slaveholders, protecting the rights of, 122
slavery
  Charles Haddon Spurgeon on, 109
  churches aligned themselves geographically on the question of, 92
  defense of as an institution, 122
  dissolving the Union on account of as absurd to Pendleton, 123
  Graves defense of, 11
  issue of, 3
  Landmark press rhetoric, 217
  Landmarkers hardened positions regarding, 213
  Landmarkism and Graves and, 120–30
  Methodist Episcopal Church, South, formed over the issue of, 24n28–25n28
  as not absolutely evil, 122
  original sin of defending, 187
  Pendleton on, 53, 128
  Protestant denominations split over, 10
  as sanctioned by the Bible, 125
Slavery: Its Origin, Nature, and History (Stringfellow), 125

slaves
    failed to join John Brown, 122n127
    as faithful to their masters, 122
Smith, Harold S., 194
"societies"
    other churches as, 75, 212
    recognition of, 179
sociohistorical dimension, of Landmarkism, 6
Son of God. *See also* Jesus Christ
    as divine and only relatively human, 209
    as only relatively human, 29
    relationship to God the Father, 28
"Sonnets of John the Baptist" (C. C. Carroll), 160
Sonship of Christ, Graves denied as eternal, 27
soul competency, 203, 203n245
Soule, Joshua, 24–25, 100
souls, all in Hades, 32
South Western Christian Advocate, circulation of in 1845, 98n30
Southern Baptist(s)
    alleged superiority and purity of white, 214
    belief in an unbroken succession of true churches, 216
    beliefs of, 203
    beliefs on inferiority of the Negro, 185
    doctrine of, 168
    exclusivist mentality of, 211
    local expressions against integration and recognition of blacks, 189
    percentage attending church on any given Sunday, 199–200
    protecting from the alleged danger posed by professors and seminary leaders, 196
    traditions outside the normative expression of true and sound Christian tradition, 215
Southern Baptist Advocate (1980), launching of, 196
Southern Baptist Bible Board, controversy regarding, 112–15

Southern Baptist churches
    average members read *The Trail of Blood* (Carroll), 75
    conducting rebaptisms, 202–3
    growth of, 97
Southern Baptist Communicator (1991), launching of, 196
Southern Baptist Convention (SBC)
    birth of, 10
    brought to the brink of dissolution, 120
    centered about the Whitsitt matter in 1897, 134
    commitment to foreign missions and taking the gospel to all people, 187
    controversies over mission work, 143
    forced its seminary to apologize for allowing King on the Louisville campus, 190
    formed out of a split among the Baptists over slavery, 213
    Graves, Pendleton, and the other Landmark voices as the true voice of, 166
    major controversies connected to Landmarkism, 1–2
    not willing to publish Carroll's book, 79
    paralyzed "silence" on the race question, 189
    racial bigotry surfacing in, 62n221
    research restricted to, 208
    resolution presented by B. H. Carroll in 1898, 231–32
    schisms within, 146
    seating of ministers from other denominations in 1855, 111
    Whitsitt sustained by the seminary board of trustees in 1898, 140
Southern Baptist Heritage (Shurden), 201
Southern Baptist Publication Society, 18, 113
Southern Baptist Seminary, 138
Southern Baptist students, responses of self-identified measured, 233

Southern Baptist Sunday School Union
  Constitution of, 227–28
  formation of, 113
  nominating committe of, 114–15
Southern Baptist Watchman (1991), 196
Southwestern Baptist Seminary, formation of, 61
Southwestern Baptist Theological Seminary, 149, 211
Southwestern Publishing House, 113
Spring Street Baptist Church, 117, 118, 119
Spurgeon, Charles Haddon, criticized by Graves, 108–9
"A Statement Concerning the Crisis in Our Nation," 187
states' rights, 3, 124
Stovel, Charles, 126
"straw-man arguments," 195
strict successionists, almost nonexistent within faculties of seminaries, 194
Strong, Augustus H., 28
student opinions, on succession of churches back to the first century, 204
student surveys
  sample, 234–35
  statistical analysis of, 236
succession of Baptist churches. *See* Baptist Church succession
"Successionist Theory," 201
successionist view, of Baptist history, 193
Sunday School Union. *See* Southern Baptist Sunday School Union
surveys
  examined and conducted on the influence of Landmarkism, 200
  measuring current beliefs and attitudes of students at predominantly Baptist colleges and universities in regard to Landmark doctrines, 233–36
Sutton, Bill, 192
syllogisms, 30, 30n62

synecdoche, according to Graves, 26

Tatnall Square Baptist Church, 185, 186
Taylor, O. W., 170–71, 180–81, 180n146
Tennessee, voted to secede from the Union, 128
Tennessee Baptist Convention, 165, 184
Tennessee Baptist (newspaper), 17
  circulation of, 90n2
  condemned the Harpers Ferry Raid, 122
  editorial stand against the Republican candidate Abraham Lincoln, 122
  on ministers leaving their flock in war, 129
  not changing the relative strength or position of Baptist churches, 110
  number of subscribers, 18n8
  stirring Baptist emotions before the Civil War, 120n121
  on Tennessee seceding, 126
  unwavering justification of slavery, and support for the Southern war effort, 126–27
  widest dissemination of Baptist succession views in Graves' day, 72–73
Tennessee Baptist Publication Society, Graves formed, 112
Tennessee Publication Society, 18, 209, 219–21
Texas Baptist Standard, 135, 149
theological directions, evaluation of, 15–17
theological influence
  of B. H. Carroll, 61
  of J. M. Carroll, 64
theology
  of the Carroll brothers, 57–64, 65
  of early Landmarkism, 15–65
  of Graves, 8, 17–39, 154, 208–10, 216
  of Pendleton, 39–57

INDEX OF SUBJECTS

Thoreau, 122n127
thousand-year reign, of Christ on the earth, 36n93
toleration, confusing with love, 49
tracts, printing for soldiers, 129
"trail of blood"
   marked the history of the true churches, 88
   phrase first used by Graves, 66
The Trail of Blood (J. M. Carroll), 7, 211, 224–26
   analysis and critique of, 76–80
   assembled from lectures given by Carroll, 75
   Carroll's thesis in, 63
   effect on wide acceptance of Baptist succession, 66
   J. M. Carroll giving lectures on, 75, 160
   number of copies published and distributed, 66–67
   publication of, 64
   read by millions of Southern Baptists, 62–63
   as a recapitulation of other writers, 68
   theological impact of, 64
Trilemma, word coined by Graves, 103n58
The Trilemma, or, Death by Three Horns (Graves), 72, 103
Trilemma argument, espoused by Graves, 110
Trinitarian doctrine, of Graves, 27–29
Trinity
   Graves' views on, 209
   Persons assuming new functions, 31
true Church of Christ (visible), 103, 104
true churches
   Baptist churches as, 67, 209, 216
   claiming to be, 16
   identifying, 81
   unbroken line of, 69
   withdrew from the apostate church and suffered persecution, 88
Tull, Selsus E., 189–90

Tully, Hugh, 173, 175, 193

unauthorized administrator, baptism administered by, 102, 169
"unchristian qualities," of Baptists, 91–92
"An Unfaithful Church in Danger of Extinction" (sermon), 43
union, of divinity with humanity, 47
Union army, occupied Nashville, 129
Union University, in Jackson, Tennessee, 204
United States of America, plunged into civil war, 124
unity, Pendleton's appeal for, 123
universal church
   B. H. Carroll argued against, 60
   not believing in, 195
   Pendleton on, 210
   student survey responses on, 205
unregenerate church members, issue of, 199
unregenerate people, admitting into membership, 102
unwise virgins, as not enemies of Christ, 38

Valdès, 85
valid baptism, 33, 34
Van Ness, I. J., 155, 155n27
Vaudois. *See also* Waldenses
   Folk on, 162
Vedder, Henry C., 71, 152, 152n15
Vindication of the Communion of Baptist Churches (Renfroe), 8n6
visible church, 16, 25
   administering scriptural baptism, 103, 104
   baptism essential to, 50
   established by Christ, 37
   Pendleton on, 42–43
visible kingdom, Jesus Christ established, 67, 72
voluntary association, of persons professing regeneration, 23
vox populi, as the impetus behind the call for Whitsitt's resignation, 138

INDEX OF SUBJECTS

Waldenses
  as Baptist churches, 71
  Benedict on, 70
  Folk on, 162
  J. M. Carroll on, 68, 85
  rejected infant baptism, 87
Waldensian period, according to Ray, 71
Waldo. *See* Valdès
Walker, Clarence, 79, 80
Waller, John L., 85, 85n80, 109
"War! Duty!" column on, 127
Ward, Wayne E., 182–83
Weaver, Rufus W., 161, 161n54
Welsh Baptists, as the seed of Gomer, eldest son of Japheth, 69
Wesley, John, 102
Western Recorder paper, 131, 135
Westward Ho (Milam), 178, 179
white race, superiority of, 185
white Southerners, alleged superiority and purity of, 188
Whitsitt, William H.
  B. H. Carroll instrumental in securing the resignation of, 74
  condemnation of, 132
  controversy over J. M. Carroll's work, 78–79
  demand for the resignation of, 138
  denied the theory of Baptist successionism, 130
  fallout over the resignation of, 63
  final address on maintaining fundamental Baptist doctrine, 143
  historical research of, 132
  hounded out of Southern Baptist Seminary, 7
  resignation of, 74, 141
  response to seminary trustees, 133
  statement before the Board of Directors at the Southern Baptist Convention (1897), 229–30
  studied theology under J. M. Pendleton, 130
  work destroyed the premise that Baptists had existed in an unbroken chain, 143
Whitsitt controversy, 11, 130–43
  B. H. Carroll's role in, 61
  demonstrated Landmarkism as a decisive element in Baptist life, 131–32
  impact of various newspapers in, 161
  similarities with, 195
Wilkins, Frank L., 151–52
Williams, Roger
  as founder of the first Baptist church in America, 107n69
  Graves on, 165
  as never a Baptist, 107, 108, 175–76
the Word, 28, 47
The Work of Christ in the Covenant of Redemption, Developed in Seven Dispensations (Graves), 7, 27, 28, 36n93, 46, 54
works, taking the place of grace, 49
Wylam Baptist Church, 193, 193n201

Zwingli, baptisms of, 104

www.ingramcontent.com/pod-product-compliance
Lightning Source LLC
Chambersburg PA
CBHW070236230426

43664CB00014B/2327